ACTA HISTORIAE NEERLANDICAE
STUDIES ON THE HISTORY OF THE NETHERLANDS

EDITORIAL BOARD:
I. Schöffer (Leiden); Johanna A. Kossmann (Groningen); H. Balthazar (Ghent); J. R. Bruijn (Leiden); A. Th. van Deursen (Amsterdam); R. Van Uytven (Antwerp).

EDITORIAL ADDRESS:
Lange Voorhout 34, The Hague, The Netherlands.

ACTA HISTORIAE NEERLANDICAE

STUDIES ON THE HISTORY OF THE NETHERLANDS

X

MARTINUS NIJHOFF
THE HAGUE/BOSTON/LONDON
1978

PRINTED IN BELGIUM

Table of Contents

Holland's Advance*

H.P.H. JANSEN

Until recently, a pronounced Hollando-centric bias dominated the teaching of history in the Netherlands, especially at primary-school level. The emphasis was placed solely on historical developments in the province of Holland, and events in the other provinces were mentioned only in so far as they were of importance for the history of Holland. This bias can be seen most clearly in the treatment of the history of the middle ages — a period when Holland was but one of the many sovereign territories, originally no more important or powerful than its neighbours, and when its development was largely autonomous. Thus today's older generation of Netherlanders often had to learn all the counts of Holland off by heart. They were told colourful stories about bold Thierry III, who defeated the army sent by the emperor to present him from setting up a toll on the Merwede; about Florence V, friend of townsman and peasant, who was murdered by the nobility; and about the party-strife of the late middle ages, known to us as the wars of the Hoeks and Kabeljauws. But the history of other provinces, such as Gelderland, Brabant, Friesland, and the bishopric of Utrecht, was condemned largely to obscurity. This partiality has often annoyed the inhabitants of the remaining provinces. Their reaction has been one of an often rather chauvinistic concentration on their own provincial history, which largely explains the growth of a variety of regional-historical associations.[1] But educational fashions changed after the Second World War. In the schools today emphasis is no longer placed either on the political history of Holland during the middle ages, or indeed on the political history

---

* This article is a slightly modified version of H.P.H. Jansen, *Holland's Voorsprong*. Inaugural Lecture Leiden University (Leiden, 1976).
1. This provincial patriotism has found expression recently in the publication of a number of large, collective, regional studies: E.C.M.A. Batta, e.a., ed., *Limburg's verleden. Geschiedenis van Nederlands Limburg tot 1815* (2 vols., Maastricht, s.a.), a publication of the Maastricht Historical and Antiquarian Society of Limburg; J.J. Kalma, J.J. Spahr van der Hoek and K. de Vries, ed., *Geschiedenis van Friesland* (Drachten, 1968); W.J. Formsma, e.a., ed., *Historie van Groningen. Stad en Land* (Groningen, 1976); B.H. Slicher van Bath, e.a., ed., *Geschiedenis van Overijssel* (Deventer, 1970); W.J. Alberts, *Geschiedenis van Gelderland van de vroegste tijden tot het einde der middeleeuwen* (The Hague, 1966). Similar provincial histories are planned for other provinces as well, with exception only of Holland.

1

of any other province. There is instead a stronger bias towards a more conceptual, rather impressionistic, treatment of a few general topics — the manor, the town, the nobility, and so forth.[2]

In what we shall for the sake of convenience call the scholarly study, the triumph over this Hollando-centric bias occurred at a much earlier date. In 1888, S. Muller delivered an address to the General Assembly of the Utrecht Society for Arts and Sciences entitled: 'Het middelpunt in de geschiedenis der Nederlandsche gewesten' (The focal-point for the history of the Netherlands provinces).[3] He argued, in no uncertain terms, that in the eleventh century it seemed likely that a North-Netherlands entity would evolve around the bishopric of Utrecht, and that therefore it would be logical to consider the medieval history of these lands from the viewpoint of the episcopal residence — the town of Utrecht. According to Muller:

> The amazing development of the province of Holland since the beginning of the seventeenth century has largely obscured the natural and most logical approach to the study of our medieval history. The Holland regents, who dominated the Republic from the Hague, and their proteges, the Holland scholars, viewed our country's history continually through Holland's eyes, and they remained unmoved when events in other provinces were torn completely out of context as a result.[4]

Muller was undoubtedly right. In the eleventh and twelfth centuries the political and economic importance of the county of Holland, situated as it was in *extrema margine mundi* was still insignificant. Muller's address, however, had otherwise no immediate effect. In 1891, one D.C. Nijhoff published a *Staatkundige Geschiedenis van Nederland*, in which he could still argue that the logical starting point of Dutch national history was the establishment of the toll at Dordrecht by Thierry III. Nevertheless, Muller's opinions gradually won more ground. P.J. Blok's *Geschiedenis van het Nederlandsche Volk*, the first two

---

2. See J.G. Toebes, 'Van een leervak naar een denk- en doevak. Een bijdrage tot de geschiedenis van het Nederlandse geschiedenisonderwijs', *Kleio. Tijdschrift van de VGN*, XVII (The Hague, 1976) 66-148. The *VGN*, the *Vereniging van leraren geschiedenis en staatsinrichting in Nederland* (The Association of teachers of history and politics in the Netherlands), has proudly set out its new educational methods in the pamphlet *Afrekenen met 1600* (Settling accounts with 1600) (Bois-le-Duc, 1975). '1600' is the traditionally best-known 'date' in Dutch schools.
3. Muller won great respect during his own lifetime and his reputation is still high today, thanks to his many source-publications and the influence which he had on the classification system employed now by Dutch archives. F.W.N. Hugenholtz is very critical of him, 'S. Muller Fzn als historicus', *Jaarboek Oud-Utrecht* (Utrecht, 1974) 215-25. For Muller as archivist see F.C.J. Ketelaar, 'Muller en de archiefwetenschap', *Nederlands Archievenblad*, LXXVIII (Groningen, 1974).
4. Quoted from the reprint in Muller's collection, *Schetsen uit de middeleeuwen* (Amsterdam, 1900) 2-3.

volumes of which appeared in 1892 and 1893, could hardly be called Hollando-centric any more.[5] But an even more radical reaction was at hand.

In 1900, Muller had his address 'The focal-point for the history of the Netherlands provinces' reprinted in his widely-read collection of essays *Schetsen uit de middeleeuwen*. A few years later, primarily through Muller's influence, the German historian, Otto Oppermann, came to Utrecht University to lecture in medieval history. He was a man educated in the scholarly traditions of the German *Urkundenforschung* and in his forty-year career as lecturer and senior lecturer he greatly influenced the study of medieval history, especially through his pupils.[6] I do not know whether he was particularly bothered by the problem of what should be taken as the focal point for the study of Dutch history. He probably thought it more profitable to subject the sparse documentation concerning the early history of the Netherlands provinces to a rigorous critical analysis, exposing much of it as spurious. He even believed a number of charters to be forgeries, which have since been proven genuine. Oppermann's first major work written in the Netherlands dealt with the history of the town and bishopric of Utrecht,[7] but he also wrote a great deal about the falsity of various sources concerning the history of Holland from the tenth to the thirteenth centuries.[8] This provoked further reactions and gave rise to the paradoxical situation in which interest in Holland's history until around 1300 was indeed stimulated, while the much more important period after 1300 was somewhat neglected. This, again, produced a distortion of perspective. It is this problem that I shall examine in more detail in this

5.   D.C. Nijhoff, *Staatkundige geschiedenis van Nederland*, I (Zutphen, 1893) 17 and 23; P.J. Blok, *Geschiedenis van het Nederlandsche Volk*, I and II (Leiden, 1892-3). Cf. the inference to be drawn from this passage in the introduction: 'The province of Utrecht, whose capital was the seat of a bishop and therefore an important ecclesiastical centre, was originally the focal-point of all interests in this area' (I, 3).

6.   The influence of Oppermann on the study of the medieval history of the Netherlands is well brought out by B.H. Slicher van Bath in his article 'Guide to the Work of Dutch Medievalists, 1919-1945', *Speculum*, XXIII (Cambridge, Mass., 1948) 236-66, reprinted in: B.H. Slicher van Bath, *Herschreven Historie* (Leiden, 1949) 30-70.

7.   O. Oppermann, 'Untersuchungen zur Geschichte von Stadt und Stift Utrecht', *Westdeutsche Zeitschrift fur Geschichte und Kunst*, XXVII (Treves, 1908) 185-263, XXVIII (1909) 155-243.

8.   O. Oppermann, *Untersuchungen zur nordniederländischen Geschichte des 10. bis 13. Jahrhunderts*. Bijdragen van het Instituut voor middeleeuwsche geschiedenis te Utrecht, III and IV (2 vols., Utrecht, 1920-21); *idem*, ed., *Fontes Egmundenses*. Werken Historisch Genootschap, derde serie, LXI (Utrecht, 1933). For the notorious attack of Johan Huizinga on the thesis of Oppermann's pupil Brandt on the borough charter of Haarlem, entitled 'Noodwendig Vertoog', see *Bijdragen voor Vaderlandsche geschiedenis en oudheidkunde*, vijfde serie, X (The Hague, 1923) 1-14, reprinted in J. Huizinga, *Verzamelde Werken*, II (Haarlem, 1948) 22-35; a rejoinder to this was written by the master himself: O. Oppermann, *Opmerkingen over Hollandsche stadsrechten der XIIIe eeuw*. Bijdragen Instituut middeleeuwsche geschiedenis Utrecht, VI (Utrecht, 1923).

inaugural address, to which I have given the somewhat challenging title *Hollands Voorsprong*.

Until well into the thirteenth century the province of Holland still lacked those characteristics which were to distinguish it in later years. It was still an agrarian country, with hardly any towns, and these could therefore have had no political influence.[9] There was no trade or commerce either with the German Hanse towns, or with England and France. There were no export-industries, and the administration of the counts was still very rudimentary. Until 1213, the province had only two, not particularly important, religious houses — Egmond and Rijnsburg, which were populated largely with the sons and daughters of a rather rustic nobility. The backwardness of the province, in comparison with Flanders, is well illustrated by the treaty of Bruges of 1167, which Florence III was forced to conclude after defeat in war. One of the terms runs as follows:

> If any Flemish merchant, while sailing through Holland, should be sued by anybody for debt, then the Fleming may reject the suit by swearing a simple oath, while remaining on board his ship to avoid being delayed. Should the plaintiff — that is, of course, the native — refuse to accept this, he must follow the Fleming to wherever he is staying, where the matter shall be settled by the local magistrates.[10]

It is as if the Flemings had acquired a sort of extra-territorial status in a colonial land. This, I believe, was possible because of the backwardness of Holland, where there was neither trade nor industry. This situation must have prevailed for some considerable time, at least until 1256, when this treaty was ratified for the last time. By the end of the fifteenth century, however, the situation had radically changed, as I hope soon to demonstrate.

The period from the thirteenth century onwards, which witnessed a series of fundamental changes, seems to me to be more interesting *per se* for the historian than the preceding centuries. But while the latter have, for a variety of reasons, continued to attract attention, the fourteenth and fifteenth centuries have been rather neglected. The history of the publication of the charters of Holland is symptomatic of this trend. As early as the second half of the eighteenth century four substantial tomes, entitled *Groot charterboek der*

---

9. Some towns did in fact play an active part in the drawing-up of a few charters before 1300: L.P.C. van den Bergh, *Oorkondenboek van Holland en Zeeland. Eerste afdeling tot het einde van het Hollandsche Huis* (2 vols., Amsterdam–The Hague, 1866-73) II, no. 321 (1276), no. 523 (1284), and no. 754 (1290). This was because they were directly involved in the issues which the charters dealt with; they certainly did not appear at this time as representatives of the towns on the council of the count. See D.Th. Enklaar, 'De opkomst van de grafelijke raad in Holland', *Bijdragen voor de geschiedenis der Nederlanden*, I (The Hague, 1946) 21.
10. A.C.F. Koch, ed., *Oorkondenboek van Holland en Zeeland tot 1299*, I, *Einde van de 7e eeuw tot 1222* (The Hague, 1970) no. 160, especially p. 307.

graaven van Holland en Zeeland en heeren van Vriesland,[11] were produced within the space of a few years by Frans van Mieris,[12] painter and principal of the art-school of his home town of Leiden. The documents printed were not edited particularly carefully, and Van Mieris appeared to have taken little trouble to get hold of the best manuscripts. He was always at loggerheads with the problem of chronology. He seems not to have realized, for instance, that from 1240 the year in Holland began at Easter.[13] However, he did make a large number of charters, up to 1436, available to the scholarly public and to the 'young men appointed to the study of letters at university',[14] and for this reason he indeed deserves to be remembered. Van Mieris had clearly intended to continue his work a little further. In the Rijksarchief in The Hague there is a supplement of five thick portfolios, none of which have ever been published. Each one is some 500 pages long, written in his beautifully clear hand, containing charters up to the year 1482. Van Mieris' first volume, which covered the period up to 1299, was in fact replaced in the second half of the nineteenth century by L.Ph.C. van den Bergh, and in 1901 a further supplement to this was produced by James de Fremery.[15] Van den Bergh and Fremery certainly studied their material more carefully than Van Mieris, had a better grasp of chronology, and published more documents. But for someone like Oppermann this was no way to publish charters. A new commission was therefore given to Henri Obreen, one-time pupil of Pirenne in Ghent, perhaps to prove that all the expertize in diplomatic need not necessarily come from Germany. One slim instalment of some 96 pages did indeed appear in 1937, but Obreen died in the same year and the publication was not continued.[16] Just recently, the first hefty volume of the *Oorkondenboek van Holland en Zeeland*, edited by A.C.F. Koch, has at last appeared.[17] It seems likely that this will finally be the definitive version. The first volume is a monument to erudition and perception, incorporating the very best in the use of diplomatic and other ancillary disciplines, and work on the subsequent volumes is making good

11. *Groot charterboek der graaven van Holland, van Zeeland en heeren van Vriesland* (4 vols., Leiden, 1753-6).
12. This is Frans van Mieris the Younger (1689-1763) — not to be confused with his grandfather, Frans van Mieris the elder (1635-81), who is today rated more highly as a painter. A study of Van Mieris as a historian is needed. At the moment we must make do with the short entry in the *Nieuw Nederlandsch Biografisch Woordenboek*, VIII (Leiden, 1930) 1154-5.
13. See J. Kruisheer, *De oorkonden en de kanselarij van de graven van Holland tot 1299.* Hollandse Studien, II (2 vols.; The Hague-Haarlem, 1971) I, 127.
14. See the unnumbered pages of Van Mieris' introduction to his *Groot charterboek*, I.
15. Van den Bergh, *Oorkondenboek*; J. de Fremery, *Supplement oorkondenboek van Holland en Zeeland tot het einde van het Hollandsche Huis* (The Hague, 1901).
16. H.G.A. Obreen, *Oorkondenboek van Holland en Zeeland tot het einde van het Hollandsche Huis (1299)* (The Hague, 1937).
17. Cf. above n. 10.

progress. But the whole work will not go beyond... 1299. For the most interesting period of Holland's history we shall have to continue to rely on the unsatisfactory texts of Van Mieris, plus a few supplements, which are in general no more reliable.[18]

I have already mentioned Holland's backwardness, due to its lack of towns, export-industries, and foreign trade, and my intention to demonstrate how, by 1500, this situation had completely changed. This is possible thanks to the information provided by the *Enqueste* of 1494, and the *Informacie* of 1514.[19] These were the names given to those surveys which were conducted in most of the towns and villages of Holland in order to arrive at a re-assessment of the tax contribution of each place. A commission of enquiry travelled the land, and in each place the parish priests and a number of other trustworthy people were examined under oath as to the number of houses in the locality, the state of the area's *neringhe* (that is, the population's means of support), and the *staet van heure faculteit* (that is, the capacity of the public finances). Additional information was requested in 1514, including for example the number of communicants, so that for this year a fairly reliable estimate of the size of the population can be made. From the testimonies given in 1494 in particular, a general picture of deep-seated misery emerges — large numbers of beggars and paupers, a slump in trade, and other such hardship and distress. Now it is true that these testimonies were in fact tax returns, and it is to be expected that people were not inclined to give a very high estimate of their wealth. Yet the witnesses were on oath, and it is to be hoped that the priests at least did not make too light of their testimonies. Indeed, on the basis of other information, it is reasonable to suppose that by 1494 Holland had been for some years in the grip of a serious economic recession.[20] Fundamentally, however, much had

18. P.J. Muller, *Regesta Hannonensia. Lijst van oorkonden betreffende Holland en Zeeland 1299-1345, die in het Charterboek van Van Mieris ontbreken* (The Hague, 1881).
19. R. Fruin, ed., *Enqueste ende Informacie upt stuck van der reductie ende reformatie van den schiltaelen, voertijts getaxeert ende gestelt geweest over de landen van Holland ende Vrieslant, gedaen in den jaere MCCCCXCIIII* (Leiden, 1870); idem, ed., *Informacie up den staet faculteyt ende gelegentheyt van de steden ende dorpen van Hollant ende Vrieslant om daernae te reguleren de nyeuwe schiltaele gedaen in den jaere MDXIV* (Leiden, 1866). The fairly extensive literature on these two documents has been summarized by A.M. van der Woude, *Het Noorderkwartier.* AAG-Bijdragen, XVI (Wageningen, 1972) 61-92.
20. In Amsterdam, the first complaints about the poverty of the textile-workers came in 1491: 'the poor, wretched artisans (can) barely scratch a living', quoted by N.W. Posthumus, *De Oosterse handel te Amsterdam. Het oudste bewaarde koopmansboek betreffende handel op de Oostzee* (Leiden, 1953) 52. The economic problems of this period have also been noted by J.C. van Loenen, *De Haarlemse brouwindustrie voor 1600* (Amsterdam, 1950) 56, who connects the drop in beer consumption with the decline in purchasing-power, caused by the rise in the cost of living at the end of the 15th century. For the prices of foodstuffs, see N.W. Posthumus, *Nederlandse prijsgeschiedenis*, II (Leiden, 1966) *e.g.* 448 (grain prices paid by St. Catherine's hospital in Leiden) and cf. 566 and the graph on xcii. The economic crisis also gave rise to serious financial

changed since the twelfth century. Then, there had been hardly any towns, but by 1514 52 per cent of the population were towndwellers. This percentage was probably somewhat smaller in 1494, although the information for this year is less complete. This much at least is clear, that by around 1500 half the population lived in towns, a much higher proportion than in any other province of the Netherlands, including Flanders.[21] Many villagers, moreover, earned their livelihood primarily from fishing and shipping; they, too, had lost their agrarian character. In the towns, which were fairly populous by medieval standards, much of the population was involved in such export industries as the manufacture of textiles in Leiden, Amsterdam, and elsewhere, and the brewing of beer in Haarlem, Delft, and Gouda. A considerable proportion of the shipping bound for the Hanse towns, for England, and to a lesser extent France, was accounted for by Holland ships. This is confirmed by other sources, especially by the toll registers of the Sound. All vessels en route to the Baltic from the west had to pass through the Sound, where the king of Denmark exacted a toll. The earliest preserved registers date from 1497. In that year, 57 per cent of the toll-paying ships were captained by Hollanders. The statistical significance of this unusually high figure may not be entirely clear, but the conclusion that the Baltic shipping routes were largely dominated by Holland is indisputable.[22]

The political influence of the towns of Holland, non-existant in the twelfth century, had grown enormously by the end of the fifteenth century through the assemblies of the provincial states. This was clearly so by 1477, when the provincial *Groot-Privilege* (Grand Privilege) was obtained.[23] In these towns power resided in the *vroedschappen*, those remarkable closed corporations whose membership was elected by co-option, and from among whom all the important magistrates were appointed.[24] In short, by the end of the fifteenth

---

problems, see J. Prins, *Het faillissement der Hollandsche steden Amsterdam, Dordrecht, Leiden en Haarlem in het jaar 1494. (Wordingsgeschiedenis van de Nederlandsche Staat)* (Amsterdam, 1922). For the unfavourable economic climate in the Netherlands in general at the end of the 15th century see R. Van Uytven, 'What is new in the sixteenth-century Netherlands', *Acta Historiae Neerlandicae*, VII (The Hague, 1974) 22-3.

21.   Compare with J.A. Van Houtte in: J.A. Van Houtte, *e.a.*, ed., *Algemene Geschiedenis der Nederlanden*, IV (Utrecht, 1952) 226.; also R. Van Uytven, 'What is new', 24, who quotes Braudel: 'au voisinage de 50 p. cent, même de 40 p. cent de population non-rurale, une région entière bascule automatiquement dans la catégorie des économies modernes'.

22.   For a treatment of all these problems, see A.E. Christensen, *Dutch Trade to the Baltic about 1600. Studies in the Sound Toll Register and Dutch Shipping Records* (Copenhagen, 1941).

23.   P.A. Meilink, 'Dagvaarten van de Staten-Generaal', *Bijdragen Geschiedenis der Nederlanden*, V (1950) 210-11.

24.   E.A.M. Eibrink Jansen's brief thesis, *De opkomst van de vroedschap in enkele Hollandsche steden* (Leiden, 1927) is a far from exhaustive or satisfactory study of this subject.

century, the economic, social and political structure that was to enable Holland to take effective control of the leadership of the Republic during the years of the Revolt, had already evolved. This supremacy, which Holland was to retain for two centuries, was, as we have seen, responsible for Hollando-centric historical image, which clearly distorted our interpretation of the period up to the end of the thirteenth century. Yet this image is, I feel, more relevant to the later middle ages.

When did this development, the results of which are revealed by the *Enqueste* of 1494, take place? 1250 could perhaps be taken as an approximate starting date, as by this time a few places in Holland had already obtained their municipal franchise. Counts William II and Florence V also demonstrated that they were alive to the economic potential of the province by granting various privileges to foreign merchants, though these measures otherwise produced few concrete results. In general, however, those places which had been enfranchized in the thirteenth century had hardly yet earned the name 'town' in the economic sense of the term. Amsterdam was certainly no town at this time, although its seventh centenary as such was celebrated with much pomp in 1975. The small group of settlers by the Amsteldam, mentioned in the toll-privilege of 1275, only obtained their municipal franchise in the fourteenth century.[25] Delft, Alkmaar, 's-Gravenzande, Schiedam, and Medemblik were also certainly no more than local agricultural centres or fishing communities in the thirteenth century, with any commercial activity being relatively insignificant. Haarlem and Leiden were probably of slightly more importance, being, in addition, favourite residences of the counts.[26] However, from the two thick volumes devoted by H. van Oerle to the urban growth of Leiden, it is abundantly clear just how small and how basically agrarian in character Leiden still was in 1294 — in practice no longer than the Breestraat plus a few alleyways —, in spite of the continually perceptible pride of the author in this hallowed ground.[27] Probably only one place in Holland was a real town in the economic

25. See J.F. Niermeyer, 'Amsterdam als dochterstad van Utrecht', *Tijdschrift voor geschiedenis*, LX (Groningen, 1947) 40-9.
26. At Leiden the counts had a court, at some distance from the site of the first urban settlement; and in Haarlem the 'old houses of the counts of Holland' were burned by the Frisians in 1132. In 1206 there were four places where the counts received the homage of their subjects — Dordrecht, Vlaardingen, Leiden, and Haarlem; see, Koch, *Oorkondenboek Holland en Zeeland*, I, no. 280, p. 463.
27. H.A. van Oerle, *Leiden binnen en buiten de stadsvesten. De geschiedenis van de stedebouwkundige ontwikkeling binnen het Leidse rechtsgebied tot aan het einde van de gouden eeuw* (2 vols., Leiden, 1975). Some writers have attributed considerable economic importance to Haarlem on the basis of a rather detailed charter, dated 1274, which granted the right to levy excise duties and listed a fairly large number of occupations, see van den Bergh, *Oorkondenboek*, II, no. 279. However, J. Huizinga has shown that this excise-grant makes no mention of any true export industries, see 'De opkomst van Haarlem', *Verzamelde Werken*, I, 265-6. In addition, it is possible

sense. This was Dordrecht, founded around 1150 on a bank of the Merwede, and enlarged during the course of the thirteenth century on land reclaimed from an arm of the river.[28] The importance of the town lay chiefly in its toll — the financial lifeline of the counts of Holland.[29] Hence the counts' policy of directing all river-traffic via Dordrecht, which led in 1299 to the establishment of the town's renowned staple-right, a privilege which was further extended during the fourteenth century.[30]

During the thirteenth century, however, the possibilities for Dordrecht were still limited because of the economic backwardness of Holland as a whole. This was apparent when, in 1294-95, the king of England transferred the wool staple to Dordrecht — a political manoeuvre aimed at forcing Flanders to side with England in a dispute with France. It lasted but a short while because, according to Melis Stoke, it was dependant upon an 'Englishman's word', and it was well known even then that nobody could set much store by the promises of 'perfidious Albion'.[31] The staple was therefore transferred to Mechlin,[32] but there was, I believe, a sound economic reason behind this move. There was no market in Dordrecht for the high quality English wool, and the result was probably the same as it was in 1337-8 when the king of England again attempted to restrict the sale of all English wool to the land of his loyal ally, William III of Holland. It simply could not be sold there, and the English merchants soon complained that they were 'in a strange country where they could conduct no business, a problem which they had even less idea how

that this excise-grant did not in fact reflect existing conditions, a suspicion reinforced by the fact that the village of Scherpenisse, which never became a place of any significance, also received a similar grant in 1340.

28. H. Sarfatij, 'Dordrecht, opgravingen in Hollands oudste stad', *Spiegel Historiael*, VII (Bussum, 1972) 624.

29. J.F. Niermeyer, *De wording van onze volkshuishouding* (The Hague, 1946) 50.

30. For the working of the Dordrecht staple-system see the large source publication edited by J.F. Niermeyer, *Bronnen voor de economische geschiedenis van het Neder-Maasgebied*. Rijks Geschiedkundige Publicatien, Grote serie, CXXVII (The Hague, 1968) and the other literature quoted therein.

31. 'Dit gheduerde ene stont,
   Maer niet langhe, als ic verhoerde,
   Want het was Ingelsche vorworde',
   (It lasted a while,
   But not long, as I heard,
   Because it was an Englishman's word),
Melis Stoke, *Rijmkroniek van Holland*, I, W.G. Brill, ed. Werken van het Historisch Genootschap, Nieuwe serie, XL (Utrecht, 1885) IV, vv. 864-6. Cf. F.W.N. Hugenholtz, *Floris V* (Bussum, 1966) 77-89. A new edition of Melis Stoke is being prepared by prof. Hugenholtz.

32. N.J.M. Kerling, *Commercial Relations of Holland and Zeeland with England from the late 13th century to the Close of the Middle Ages* (Leiden, 1954) 8.

to solve'.[33] I conclude that in the thirteenth century a hesitant beginning had indeed been made, but that as yet Holland was in no sense an urbanized country with a primarily non-agrarian population supported by foreign trade and commerce and export-based industries. The towns still had hardly any political influence. This was clearly the case during the struggle for power in Holland in the turbulent years from 1296 to 1304, which followed the assassination of Florence. During similar conflicts in other provinces, notably Flanders, the towns were accustomed to firmly indicating their preference, but in Holland during these years the towns were summoned on a few occasions only to witness the issuing of certain decrees. For the rest the towns allowed events to pass them by,[34] with the exception again of Dordrecht, which received the above-mentioned staple-right as a reward for its support of the Avesnes of Hainault. However, by the succession-struggle of the years 1345-54 the power structure had already completely changed, and this time the Holland towns clearly did influence the politics of the province.

Turning to the question of economic developments, it is clear that the transformation, which produced the modern fabric revealed by the *Enqueste* of 1494, took place between the years 1350 and 1400. The expansion of a number of towns during the second half of the fourteenth century indicates that only during this period did urbanization get fully under way. Leiden was enlarged in 1355, and again in 1386, by which time it had attained the form in which it was to survive the famous siege of 1574. Haarlem was enlarged in 1355 as well, and this also appears to have been sufficient until the sixteenth century. These are just two of many examples.[35]

Only in the second half of the fourteenth century was Holland's foreign trade and shipping of any real importance. This can be readily substantiated with the aid of a number of important source publications concerning the Netherlands trade with the Baltic, France, and more especially with England

33. *Idem*, 'Afrekening van de Engelse koopman Reginald de Conductu betreffende de onkosten gemaakt voor vervoer en berging van Engelse wol naar en in Dordrecht (1335-1338)', *Bijdragen en Mededelingen van het Historisch Genootschap*, LXVIII (Utrecht, 1951) 81, nt. 17.

34. After the assassination of Florence V, Edward I of England requested Holland to send some delegates to an assembly in England. As was his custom when summoning the English Commons, he asked for two delegates to be sent from each 'good town' and 3 or 4 *homines nobiles* from each *patria* (clearly meaning something like 'county'): Van den Bergh, *Oorkondenboek*, II, no. 958. According to Melis Stoke an embassy did in fact set out for England, but it was composed only of 'a small company of noblemen' — the towns were clearly not ready yet for such an undertaking. Compare also D.Th. Enklaar, 'Opkomst', 26-7.

35. Van Oerle, *Leiden, passim*; F. Leiden, 'Nederlandsche plattegrondstudies, V', *Historisch Tijdschrift*, XIX (Tilburg, 1939) 175-84; C.H. Peters and H. Brugmans, *Oud-Nederlandsche steden in haar ontstaan, groei en ontwikkeling*, I (Leiden, 1909) 304 and 309, mention the expansion of yet more towns in the 14th century, *e.g.* Amsterdam in 1367 and 1383, and Enkhuizen in 1390.

and Scotland.[36] Thanks to the labours of Poelman, Sneller, Unger, and Smit, these publications provide a fairly complete synopsis of the existing material. The data collected by dr. Smit from various English archives, which lends itself somewhat to statistical analysis, is especially valuable. Around 1300 there were a number of Zeeland ships involved in the trade with England and France, and to a lesser extent with the Baltic, while Holland vessels, with the exception again of ships from Dordrecht, were only occasionally involved. Shortly after 1350 this situation changed. Within a few years Holland's ships had penetrated the Baltic. The earliest document which proves that Amsterdammers were active in the Baltic area dates from around 1360.[37] A few years later this trade had become so important for Amsterdam that the town took an active part in the war of 1367-70 against Waldemar IV of Denmark in order to keep the Sound open.[38] Similar developments can be observed in almost all the other towns of Holland, and also with relation to the trade with England and France. Before 1350 there was hardly any evidence of foreign trade; a few decades thereafter it had become a phenomenon of considerable importance.

Similarly, only after 1350 were there any true export-industries of any importance. The textile industry of Leiden provides us with the best example. Before this date the information is sparse. There was probably some textile manufacture in the town, but only to meet local demand, using home-grown wool, referred to disdainfully as 'pig's wool', as the raw material. Shortly after 1350, however, the manufacturers began to use English wool, which had to be bought at the staple in Calais. This was the beginning of the development towards the semi-capitalistic organization of the textile industry. Drapers played the role of entrepreneur, and contracted out work to self-employed weavers, fullers, dyers, cloth-shearers, and many other tradesmen. Thus was born the putting-out system, which we are acquainted with from other textile towns such as Ghent and Florence, and which at times was responsible for the existence of socially unacceptable conditions. Yet it did produce an exportable product, capable of competing in foreign markets with Flemish, Brabant, and English textiles, and this in turn gave an added stimulus to Holland's foreign trade.[39]

36. H.A. Poelman, ed., *Bronnen tot de geschiedenis van den Oostzeehandel, 1122-1499*. Rijks Geschiedkundige Publicatien, Grote serie, XXXV-VI (2 vols., 1917); Z.W. Sneller and W.S. Unger, ed., *Bronnen tot de geschiedenis van den handel met Frankrijk*, I, *753-1585*. RGP, Grote serie, LXX (The Hague, 1930); H.J. Smit, ed., *Bronnen tot de geschiedenis van den handel met Engeland, Schotland en Ierland*, I, 2 parts. RGP, Grote serie, LXV-VI (The Hague, 1928).
37. Poelman, *Bronnen Oostzeehandel*, I, no. 246.
38. Amsterdam was one of the participants in the so-called Conference of Cologne in 1367, *ibidem*, no. 296.
39. N.W. Posthumus, *Geschiedenis van de Leidsche lakenindustrie*, I, *De middeleeuwen (XIVe tot XVIe eeuw)* (The Hague, 1908); H. Ammann, 'Deutschland und die Tuchindustrie Nordwest-europas im Mittelalter', *Hansische Geschichtsblätter*, LXXII (Cologne, 1954) 1-63.

Indeed, Leiden was not the only textile town in Holland. Delft, Haarlem, Amsterdam, The Hague, and a number of other places all produced textiles during the latter half of the fourteenth century which could compete in foreign markets.[40] The second export industry of importance was beer brewing. The sales potential of beer in the middle ages should not be underestimated. With water being largely undrinkable, and wine too dear, it was drunk in vast quantities. Originally each housewife in Holland brewed her own beer, a mild brew, known as *kuitbier*. It could only be kept for limited periods, and the taste was not particularly appealing, even after the addition of some ground herbs or *gruit*, which could only be obtained from the *gruit* dealer of the count. But then a heavier beer, brewed with hops, was produced in Hamburg, and it quickly became a much sought-after commodity everywhere, including Holland. In 1323 the count set up a beer toll in Amsterdam, which gave the town a complete monopoly over the import of Hamburg beer, and partly explains its rise to prosperity.[41] After 1350, however, hop-flavoured beer was also produced in Haarlem, Delft, and Gouda. The grain was imported, peat provided the fuel, and, according to a report dated 1380, hops were being cultivated in large quantities in the seigniory of Heusden, recently acquired by the counts of Holland. A third branch of industry — shipbuilding — has became better known to us thanks to the recent studies of the American, Richard Unger.[42] Shipbuilding in Holland in the middle ages was perhaps not strictly an export industry, although in the early-fifteenth century ships built in Haarlem were sold in Brabant; but shipbuilding did make export possible. In this connection a centuries old tradition probably prevailed in Holland, as, for its ship service to the lord, each village had to provide a *heerkogge*, an oared vessel which was used as a troop transport in wartime.[43] These ships were relatively small, like the Holland fishing boats which could be built in one's backyard;

---

40. Ammann, 'Deutschland und die Tuchindustrie', 44: map 10, gives the towns that found markets for their textiles in the Hanse area in the 14th century, namely, Amsterdam, Leiden, Schiedam, Dordrecht, and Geertruidenberg. In the 15th century this list included Haarlem, Hoorn, Naarden, The Hague, Gouda, Delft, and Rotterdam as well. See also Posthumus, *Geschiedenis Leidsche lakenindustrie*, I, 1-45. In the trading-accounts of the German Order from 1391 to 1423, only Leiden, Amsterdam, and Dordrecht are still referred to as textile-producers: Ammann, 'Deutschland und die Tuchindustrie', 51.
41. Van Mieris, *Groot charterboek*, II, 321. For the beer-toll see H. J. Smit, *De opkomst van den handel van Amsterdam* (Amsterdam, 1914).
42. R.W. Unger, 'Regulations of Dutch Shipcarpenters in the Fifteenth and Sixteenth Centuries', *Tijdschrift voor geschiedenis*, LXXXVII (1974) 503-20; *idem*, 'Dutch Ship Design in the Fifteenth and Sixteenth Centuries', *Viator*, IV (Berkeley, 1973).
43. For the remarkable organization of the ship-service in Holland, by which every village had to provide a ship as its contribution to the war-effort, see I.H. Gosses, *Welgeborenen en huislieden. Onderzoekingen over standen en staat in het graafschap Holland* (The Hague, 1926) 65-70 and *passim*.

larger ships were usually bought in Germany. By 1351, however, there were professional ship's carpenters in Dordrecht as well, where they had organized themselves into a guild. Large quantities of wood were imported into Dordrecht from the Rhine lands and, shortly after, shipbuilding on a similar scale, with shipyards and cranes, must have developped in other Holland towns as well. It was these Holland shipbuilders who made the expansion of the North Sea herring-fishery possible. Before the fourteenth century, herrings could not be preserved on board the small ships which were used in the fishing fleets. This meant that the herring packaries of Schonen, where the herrings could be caught right on the coast, had a virtual monopoly in the curing and packing of herring. Around 1400, however, the *haringbuis* was developped, a new, larger type of ship which made the packing and curing of herrings on board possible, thus bringing the fishing grounds of the Doggerbank within reach of the Holland fishermen.[44] The expansion of the fisheries and the growth of ship-building influenced each other and, furthermore, these fishing boats could also be used in the transportation of other cargoes.

All the above-mentioned industries — textiles, brewing, and shipbuilding — took root in the towns, and it is to be expected that the latter attracted large numbers of immigrants in the second half of the fourteenth century. This is confirmed by the above-mentioned urban expansion, and also by the *poorterboek* of Leiden, which records the names of all those who acquired civic rights from 1365 onwards. In the fourteenth century more than half of Leiden's immigrants evidently came from Rijnland, that is from the immediate vicinity of the town. Moreover, it appears that from 1365 to 1400 on average 50 new citizens a year were admitted, a figure which was only once attained in the fifteenth century, during the decade 1450-9, and which was never reached in the sixteenth century.[45] Since only a minority of the immigrants troubled to buy civic rights, the total number of new inhabitants in Leiden in the second half of the fourteenth century was probably quite considerable, and it is, I believe, justifiable to assume that the example of Leiden was repeated throughout the rest of the province. The present state of research scarcely permits an accurate census of the urban population at the end of the fourteenth century. There are, however, two lists preserved from this period which record the numbers of men-at-arms who were summoned from each town to fight

---

44. For this question see the various articles of R. Degrijse, *e.g.* 'Oorsprong van het haring-kaken in Vlaanderen', *Nederlandsche Historiebladen*, I (Antwerp, 1938) 201-19.
45. Posthumus, *Geschiedenis Leidsche lakenindustrie*, I, 377 ff. and D.E.H. de Boer, 'De ver-houding Leiden-Rijnland, 1365-1414. Veranderingen in een relatie', *Economisch- en sociaal-historisch jaarboek*, XXXVIII (The Hague, 1975) especially 63-8.

in the Frisian wars,[46] and on the basis of these it is at least possible to assess the relative size of towns. Blok estimated the population of Leiden around the year 1400 at 5,000.[47] On this basis, we arrive at a figure of around 40,000 for the population of the seven largest towns of Holland, and around 25,000 for the smaller towns. I am reluctant to give an estimate of the total population of the province for this period, but this much at least is certain: that already a considerable proportion of the population were towndwellers.

It is also to be expected that during the second half of the fourteenth century these towns acquired some political influence, like the towns of Flanders and Brabant. This is clearly indicated during the years when the succession was in doubt, following the death of William IV in 1345,[48] and William V's attack of madness in 1358. The territorial integrity of the three counties — Holland, Zeeland, and Hainault — was then threatened, and delegates of the towns were repeatedly summoned, together with those of the nobility, to discuss the situation. At such assemblies the prince made far-reaching concessions. In a charter granted to South Holland in 1346, the Empress Margaret promised not to embark on any foreign wars without the consent of the nobility and towns; and from 1352 to 1354 the county of Holland was in practice under the financial guardianship of a number of its towns, which were continually represented at the auditing of the accounts. It is true that the title 'States of Holland' was not in use at this time — not until the Treaty of Delft of 1428 was mention made of the *Drie Staeten der Landen* (the Three Estates of the Country) —, but in practice the role of these 'estates' was no different from those of Flanders and Brabant at this time. Due to a lack of previous studies we know little about the further development of this situation after 1364, when Albert was firmly in the saddle.[49]

There appear to have been no fundamental changes in the political and economic life of Holland during the course of the fifteenth century. The process of urbanization doubtless became more intensive, and foreign trade and commerce certainly increased considerably, but the basic fabric, once attained, was not altered as a result. Indeed, the economic situation was not always so favourable during this century. I have already mentioned the economic crisis

46. See appendix I. Van Mieris, *Groot charterboek*, II, 670-1 and G.F. Thoe Schwartzenberg en Hohenlansberg, Groot placaat- en charterboek van Vriesland, I (Leeuwarden, 1768) 338. Compare with J.C. Ramaer, 'Middelpunten der bewoning in Nederland, voorheen en thans', *Tijdschrift van het Aardrijkskundig Genootschap*, tweede serie, XXXVIII (The Hague, 1921) 11 ff.
47. P.J. Blok, *Geschiedenis eener Hollandsche stad*, I (2nd edition, The Hague, 1910) 74, partly on the basis of the number of men-at-arms in 1418 (650).
48. H.P.H. Jansen, 'Willem V', *Spiegel Historiael*, VI (1971) 424-30.
49. P.J. Blok, 'De eerste regeeringsjaren van hertog Albrecht, 1358-1374', *Bijdragen vaderlandsche geschiedenis*, derde serie, II (1885) 244-84.

of the years preceding the *Enqueste* of 1494, and Jansma has shown that during the first decade of the rule of Philip the Good Holland was not prospering as well as might be expected.[50] The exceedingly high number of immigrants from Holland who were resident in London in 1436 — 534 adult males, more than from any other province of the Netherlands[51] — is possibly connected with this unfavourable economic climate. Moreover, the fact that Hollanders emigrated to England in large numbers demonstrates conclusively that the agrarian character of their native land was disintegrating. Many of them, for example, were brewers who began producing hop-flavoured beer in the vicinity of London. It was probably only during the rule of Charles the Bold (1467-77) that Holland enjoyed a few golden years of prosperity. In the *Enqueste*, for example, there were repeated nostalgic references to the great prosperity of 'Duke Charles's days'. The division of the six-year grant of 1473, which amounted to 500,000 *schilden* per annum, gives us an idea of the extent of Holland's wealth in these years. Holland promised to pay 127,000, as much as Flanders and more than Brabant.[52] This foreshadowed the situation that was to develop during the days of the Republic, when Holland's power was largely derived from its quota of 57 per cent in the budget of the generality. True, in normal times during the fifteenth and sixteenth centuries Holland contributed considerably less, but in these cases the 'transport' of 1462 was always enacted, by which Holland still paid more than provinces such as Namur, Luxemburg, and Zeeland.

It is therefore not surprising that the political centre of gravity shifted to The Hague around 1400, as even Muller admitted in his much-quoted essay. According to him, however, this was not so much due to any special merits of Holland but rather to the initiative of the dukes of Burgundy.[53] This I doubt. The Burgundians in fact only laid claim to the government of Holland in 1425, and in their attempts to extend their influence into Friesland and the bishopric of Utrecht they assumed the role of counts of Holland, rather than

---

50. T.S. Jansma, *Het vraagstuk van Hollands welvaren tijdens hertog Philips van Bourgondië* (Groningen, 1950), also in : *Economisch-historische herdrukken... verzameld door de vereniging Het Nederlands Economisch-Historisch Archief* (The Hague, 1964) 55-74.
51. M.R. Thielemans, *Bourgogne et Angleterre. Relations politiques et economiques entre les Pays-Bas bourguignons et l'Angleterre 1435-1467* (Brussels, 1966) 548-9 and Appendix II below.
52. J. Cuvelier, J. Dhondt, R. Doehaard, ed., *Actes des Etats Generaux des Anciens Pays-Bas*, I *1427-1477* (Brussels, 1948) 208.
53. S. Muller, Fzn., *Schetsen*, 24. F. Quicke, *Les Pays-Bas à la veille de l'unification bourguignonne (1356-1384)* (Brussels, 1947) 173 and *passim* recognizes the existence of three great powers in the Netherlands in the second half of the 14th century — Flanders, Brabant, and Holland-Zeeland-Hainault. Albert clearly was aware of the fact that, of the latter, Holland had become the most important. He turned The Hague more and more into a sort of capital, and from 1389 onwards he in fact took up permanent residence in Holland.

dukes of Burgundy.[54] These policies were traditionally Holland's policies, and it was not, I feel, so much the particular merits of the dukes themselves which won them so much success, but rather the increased power and wealth of Holland. This again foreshadowed the developments which were to take place during the days of the Republic.

At this stage I should like to summarize and attempt to explain my remarks so far. I have tried to establish that in the period 1350-1400 Holland was completely transformed from a largely agrarian and rural society to an urban, commercial, and industrial one, and that only during these years did Holland acquire a dominant position in the foreign trade and commerce of the Netherlands. In conjunction with these developments the towns obtained an increasing share in the government of the province, and the province of Holland a leading role in the northern Netherlands. These processes indeed became more marked and more intensive during the fifteenth and sixteenth centuries, but they remained fundamentally unchanged.

If all this is true, it must first be explained why this transformation should have taken place when it did, considering Holland's exceedingly favourable location for every possible type of commercial enterprise. Well, it should first be remembered that in the eleventh century the country must still have been extremely sparsely populated, with a few scattered hamlets on the *geest* lands along the coast and the clay-lands along the river banks. The whole interior of the country consisted of unworked marsh lands, which were systematically reclaimed from the eleventh to the thirteenth centuries. During the early stages of the process, before the land had had time to settle, it was possible to grow corn in these peat-workings, thereby obviating the need for the Hollanders, unlike the hill-villagers of Friesland, to engage in any commercial activity.[55] For centuries, these reclamations provided an occupation for the surplus population, and those who yearned for more adventure could always go off and join in the colonization of eastern Germany. Only in the fourteenth century, when these waste lands had largely disappeared, could the process of urbanization proceed, a development promoted since the thirteenth century by such princes as William II and Florence V, and continued after them by the counts of Hainault. The latter also improved the administration of their own property and revenue, with the help of a number of families of state officials from towns such as Dordrecht and Leiden.

---

54. A.G. Jongkees, 'Bourgondië en de Friese Vrijheid', *De Vrije Fries*, XXXIII (Leeuwarden, 1953) 63.
55. H. van der Linden, *De Cope. Bijdrage tot de rechtsgeschiedenis van de openlegging der Hollandse-Utrechtse laagvlakte* (Assen, 1956) 68.

In addition, it should be explained how this transformation could have occurred between 1350 and 1400, precisely the period which was marked elsewhere in Europe by economic decline — the result partially of the depopulation caused by the Black Death. One might therefore conclude that Holland was not affected, or at least not seriously affected, by the ravages of this disease,[56] and that the province was able to profit from the difficulties encountered by Flanders, Utrecht, and several of the Hanse towns. There are a number of reports about the low standards of pay of Holland sailors in the late Middle Ages. Could it not be that Holland, unaffected by depopulation, was better able to compete against the surrounding areas with their decimated populations and their occasionally hostile guild organizations?

I might justly be accused so far of having thrown together a number of hypotheses, which have yet to be substantiated. This I would readily concede, but I would plead in my defence the fact that so little has been written on the crucial issues in this period of Holland's history from an up-to-date point of view. I am fairly confident of my case concerning the question of economic developments, but the social, institutional, and political aspects of it contain a number of shortcomings. The material for these problems does exist, however, in the often incomplete series of registers and memorandum books of the *Leenkamer* (feudal council) of Holland, and the enormous series of accounts of the financial administration of the county, both of which are preserved in the Rijksarchief in The Hague. Of course, not everyone has been idle in past years — I have already mentioned the work undertaken in the field of economic history. Two pupils of Oppermann dealt respectively in their theses with Council and Exchequer, and Church and State under the Burgundians, making excellent use of the material from the *Leenkamer* and exchequer.[57] But there is still much more to be done. It is therefore encouraging to note a revival of interest in this period of history in recent years. I am thinking especially of the periodical *Holland* with its attendant series of Holland Studies, of the establishment of

56. H. Van Werveke, *De Zwarte Dood in de Zuidelijke Nederlanden*. Mededelingen van de Koninklijke Vlaamse Academie voor Wetenschappen, Klasse der Letteren, XII, iii (Brussels, 1950).
57. T.S. Jansma, *Raad en Rekenkamer in Holland en Zeeland tijdens hertog Philips van Boergondië*. Bijdragen Instituut Middeleeuwsche Geschiedenis Utrecht, XVIII (Groningen, 1932); A.G. Jongkees, *Staat en Kerk in Holland en Zeeland onder de Bourgondische hertogen, 1425-1477, ibidem*, XXI (Groningen, 1942). J. Kruisheer, in his article 'de registers van Pieter van Leiden: het papieren cartularium van de graven van Holland (1299) en het begin van de systematische registratie ter kanselarij', *Nederlands Archievenblad*, LXXII (1968) 27-110, points out (28) the remarkable fact that since the publication of Th. van Riemsdijk's *De tresorie en kanselarij van de graven van Holland en Zeeland uit het Henegouwsche en Beyersche Huis* (The Hague, 1908), virtually nothing more has been written about the archive of the *Leenkamer* (feudal council), which has been preserved almost completely intact. Kruisheer, whose article marks a welcome reversal of this trend, himself describes this collection as 'unique'.

the study-group 'Holland in the late-middle ages', and of the valuable studies not only of foreigners, such as Spading[58] and Unger, but also of Dutchmen, such as the penetrating study of Philip of Leiden by Leupen.[59] I have also noted with pleasure the interest in the study of Holland in the late middle ages here at Leiden University, and I hope to be able to contribute to this in my teaching and research.

APPENDIX I

In 1398 both artisans and men-at-arms were called up; in 1404 only men-at-arms were summoned. By including the artisans with the men-at-arms we arrive at the following table:

town	1398	1404
Dordrecht	640	200 + 200
Haarlem	640	375
Delft	540	300
Leiden	421	225
Alkmaar	315	150
Amsterdam	315	225
Rotterdam	208	120
Schiedam	110	40
Oudewater	160	40
Schoonhoven	264	60
Gouda	420	160
Beverwijk and Wijk-by-Sea	112	40
Geertruidenberg	36	20
Heusden	88	—
's-Gravenzande	24	6
Vlaardingen	24	6
Medemblik	110	70
Monnikendam	108	60
Edam	56	40
Enkhuizen	156	70
Grotebroek	56	50
Woudrichem	67	—
Weesp	31	50 (Weesperkarspel)
Brielle and Voorne	112	100
The Hague	100	—
Hoorn	—	150
Naarden	—	30
Muiden	—	10
Woerden	—	12

58. K. Spading, *Holland und die Hanse im 15. Jahrhundert*. Abhandlungen zur Handels- und Sozialgeschichte, XII (Weimar, 1973).
59. P.H.D. Leupen, 'Filips van Leiden. Een onderzoek naar ontstaan, vorm en inhoud van zijn tractaat 'De cura reipublicae et sorte principantis' (Unpublished thesis, Amsterdam, 1975).

If one accepts that, in 1398 at least, the number of men-at-arms summoned was in direct proportion to the size of the population, we arrive at the conclusion, based on the evidence for Leiden, that one twelfth of the population was called up. The combined population of the towns of Dordrecht, Haarlem, Delft, Leiden, Alkmaar, Amsterdam, and Gouda would then have totalled 40,692. I am well aware, however, that this estimate is suspect, as the proportions in the second list, which are occasionally completely different, indicate only too clearly. Gouda also appears to have been relatively heavily burdened in 1398. It is possible that in 1382 the town had no more than 820 houses: Ramaer, 'Middelpunten', 11.

APPENDIX II

On 29th March, 1436, during the war between Henry VI and Philip of Burgundy which followed the treaty of Arras of 1435, the English king demanded an oath of allegiance from all Philip's subjects who were then permanently resident in England. The same oath was demanded of all immigrants from the Netherlands, irrespective of whether they came from those provinces which were already under Burgundian dominion, or from provinces such as Gelderland, Liège, Friesland, and the Bishopric of Utrecht, which were still free. The lists of those who took this oath are preserved in the *Calender of Patent Rolls Henry VI*, II, *1429-1436* (London, 1907) 537, 539, 541-88, cited by Thielemans, *Bourgogne et Angleterre*, 283 fn. 666. In her book, on pages 283-306 and 494-559, Miss Thielemans gives a penetrating, statistical analysis of this information. She emphasizes the fact that each name is that of one adult male, and in practice, therefore, represents one 'hearth'; and that the totals given are minimal, since it is probable that a number of people refused, or forgot to take the oath. Miss Thielemans argues that the lists only record the names of foreigners who were permanently resident in England, and not merchants who were only temporarily resident and she attributes the high number of emigrants to the unfavourable climate of the Netherlands. The lists also record the place of origin of these immigrants, although in a few cases only the province is given.

A division of the immigrants into their provinces of origin gives the following results:

Duchy of Brabant	385
County of Flanders	94
County of Hainault	14
County of Holland	534
Duchy of Limburg	1
Maastricht	37
Seignory of Mechlin	37
County of Zeeland	145
Seignory of Friesland	14
Duchy of Gelderland	125
Bishopric of Liège	84
Tournai	2
Bishopric of Utrecht	62

The majority of the immigrants settled in London (325) and in the eastern counties along the seacoast: Norfolk (139), Suffolk (95), Essex (82), Surrey (165) and Kent (139).

19

Poverty in Flanders and Brabant from the Fourteenth to the Mid-Sixteenth Century: Sources and Problems *

W.P. BLOCKMANS and W. PREVENIER

I. THE LIMITS OF POVERTY

'Poor' and 'poverty' are such general words — and their use in the sources is no exception — that their application in a scholarly treatise requires a more precise definition. In our view, this can best be approached from the concepts of need or deprivation, which express a lack which may relate to various aspects of the human scale of values and of which the connotation varies according to the social environment. By defining the terms thus, we eliminate a category which contemporaries and also many historians have included in the notion of poverty, namely certain groups which of their own free will chose a sober way of life.[1] For them, spiritual compensations in fact precluded need.

In determining the threshold of need, it is difficult to avoid a subjectively arbitrary choice. Some authors have suggested a vital social minimum, or a mean standard of living, based on the pattern of consumption pertaining to a given social stratum. If one takes account of the fact that the society under the *ancien régime* was essentially agrarian in character and therefore already subject to cyclical crises, whereas in the Netherlands from the fourteenth century onwards the comparatively excessive urbanization, in particular, increased this vulnerability, the biological minimum would appear to be a justifiable criterion. Contemporaries employed other standards, and these also require evaluation.

STANDARD OF LIVING AND VITAL MINIMUM

Better than any specific source emanating from poor relief, or any fiscal or literary document which reflects the opinions of more well-to-do contempo-

* This is an abridged translation of 'Armoede in de Nederlanden van de 14e tot het midden van de 16e eeuw: bronnen en problemen', in *Tijdschrift voor geschiedenis*, LXXXVIII (Groningen, 1975) 501-38. More material, notably in a number of Tables, graphs and a map, will be found in the original version. Conversely, this version embodies a number of additions and corrections.
1. M. Mollat, 'Les problèmes de la pauvreté', in: M. Mollat, ed., *Études sur l'histoire de la pauvreté (Moyen Age-XVIe siècle)* (Paris, 1974) 12-3.

raries, an analysis of cyclical economic developments and purchasing power reveals that poverty is an exceptionally relative and variable concept. Relative because the awareness of poverty is governed by the pattern of needs and values which exists in a given society. Variable because all manner of variable factors, which we shall proceed to analyse, continually influence the living standards of populations.

The starting point is the minimal human requirement for food, satisfied in the cheapest possible manner. Experts in the science of nutrition calculated some time ago that an adult needs between 2,000 and 3,500 calories daily, according to the nature of the work which he or she performs and his or her age. A child below the age of 15 can on average manage on 2,000 calories. For a family consisting of two adults and two children, the calorific requirement can thus be put at roughly 10,000 per day.[2] In the Netherlands, prior to the eighteenth century, the cheapest source of these calories was bread, after which came pulses.[3] Variation in diet is even more important than the volume consumed. No single product supplies sufficient energy plus the full range of proteins, fats, minerals and vitamins required. Therefore, a poverty limit may not be calculated on the basis of the satisfaction of the calorific requirement with bread alone,[4] a situation which, especially with children, would eventually lead to a shortage of essential dietary components and thus to damage to health. This phenomenon must undoubtedly be regarded as a form of need. The possibility that a body which suffers protracted undernourishment develops a slower than normal digestive process, which extracts more than the normal quantity of energy from a given amount of food, is, and must remain, an unknown factor in this context.

Besides food, the bare necessities of life include clothing and housing, two items on which compromises can be accepted in the interests of food, but not without stepping into an area of need. A theoretically interesting line of investigation would be to prosopographically assemble, on the basis of legacy declarations, types of wealth and goods and chattels for certain professional categories. Then, the sum of experiences of life would be materially revealed.

2. R. Masseyeff, *La faim* (Paris, 1956); F. Lévy, *L'alimentation* (Paris, 1962) 61; J. Fourastié, *Machinisme et bien-être* (Paris, 1951) 32ff.; C.M. De La Roncière, 'Pauvres et pauvreté à Florence au XIVᵉ siècle', in: *Études sur l'histoire de la pauvreté*, II, 674-6; C. Catfield, *Food Composition Tables for International Use* (New York, 1949).
3. J. Craeybeckx, 'Brood en levensstandaard', in: *Bijdragen tot de prijzengeschiedenis*, III (Louvain, 1948) 134-9.
4. R. Gascon, 'Economie et pauvreté aux XVIᵉ et XVIIᵉ siècles, Lyon, ville exemplaire et prophétique', in: *Études sur l'histoire de la pauvreté*, II, 748-51, fixes the limit of expenditure on bread for a family of four at 70% of the daily disposable income, which is deemed to be the threshold of poverty. This ratio, however, minimizes other types of food and items of expenditure.

It must, however, be feared that even in the best-documented cases the methodological difficulties would be immense (uncertainties regarding identification, lack of indications concerning rank in a craft trade). By employing the typical (statistically most common) patterns of consumption for each social category as a norm, we allow subjective appreciation, which cannot be dissociated from the concept of need, to assume its rightful proportions.

In the typical working-class budgets of the *ancien régime*, the best-qualified authors, who base their findings on divergent data, put food at 70-80 per cent, rent at 5-15 per cent, lighting and heating at 5-10 per cent and clothing similarly at 5-10 per cent. Of the expenditure on food, some 15 per cent related to items of animal origin, about 11 per cent to produce of vegetable origin and 44 per cent to bread.[5] If we accept this pattern as typical for the bricklayer or worker of comparable status with a wife and two as yet non-working children to support — a family which the majority of authors took as a model — we can say that if the price of the customary quantity of bread, which represented 44 per cent of the budget, was exceeded, a needy situation existed. This quantity can be put at about 2.5 kg per day,[6] or in calorie equivalent 6,250 of the 10,000 required. However, we view this balance between bread and other foodstuffs as being relatively favourable and probably specific for the higher categories of workers (qualified men, master craftsmen and journeymen). Doubtless the diet of the lower socio-professional classes contained a larger proportion of bread. For the family of four which we have chosen as being typical, we would go so far as to put the consumption at 3.2 kg per day, leaving 20 per cent of the calories to be obtained from other food items.

In addition to the differences in patterns of consumption brought about by discrepancies in incomes, the vicissitudes of the times, which can upset the composition of the budgets, must be taken into account. Cyclical variations in agricultural production, changes in the level of wages and fluctuations in the purchasing power of incomes — of which the last-named largely derives from the first two — are the principal factors governing fluctuations in the living standard. The volume of wages is greatly influenced by the relationship between the demand for labour and the supply. On the one hand, the level of wages reflects this relationship; on the other hand, it is expressed, via the level of employment, in the total income of a population. But purchasing power is also governed in part by the monetary situation. It is known that, as a result

---

5.   E. Scholliers, *De levensstandaard in de XVe en XVIe eeuw te Antwerpen* (Antwerp, 1960) 167; F. Braudel, *Civilisation matérielle et capitalisme* (Paris, 1967) 99; W. Abel, *Massenarmut und Hungerkrisen im vorindustriellen Europa* (Hamburg, 1974) 395-6: the exact figures are derived from this source, even though the budget relates to a family consisting of a bricklayer, his wife and three children in Berlin in 1800.
6.   Gascon, 'Economie et pauvreté', 751.

of the accelerated fall in the value of money during the approximate periods 1350-90, 1410-30 and 1475-90, and in 1520 and the succeeding years, purchasing power fell sharply owing to the slowness, inadequacy and selective nature of wage adjustments.[7]

These elementary factors of economic life governed the fluctuations in the living standard — and with these the rise and fall of the number of needy persons — in the highly vulnerable agrarian society of the *ancien régime*. This approach places less emphasis on the traditional definition of poverty, consecrated by ecclesiastical doctrine, as embracing widows, orphans, the elderly, the infirm and the sick — categories which in early-modern times continued to be among the groups receiving relief. Rather, our method highlights the numerically far more important groups of people who, having lost their social position or been pushed out of declining sectors of the production process, or having suffered successive food crises, were living almost at subsistence level. These categories had in common an absence of reserves with which to support themselves and limited opportunities for the deployment of their labour. The description of this group of *paupérisables* is by definition mobile, *i.e.* it is determined by the economic climate in a well-defined, not too extensive geographical context — for example, a town and its environs and/or commercial hinterland.

The sources demanded by this method have been sufficiently publicized and critically weighed in the economic study. Series of price and wage statistics reveal their specific interpretative possibilities[8] which, notably for the southern Netherlands, are realized in the publication of numerous and diverse series. By combining series of prices and wages which are homogeneous and representative in terms of time, place and nature, it is possible to express the purchasing power *in natura* of wages in various sectors for many towns.[9] For heuristic reasons, however, the majority of the available wage series relate to the building sector, which cannot in itself be regarded as representative of an entire urban economy.

For the investigation, a far more serious difficulty lies in the complete un-

7. The study by H. Van Werveke, 'De economische en sociale gevolgen van de muntpolitiek der graven van Vlaanderen (1337-1433)', in his *Miscellanea Mediaevalia* (Ghent, 1968) 243-54, still constitutes an example in this area.
8. The reader is referred, solely for purposes of orientation, to H. Van der Wee, 'Problèmes de statistique historique', *Belgisch tijdschrift voor filologie en geschiedenis*, XLVI (Brussels, 1968) 490-512, and, in this connexion, *idem*, 'Les archives hospitalières et l'étude de la pauvreté aux Pays-Bas du XVe au XVIIIe siècle', *Revue du Nord*, XLVIII (1966) 5-16.
9. Broadly conceived examples of this method were recently provided by E. Scholliers, 'Le pouvoir d'achat dans les Pays-Bas au XVIe siècle', in : *Album Charles Verlinden* (Ghent, 1975) 305-30, and *idem*, 'De materiële verschijningsvormen van de armoede voor de industriële revolutie. Omvang, evolutie en oorzaken', *Tijdschrift voor geschiedenis*, LXXXVIII (1975) 451-67.

certainty regarding the level of employment, which of course exerts an immense influence on the income of the working population. Studies of the amount of labour expended for a given employer, *e.g.* a town as public entrepreneur, repeatedly show that the employment provided, on an individual basis, is irregular and discontinuous in the extreme and consistently inadequate.[10] The trend elaborated by H. Van der Wee for the Antwerp region is extremely valuable and illustrative.[11] This shows that the 270 potential working days per year were never fully utilized and that between 1437 and 1516 the actual number of days worked fluctuated between 200 and 220, falling to 191-195 in the crisis of 1484-94. Thereafter, the trend was primarily upward, reaching a maximum of 252-260 in the period 1544-49. We would, however, stress that the statistics quoted here must not be seen as indicative of other regions. The Antwerp market area was an exception in terms of scale in Europe, and the expansion which it underwent during the first two-thirds of the sixteenth century may certainly not be assumed to have been matched in the rest of the Netherlands. Indeed, the nearby town of Mechlin, which initially flourished in the wake of the metropolis, experienced an economic decline: commencing at the end of the fifteenth century, this accelerated in the years after 1520 and by 1540 had assumed catastrophic proportions. This, then, was exactly the opposite of the situation in Antwerp, and it has the advantage that it is based on material concerning other, more dominant sectors of the urban economy, namely the linen industry, commerce and services.[12] Clearly, under a system of payment by the day, employment remains an unknown factor, but one which is of decisive importance for determining income.

Similarly, uncertainty exists with regard to the composition of the family and the number of members in receipt of a regular income. Most authors work on the basis of one breadwinner in a family of four. Abel, Labrousse and Scholliers, in contrast, assume the existence of three children.[13] Illustrative in this context are the numbers of children in 41 families which in 1534-9 received assistance from the *aumône générale* of Lyons. Thirteen families, *i.e.* nearly one-third of the total, had two children, and these formed by far the

---

10. Examples in the dissertation of J.P. Sosson, *L'industrie du bâtiment à Bruges aux XIVe et XVe siècles*, to be published by Pro Civitate, Brussels.
11. H. Van der Wee, *The growth of the Antwerp market (14th-16th century)*, I (The Hague, 1963) 540-3.
12. R. Van Uytven, 'De omvang van de Mechelse lakenproduktie vanaf de 14e tot de 16e eeuw', in: *Noordgouw*, V (Antwerp, 1965) 112-7, 118, 122-3, 129-30.
13. Abel, *Massenarmut*, 396; Scholliers, *Levensstandaard*, 158-9.

largest group; but both the average and the median were 3, for not only were there 9 families with this number of children, but also 12 with between 4 and 7.[14] The number of children and, more important still, their ages undoubtedly played a vital role in the family budget. In general terms, the first fifteen years of a marriage, in which two or three children survived, may be regarded as the most problematical period in the career of the potential pauper. Thereafter, things would improve as a result of additional income from juvenile labour — always assuming, of course, that the marriage was not terminated by the death of one of the parents, something which, according to demographic statistics, occurred on a large scale. The death, illness or disability of the husband were the greatest causes of need, as can be deduced from the disproportionate number of widows and wives appearing in every form of documentation pertaining to poverty. The phenomenon of poverty must therefore be viewed against the dynamic background of the life cycle.

A precise demarcation of the needy elements in a population would thus require a complete picture of the economic circumstances and also a social stratification of the population based on professional category, income and demographic factors. It is evident that, strictly speaking, the data at our disposal in this area concerning the Netherlands in the fourteenth to sixteenth centuries are inadequate. However, much more can be achieved by means of comparative research, albeit the results will be virtually limited to the towns.

As the social structure and economic developments in the rural areas differ from those in the towns, they demand a separate heuristic and treatment. Need in a rural area cannot be measured by expressing wages (which in themselves are problematical as a datum) in quantities of bread. What is required is to determine the wealth structure, the crop yields, the conditions of exploitation and — an almost impossible task — the amount of labour produced. The forms in which poverty is manifested are less varied in rural areas than in the towns. Moreover, the scattered nature of rural dwellings was an obstacle to consciousness of poverty, with the result that secondary conflicts between village communities frequently camouflaged objective contrasts.[15]

Three examples will serve to elucidate this method.

---

14. Z. Davis, 'Assistance, humanisme et hérésie: le cas de Lyon', in: *Études sur l'histoire de la pauvreté*, II, 768.
15. F. Graus, 'Au bas moyen-âge : pauvres des villes et pauvres des campagnes', *Annales E.S.C.*, XVI (Paris, 1961) 1059-61.

Special building accounts drawn up by the municipal authorities in Ghent and dating from a very early period have survived,[16] as have the accounts of the *Hl. Geesttafel*, 'Table of the Holy Ghost', the poor relief organization, of a centrally located parish, St. Nicholas, in which the annual selling prices of rye are recorded.[17] These reveal a wide fluctuation in the period 1321-6, the minimum and maximum prices over the six years differing by a factor of 3.4 (Table I). Taking a groundworker (journeyman digger) as an example, the data are as follows : day wage (summer) 18 d.par.; day wage (winter) 16 d.par.; maximum annual wage (270 days) 4,680 d.par.; normal annual requirement of rye bread for four persons 1,168 kg., for which 25.28 *halsters* (a measure employed in Ghent) of rye were needed.

TABLE I. *Annual expenditure on bread, as a percentage of maximum annual wage, of workers in Ghent (first quarter of the fourteenth century)*

	Price of rye per halster	Baking cost	Cost price of bread	% of max.annual wage
1320-1	60 d.par.	253 d.par.	1,770 d.par.	37.3
1321-2	96	253	2,680	57.3
1322-3	50	253	1,517	32.4
1323-4	36	253	1,163	24.8
1324-5	38	253	1,214	25.9
1325-6	28	253	961	20.5

The period may in general be described as favourable. This is evidenced by the major building works carried out for the city, which included the Town Hall and the Belfry. Nevertheless, 1321-2 was a highly problematical year; 1320-1 was also difficult. If our digger had then worked, not 270 days but only 232 — a hypothesis which, as demonstrated, is still very favourable — he would again have crossed the threshold of need.

16. J. Vuylsteke, *Gentsche stads- en baljuwsrekeningen 1280-1336*, (Ghent, 1900) 191-233, 281-319, 473-97.
17. Rijksarchief, Ghent, S 498-504; annual purchases and sales of 4 *halsters* of rye (1 *halster* = 53 litres).

BRUGES, FOURTEENTH-FIFTEENTH CENTURY

We can base our observations on the wage statistics given in the dissertation of J.P. Sosson[18] and the published series of prices.[19] In the following Table, our primary aim is to demonstrate the effects of the creeping devaluation of the mid-fifteenth century and the accelerated devaluation of the second half of the fourteenth and the late-fifteenth centuries (Table II). For the fifteenth century, we chose the years in which grain prices were highest. The maximum

TABLE II. *Annual expenditure on bread, as a percentage of maximum annual wage, of workers in Bruges (fourteenth and fifteenth centuries)*

	Price of rye per *hoet*	Cost price of bread	Day wage		Max. annual wage		% of max. annual wage required for bread	
			D	B	D	B	D	B
	gr.	gr.	gr.	gr.	gr.	gr.	%	%
1362-3 min.	24	217	3	3	810	810	27	27
max.	29	258					32	32
average	27	242					30	30
1363-4 min.	44	381	3.5	3.5	945	945	40	40
max.	53	454					48	48
average	47	405					43	43
1416-7 min.	60	512	4	5	1,080	1,350	47	38
max.	88	741					69	55
average	77	651					60	48
1438-9 min.	60	512	5	5	1,350	1,350	38	38
max.	120	1,002					74	74
average	96	806					60	60
1455-6 min.	60	512	S 6	6	1,530	1,620	33	32
max.	62	528	W 5				35	33
average	61	520					34	32
1482-3 min.	96	806	S 6	S 6	1,530	1,530	53	53
max.	143	1,191	W 5	W 5			78	78
average	116	970					63	63

D = digger (journeyman)   B = bricklayer's assistant   S = summer wage   W = winter wage

18. Sosson, *Industrie*, appendices 55-6 and 65-6. The wages in these trades are representative of many others in the construction sector.
19. A. Verhulst, 'Prijzen van granen, boter en kaas te Brugge volgens de "slag" van het Sint-Donaaskapittel (1348-1801)', in: C. Verlinden *et alii*, ed., *Dokumenten voor de geschiedenis van prijzen en lonen* (Bruges, 1959-75) II A, 43-5.

number of days worked was again put at 270, although it should be borne in mind that the actual figure was usually about one-quarter lower. The prices were quoted three times a year; of these, we have taken the lowest and highest quotations and the average of the three. The normal annual requirement for rye bread for 4 persons was met with 8.179 Bruges *hoets* (*hoet* averaged 168 litres). We added 21 gr. to cover baking costs.

It can be deduced from the Table that wage adjustments, such as the one in 1363, were not adequate to enable workers in the lower categories to get through the many expensive years of the second half of the fourteenth century free of problems. On the other hand, the relatively prosperous nature of the middle part of the fifteenth century is revealed. The sole period of high prices in the space of forty years (1455-7) passed without encroaching upon the vital minimum for the groups concerned. A much more serious situation existed during the long crisis from 1475 to 1490, which formed a prelude to the process of pauperization which was to take place in large areas of the southern Netherlands during the sixteenth century.

MECHLIN IN THE FIRST HALF OF THE SIXTEENTH CENTURY

With this example, we seek principally to highlight the social impact of the pauperization process. Assuming an employment rate of 270 days, the Table shows the number of years during which the socio-professional classes which have been distinguished failed to attain the vital minimum as earlier defined[20] (Table III).

TABLE III. *Number of years during which the purchasing power in Mechlin remained below the vital minimum (1501-45)*

	farm worker	digger	bricklayer's assistant	paviour (journeyman)	bricklayer (journeyman)
1501-10	3	–	–	–	–
1511-20	6	3	1	–	–
1521-5	5	4	4	–	–
1526-30	5	5	4	1	–
1531-5	5	5	2	–	–
1536-40	5	5	3	–	–
1541-5	5	5	4	1	1
Total	34	27	18	2	1

20. As no grain price series have so far been published for Mechlin, we used the average prices for rye in Antwerp, even though these on the whole appeared to be slightly higher: E.

Besides the increase in pauperization from 1520 onwards, the Table reveals, in particular, the differentiation of the social consequences of the process. The better organized and less easily replaceable a professional group, the greater was the extent to which its purchasing power was protected against the galloping inflation. Until 1545, the limit of the group of *paupérisables* remained beneath the level of journeymen. The frequency and continuity of the years in which the threshold of need was crossed evidently confronted whole professional categories with crises in which their very existence was at stake and from which they were unable to recover. This affords a more penetrating description of poverty than can be obtained from any other source material.

The limit of poverty may often be an individually subjective datum and one with a high degree of relativity (fluctuating in time and space), but it is nonetheless useful to establish where contemporaries envisaged that limit or actually placed it.

THE LIMIT OF FISCAL POVERTY

In Flanders and Brabant, those in receipt of poor relief usually appear as a separate group in the fifteenth- and sixteenth-century hearth censuses, evidently because account was taken of them fiscally and because the group presumably did not pay taxes. In Artois, Hainaut and Luxembourg, on the other hand, the poor were in most cases included in the lists of taxpayers and taxed with them. Of the 27,203 hearths counted in Hainaut in 1365, only 171 (0.6 per cent) were exempted from payment on grounds of poverty. If we look at data from other sources and of later date, this percentage cannot possibly embrace all those in receipt of relief; in 1413, not a single poor hearth was mentioned separately: the poor were included in the overall list. M. Arnould rightly postulates that in 1365 and 1413 the aim was evidently to draw everyone into the fiscal net, if necessary only marginally.[21] In this system, the fiscal limit of poverty is non-existent, or nearly so, in the sense that no one is out of range. A contemporary defined the situation as one in which: 'le riche portait le

Scholliers, 'Prijzen en lonen te Antwerpen (15e-16e eeuw)', in: Verlinden, *Dokumenten*, I, 277; *idem*, 'Lonen te Mechelen in de XVe en XVIe eeuw', *ibidem*, IIB, 1279-81. For a more thorough analysis of these data, the reader is referred to: W.P. Blockmans, 'Armenzorg en levensstandaard te Mechelen vóór de hervorming van de openbare onderstand (1545)', *Handelingen van de koninklijke kring voor oudheidkunde te Mechelen* (Mechlin, 1976) 141-73.
21. M.A. Arnould, ed., *Les dénombrements de foyers dans le comté de Hainaut*. Commission Royale d'Histoire (Brussels, 1956) 141, 279; in 1540 the poor were explicitly registered as a separate group, which fact produces the fairly normal ratio of 9,219:34,286 = 26.9 %.

pauvre'; this implied that in time of need the well-to-do, by way of a tax surcharge, subsidized their less fortunate fellow villagers.[22]

Later, a different fiscal limit emerged, namely in the degrees of liability for tax. In 1540 the authorities in Hainaut distinguished the poor among the three rural categories, *i.e.* 1) the *laboureurs* and *censiers*; 2) the *heritiers* and *louaigiers*, the so-called well-to-do; and 3) the poor, which category proves to consist of *pauvres vivans de l'aumosne* and includes a number of beggars *allans mendyer*, those receiving relief from the *Hl. Geesttafels* or *armendissen*. But these poor people are taxed. They can be divided into two sub-groups, whose quota amounts to 10 or 20 per cent of the highest rate of 60 patars (3 Carolus florins), namely 6 or 12 patars. In practice, however, a number of them were unable to pay, and in the issue of local demands an effort was made to omit the poorest families in order to reduce the total number of hearths; but this led to a game of evasion to the benefit of the more well-to-do, to whom the principle 'le riche portait le pauvre' ceased to apply.[23] At any rate, the needy of no fixed abode (itinerant beggars) — who, indeed, were fairly hard to track down — were not included for the purpose of the censuses (Hainaut, 1540; Artois, 1475), and certainly not for the parish quota.[24] Between them and the *disarmen* (those regularly in receipt of full poor relief from the *armendissen*), lay the official fiscal poverty line. The records show that in Artois, *e.g.* in the village of Dainville in 1475, 19 poor households together paid 18 sol. as against the 3 lb. 16 s. paid by 16 well-to-do hearths, a ratio of 1:5. A standard of judgement is also found in the fact that in other Artesian villages the annual quota for the poor varies between 1 and 4 s. par. — the daily wage of a very humble workman.[25] This implies that a worker who was not employed throughout the year on a day wage basis, by reason of lack of employment or crop failure, should immediately fall below the limit for tax liability.

In Flanders, where the poor apparently did not pay, the limit is as follows. In the 1469 hearth census in the small town of Lo, three fiscal categories were

---

22. In Walloon Flanders, 1449; Luxembourg, 1495 and 1501; Burgundy, 1483. A. Bocquet, *Recherches sur la population rurale de l'Artois et du Boulonnais, 1348-1477* (Arras, 1969), 133; J. Grob and J. Vannérus, *Dénombrement des feux des duché de Luxembourg et comté de Chiny.* Commission Royale d'Histoire (Brussels, 1921) 98; J. Favier, *Finance et fiscalité au bas moyen-âge* (Paris, 1971) 200-1.
23. Arnould, *Dénombrements*, 141, 180-3.
24. *Ibidem*, 41, note 4 (occasionally a number is quoted, e.g. 33 beggars in Morlanwelz in 1531); Bocquet, *Recherches*, 139.
25. Bocquet, *Recherches*, 139; round about 1475, a bricklayer's assistant in Ghent could earn as much as 6 s. par. per day, and an unskilled labourer 2-3 s.: E. Scholliers, 'Lonen te Gent XVe-XIXe eeuw' in: Verlinden, *Dokumenten*, IIA, 423, 426; regarding the Franc of Bruges, see also 94-5.

distinguished. The highest (67 persons) paid more than 4 s. par.[26] The middle group (40 persons) paid 4 s. par. or less. The *disarmen* (37 persons) and three unpropertied persons were exempted.[27] Thus the middle group, in terms of tax burden, correspond to the group of *disarmen* in Artois. In the tax lists of the town of Ostend for 1411-2, the lowest group, numbering 96 out of a total of 575 (16.7 per cent), paid $^{1}/_{4}$ lod, slightly more than $2^{1}/_{2}$ s.par.; in the light of the Flemish context, this would constitute the border with the untaxed *disarmen*, who indeed existed in Ostend — at least in 1469.[28] In the rural textile centre of Hondschoote, three categories were distinguished in 1469: the well-to-do (260 persons) paid 40 s.par. or more; the middle group (209 persons) paid 4 s.par. or less; and the poor (43 persons) were exempted.[29]

With the special levies in Ghent in 1492-4, the situation was different again. A single tax of one guilder per family was imposed, but exemption was granted to all 'who were very poor or lived on parish relief' — a form of words which clearly confirmed that the relief did not fully cover the actual poverty. The extent of this group can be measured by comparison with a two year older fiscal document, in which the *disarmen* did not constitute an exempt category: 53 per cent of the families included in the levy of 1492 do not reappear in 1494. Although the *disarmen* were assessed by the same standards as all other inhabitants, they at that time enjoyed a remission of fifty per cent, as was accorded to all clerical persons.[30] The explanation is simple: regular assistance from a parochial relief organization implied that the property of the recipient became part of the patrimony of the organization concerned.

The very wide divergence and variability of the criteria for fiscal exemption make these limits difficult to apply, the more so since they do not coincide with the limits applying to relief.[31] Here, too, the most valuable datum proves to be the standard of living, *i.e.* the expression of the minimum assessment in a wage category.

26. 12 of the 67 persons in this upper group have an income in excess of 6 lb. gro.; the remainder are craftsmen and *labeurders* (labourers).
27. Algemeen Rijksarchief, Brussels, Trésor de Flandre, no. 1356.
28. Algemeen Rijksarchief, Brussels, Rekenkamers. Reg. no. 16,102-3; in 1469 there were 105 paupers out of a total of 495.
29. 'Are so poor that they cannot pay ...' (Archives départementales du Nord, Lille, B 195/25).
30. W. Blockmans, 'Peilingen naar de sociale strukturen te Gent tijdens de late 15e eeuw', in *Studiën betreffende de sociale strukturen te Brugge, Kortrijk en Gent in de 14e en 15e eeuw*, I. Standen en Landen, LIV (Heule, 1971) 227, 231-2. The taxing of *disarmen*, exceptional in Flanders, in 1492 may be a product of the acute financial situation in the town at that time.
31. Cf. critical comments in the same vein by Mollat, 'Les problèmes de la pauvreté', 21-2.

The *enquêtes* conducted in rural areas in the fifteenth and sixteenth centuries do not afford an explanation of the criteria on which the eligibility for relief was assessed. In attempting to deduce these, we run into methodological problems which demand more thorough research than was possible. Here are some approximations based on the *enquête* held in the castelry of Lille in 1543, which gives an inventory of the area of land cultivated by each villager, the tributes paid, the quantity of goods rented, the value of parcels of land when sold, the number of animals kept, etc.

In the case of the village of Capinghem, it appears that the area of land in use constituted the criterion.[32] The gap between the largest and smallest holdings, which were of 33 hectares 65 ares and 26 ares respectively — a ratio of 126:1 — is sufficiently large to span the entire range from maximum to minimum. The 33 ha. correspond to J.M. Duvosquel's interpretation of a full agricultural pursuit in that area, while in the neighbouring Hainaut, according to Sivéry, 5 ha. was the bare minimum on which to support a family.[33] The 26-are plot can have been no more than a kitchen garden, the tenders of which must have been labourers, paid by the day. As 6 of the 27 hearths in the village were eligible for assistance, we can put the poverty line in this case at between 39 and 43 ares. The lowest tribute among the well-to-do is 7 lb.par.

If, however, we seek to combine the criterion of land area with other criteria, such as annual tribute, realizable value of land worked or owned, etc., the picture becomes obscure owing to the absence of a number of elements of information. If in the case of the Escobeques files we employ land area as the criterion, we find that there is a ratio of 49:1 and that the poverty line (for the 6 poor hearths among the 18) lies between 164 and 251 ares. If, however, we classify the files on the basis of market value of land, we find that plots of 43, 78, 104 and 113 ares were at times priced at the same figure, namely 100 Carolus florins; in all probability this was due to differences in the quality of the land. The dividing line appears to lie *below* an area of 1 ha. 42a., worked for a tribute of 6.5 Carolus florins and having a market value of 300 florins.

Wage earners in the rural areas were very likely to fall below the poverty line unless they could supplement their income by cultivating tribute land with an area of more than 38 are (in some villages as much as 163 are).

For the towns, data concerning the relationship between wealth and any

---

32. Archives départementales du Nord, B 3752 (no. 24) and 3753 (no. 4).

33. J.M. Duvosquel, *Un document d'histoire rurale: le dénombrement de la seigneurie de Comines, 1470* (Leuven and Ghent 1971) 10 (between 21 and 31 hectares); G. Sivéry, *Structures agraires et vie rurale dans le Hainaut à la fin du Moyen-Age* (2 vols., Lille, 1973).

relief are far scarcer. It can be deduced from the levy imposed in Ghent in 1492 that 18 per cent of the families living in the parish of St. James received assistance from the parochial relief organizations. Of the 91 families receiving assistance, eleven were not in the lowest fiscal category. Only 37 per cent of the remaining 80 families were actually in receipt of relief. One *disarme* stood on the third of the five rungs of the fiscal ladder. The rentable value of the houses occupied by the *disarmen* varied from 48 to 312 groats annually, a ratio of 1:6.5. Three families in receipt of relief occupied houses with a rentable value in excess of the general average for the parish of 217 groats.[34] Of greater interest, however, is the finding that an unskilled worker or bricklayer's assistant who, being adequately employed, spent 10 per cent of his annual wage of 1,200 groats or thereabouts on rent would just fall into the lowest fiscal category.[35] It is thus obvious that the eleven assisted families on the higher rungs of the ladder must have been in higher income groups.

The inference is thus clear: the rentable value of the houses reveals in an undoubtedly representative manner very wide differences in status among those receiving assistance. One could justify this discrepancy by assuming that the better-off among this group had become impoverished as a result of loss of income through illness, disability, acts of war, riots, etc. This, however, did nothing to sweeten the pill for the 63 per cent of the poor who received no assistance. At any rate, the sources concerning poor relief in the towns afford little to go on in fixing a poverty line.

II. TAXATION AND POVERTY

Disarmen and fiscal paupers are not always synonymous. Under a system employed in Brabant, the total tax liability of every town was reduced by 10 per cent, and that of every village by 20 per cent, to allow for the poor in fiscal terms.[36] Consequently the percentage of 'poor' hearths in the censuses cannot be a reflection of the evolution of real need. The frequent use which a number of authors have made of them with the aim of discovering trends

---

34. W. Blockmans, 'De vermogensstruktuur in de St. Jacobsparochie te Gent in 1492-4', in: *Studiën betreffende de sociale strukturen te Brugge, Kortrijk en Gent*, III. Standen en Landen, LXIII (Heule, 1973) 150-98, in which data in Blockmans, 'Peilingen', 232, are amended.

35. Scholliers, 'Lonen te Gent', 388, 392, 412, 415-6, 423; the summer wage amounted to 5-6 gr. per day, and the winter wage to 3-5.

36. J. Cuvelier, *Les dénombrements de foyers en Brabant* (Brussels, 1912) cxliii and ccxiii (1464 and 1496). In the Bois-le-Duc region, a different *forfait*, namely 12.5%, was applied: Blockmans and Prevenier, 'Openbare armenzorg te 's-Hertogenbosch tijdens een groeifase, 1435-1535', *Annalen van de Belgische vereniging voor hospitaalgeschiedenis*, XII (Brussels, 1976) 22-4.

towards pauperization is therefore unjustified.[37] On the other hand, the population censuses themselves were evidently carried out in a fairly reliable manner, and the tax quotas were consistently adapted to meet changes in the socioeconomic situation.

We are not so well informed with regard to the major towns in the county of Flanders. For Ypres, there is only one statistic dating from 1431; this relates to one of the wards, the *Ghemeene Neringhe* (common crafts).[38] Out of 850 families, 51 householders are stated to be poor and mendicant (6.0 per cent) and 38 others to be in almshouses (4.5 per cent), making a total of 89 householders or past householders out of 850 (10.5 per cent).[39] In the same ward, only 178 families out of 850 are liable for tax (20.9 per cent); in other words, 672 families are poor in fiscal terms, and of these, 89 (13.2 per cent) are in receipt of assistance. For Bruges, there are tax registers for 1394-6, which show that only 0.16 per cent (in three of the six wards) were exempt from taxation. At the same time, nearly 12 per cent pay less than 1 s.par.[40] In the very drastic levy imposed in the parish of St. James, in Ghent, in 1492, in which every family was regarded as taxable, 49 per cent defaulted, even though the minimum assessment (10 per cent on the lowest house rent of 48 groats) amounted to no more than one day's wages for an unskilled worker.[41]

For the small towns, though not all, and part of the rural area, our material is virtually limited to a momentary picture dating from 1469.[42] The percentage of poor in these towns varied between 2.6 and 40.7, the overall average being 26 per cent.

For one such town, Courtrai, we have information spanning a longer period. In a tax levy of 1440, there are among 1,782 burgher hearths 15 poor householders (0.8 per cent) who pay no tax, but a further 94 (5.3 per cent) who are assessed at the minimum rate of 5 s. 4 d.par. — the equivalent of one day's

37. J.A. Van Houtte, 'Maatschappelijke toestanden' in: *Algemene Geschiedenis der Nederlanden*, IV (Utrecht, 1952) 239-40; Van der Wee, *The growth of the Antwerp market*, II, 70, 90-1, 113-4.
38. H. Pirenne, 'Les dénombrements de la population d'Ypres au XVe siècle', *Vierteljahrschrift für Sozial- und Wirtschaftsgeschichte*, I (Wiesbaden, 1903) 13, 27, 30-2.
39. The data mentioned by Pirenne are not absolutely exact, and are misleading to the extent that the 51 poor families mentioned appear to be incomplete (39 are headed by a woman) and that 38 of the occupants of institutions have no partners. Strictly speaking, we should therefore compare 38 + 51 (× 1 or 2) with 850 (— 89) times the family coefficient of 3.5. This applies to all the other data.
40. I. De Meyer, 'De sociale strukturen te Brugge in de 14e eeuw' in: *Studiën betreffende de sociale strukturen*, I, 41. Cf. *passim*, discussion of fiscal categories.
41. Blockmans, 'Peilingen naar de sociale strukturen', 228.
42. Archives départementales du Nord, B 195 and 197; Algemeen Rijksarchief, Brussels, Rekenkamer, Reg. 45,978; *ibidem*, Trés. de Fl. no. 1356. The work by J. de Smet, 'Le dénombrement des foyers en Flandre en 1469', *Bulletin Commission Royale d'Histoire*, XCIX (Brussels, 1935) 105-50, is inaccurate in many respects.

wages for an unskilled worker. This group, which grew from 5 to 18 per cent by the end of the fifteenth century, was gradually exempted from taxation. In addition to, and separate from, this taxable group are paupers not having the status of burghers, who, numbered 67 in 1447, 105 in 1451, 330 in 1476 and 340 in 1490. Thus the number of paupers round about 1440 may be put at $94 + 67 + 15 = 176$, or approximately ten per cent of the population.[43]

For the Flemish countryside, the overall percentage of paupers in villages where their numbers are known is exactly 25 (if we include the many villages for which information is lacking, we arrive at an absolute minimum of 18.3 per cent), but the individual figures vary from 8.5 to 40 per cent. The figure of 25 per cent lies very close to the 26 per cent for the small towns, and in both cases there are very wide fluctuations between the various areas and towns.[44]

Nine fiscal *enquêtes* conducted in thirteen villages in Walloon Flanders (the castelries of Lille, Orchies and Douai) show that the average proportion of paupers in the total population grew from 22 per cent in 1432 to 40.5 per cent in 1544.[45]

The data for Brabant, obtained from the hearth censuses published by Cuvelier — which, however, have not been verified by us from the sources, nor subjected to the criticism of Mrs. Tits-Dieuaide[46] — are:

% 'poor' hearths	1437	1480	1526
Total	23.4	27.3	25.8
Large towns	10.5	13.7	19.2
Small towns	9.2	27	28.6
Rural areas	29.7	30.3	27.3

In 1365, the poor in Hainaut were evidently not taxed. In 1540 they represented 26.9 per cent of the total number of hearths, and in 1562 21.7 per cent.[47]

It would be premature to attempt to indicate the mechanisms which explain

43. C. Pauwelijn, 'De gegoede burgerij van Kortrijk in de 15e eeuw', in: *Studiën betreffende de sociale strukturen*, I, 165, notes 25 and 175-6.
44. This is strikingly evident from the rural map and Tables IV and V relating to the small towns and villages in each castelry in 1469: Blockmans and Prevenier, 'Armoede in de Nederlanden', 513-5.
45. *Ibidem*, Table VI.
46. *Ibidem*, Table VII, which contains figures derived from Cuvelier, *Dénombrements*, 432-87 and *passim*. Limitations with respect to the applicability of this work are dealt with in M.J. Tits-Dieuaide, 'L'assistance aux pauvres à Louvain au XVe siècle', in: *Hommage P. Bonenfant* (Brussels, 1965) 437-8, note 4; during verification of the sources for the Bois-le-Duc quarter, it was found that the data supplied by Cuvelier were incomplete, which implies that the results require revision. Blockmans and Prevenier, 'Openbare armenzorg', 22-31.
47. Arnould, *Dénombrements*, 181-3 and 200.

the scope and dynamics of this statistical material. We shall therefore content ourselves with one or two suggestions for further investigation.

It could be said that a correlation between economic prosperity and expansion on the one hand, and the number of fiscal paupers on the other, is logical. The example in the Brabant table[48] for the town of Antwerp would appear to confirm this; the percentage of paupers there declined between 1437 and 1480 from 13.5 to 10.5 per cent, whereas in the large and small towns the trend was upwards. In any case, this mechanism, even in this form, requires critical appraisal. For most areas, however, it is totally inapplicable, since the majority of figures relate to *disarmen*, and one might expect that an economic crisis would be accompanied by a decrease in the ranks of *disarmen* rather than an increase, observing that the resources of the well-to-do section of the population would be reduced, as would the patrimony of the institutions for the poor. With the aid of accounts of institutions, we shall also demonstrate that the numbers in receipt of assistance during and after a crisis can actually remain constant, even though the quality and extent of the assistance are drastically restricted. The percentage of *disarmen* in Lécluse (Walloon Flanders) fell from 65 in 1491 to 3 in 1498, after which it rose to reach 50 in 1505.[49] The remainder of the *enquête* does not indicate that this pattern was due to an improved economic situation in 1498, and indeed the reverse was the case; however, the crisis of 1491 made it impossible for the better-off farmers and workers to contribute adequately to the poor relief fund, and also reduced the ground rents accruing to the funds. A decline in the amount of assistance can thus coincide with a rise in destitution. What we do not know in the present state of research is the extent to which familial solidarity and mendicancy outside the person's own village provided adequate compensation for temporary interruptions in relief. Cuvelier's thesis concerning Brabant, that an increase in the number of poor persons in the table implies pauperization,[50] and Arnould's postulation that the decline in the number of poor persons in Hainaut between 1540 and 1562 is indicative of an impoverishment of well-to-do and poor alike (and thus of a reduction in relief)[51] must in consequence be examined critically. It is probable that a long series of exhausting wars and crises results in growing pauperization. Cuvelier[52] points to the example of the rural areas in Walloon

---

48. Blockmans and Prevenier, 'Armoede in de Nederlanden', 517 (Table VII).
49. Archives départementales du Nord, B 20 182, 3761, 3762. For example, a portion of the poor relief fund was used to restore the church, which was destroyed during the disturbances at the end of the 15th century.
50. Cuvelier, *Dénombrements*, cclxxxii.
51. Arnould, *Dénombrements*, 283.
52. Cuvelier, *Dénombrements*, cxxxi-iii.

Brabant between 1437 and 1526. Another example is to be found in Walloon Flanders where, under the influence of the conflicts of the second half of the fifteenth century, the figure rose from a normal 26 per cent (in 1449) to a peak of 37 per cent in 1485, while a reduction of the tension after 1491 produced a fall to 29 per cent. Thus war as well as crisis can lead to a decrease in the number of poor persons (cf. Lécluse, above) or to an increase.[53]

In our view, another avenue for research lies in the correlation between the number of poor persons and the evolution of the population as a whole. If, however, in the Brabant hearth censuses one counts the number of instances in which an increase of the population is accompanied by a rise in the number of poor persons, and a decrease by a fall, one finds that this occurred thirteen times in terms of absolute figures and six times in terms of percentage. The reverse occurred seven times in the absolute figures and fourteen times in the percentages. For Walloon Flanders a positive correlation (increase + increase, or vice versa) occurred 31 times absolutely and 23 times percentagewise; an inverse correlation occurred 31 times absolutely and 36 times percentagewise. Little can be concluded from this, but here, too, further investigation is needed. If we look at the total population figures for the whole of the rural area of Walloon Flanders,[54] we find that the decline between 1449 and 1485 is accompanied by rising numbers of paupers, while the reverse is the case between 1485 and 1498; however, the population growth which occurred between 1498 and 1505 and between 1505 and 1544-9 was also accompanied by a rise in the number of paupers. It is thus clear that the mechanism can be bidirectional. Cuvelier has pointed to the fact that the rise or fall in the number of well-to-do hearths in Brabant between 1374 and 1437 had a manifest influence on the degree of pauperization at the end of that phase (*i.e.,* in 1437): the regions with a favourable demographic evolution (the Antwerp quarter and the Flemish part of the Brussels quarter) ultimately (in 1437) had the lowest percentage of paupers, while the rural areas of Walloon Brabant, which experienced a greatly inferior evolution, indeed had the highest (38.5 per cent).[55]

As all this ambiguity stems from the fact that the numbers of paupers in the hearth censuses in most cases reflect assistance provided by the *dissen*, the questions posed cannot be answered until the nature and evolution of the poor relief in a number of places has been analyzed.

---

53. An example of an increase in poverty is found in Comines in 1437, following its destruction by military action and fire. 'Il n'y a mie le tierch de peuple qu'il y soloit avoir, et yceulx sont si tres povre qu'il ne sceuent que faire de povreté', Archives départementales du Nord, B 17656.
54. M. Braure, 'Etude économique sur les châtellenies de Lille, Douai et Orchies d'après les enquêtes fiscales des XVe-XVIe siècles', *Revue du Nord*, XIV (1928) 199, *passim*.
55. Cuvelier, *Dénombrements*, cxv.

The geographical correlation is remarkable. Take, for example, Brabant with the increasingly impoverished Walloon area and the very stable Flemish part of the Louvain and Brussels quarters. The map of the Flemish country-side[56] similarly reveals striking contrasts between districts with very large numbers of 'fiscal' paupers, such as Dendermonde (Termonde), Oudburg and Waas; areas in which there were probably fewer in receipt of relief, like Courtrai and Bergues (near Dunkirk) and others which perhaps contained no paupers, such as Bourbourg and the Vier Ambachten (Assenede, Boekhoute, Hulst and Axel). A whole field for research lies open here. Is agrarian prosperity linked to a higher level of assistance to the poor? Do the quality of the soil and the flexibility of the area farmed play a part? A noteworthy phenomenon in this field is the intensification of poor relief in the urban centres, which can apparently be explained by the tendency on the part of the poor to abandon the countryside to seek more effective relief in the better organized urban *dissen*.[57] In the case of Comines, this was explicitly borne out in the source in 1498: in a town (or in an important textile centre like Comines), there is more assistance, more work and better and cheaper housing.[58] For North Brabant, too, various sources demonstrate the attraction exerted on the inhabitants of the rural areas by the poor relief schemes in the towns.[59] This calls for a study of the migrations between the countryside and the towns, and from town to town or village to village, in the light of the potential and the possibilities for the absorption of paupers. However, the temporary nature of these movements is an obstacle to their numerical evaluation.

A useful direction for further research lies in determining the evolution of the burden of taxation on the local communities. The process by which States were formed, it is argued — though overall figures are very scarce — was accompanied by an increase in the volume of taxes imposed on the subjects. Figures which are clear in this sense are available for the county of Flanders, and these also show that the rural areas suffered more from this evolution

56. Blockmans and Prevenier, 'Armoede in de Nederlanden', 514.
57. Cuvelier, *Denombrements*, cclxxxvi; C. Ligtenberg, *Armenzorg te Leiden tot het einde van de 16de eeuw* (Utrecht, 1908) 287 (mid-fifteenth century).
58. Archives départementales du Nord B 3761, fol. 41: many paupers made their way to Comines in view of the twice- or thrice-weekly 'ouvreture du tran a passage, ou les dis povres gens prennent ... ung petit gaingnage ... et aussi que les dits povres gens trouvent les maisons à tres bon marché de louage'.
59. H.F.J.M. van den Eerenbeemt, 'Sociale spanningen en overheidsbeleid. Bestrijding der bedelarij in het Noorden van Brabant in de vijftiende en zestiende eeuw', *Varia Historica Brabantica*, I (Bois-le-Duc, 1962) 152-9.

than did the towns.[60] Increasing taxation can exacerbate a process of pauperization and limit the value, for historiographical purposes, of the fiscal categories.

III. INSTITUTIONALIZED POOR RELIEF

A characteristic feature of the evolution of poor relief in the late middle ages is the extremely fragmented nature of the underlying initiatives, which in many instances emanated from individual foundations and were therefore of very modest proportions. Undoubtedly this variety of aid organizations afforded a minority an opportunity to sup at more than one table, or even to go from one institution to another — a situation against which the rationalization plans of the fifteenth and sixteenth centuries were aimed. At the same time, it would be wrong to interpret the multiplicity of institutions as a sign of abundant beneficence before thoroughly investigating the true nature and extent of the aid furnished.

Generally speaking, the Christian religion may be said to have stimulated aid to the poor; it certainly determined the form which this took. It can scarcely be a coincidence that Pieter Brueghel's drawing 'De werken van Barmhartigheid' (The works of Charity), anno 1559, accurately depicts the entire spectrum of the work of the charitable institutions. To a devout person, as to an institution, distributing alms afforded an opportunity to earn a place in Heaven. It is typical of all forms of poor relief in the period concerned that they followed the rhythm of the Church's year. Clearly, the object — particularly at festivals (Christmas, Easter, Whitsun, All Saints' Day, and in some cases also at Lady Mass) and during Lent — was to remind the poor of the Church and the faith, and at the same time to secure the salvation of the donors. This approach to the subject of assistance, needless to say, was not the most

---

60. The sums of taxation permitted to be levied on the third estate in Flanders rose steeply under Charles the Bold:

1440-1468:	less than 100,000 lb.par.	12 years	1469-1506:	less than 100,000 lb.par.	2 years
	100,000-200,000 lb.par.	10 years		100,000-200,000 lb.par.	5 years
	200,000-300,000 lb.par.	5 years		200,000-300,000 lb.par.	12 years
	more than 300,000 lb.par.	2 years		300,000-400,000 lb.par.	8 years
				400,000-600,000	3 years
				600,000-900,000	8 years

W.P. Blockmans, *De volksvertegenwoordiging in Vlaanderen tijdens de overgang van middeleeuwen naar nieuwe tijden*. Verhandeling Kon. Academie van België, Klasse der Letteren (now being printed); N. Maddens, 'De beden in het graafschap Vlaanderen tijdens de regering van Keizer Karel V (1515-1550)' (dissertation, University of Louvain, in print). The rising burden of taxation is compared with the revenues from a Hainaut village. M.A. Arnould, 'L'incidence de l'impôt sur les finances d'un village à l'époque bourguignonne. Boussoit-sur-Haine, 1400-1555', *Contributions à l'histoire économique et sociale*, I (Brussels, 1962) 41-105.

efficient. We shall attempt to define the real importance of the activities of a number of types of relief institution. We must of necessity content ourselves with examples.

TYPOLOGY OF RELIEF ORGANIZATIONS

A good example in this sense is to be found in the municipal accounts of Ghent. Every year the administrators allocated a sum for alms. In the early part of the fourteenth century, only mendicant orders, brotherhoods and incidental paupers were remembered.[61] Later, the assistance provided by the city fathers was extended to include wine, herring and turf, not only for the mendicant orders but also hospitals and other institutions for the care of the sick, and the poor relief funds of the principal guilds. In addition, these institutions, and also poor prisoners and paupers living on their own (*huisarmen*) received a gift of a cask of wine from the city four times a year.[62] The magnitude of the sums involved is significant: expressed in daily wages of a groundworker or bricklayer's assistant,[63] the city in 1360-1 spent the equivalent of 470 days on the distribution of herring, 528 days on turf and 1,410 on wine — all in all a substantial expenditure (this exceeded one per cent of the total budget) which, however, largely benefited the mendicant orders, and of which the largest item, the wine, can have possessed only psychological significance. The subsidizing of the relief funds of the guilds — about which our information as a whole is still very limited, making further research desirable[64] — reflected their growing influence in the municipal administration and, of course, was aimed at further strengthening their position. The purpose of the assistance provided by the city fathers was apparently to predispose the poor section of the population in favour of the administration, the instruments being the preaching of the mendicant orders and spectacular distributions of wine. The city thus furnished no systematic and direct relief. It was, however, the custom, notably in reconciliation proceedings, for municipal judges to assign certain

61. Vuylsteke, *Gentsche stads- en baljuwsrekeningen*, I, 163 l. 1-2 (1321-22); II, 890 l. 26-33, 891 l. 30-1, 915 l. 23 (1333-34).
62. A. Van Werveke, *Gentse stads- en baljuwsrekeningen (1351-1364)*, KCG (Brussels, 1970), 100-1 (1353-4), 323-5 (1357-8), 384-5 (1358-9), 459-61 (1360-1), 562-4 (1362-3). Wine was distributed on All Saints' Day, Christmas Day, Easter Day and Whitsunday. Herring was distributed during the winter. On occasions, the town made an extra donation: 'Item distributed amongst the poor living at home as alms in view of the severe cold: 3 lb.5s.gr. (Municipal Archive, Ghent, stadsrekening 1407-8, fol. 148, r°.).
63. 13s. 4d. payment: Van Werveke, *Gentse Stads- en baljuwsrekeningen*, 583 ff.
64. A number of useful normative data pertaining to Amsterdam can be found in C.A. van Manen, *Armenpflege in Amsterdam in ihrer historischen Entwicklung* (Leiden, 1913) 16-22.

fines to mendicant orders, hospitals, hospices and *armendissen,* or to impose fines payable as alms in cash or in kind. In amicable settlements of family feuds, in particular, the municipal authorities would often decree that monies should be spent in this way. Although this source was employed in both the northern and southern parts of the Netherlands, its quantitative significance within the whole framework of poor relief cannot be estimated.[65]

Poverty and sickness were allied problems. A manual worker who became ill or disabled lost, temporarily or permanently, his livelihood and thus became needy. Numerous institutions were established to care for the sick, the poor and the poor sick. *Hl. Geesttafels,* which normally cared only for the poor, regularly assisted the bedridden with special gifts, even though they were not regular almsmen.[66] From a number of monographies concerning hospitals it can be deduced that the poor were gradually squeezed out by the practice among the better-off of purchasing a prebend in order to obtain a sort of insurance against sickness.[67] From the accounts of the hospitals, it is difficult to ascertain how many poor persons actually remained there and how many enjoyed other forms of assistance. At the *Drievuldigheidsgasthuis* in Mechlin, the annual distribution to 65 poor persons in the fifteenth century did not exceed 1 groat and a quantity of butter averaging 180 kg, representing a total fixed sum of 3 lb. 10 s. 5 d.gr. At the beginning of the sixteenth century, in contrast, weekly portions of meat varying from 15 to 21 kg for the poor are explicitly referred to; at Easter, the quantity was increased to 35 kg.[68]

---

65. Example in Ghent: the penalty imposed in a case of affront included the payment of 100 French guilders in the form of alms; each of the four mendicant orders and the seven *Hl. Geesttafels* received herring, wheat and peas. These were to be distributed by the insulted party, together with her friends and relatives (Municipal Archive, Ghent, Zoendincboek, Reg. van Staten van Goed 13, 1405-6, fol. 256 r°). Cf. D.M. Nicholas, 'Crime and Punishment in Fourteenth-Century Ghent', *Belgisch tijdschrift voor filologie en geschiedenis,* LXVIII (1970) 293; the leper house, the Franciscan monastery and the poor institutions in Gouda were also named as beneficiaries on a number of occasions.
66. During the fifteenth century, the *Hl. Geesttafel* in the parish of St. Nicholas, in Ghent, distributed varying sums of money in individual cases of sickness, childbirth in difficult circumstances, and disability. The *Hl. Geesttafel* of Our Lady in Mechlin annually devoted substantial sums to caring for the sick in their own homes (if necessary providing an attendant) and to placing the mentally handicapped in the care of monks or nuns. The weekly allowance of 3-4 *stuivers* slightly exceeded the daily wage of a bricklayer's assistant and may thus be regarded as the minimum on which one person could survive (Archief van de Commissie voor Openbare Onderstand, Mechlin, 8411-8419, anno 1521-45).
67. R. Van der Made, *Le Grand Hôpital de Huy. Organisation et fonctionnement, 1263-1795.* Standen en Landen XX (Louvain, 1960) 108-11; G. Maréchal, 'Het hospitaalwezen te Brugge in de Middeleeuwen. Een institutionele en sociale studie' (unpublished dissertation, University of Ghent, 1974-75, I, 10-001; publication forthcoming).
68. Archief van de Commissie voor Openbare Onderstand, Mechlin, 8952 (from 1446-7) to 8957 (up to 1542). The portions of meat distributed to the poor are very clearly distinguished in the 1526-7 accounts.

In most cases, the functions of poor relief and medical care do not appear to be sharply demarcated. The *Potterie* hospital at Bruges also functioned as a hospice, albeit on a limited scale, distributing bread, meat or herring, clothing and footwear to perhaps 24-36 almsmen at religious festivals.[69] In the mid-sixteenth century, the great St. John's Hospital was still taking in pilgrims, authentic or otherwise, even though specialized institutions existed for them. During the winter of 1547-8, they numbered between 22 and 28 a day out of a total of 150 beds.[70] The *Potterie* hospital was principally for invalids and the elderly, but transients were also accepted.[71] The *Grand Hôpital* at Huy was also open to persons in the last-named category.[72]

Every town of any significance had at least one establishment, which was usually dedicated to St. Julian, where needy travellers could spend a maximum of three evenings and nights. Transients who did not enjoy assistance from other sources were thus driven to an itinerant existence. The four *passantenhuizen* in Bruges were together able to accomodate about 200 persons.[73]

Comparison of the assistance provided by institutions of this type in Bruges and Mechlin reveals that the hospitality in the former town was substantially greater than that in the latter. The food in Bruges was more varied and the period of distribution was four times as long as in Mechlin. The capacity at Bruges was undoubtedly greater (perhaps double that at Mechlin) and the reason for this appears to be that the town was more attractive to foreigners. All these factors lead one to the conclusion that the *passantenhuizen* performed a minimal function in terms of assistance owing to the limited lodging facilities, especially in terms of duration[74] the meagre distribution of food (only during a certain period of the year, totalling 40 days at Mechlin and at most 176 days at Bruges) and the orientation towards foreigners.

The existence of yet another type of institution, the brotherhood, also merits attention. A recent study on the *O.L. Vrouwe Broederschap* in Bois-le-Duc reveals that this highly distinguished body was greatly concerned about the care of the poor. Commencing in 1372, it organized annual distributions of rye bread. From 1396 onwards, these were increased to four per year, on religious festivals, 1,224 kg. of bread being distributed on each occasion. This quantity did not change, even in the sixteenth century, despite the fact that the income of the brotherhood increased substantially. This, however, was increasingly used to pay for lavish meals for the brothers. Besides its own

69. Maréchal, 'Hospitaalwezen', 11-040 - 11-043.
70. *Ibidem*, 11-056-62 and 11-088.
71. *Ibidem*, 11-063-4.
72. Van der Made, *Grand Hôpital*, 128-9.
73. Maréchal, 'Hospitaalwezen', 11-022-38.
74. Van Manen, *Armenpflege*, 10.

distributions, the brotherhood made others by virtue of foundations by its members; in this manner, 12 distributions, each of 1,224 kg., were made annually. In all, the brotherhood and its members distributed something like 14,688 kg. of rye bread per year — enough for 50 persons. In addition, they provided footwear, clothing and alms on a limited scale.[75] The overall appraisal of this example is that this institution can admittedly be credited with tangible accomplishments, but that these did not meet the evolution of poverty and were far below what could have been achieved.

Let us now turn our attention to an ecclesiastical institution. In view of the richness of the source material, we chose the St. Peter's Abbey in Ghent, one of the oldest and richest in the Netherlands. The almoner's accounts reveal that during the second half of the fourteenth century the abbey expended considerable sums on distributions for the poor and in donations to certain charitable institutions and mendicant orders. In both cases the emphasis lay on bread, money and linen cloth, but the gifts also included pork, herring, wine, beer and footwear. Comparison of the magnitude of this relief with the aid distributed in the same period by the *Hl. Geesttafel* in the parish of St. Nicholas (about which more anon) shows that the latter, as a whole, lay far below that provided by the abbey. Only in the quantity of pork provided did the *dis* surpass the abbey, but against this the distributions of bread from the abbey were more than ten times greater than those of the *dis*. They were met from income in kind and remained substantial, tending to increase towards the middle of the fifteenth century. From the end of the fourteenth century, however, expenditure by the almoner declined sharply, economies being made on all items. The pecuniary distributions survived the best. During the first decade of the fifteenth century, they varied from 220 to 452 days' wages for a bricklayer's assistant. In the fourteenth century, the highest figure, including donations to institutions, had equalled 728 days' wages. The remaining categories of distribution tended to assume a symbolic character. These economies are somewhat surprising, observing that in the period 1410-50, the income in the form of money rose much more sharply than expenditure. The surplus was put to other uses, such as contributions to the Holy See aimed at influencing the appointment of abbots.[76] Another noticeable shortcoming is the halving of the distributions of bread in the period 1399-1402, when prices

75. G.C.M. van Dijck, *De Bossche Optimaten. Geschiedenis van de Illustere Lieve Vrouwe broeder-schap te 's-Hertogenbosch 1318-1973*. Bijdragen tot de geschiedenis van het Zuiden van Nederland, XXVII (Tilburg, 1973) 56, 163-7, 285-9.
76. G. De Mey, 'De financiële organisatie van de Sint-Pietersabdij te Gent in de tweede helft van de 14e eeuw en de eerste helft van de 15e eeuw' (unpublished licentiate treatise, University of Ghent, 1970) 106-13. The almoners accounts in Rijksarchief Ghent, Fonds St. Pieters I, 645-80, 25, 2272-3.

were high and plague rampant. The explanation given for the measure is a reduction in income in the form of grain; nevertheless, it implied a minimum response to need when this was greatest. Finally, the almoner of the St. Peter's Abbey, like others, was guilty of concentrating on bread and pecuniary assistance, the disadvantages of which have already been referred to. This single example shows that the presence of an important abbey can exert a major influence on poor relief. The extent to which this occurred elsewhere remains to be investigated, but it is already clear that the picture would be very incomplete without this component. In this context, we would also mention the indirect role played by the abbey in the shape of support for various *dissen* and hospitals.

PAROCHIAL POOR RELIEF ORGANIZATIONS

In terms of the scale of relief provided for the poor in the Netherlands, the parochial *dissen* undoubtedly take pride of place. Their work has been dealt with in earlier studies, mainly from the institutional point of view.[77] However, a far more relevant approach is revealed in a number of recent contributions in which the extent of the aid per recipient is expressed in figures.[78] The variety, distribution and quantity of the food handed out are of particular importance. Generally speaking, it can be said that the fact of the distributions being concentrated around the religious festivals resulted in an unequal distribution of calories over the year, and in particular that the exceptional regime during the 40 days of Lent made these the best of the whole year in both quantitative and qualitative terms. Insufficient attention has been given to the evolution of relief in the long term, the support given in times of diminished purchasing power and the financial policy of the *Hl. Geesttafels*.

While there is a high degree of uniformity in regard to the nature of the commodities distributed — bread, clothing, footwear, meat, fuel, money, herring, peas, fats, wine and beer — the relative magnitude of the items varies from one parish to another; moreover, there are omissions and additions, the latter

77. Ligtenberg, *Armenzorg*, 158, 233; J. Withof, 'De Tafels van de Heilige Geest te Mechelen', *Handelingen van de Mechelse kring voor oudheidkunde, letteren en kunst*, XXXII-III (Mechlin, 1927-28) 85-134 and 35-89.

78. Tits-Dieuaide, 'Assistance'; Ch. De Geest, 'Les distributions aux pauvres assurées par la paroisse Sainte-Gudule à Bruxelles au XVe siècle', *Annalen van de Belgische vereniging voor hospitaalgeschiedenis*, VII (Brussels, 1969) 41-84; Blockmans, 'Armenzorg en levensstandaard te Mechelen'; Blockmans and Prevenier, 'Openbare Armenzorg te 's-Hertogenbosch'; M.J. Tits-Dieuaide, 'Les tables des pauvres dans les anciennes principautés belges au moyen âge', *Tijdschrift voor geschiedenis*, LXXXVIII (Groningen, 1975) 562-83.

sometimes including cheese, eggs, butter and figs. It is noticeable that the bread distributed was usually made with rye — except, that is, on special days, notably during Lent and at Easter, when wheat bread was used. Ghent and Bruges were exceptions in this respect: there, rye bread was resorted to only in times of great need (the years round about 1490).[79] This luxury is also found to have existed in Florence[80] and in the Flemish village of Pittem, whose *dis* accounts were also investigated by way of a random test.[81] In Brussels, the records show, barley was substituted for rye in time of crisis.[82] Everywhere, bread was the staple item and the one distributed most regularly and in the largest quantities which, moreover, displayed no tendency to decline in the long term.

We have investigated the operation of a number of *Hl. Geesttafels* with the aim of shedding a little more light on the foregoing issues. Particular value attaches to the series of accounts of the *tafel* in the centrally situated parish of St. Nicholas in Ghent, which go back as far as the beginning of the fourteenth century.[83] We also investigated the only *tafel* in Bois-le-Duc, for which accounts are available from 1435;[84] four *tafels* in Mechlin (out of a total of seven), of which accounts dating from before the middle of the sixteenth century have survived (only in one case from the last one-third of the fifteenth century);[85] the three surviving accounts of the only *tafel* in Aalst;[86] and finally the fifteenth-century accounts of a rural *dis*, namely the one in Pittem, in West Flanders.[87]

The quantities of grain provided by these institutions for use in baking bread for the poor vary widely from period to period and from one institution to another. The bread distributions made by the *Hl. Geesttafel* in Bois-le-Duc were noticeable larger than those anywhere else. In 1527, there were 574

79. Rijksarchief Ghent, S 14-15 (*Hl. Geesttafel*, parish of St. Nicholas); Maréchal, 'Hospitaal-wezen', 11-035.
80. De la Roncière, 'Pauvres et pauvreté à Florence', 676 note 29.
81. Rijksarchief Courtrai, Municipal Archive of Pittem, 257a (except that in 1489-90 only half the customary amount of wheat bread was distributed, plus a quantity of rye bread).
82. De Geest, 'Distributions', 68-9.
83. A well-preserved series dating from 1311-2, Rijksarchief Ghent, S 496-522; rolls 119-38, 157; S 169-212; S 11-45 (1533-4).
84. Archief van de Godshuizen, Bois-le-Duc, 406-22 (1453-4 to 1534-5). Registers showing income and expenditure in 1435 and subsequent years are available. The figures have been incorporated in tables and graphs in Blockmans and Prevenier. 'Openbare armenzorg te 's-Hertogenbosch'.
85. Archief van de Commissie voor Openbare Onderstand, Mechlin, 8207-12 (St. Rumoldi, from 1530), 8411-5 (Our Lady from 1521), 8481-90 (St. John from 1528); archive of the parish of St. Peter and St. Paul (from 1466). The figures are to be found in the Appendix to Blockmans, 'Armen-zorg en levensstandaard te Mechelen', 165-73.
86. Municipal Archive, Alost, 1991-3 (1464-5, 1466-7 and 1534-5).
87. Rijksarchief Courtrai, Municipal Archive of Pittem, 275a (from 1485-7).

families in receipt of relief, each of which received 430 kg. of rye bread per year, or 1.177 kg. per day — an adequate family ration, assuming that sufficient food of other types was also provided (see Table IV).

TABLE IV. *Quantities of bread distributed by parochial relief organizations*

	Period	Number of beneficiaries	Grain (litres)	Bread (kg.)	Annual portion (kg.)	Daily port. (gr.)
Ghent	ca. 1330	1,000[88]	± 3,000	± 2,700	2.7	
(St. Nicholas)	ca. 1360	369	± 3,000	± 2,700	7.317	
	1400-1430	154	± 4,000	± 3,600	23.377	
	from 1458	50	(6,466)	(5,819)		
			3,195	3,028	60.560[89]	166
Alost	ca. 1465	200	4,045	3,641	182	500
Pittem	ca. 1486	28	1,180	1,062	37.132	101
Mechlin						
(St. Peter)	1530-36	125	5,716	4,859	38.872	106
(Our Lady)	1530	100	9,916	8,429	84.286	231
	1536	125	15,761	13,397	107.176	294
(St. Rumold)	1530	100	18,013	15,311	153.11	419
	1536	100	20,394	17,335	173.349	475
Bois-le-Duc	1527	574	290,400	246,840	430	1,177

The data can also be compared with those relating to the central *dis* in Louvain and the parish of St. Gudule in Brussels, *i.e.* 215 gr. of bread daily (during the period of stable, large distributions, 1470-88) and 611 gr. (1440-60) respectively.[90] The differences between the dissen are seen to have been significant.[91] The *tafel* in Bois-le-Duc distributed approximately twice as much bread as the next most generous dis, the one at St. Gudule in Brussels. Nowhere except in Bois-le-Duc was the ration of bread adequate for an adult, even one who ate a normal proportion of other products. The portions given in the parish of St. Nicholas, in Ghent, during the fourteenth century and the first half of the fifteenth were remarkably small. The subsequent, noticeable, increase was

88. On the basis of the number of items of footwear. Commencing in 1458, the number of almsmen was stated.
89. On feastdays, the distributions of bread extended to 350 almsmen; we calculated their possible significance for the 50 paupers who were assisted weekly. No good purpose would be served by making an annual calculation for the remaining 300.
90. Tits-Dieuaide, 'Assistance', 436-7; De Geest, 'Distributions', 79; we counted 1 pound (470 grams) per day, together with 109.5 pounds per year which were spread over a number of days (dividing this by 365 gives 141 grams). This figure, like so many others, is therefore an average.
91. Tits-Dieuaide, 'Tables des Pauvres', 579, affords further material for comparison.

achieved at the expense of other products and of the number of recipients, and thus the operation as a whole implied a considerable cutback.

In most institutions, meat and linen cloth were the principal items which were paid for with money. Bois-le-Duc was a notable exception to this rule, consistently devoting ten per cent or thereabouts of its budget to footwear and only a fraction (from 1470 onwards, seldom more than one per cent) to meat. This item was deleted altogether in 1484. In the Ghent parish of St. Nicholas, large quantities of footwear accounted for 30-40 per cent of the expenditure during the first half of the fourteenth century. The high price and nutritional value of meat merit special attention (see Table V).

TABLE V. *Quantities of meat distributed by parochial relief organizations*

	Period	Number of beneficiaries	No. of pigs per year	Hypothetical total weight (kg.)	Individual portions per year (kg.)
Ghent	ca. 1330	1,000	14	420	0.420
(St. Nicholas)	ca. 1360	369	14	420	1.138
	1400-1430	154	13	390	2.532
	after 1430	—	—	—	—
Alost	ca. 1465	200	18	540	2.7
Pittem	ca. 1490	28	2	60	2.143
Mechlin					
(St. Peter)	1494	110	41	1,230	11.181
	1529	110	16	480	4.364
(St. Rumold)	1532	100	18	540	5.4
Bois-le-Duc	1465	325	34	1,020	3.138

The number of pigs distributed in Louvain and in the Brussels parish of St. Gudule was considerably higher, amounting to 100-220 and 50-80 respectively.[92] Although weight was estimated in a completely fictious manner (an average of 30 kg. of meat per animal), these calculations, comparatively speaking, possess a true significance. It is immediately apparent just how relative all these distributions of meat were. On one, two, three or four occasions during the year, the almsmen received a quantity which was scarcely sufficient for a few days. Even in the most favourable case, that of the parish of St. Peter in Mechlin in 1494, this amounted to no more than 37 grams per day. But then the allocations of meat everywhere tended to decrease or disappear. In the

92. Tits-Dieuaide, 'Assistance', 431; De Geest, 'Distributions', 58 and 79. According to our calculation, if a pig was estimated to yield 30 kg. of meat, the rations at St. Gudule would have been only half the figure by the author, *i.e.* 5.625 kg.

parish of St. Nicholas, in Ghent, they ceased about 1458, in Bois-le-Duc in 1484 and in the *tafels* in Mechlin in 1535, while in Alost the quantity fell from 18 pigs in 1467 to 3 in 1535.

Regarding other forms of food, we can be brief. These were virtually limited to Lent and, by providing a more varied and more ample diet, were intended to remind the recipients of their duty to attend services of worship. Although, paradoxically enough, the quantity of the food distributed at Lent was greater, and the quality higher, it fell far short of being adequate.[93] The situation in regard to other gifts, such as clothing, footwear and fuel, reveals wide discrepancies. In the parish of St. Nicholas in Ghent, the first two had ceased to be distributed by the middle of the fifteenth century.

At a number of *tafels*, distributions in the form of money were raised to partly offset the reductions in those in kind. In Ghent, under an alms reform carried out in 1458 or thereabouts, the items were reduced to bread, money, herring, peat and linen cloth, of which only the first two appeared regularly and in considerable quantity. From then on, money, which had previously accounted for only one or two per cent of the budget, made up 20-30 per cent (including the price paid for grain). This development spread to Mechlin in 1535, coinciding with the elimination of other items. In Alost, the value of alms in the form of money had by this time risen to twice the 1467 level, at the expense of meat. Everywhere this evolution was accompanied by a wider distribution of alms and an increase in their frequency to a weekly pattern, both for bread and money. While this reform in no case led to nominal economies, the beneficiaries undoubtedly lost out in the long run, since its implementation always coincided with a period of rapidly rising prices for meat and other commodities. In Ghent, moreover, the number of almsmen was reduced from 149 in 1430 to 50 as from 1459, although this swelled to 350 during Lent and on religious festivals. These measures were inspired by two factors: on the one hand, there was the continuing, strong concern to emphasize the role of the Church by spectacular distributions at festivals; on the other hand, more frequent (and consequently smaller) distributions afforded more efficient control of the recipients. It is not surprising that this tendency towards economy and stricter control was first manifested in a very large town, and only later in urban centres with a slower rate of development. At any rate, it formed a prelude to the measures which the imperial ordinance of 1531 sought to make generally applicable.[94]

---

93. De Geest, *ibidem*; Tits-Dieuaide, 'Assistance', 436-7 (concerning oil, herring, peas and beans); Blockmans, 'Armenzorg en levensstandaard', 147-9.

94. It will be observed that in the ordinance of 7th October 1531, the magistrates proposed that the distributions should take place weekly, and also that money, bread, wood and clothing

The financial policy of the parochial poor relief funds also helps to explain the measures of 1531. Swollen by the accumulation of gifts which carried obligations, the overall costs and the expenditure on religious ceremonies to the honour of the donors demanded a substantial and ever increasing portion of the budget. In Bois-le-Duc, direct aid to the poor represented only between 12 and 31 per cent of the monetary outgoings (the distributions of bread are thus excluded). In Alost, in 1535, church services accounted for 31 per cent of the total expenditure of the *tafel*, and at Pittem, in 1486-7, 29 per cent. For Ghent, the figure was 24 per cent in 1411-2 and 37 per cent in 1463-4. The yearly purchases of costly linen for the choir which added lustre to the services amounted to twice the sum spent on linen for the poor of this *tafel*. This item was exempted from economies, even in the worst starvation years.

Contrasting with this is the efficiency of a new type of *dis*, the *Tafel van de Huisarmen* (poor living on their own) of the parish of St. Rumold, which emerged in Mechlin in 1499. There, on average, 77 per cent of a budget which equalled that of the *Hl. Geesttafel* was devoted to direct assistance to the poor.[95] Institutions of this type had earlier been established in Antwerp (1458) and Bois-le-Duc (1477).[96] In the latter town — at least as far as the central district surrounding the market was concerned — the aid was much more selective and more closely related to the individual, and consisted to a greater extent of money, than was the case with the *Hl. Geesttafel*. Moreover, the method of operation was considerably more efficient: normally, 72 per cent or thereabouts of the budget was devoted to actual poor relief, compared with 21 per cent for the *Hl. Geesttafel*.

Pursuing this line, we come to the question of the effect of agricultural crises on poor relief. In a large number of cases it can be demonstrated that the cautious policy on the part of the *Hl. Geesttafels*, most of which maintained substantial stocks of grain in their lofts, enabled them to get through the majority of the crises without reducing their customary distributions. In some instances they even succeeded in increasing the distributions of bread (Ghent 1400-1403, 1418, 1482; Bois-le-Duc 1521-4; Mechlin, St. Peter, 1431-2). The extremely severe, protracted and widespread nature of the crisis of 1480-90, however, brought difficulties for all institutions. In Bois-le-Duc, bread distributions were halved and until 1511 remained below the level of the 1470s. Shortages and failures in deliveries to the *tafel* produced a debt of such

are referred to — in that order — but not meat; E. Lameere, *Recueil des ordonnances des Pays-Bas*, 2nd series, *1506-1700*, III (Brussels, 1902) 269.

95. Blockmans, 'Armenzorg en levensstandaard', 152.

96. E. Païs-Minne, 'Weldadigheidsinstellingen en ondersteunden', in: *Antwerpen in de XVIe eeuw* (Antwerp, 1975) 182. For Bois-le-Duc cf. Blockmans and Prevenier, 'Openbare Armenzorg', 55-9.

magnitude that for 20 years, from 1486, it matched the income for a normal year.

This deficit was not reduced until the 1520s, and then only very gradually. In the budget expressed in money, the arrears to the *Tafel* ran at 100-150 per cent of income for several decades, and during the 1490s budget deficits of 20-40 per cent were common. A similar picture is observed at the *Hl. Geesttafel* in the parish of St. Nicholas in Ghent: deficiences equalling, or exceeding, annual revenues — a situation which was not reversed until the second decade of the sixteenth century. Two conclusions can be drawn from this: first, that the *tafels* failed utterly during periods of greatest need since they were then obliged to severely curtail their assistance at a time of rising poverty; second, that the crisis of the late-fifteenth century had a prolonged effect on budgets until far into the sixteenth century. Both symptoms of a less than efficient policy undoubtedly favoured the tendencies towards reform which were manifested after the 1520s.

It is clear that the data concerning the assistance provided by the *Hl. Geesttafels* must be viewed in the light of the trends in the economy of the town or region concerned. The reduction in the purchasing power in the years following 1475 and again, in more severe form, from 1520 onwards was a general factor of pauperization, and consequently a factor in the higher than average mortality rate among the least well-off.[97] In a number of towns, the decline in the basic sectors of the economy played a decisive role. This has been shown to have been the case in Leiden and Mechlin in the first half of the sixteenth century.[98] This correlation can be demonstrated for Dixmude as early as the fifteenth century. There, the traditional linen industry collapsed during the first two decades of the century; the tax revenue from linen manufacture declined from 9,568 s.par. in 1380-1 to 572 s.par. in 1420-1, while the number of municipal fiscal seals attached to the cloths fell from 10,500 in 1403-4 to 400 in 1420-1. Records of a series of levies imposed by the municipality, which included fiscal paupers, show that up to 40 per cent were in default in the period 1454-9.[99] A hearth census taken in 1469 revealed that in Dixmude there were 225 'poor' hearths and 83 empty homes (another phenomenon of decadence) among a total of 636. Counting only the 553 occupied houses, this source reveals that more

---

97. The study by H. Neveux, 'La mortalité des pauvres à Cambrai (1377-1473)', *Annales de démographie historique* (Paris, 1968) 73-97, can serve as a model in the matter of the relationship between the causes and effects, mainly economic, of the abnormal mortality rate among paupers.
98. Ligtenberg, *Armenzorg*, 14; Blockmans, 'Armenzorg en levensstandaard', 161-4.
99. G. Schacht, 'Sociaal-ekonomische strukturen te Diksmuide in de 15e eeuw' (unpublished licentiate treatise, University of Ghent, 1974) 55-6, 121-5.

than 40 per cent of families were considered as poor;[100] this high figure is explained by the social degradation of workers in a declining branch of industry.

By combining fiscal *enquêtes* and documents pertaining to the practical aspects of poor relief, it is possible to determine the diversity of, and fluctuations in, the recipient group. In 1469, 72 heads of poor families in Mesen were divided into three sub-groups — *disarmen*, paupers who lived by manual labour and those who bore the burden of heavy tributes, rents and leases ... 'for they have little property'. The last-named were small tenants who sporadically succumbed to the pressure of commitments.[101] Here it should be borne in mind that the majority of these data fall outside the actual crisis years, so that the cyclical peaks of poverty, which hit the unassisted manual workers and tenants, are hidden from our view.

It is obvious that, in addition to the cyclical poverty referred to here, there must have been a structural form since, as the examples of Dixmude, Mechlin and Leiden show, the economic situation brought prolonged unemployment for a section of the population.

The existence of organized poor relief in the rural areas is known explicitly from fourteenth- and fifteenth-century fiscal documents pertaining to the majority of villages in Flanders, Hainaut and Brabant.[102] While there is a complete absence of information concerning the existence of *dissen* in Artois, it is conceivable that they were present.[103] The accounts of the *Hl. Geesttafel* in the village of Pittem reveal a method of operation completely analogous to that in the towns, albeit somewhat more personal by reason of the smaller scale.

The hearth census of 1469 in Pittem shows 40 'poor' hearths out of a total of 232.[104] Distributions of bread amount to nine per year, two of 40 loaves, six of between 24 and 26 and one of 36 loaves. Distributions of footwear benefited 23 adults and 21 children in 1486-7; 19 and 24 in 1487-8; 22 and 32 in 1489-90; 8 and 2 in 1492-3. An annual gift of money was made, in which all 40 paupers shared. It is thus clear that the figure for fiscal poverty cannot be accepted without question, even as an indication of the number of *disarmen*. The number eligible for the principal gifts, *e.g.* linen, was smaller.

100. L. Gilliodts van Severen, *Coutumes des pays et comté de Flandre. Petites villes*, VI (Brussels, 1893) 579-80.
101. Archives départementales du Nord, B 195/36.
102. *Ibidem*, B 197 *passim*; Algemeen Rijksarchief, Brussels, Rekenkamer, Reg. no. 45,978; Arnould, *Dénombrements*, 181; Cuvelier, *Dénombrements*, e.g. 290.
103. Bocquet, *Recherches*, 139.
104. De Smet, 'Dénombrement', 131 (datum collated with the document; the exempted hearths owned by inhabitants of the town numbered 12).

Nevertheless, the agreement between 40 poor hearths and 40 distributions of bread and money is noteworthy. This shows that the figures for the hearth censuses are a fairly good reflection of the maximum achievements of the *dissen*. At the same time, due regard must be paid to the fact that the distributions were in many cases on a smaller scale, and also that the number of recipients (here 40) by no means implies that all who were in need of assistance received it and therefore does not indicate the threshold of need.

The fiscal documents for the villages in Brabant in 1526 reveal that there were no less than five categories of paupers, which are not clearly discernable, namely *disarmen*, *huisarmen* who received assistance from the *dis*, paupers with a trade who received assistance to supplement their wages, paupers living in institutions, and itinerant beggars.[105]

The income of the *dissen* — which in essence consisted of donations from the well-to-do and property donated by way of tribute[106] — was in many cases inadequate. The inadequacy of the assistance provided by the *dissen*, in turn, necessitated begging. It appears that between 25 and 50 per cent of those who received assistance from the *dissen* in Walloon Flanders between 1498 and 1544 were also obliged to resort to mendicancy.[107] Some, out of shame, were driven to beg outside their own village.

The number of persons receiving assistance from the rural *dissen* is not always proportional to the true extent of the need, though perhaps it is in proportion to the financial resources or the willingness on the part of well-to-do villagers to contribute. This can be investigated with the aid of fiscal *enquêtes* for Walloon Flanders dating from the fourteenth and fifteenth centuries. In Lomme — near Lille — (1432), the 66 hearths are divided into 20 *disarmen*, 8 families living in freehold properties and 38 tenants. In Lécluse (1498), the 96 hearths comprise 2-3 beggars, 20-24 farmers with freehold or rented land and 69-74 'manouvriers vivans du mieulx qu'ilz peuent'.[108]

The most vulnerable groups in the society had the largest share in the relief. These were the single women and widows. In Ypres (1431), 39 of the 51 beggars were women, while of the 38 paupers in institutions, 25 were widows.[109]

105. Cuvelier, *Dénombrements*, 493 and 415.
106. Archives départementales du Nord, B 3752; *Bulletin de la Commission Flamande de France*, XXVII (Arras, 1928) 13-82 : at the beginning of the fifteenth century, 165 *gemeten* (4423m²) out of a total of 3,718 formed part of the patrimony of the *dis* in the parish of Meteren.
107. Cf. Table X in Blockmans and Prevenier, 'Armoede in de Nederlanden', 531.
108. Archives départementales du Nord, B 1110, liasse Lomme; B 3761, fol. 86 v°.
109. H. Pirenne, 'Dénombrements', 31-2.

IV. SOCIAL ATTITUDES TOWARDS THE NEEDY

There are various paths by which to discover the image of the needy section of the population in the mind of the public at large. To start with, every literary or artistic expression, as a work which in all probability was conceived in a well-to-do environment, was in any case destined for one and was therefore adapted to the scale of values of that environment, is a highly suitable instrument of cursory acquaintance with opinions which were common-place, or which were held to be particularly objectionable or commendable.[110] Analysis of the preachings and of all manner of moralizing texts would un-doubtedly prove very interesting also. In this context, the socializing role played by schools, notably in the early part of the sixteenth century, merits attention. Without doubt, these sets of ideas influenced the policies of govern-ments and the attitudes of individuals towards the poor. We have as yet been unable to elaborate this aspect; however, in doing so it is essential to start by investigating the social effect actually produced by the intentions and measures. From the point of view of research, testamentary dispositions relating to poverty, like the subjects referred to earlier, still constitute well-nigh virgin, but very fertile, terrain. Can the conclusion regarding Douai in the fourteenth century — namely that the citizens devoted at most 10 per cent of their patrimony to the poor; that they regarded such gifts as a means of achieving salvation; and that they would rather donate twenty or even forty times as much for Masses — be generalized?[111] On the other hand, the value of wills as a measure of charity on the part of the citizenry must not be overestimated in view of the constraints imposed by local authorities on the transfer of property and ground-rent in mortmain. We doubtless lack a great deal of information concerning many other forms of charity on a more restricted and individual scale, which are difficult to quantify owing to the nature of the relevant documentation, which rarely allows genuine gifts to be distinguished from sales ostensibly stemming from motives of piety.[112] While here and there hitherto unobserved forms of poor relief emerge from the sources,[113] the work of the major institutions, as the sum of countless individual actions, must be seen as reflecting the trend.

We would remind the reader of the *modus operandi* of the *Hl. Geesttafels* which, as a mirror reflecting the foundations by burghers, were also obliged

110. A sensitive approach to the source material dealing with the attitude to the needy is to be found in De la Roncière, 'Pauvres et pauvreté à Florence', 685-734.
111. F. Leclère, 'Recherches sur la charité des bourgeois envers les pauvres au XIVᵉ siècle à Douai', *Revue du Nord*, XLVIII (1966) 139-54.
112. Tits-Dieuaide, 'Tables de Pauvres', 566-7.
113. Blockmans and Prevenier, 'Openbare Armenzorg', 37-40.

to devote a substantial part of their budgets to Masses and other religious ceremonies, and of the fact that they economized on distributions to the poor in preference to failing in their obligations towards the donors. We would also recall that, in terms of date, quality and place (at the rear of the church, often following a Mass for a departed soul), the entire pattern of poor relief was aimed at accentuating the ritual of the Church.

Finally, we would observe, as O. Mus has done in relation to Ypres,[114] that the conjuncture of certain charitable initiatives appears to have stemmed primarily from a desire to preserve the established social order. The establishment, at the initiative of the entrepreneurial ruling classes, of hospices for the temporarily unemployed coincided precisely with the brief spells of economic depression which occurred during the long period of expansion in the thirteenth century. In that century, new hospitals were built, or existing ones enlarged, in nearly all the towns in the southern Netherlands. Their prime function at that time lay in providing temporary relief for paupers who, by reason of sickness, disability or pregnancy, were prevented from begging. Later, these establishments were occupied almost exclusively by well-to-do citizens who, by making a substantial donation, had assured themselves of a carefree old age.[115] The thirteenth century also witnessed a significant increase in the patrimony of the *Hl. Geesttafels* as a result of the sale by institutions on a large scale of life annuities, which were not infrequently paid out in the form of prebends.[116]

A far-reaching study of Ghent revealed that round about 1500 there was indeed a rise in the number of new foundations, but that these did not result in an increase of poor relief as a whole.[117] Against this, from 1335 or so onwards there was a manifest reduction of overall relief, coupled with stricter control on would-be recipients, and exclusion and repression of all who made up the reserve of labour. In other towns, such as Louvain, Brussels, Antwerp, Mechlin and Bois-le-Duc nothing of this nature occurred even in the fifteenth century; on the contrary, new foundations were established. But, in the cases of Mechlin and Bois-le-Duc at least, we have established that the sixteenth century witnessed a curtailment such as had occurred in Ghent two centuries earlier.

---

114. O. Mus, 'Rijkdom en armoede. Zeven eeuwen leven en werken in Ieper', in: *Prisma van de geschiedenis van Ieper* (Ypres, 1974) 10-3.
115. G. Maréchal, 'Motieven achter het ontstaan en de evolutie van de stedelijke hospitalen in de XIIde en XIIIde eeuw', in: *Septingentesimum Iubilaeum Hospicii dicti Belle. Bijdragen tot de geschiedenis van de Liefdadigheidsinstellingen te Ieper* (Ypres, 1976) 18-23 (with additional literature references).
116. Tits-Dieuaide, 'Tables des Pauvres', 565-8.
117. G. de Wilde, 'De parochiale armenzorg te Gent van de 14e tot het begin van de 16e eeuw' (unpublished licentiate treatise, University of Ghent, 1976) 41, 143.

There is a need to investigate the shift in other cases, in its relationship to the demographic and economic evolution of the towns concerned.

The tendency is apparent in the very numerous regulations and ordinances, which were chiefly issued during periods of famine, when the migration of paupers to the towns evoked there a repulsive reaction born of self-preservation.[118] The fact that such measures, which were primarily directed towards able-bodied mendicants, were repeatedly adopted shows that they were ineffective.[119] As simultaneous action of this nature in all the cities failed to solve the problem, the local administrations raised the issue of combatting beggary at provincial level as soon as the process of State formation allowed. This first occurred in Brabant in 1459, when the province, following a period of high prices, was plagued by bands of men discharged from the army.[120] It is important to emphasize that in the first provincial ordinance on the subject of poor relief, the first 23 articles deal with vandalism in various forms. This is indeed the context in which the government placed the problem of poor relief; its solution lay in imposing on all able-bodied men an obligation to find work within three days, after which any beggars not carrying a mark of identification from a *Hl. Geesttafel* were liable to be sent to the galleys.

It is hard to believe that the authorities deemed their coercive measures to be practicable. They must have been sufficiently well acquainted with the situation on the labour market to know that, for example, the craft regulations severely limited the opportunities for employment. Did they perhaps hope by this means to increase the reserve of labour and thus depress wages? They were undoubtedly aware that, with their approval, the wages of workers in vital categories had been brought much more closely into line with the increased cost of living than those of other, more easily replaceable men. This wage policy

---

118.   April 1403, February 1409 and 1438 for Mons; P. Heupgen, *Documents relatifs à la réglementation de l'assistance publique à Mons du XVe au XVIIIe siècle.* Commission Royale d'Histoire (Brussels, 1929) 1-6.

119.   The regulations issued in Ghent contain repeated ordinances forbidding begging, except for those in possession of an authorization issued by the masters of the *Hl. Geesttafels*. These ordinances span the period from 1414 to 1428. In 1432, a year of high prices, orders banning alien beggars were issued on 5th and 20th Sept. (Municipal Archive, Ghent, Voorgeboden, 108, Reg. no. 2, fol. 43 v°, etc.).

120.   *Placcaerten van Brabant*. IV (Brussels, 1724) 394-405. The text used in Brabant, with only minor amendments, was promulgated in Flanders on 4th September 1461 : A. Vandenpeereboom, *Le Conseil de Flandre à Ypres* (Ypres, 1874) xc-xcvii. As the introductory passage shows, the initiative for this stemmed from the Four Members of Flanders, following consultations with the States of Brabant, the towns in Holland and Zeeland, and the duke (between 9th Jan. and 1st July 1461). Algemeen Rijksarchief, Brussels, Rekenkamer, 42,572 (Franc of Bruges, account 1460-1) fol. 43 r°, 47 r°, 48 r°, 34 v°; 38,685 (Ypres, account 1461) fol. 9 v°. In the light of the contact with Holland and Zeeland, in January, it may be assumed that similar oridinances were promulgated in those regions.

was part of a social policy which was clearly inspired, not by the principles of Christian charity but by those of capitalist enterprise.

One thing which is certain is that from that time onwards poor relief was deliberately curtailed on the grounds that undeserving cases profited excessively from it. This contraction already applied in the parish of St. Nicholas in Ghent, in 1458; in any case, the scale of the assistance was severely reduced everywhere after the crisis which commenced in 1477. Charity on the part of the burghers produced no significant change in the situation, except perhaps in the still prosperous towns of Antwerp, Bois-le-Duc and Mechlin where, with the aid of fresh capital, a new, efficient and intensive form of weekly assistance was instituted. Here we see again the positive correlation between poor relief and prosperity such as existed in Ypres in the thirteenth century. The explanation for these conclusions, which conflict with traditional views on charity, lies in the part played by public poor relief in controlling the relative surplus of population in the towns and exercising supervision of the labour market. In time of boom, the maintenance of a reserve of labour by means of relief mechanisms was not only highly feasible, thanks to the relative prosperity, but also justifiable in economic terms. During longer-term depressions, the existing institutions were allowed to fade away, or to perform other functions, and relief was restricted to a minimal number of cases which, moreover, were carefully scrutinized. This difference of approach is governed, not by a specific time category but by a specific social and economic constellation which occurs in various places at different times.[121]

Finally, one could attempt to discover the attitude of the needy towards their situation. It has proved possible to do this for the paupers of fourteenth century Florence by means of, *inter alia*, their complaints to the authorities.[122] In this country, such an investigation could be conducted with the aid of judicial documents which specify the sentences passed on paupers. Narrative sources, *e.g.* those pertaining to rebellious phases in which undercurrents clearly emerged, could produce a great deal of fresh material in this context. If we examine the numerous revolts which were an expression of the people's discontent at their deprivation, do we find the poor protesting the most vehemently? Decidedly not: they were not willing to jeopardize their miserable

---

121. F.F. Piven and R. Cloward, *Regulating the Poor. The Functions of Public Welfare* (London, 1972); C. Lis and H. Soly, 'Verarming en sociale politiek tijdens twee versnellingsfasen in de kapitalistische ontwikkeling', *Handelingen XXXe Vlaams Filologencongres* (Ghent, 1975) 243-6; H. Soly, 'Economische ontwikkeling en sociale politiek in Europa tijdens de overgang van middeleeuwen naar nieuwe tijden', *Tijdschrift voor geschiedenis*, LXXXVIII (1975) 584-97. This mechanism has been clearly demonstrated for Mechlin and Bois-le-Duc: Blockmans, 'Armenzorg en levensstandaard', 161-2; Blockmans and Prevenier, 'Openbare armenzorg te 's-Hertogenbosch', 58-60.
122. De la Roncière, 'Pauvres et pauvreté à Florence', 735-40.

allowance. In urban revolts, we find among the ringleaders craftsmen in well-defined categories who had suffered loss of income or status.[123] The same conclusion can be drawn from an analysis of confiscation lists following revolts: it was not the paupers who led the fray, but groups with a certain level of prosperity which they felt was threatened.[124]

This is in conformity with an important conclusion emanating from this study, namely to apply the term 'need' to all groups, in particular socio-professional categories, whose minimum standard of living was threatened regularly — and during the late-fifteenth and sixteenth centuries increasingly — by unfavourable developments in the economy. The fluctuations above and below the poverty line greatly increased the number of such groups and made them more keenly aware of their situation than were those who, often as a result of natural setbacks, were condemned to remain permanently below the line.

In addition, we have stressed the fact that the assistance given to the poor was at no time adequate, added to which it was deliberately curtailed and more closely supervised as the number of would-be recipients increased in times of structural unemployment, and that, in contrast, the scale was increased during phases of economic expansion. Here we see the interaction between, on the one hand, objective factors such as climate, which can result in crop failures, and mechanisms which are outside the control of man and which produce a downturn in the economy, and on the other, human actions aimed at spreading existing shortages as favourably as possible from the point of view of the better-off.

123. On 25th Oct. 1436 in Bruges, weavers, fullers, shearers and dyers; on 18th Apr. 1437 in Bruges, smiths; on 10th and 12th Oct. 1437 in Ghent, smiths, barge masters; in Nov. 1487 in Ghent, artisans in craft establishments, on 2nd February 1488 in Bruges, aldermen of the craft guilds and craftsmen; Niklaas Despars, *Cronijcke van Vlaenderen 405-1492*, ed. by J. de Jonghe (Bruges, 1840) III, 378-9, 388-90, 399-400; IV, 293-7; Olivier van Dixmude, *Merkwaerdige gebeurtenissen 1377-1443*, ed. by J.J. Lambin (Ypres, 1835) 156-7; Jean Molinet, *Chroniques*, ed. by G. Doutrepont and O. Jodogne, I (Brussels, 1935) 589.

124. J. Mertens, 'De economische en sociale toestand van de opstandelingen uit het Brugse Vrije wier goederen na de slag bij Cassel (1328) verbeurd verklaard werden', *Belgisch tijdschrift voor filologie en geschiedenis*, XLVII (1969) 1132-53; *Idem*, 'Twee (Wevers) opstanden te Brugge (1387-1391)', *Handelingen van het genootschap Société d'Emulation te Brugge*, CX (Bruges, 1973) 5-20; A. van Oost, 'Sociale stratifikatie van de Gentse opstandelingen van 1379-85', *Handelingen van de Maatschappij voor geschiedenis en oudheidkunde te Gent*, XXIX (Ghent, 1975) 59-92.

57

Prices and Wages as Development Variables: A Comparison between England and the Southern Netherlands, 1400-1700 *

H. VAN DER WEE

The study of prices and wages has become of the highest importance in Belgium since the second World War, due *inter alia* to the stimulus of C. Verlinden and his collaborators. The great amount of information on prices, wages, and rents that has been collected and published, provided a basis for the study of the relationship between prices and the quantity of money available, to determine whether 'quantitive theory' is applicable to the history of prices in the southern Netherlands during the *ancien régime*. Prices, wages, and rents have also been even more useful in the study of social and economic conditions, making possible an answer to the following questions : Which factors governed the long-term movement of prices or the short-run price cycle? What was the latter's influence on rural incomes, on the incomes of commercial speculators and of urban wage earners? Which variables governed the movement of house rents and land leases?

Belgian price historians have paid less attention to the problem of economic development. This is understandable. Modern development theories primarily rely on volume-statistics of production, consumption, savings, investment, employment, population, etc., and few representative and dependable volume-statistics are available for the *ancien régime*. On the other hand, price and wage statistics are copious for the latter period and can also be approached more critically and with greater precision. It may be considered therefore whether prices and wages cannot be used in the study of economic development, as a substitute for the missing volume-statistics and as the basic information for the elaboration of explicative work hypotheses. The present study is an attempt to determine whether an inter-regional comparison of prices and wages in Brabant and southern England for the period 1400-1700 can, by

* This article is a translation of 'Prijzen en lonen als ontwikkelingsvariabelen. Een vergelijkend onderzoek tussen Engeland en de Zuidelijke Nederlanden, 1400-1700' in: *Album offert à Charles Verlinden à l'occasion de ses trente ans de professorat* (Ghent, 1975) 413-35. The price and wage series on which this article is based have been published in *Album Verlinden*, 436-47. The author would like to thank Mr. M. Grow and Mrs. M. Pappas for their assistance and, particularly, professors J. Munro, S. Eddie and C. Harley of the University of Toronto for their most useful comments.

reflecting the evolution of real wages, suggest certain development variables in the pre-industrial economy.

The period 1400-1700 was chosen for the following reasons: during the fifteenth and sixteenth centuries southern England and Brabant had narrow commercial ties but different economic infrastructures, clearly less primitive in Brabant than in England. During the seventeenth century both regions continued to develop within the framework of a pre-industrial economy, but the common factors weakened; moreover, Brabant stagnated and showed signs of regression in some sectors while England gradually evolved into a leading European economy. An investigation of the causes or mechanisms of these movements within a homogeneous technical structure could shed light on the conditions necessary for the transformation from a pre-industrial to an industrial society.

STATISTICAL INFORMATION: HEURISTIC AND METHODOLOGICAL REMARKS

Four studies by E.H. Phelps Brown and Sheila V. Hopkins published in *Economica* from 1955 to 1959 were taken as a point of departure for a comparative analysis.[1] Phelps Brown and Hopkins examined the development of prices of consumption goods in comparison with the evolution of wages in the building sector for the period 1264-1954 in southern England, and tested their results against analogous information from France, Alsace, Munster (Westphalia), Augsburg, Vienna, and Valencia. Our aim is to compare the information from southern England with price and wage material from Brabant between 1400 and 1700.

To preserve the homogeneity of our comparative study, the method Phelps Brown and Hopkins created with the economic historians of the London School of Economics is taken as a guide. The authors used six sub-groups of essential consumer goods to make up their annual price index. The choice of the essential consumer goods inside each sub-group and the probable amount of each product used per adult male person per year were based on historical budget information. The total annual cost per sub-group was reduced each time to one index figure with the average of the stable years 1451-1475 as a base period. The six partial index figures thus arrived at were combined to

1. E.H. Phelps Brown and S.V. Hopkins, 'Seven Centuries of Building Wages', *Economica*, N.S. XXII, no. 87 (London, August 1955) 195-206; *ibidem*, 'Seven Centuries of the Mirices of Consumables compared with Builders' Wage-Rates', *ibidem*, XXIII, no. 92 (November, 1956) 296-314; *ibidem*, 'Wage-rates and Prices : Evidence for Population Pressure in the Sixteenth Century', *ibidem*, XXIV, no. 96 (November, 1957) 289-306; *ibidem*, 'Builders' Wage-Rates, Prices and Populations : some Further Evidence', *ibidem*, XXVI no. 101 (February, 1959) 18-38.

form one average annual global index figure, with the help of a weighting coefficient which referred to budgets of the period studied. Lord W. Beveridge's price lists provided the English price series between 1400 and 1700, together with as yet unpublished information from the Beveridge archives. Thorold Rogers' publications provided series of wages. Two annual budget tables and one weighting table were used for the choice of products and the weighting coefficient, as can be seen in Table I.

TABLE I. *Annual budgetary basket of essential consumer goods for an adult male, southern England, 1200-1700*

	1275	1500	Weighting coefficient per sub-group to calculate the annual index
1. Meal products	1 1/4 bushels wheat 1　　bushels rye 1/2　bushels barley 2/3　bushels peas	1 1/4 bushels wheat 1　　bushels rye 1/2　bushels barley 2/3　bushels peas	20%
2. Meat and fish	1/2 pig 1/2 sheep 40 herrings	1 1/2 sheep 15 white herrings 25 red herrings	25%
3. Butter and cheese	10 lbs. butter 10 lbs. cheese	nihil	12-1/2%
4. Drink	4-1/2 bushels malt	4-1/2 bushels malt	22-1/2%
5. Heating and lighting	nihil	4-1/2 bushels charcoal 2-3/4 lbs. candles 1/2 pint oil	8-1/2%
6. Textiles	3-1/4 yds canvas	2/3 yds canvas 1/2 yd shirting 1/3 yd woollen cloth	12-1/2%

In their 1959 publication Phelps Brown and Hopkins indicated that meal products had received too low a weight in the weighting coefficients for the essential foodstuffs while drink, meat, and fish had received too high a figure. Mutual changes of these coefficients for meal products and drink would have little effect on the result because both groups are based on grain prices. The observation is chiefly relevant in the case of meat and fish consumption for the period after 1700, but our study does not extend beyond that date. Moreover, budget information for the southern Netherlands for the period 1400-1800 indicates a high meat and fish consumption.[2] We have, therefore, retained the Phelps Brown and Hopkins calculations.

2. H. Van der Wee, 'Voeding en dieet in het *Ancient Régime*', *Spiegel Historiael*, I (Bussum, 1966) 94-101.

On the basis of the daily summer money wage of a master-mason in southern England, an annual money wage index figure based on the average money wage during the period 1451-1475 was calculated. The annual global price index figure for basic maintenance was then put beside the annual money wage index figure, producing an annual index series which expressed the real wage income of an English master-mason in terms of a basket of essential consumer goods as described above.

For the statistics concerning prices and wages in Brabant and Antwerp published and still unpublished information from our study of Antwerp,[3] supplemented by figures published by E. Scholliers and J. Craeybeckx in the series edited by C. Verlinden and his collaborators, has been used.[4] Just as in the work of Phelps Brown and Hopkins, a budgetary basket of essential consumer goods was composed, but the availability of price series had to be taken into account for determining the articles selected. Because the budgetary difference between the southern English tables of 1275 and 1500 was so slight, only one annual budgetary basket was composed for Brabant (table II).

There was little sense in arranging the calculations concerning the annual price index-figures in Antwerp and Brabant in two stages, as Phelps Brown and Hopkins did, because the number of selected consumer goods available per sub-group was so small. Prices from Antwerp and Brabant were therefore only weighted once, by multiplying the price of each relevant product by the amount given in the annual budget. The average of the stable years 1451-1475 again served as a base period. The calculation of the annual money wage index figures was based on the daily summer wage of a master-mason in Antwerp and used the same 1451-1475 base period. The two index series were compared in the same way as those for southern England. Both the annual money wage index series (graph II) and the annual price index series (graph I) and their mutual comparison were expressed in graphs in a semi-logarithmic scale.

---

3. H. Van der Wee, *The Growth of the Antwerp Market and the European Economy (fourteenth-sixteenth centuries)* (The Hague, 1963) I, 173-8 (rye in Antwerp), 189-93 (barley in Antwerp), 210-6 (butter in Brussels), 217-24 (cheese in Antwerp), 225-7 (salt beef in Mechlin), 249-53 (tallow candles in West Brabant), 254-6 (charcoal in Antwerp), 269-72 (Weerts' grey serge in Antwerp), 273-6 (sail cloth in Mechlin), 277-86 (dried herring in Mechlin), 336-49 and 457-63 (summer daily wage of master mason in Antwerp). This information was supplemented with non-published figures from the same sources. For grain and cloth prices in the seventeenth century, non-published accounts from charitable and ecclesiastical institutions in Brussels and Antwerp and the official urban list of grain prices in Brussels, were used.

4. Ch. Verlinden, J. Craeybeckx, E. Scholliers and others, *Dokumenten voor de geschiedenis van prijzen en lonen in Vlaanderen en Brabant (XVe-XVIIIe eeuw)* (4 vols, Bruges, 1959-1973) I, 501-3 (barley in Brussels); II (19), 692-712 (meat in Antwerp), 726-37 (herring in Antwerp), 712-21 (butter in Antwerp), 723-5 (cheese in Antwerp), 843-5 (flax in Antwerp), 977-1056 (wages in Antwerp), 92-135 and 360-461 (wages in Bruges and Ghent for comparison).

TABLE II. *Annual budgetary basket of essential consumer goods for an adult male, Brabant, 1400-1700*

Essential consumer goods	Annual budget per person	Daily budget per person
1. Meal products	rye: 126 litres	0.345 litres
2. Drink	barley: 162 litres	0.444 litres
3. Meat and fish	beef: 23.5 kg. (salted)	0.065 kg.
	herrings: 40	0.11
4. Butter and cheese	butter: 4.8 kg	0.013 kg
	cheese: 4.7 kg	0.013 kg
5. Heating and lighting	charcoal: 162 litres	0.444 litres
	tallow candles: 1 1/3 kg	0.004 kg
6. Textiles	woollens from Weert, etc. 1.125 metres	0.003 metres
	linen: 1.80 metres [5]	0.005 metres

Moreover, the price trend was calculated by interquartile moving averages over thirteen years, which are also expressed on the graphs.

Complete price series existed for most of the consumer goods selected. The occasional gaps were filled by indirect information. Such interpolations have been given in brackets in the published series. For budget groups one and two, the principal ingredients of the end products such as bread and beer were included rather than the end products themselves. In periods of falling price trends and of wage inertia, such calculations based on ingredients distort the increase in purchasing power in an upward direction, while in periods of rising prices and slower wage increases they over-accentuate the decrease of purchasing power. On the other hand, the wage index series does not take employment into account. This is unfortunate, because employment was not static throughout and because there were differences in the situation in Brabant and southern England. An employment index for Brabant in the building sector is available,[6] but for England there is no such information; to retain a homogeneous study the Brabant information was not included in the calculations, but was used for the interpretation of the figures. In any event, the differences are not, globally speaking, large enough to distort the main conclusions.

The choice of the price and wage information from Antwerp-Brabant and in particular the selection of building wages must also be justified. In the

5. Because there was no continuous series for linen, it was replaced by coarse linen sail-cloth. Because this has about half the value, the annual amount of 1.80 m. linen was replaced by 3.60 m. sail cloth.

6. Van der Wee, *Growth of the Antwerp Market*, I, appendix 48, 539-44.

first place the price series from Antwerp and Brabant are the most complete and homogeneous available for the period in Brabant. They are also representative of the western urban region of the duchy, a region which from about 1400 showed a marked tendency towards market unity. On the other hand, Antwerp building money wages represent more exclusively the wage sector of the town itself. They reflect, for the fifteenth and sixteenth centuries, the economic rise of the trading metropolis of Brabant, and, because of the building multiplicator in Antwerp, they even tend to exaggerate it too much. The relationship was reversed in the following century of commercial decline. Various sectors, such as printing, weaving, etc., defended themselves much better in Antwerp than the building sector, and therefore enjoyed a more favourable money wage development — in other words, the figures for building wages in Antwerp in the seventeenth century tend to understate global money wage development.

Comparisons between money wages in Antwerp and the other towns of Brabant tend to favour Antwerp as far as rate is concerned, but certain costs, like house-rents, were markedly higher there too. Antwerp did not always have the highest rate of increase; Brussels' linen weavers' money wages, for example, as well as rural money wages around Lier and even some building money wages outside Antwerp, rose more quickly between 1480 and 1650 than did masons' money wages in Antwerp. *Grosso modo* therefore information about money wages in Antwerp was sufficiently representative for all western Brabant.

Finally, on a separate graph, the trend of rye prices in Antwerp is compared with the price of building materials and building money wages, with the price of textiles and textile money wages, and with rents and rural money wages (graph IV). For the method of calculation, see our study of Antwerp.[7]

ANALYSIS OF THE STATISTICAL RESULTS

The curves for the fifteenth, sixteenth, and early seventeenth centuries are analyzed together, because they can be treated as a single cycle of inter-secular development. The comparison of the trend of the nominal prices for a basket of essential consumer goods in southern England and in Brabant between 1400 and 1650 (graph I) reveals — in spite of a fundamental analogy in their inter-secular movement — substantial mutual differences, especially in connection with the inter-decennial situation. In contrast to Brabant the trend in

7. This graph is no. 53 in Van der Wee, *Growth of the Antwerp Market*, which through a printer's error did not appear, together with no. 54, in the book.

southern England is very continuous and clear: slowly falling prices moving into stagnation from 1400 to 1510; regularly rising prices between 1510 and 1610 (except the noticeable quickening during the Great Debasement period in the forties and early fifties) and a weakening of price rises between 1610 and 1650. When the English price series are divided between groups of goods, the picture of the important waves of different price categories remains the same, although prices for essential foods fall more quickly between 1400 and 1510 than prices of non-essential agricultural produce and industrial goods; on the other hand essential food prices rose during the following Price Revolution more quickly than the two other groups of goods.[8] Finally, English daily money wages rose at the beginning of the fifteenth century and remained at a high level in spite of the falling and stagnant price trend until 1510 (graph II). In other words, the purchasing power of wages increased and retained its position well in relation to a basket of essential consumer goods in England throughout the century (graph III). During the sixteenth century, on the other hand, the situation was reversed: English daily money wages failed to keep up with price rises and did so only with a marked difference in timing (graph II) so that the purchasing power of wages collapsed in an alarming manner, until by the first quarter of the seventeenth century it had fallen to less than 40 per cent of its fifteenth-century level (graph III).

The evolution of population in England coincided closely with this price-wage movement. Demographic stagnation followed the sharp fall in population caused by the Black Death of the mid-fourteenth century, while a slow recovery took place in the second half of the fifteenth century; the recovery widened into a strong growth in population during the sixteenth century with saturation about 1600.[9] A Malthusian macro-interpretation is obvious: a relative abundance of land and a relative scarcity of labour explain the development of prices, money wages, and purchasing power during the fifteenth century, while the relative abundance of labour and consequent increasing scarcity of land can be seen as decisive factors in the development of the following period. The *strategic variable* was, therefore, population, and quantity of money, devaluations, investment, etc. were only secondary factors.[10]

8. F. Simiand, *Recherches anciennes et nouvelles sur le mouvement des prix du XVe au XIXe siècle* (Paris, 1932); I. Hammarström, 'The Price Revolution of the Sixteenth Century: some Swedish Evidence', in: P.H. Ramsey, ed., *The Price Revolution in Sixteenth Century England* (London, 1971) 63-5.
9. M. Reinhard, A. Armengaud and J. Dupaquier, *Histoire générale de la population mondiale* (Paris, 1968) 98, 100-1, 118.
10. See in this connection M.J. Elsas, *Umriss einer Geschichte der Preise und Löhne in Deutschland vom ausgehenden Mittelalter bis zum Beginn des neunzehnten Jahrhunderts* (Leiden, 1936-49); M. Postan, 'The Trade of Medieval Europe; the North', in: M. Postan and E.E. Rich, edd.,

The trend in Brabant of prices, money wages, and buying power was obviously less continuous. Population development remained an important variable in explaining price, money wage, and buying power movements in the long term, but other variables were also active both in deciding the secular movement and in the inter-decennial cycles. Moreover, it is useful to include the graphs of nominal prices (graphs I, II, III) and those transposed into precious metals equivalents (graph IV) in the Brabant analysis. In graph I the fifteenth century trend can be seen as a hesitating preamble to the price rises of the sixteenth, although declines after 1438 and 1495 are undeniable. In graph IV the trend in silver equivalent prices can be seen to rise in the fifteenth century until the crisis of 1437-38; thereafter the drop is more obvious than in the graphs of nominal prices.

The demographic factor cannot be ignored for Brabant. Probably influenced by still flourishing industry and trade in the larger and smaller towns of the duchy, the population of Brabant increased in the late fourteenth-early fifteenth centuries, but if stagnated after the famine of 1437-38, and diminished quite impressively during the last third of the fifteenth century.[11] The increase in nominal and real prices until 1437-38 (graphs I and IV) and the fall in purchasing power of wage earners' incomes during the first quarter of the fifteenth century (graph III) agrees with this. The price stagnation after 1437-38 and price declines after 1495 (graphs I and IV), as well as favourable purchasing power between 1440 and 1480 (graph III), can also be generally reconciled with a demographic interpretation. But the sharp rises of nominal and real prices at the beginning of the fifteenth century and during the 1480's were also closely connected with money policies and their psychological implications: in other words, with the gradual devaluation of the Brabant groat from 1.02 to 0.54 grs. fine silver between 1400 and 1435 and with the heavy devaluations under Maximilian of Austria when the Brabant groat fell from 0.35 to 0.16 grs. fine silver between 1480 and 1489.[12]

The demographic interpretation, however, does not explain the sharp rise in money wages during the first third of the fifteenth century, a period of marked population growth (graph II). This deviation must be considered in the special context of the economy of the Low Countries in comparison with the rest of Europe north of the Alps. While the fourteenth and fifteenth centuries saw

The Cambridge Economic History of Europe, II (Cambridge, 1952) 119-256; W. Abel, *Agrarkrisen und Agrarkonjunktur* (Hamburg, 1966).

11. J. Cuvelier, *Les dénombrements de foyers en Brabant (XIVe-XVIe siècles)* (Brussels, 1912). For statistical adaptation see H. Van der Wee, *Growth of the Antwerp Market*, I, appendix 49, 545-48.

12. *Ibidem*, 127-8.

demographic stagnation and economic malaise throughout Europe, urban Brabant, although not immune, had sufficient power to resist.

Although the price trend was clearly influenced by the unfavourable European situation, it nevertheless showed a tendency to rise. In addition, a more dynamic development of money wages took place, although still not sufficient to maintain the purchasing power of workmen's money wages at a high level throughout the whole century. From this point of view, an institutional factor seems in Brabant to be the strategic independent variable, while the population factor is reduced to the position of a secondary explaining variable (see *infra*).

During the sixteenth century Brabant's exceptional economic position became still more pronounced. To be sure, the important population increase until the Revolt ran parallel, as in the rest of Europe, with the rise in prices and in land rents during the second and third quarter of the sixteenth century. Moreover, Brabant prices for essential foodstuffs also increased faster than those for non-essential foodstuffs and industrial goods (graphs I and IV). Nevertheless, population cannot be considered the determining variable in explaining the sharp increase of nominal wages and the gradual improvement of purchasing power of the wage-earner's income during the same period (graphs II and III).

During the early Revolt, it is even more difficult to use the population variable as the decisive explicatory factor. Although the population increase obviously diminished and soon turned into a drastic decrease depressing demand, prices still rose considerably. The demographic decrease had a braking effect on prices only near the end of the century, especially during the re-conquest of the south by Farnese and during the Twelve Year Truce, but the price revolution continued unabated when war began again in 1621.[13]

After the Eighty Years' War and the English civil war, the relationship between population, economy, and price-wage movements, as far as those factors can be compared in southern England and Brabant, reversed itself. In England, where the population rose until the second half of the seventeenth century and did not fall seriously afterwards,[14] prices started to stagnate, money wage rises occurred, and the purchasing power of the working man's income began to improve. In Brabant, on the other hand, population, even

13. In fact there was a slow demographic improvement after the brutal decrease of the seventies and eighties caused by the war, plundering of the country areas, emigration and the great famine of 1586-7; but this was initially on a lower level than before the Revolt and only gathered momentum during the second quarter of the century. (P. Klep, 'Urbanization in a Pre-industrial Economy. The Case of Brabant, 1374-1930', *Belgisch tijdschrift voor nieuwste geschiedenis*, VII (1976) 1-2, 153-168.
14. Reinhard, Armengaud and Dupaquier, *Histoire générale*, 169-70.

when regaining its losses, stagnated again after the 1660's, while prices, except during the war years around 1700, tended to fall, with money wages holding their own, *id est*, with a favourable effect on the purchasing power of the wage-earners. As far as the seventeenth century is concerned, the Malthusian interpretation, which stresses population as the strategic variable, can thus be better applied to the development of Brabant than to the English situation. Brabant seemed to be integrated into the less-developed European agricultural economy, while England moved forward to develop a modern economy.

FROM ECONOMIC INTERPRETATION TO WORKING HYPOTHESIS

To transform the conclusions reached above into a unifying working hypothesis, the dual economic structure of pre-industrial Europe must be accepted as a basic assumption: certain regions, like northern Italy and Flanders-Brabant, already then possessed a very modern money economy in contrast with most other European areas which still had a primitive agrarian economy. The degree of urbanization can be taken as the main criterium of distinction between the regions. In Flanders-Brabant, for example, urban population already comprised 35 to 40 per cent of the total in the fifteenth and sixteenth centuries, while in less developed areas the urban sector fluctuated around 5 per cent and only reached 10 per cent very rarely. The less developed areas were, moreover, dominated by autarchic agriculture and only gradually experienced the expansion of urban money and credit in contrast to more modern zones, where agriculture was closely connected with the urban money economies both geographically and sectorially.

Fifteenth and sixteenth century trends of prices and real wages suggest that southern England was obviously one of the less developed regions. Such a conclusion coincides with those of Phelps Brown and Hopkins, who showed clear analogies between southern England and France, Alsace, northwestern Germany, Austria, and Spain.[15] The English fifteenth and sixteenth century experience can therefore be considered as typical for less developed European economies, dominated by primitive agriculture. Brabant, on the other hand, can be considered a European centre of more highly developed, already largely urban, money economies.

15. Phelps Brown and Hopkins, 'Wage-Rates and Prices', 291-9; *ibidem*, 'Builders' wage-rates', 18-29.

As indicated above, the population factor, with its own internal dynamics, serves as the *strategic* variable in explaining the inter-secular development of the primitive European economy. Because of the demographic relapse of the fourteenth and fifteenth centuries (itself a complex result of the tendency towards relative overpopulation during preceding centuries), subsequent increasing labour productivity led both to higher or stable wages for labourers and to falling prices for essential foodstuffs, so that real *per capita* incomes (employment prospects considered as remaining constant), increased substantially in the urban and rural wage sector. In the towns, favourable wage development was vigorously supported by increased corporatism and the expansion of craft guilds.

On the other hand, the new relationship between population and acreage (*i.e.*, the changed land/labour ratio) and the rise in marginal labour productivity which resulted from it, did not automatically lead to a speedy recovery of agricultural incomes for various reasons. Falling productivity of cultivated land caused by the catastrophic character of the depopulation, offset the rising labour productivity in the agricultural sector. For big land-owners, higher wages also meant higher costs for the domains they themselves exploited while cheaper land leases implied that they received lower incomes from their tenants. For independent farmers, falling agricultural prices meant a lower monetary return from their own acres. Another reason for the decline in income of the land-owners and independent farmers was rigidity: productivity gains which might have occurred from a shift to lands of better quality or from a consolidation of parcels into larger units failed to materialize, due to the built-in rigidity and immobilism which characterized primitive, self-sufficient agriculture.

The falling prices for agricultural produce meant as we have seen substantial market losses for land-owners. Since social relations in the agricultural economy still depended to some extent on seignorial relationships even when land was leased to tenants, allowing the land-owners to retain some authority over the farmers and tenants, the former tried to compensate for the threat to their profits by making new claims on the latter. In other words, while the increase in marginal labour productivity meant, in principle, higher incomes for farmers and tenants, there were nevertheless attempts by the landlords to skim off some of that income by introducing new feudal duties or imposing new feudal charges. When the landlords succeeded, which they often did, the richer groups (which as land-owners should have suffered most from falling rents) were not the worst off and were not forced to use their savings for consumption but instead could maintain their established habits of saving. On balance the new transfers of income meant a continuing impoverishment of the mass of farmers and tenants whose loss of income was not compensated by an increased inflow of money from the reserves of the rich into the urban and rural wage-sector and then back to the agricultural producers. Although the favourable development of urban and rural wages included the possibility of creating potential inflow of money into the urban economy, both income sectors were in fact too narrow in the less developed areas of Europe to allow a sufficiently dynamic demand effect.

Finally, the political factor must not be forgotten. Europe's demographic decline in the fourteenth and fifteenth centuries, by drastically reducing fiscal income, severely threatened the maintenance of the administrative structure of the State. Many European rulers sought recourse in war believing that territorial expansion would help compensate for the loss in revenues. The net result was usually disastrous: conflicts dragged on for years and were accompanied by the endless plundering of the country-side, higher taxes, increasing misery for the peasantry, and growing rural depopulation. Many peasant revolts were provoked by fiscal regulations imposed by the rulers during war or as a result of the landlords' abuses of power described above.

The population factor and the other variables connected with it were strong enough to ensure an extended stagnation of European development in the fourteenth and fifteenth centuries; therefore the normal internal dynamic for re-establishing income equilibrium through a better land-labour ratio could not easily work. In England, moreover, particular factors in the economic structure meant that efforts to cope with the threat to farmers' and landowners' incomes took a specific direction. The slower decline in wool and meat prices in comparison with grain prices prompted landowners to enclose their land and turn it into pastures to breed more sheep. The unemployment and loss in income that resulted for the rural population was compensated, to some extent, by the creation of an English cloth industry based on rural labour. The growth of the cloth industry in the countryside was therefore an important factor in the revival of English agriculture beginning in the second half of the fifteenth century.

Stagnation in the rest of Europe seemed to end at about the same moment: the gap between the relative factor prices seemed to have assumed such proportions that the obstacles started to yield to the forces of adjustment. The rising marginal labour productivity also led to higher incomes of farmers and tenants, creating a stimulus to demographic revival, which initially meant increasing returns in European agricultural produce. Agricultural renewal, strengthened by special exogenous commercial factors, led to the powerful expansion of the sixteenth century. Unavoidably, this cumulative development eventually passed its peak; in the course of the sixteenth century the threat of relative over-population again appeared in many parts of western Europe, with relative factor proportions evolving towards relative land shortage and an excess of labour. Land rents rose while marginal labour productivity gradually edged toward zero as a result of relative overpopulation.

The effect on wage incomes in the more primitive economies was particularly negative. The corporate structure in the towns was not yet strong enough to push wages above prices. There was a painful fall in the purchasing power of *per capita* wage income. On the other hand, the outflow of money that financed the urban purchases of the more expensive foodstuffs only partially returned to the towns in the form of purchases of urban manufactured goods and services by the rural population. In the less developed parts of Europe, considerable delays occurred owing to traditions of autarchy and hoarding among rural people. In addition, the great landowners tended to display an increasing marginal propensity to save and/or orientate their consumption towards the importation of luxury articles from the more highly developed areas of Europe and towards the importation of exotic products. In eastern and central Europe these circumstances led to an obvious weakening of the urban economy in the course of the sixteenth century.[16]

In the agricultural sector of the primitive economies the purchasing power of money wages slipped speedily back for the same reasons. On the contrary, independent farmers and to a greater extent, landowners had sufficient reserves to sell at the best moment, and profited from the increase in land rents; tenants were also favoured by quickly rising prices for foodstuffs, in so far as these benefits were not reduced by higher leases or taxes paid to the owners. *Grosso modo* it can be stated that the profit from rising land rents led to a greater concentration of incomes when the agricultural economy was more primitive as in eastern and central Europe. Alternatively, the more modernized the agriculture as in western Europe, the wider the benefits of a higher land rent were spread over the rural population. In England, where traditional rural industry was essentially aimed at export, falling wage costs were an extra impetus to export, so that merchant-entrepreneurs felt no need to adapt their production and accordingly made few creative changes in rural industry.

The region of Flanders and Brabant, as a nucleus of economic growth in north western Europe, developed differently. The strategic variable in this case was less the population than an institutional factor generating a more dynamic macro-behaviour in economic affairs. The more progressive institutional environment indeed created a most powerful stimulus for creative change and structural progress in response to the threat that future income levels would not meet expectations based on past favourable results.

16. Communicated to me by professor Z.P. Pach for which I thank him very much.

The continuing importance of urban trade and industry in Brabant through-out the fourteenth and early fifteenth centuries ensured permanent possibilities for emigration from the country; it was an additional element in weakening the landlords' authority over the farmers, who were not exposed to the pressure of new feudal taxes or duties, and also helped perpetuate a very intense movement of money between agriculture, industry, and the tertiary sector. Because of these special circumstances surrounding agricultural incomes, the population in Brabant grew until 1437-38 and even maintained a high level during the second third of the fifteenth century. Acreage therefore remained relatively scarce and there was plenty of labour in contrast with the situation in the less developed parts of Europe, where the relative factor prices were evolving in the opposite direction.

The wage-earners of Brabant should, in such circumstances, have been victimized by their great numbers. Workers' real income should normally, under the influence of the factor prices, have evolved negatively; and indeed, for precisely this reason the curve of the purchasing power of the workers' *per capita* income in Brabant in the fifteenth century (graph I) shows a greater nervousness than in England. But on the whole, the impression concerning the real wage situation in Brabant is quite favourable throughout the fifteenth century; in spite of the unfavourable land/labor ratio, real incomes of wage-earners in Brabant reached a high level.[17]

The crucial impact of the institutional factor must, therefore, be stressed. The broad artisanal sector, particularly in the towns of Brabant, felt itself threatened as far as future income was concerned. Because of the happy in-come experience before, the artisans fell back on the now strongly rooted corporatism in Brabant in order to insist successfully on higher wages. At the same time, the Brabant towns began to build up a new industrial structure principally aimed at a diversification of production, at the improvement of skills, at an increase in the economic productivity of labour and resources (which meant more value for the same physical use of labor and raw material), and at a reorientation from external to internal markets. This institutional factor was during the fifteenth century particularly important in saving real wage incomes in advanced areas such as Brabant, carrying the whole economy forward in its wake.

Agriculture in Brabant developed in a similar way. Because of a continuing high population density, land remained relatively scarce and labour relatively

17. Some would explain this particular situation by an exogenous circumstance: the decline in foodstuff prices in Europe undoubtedly also slowed down prices in the Low Countries and, by so doing, indirectly pushed up real wage incomes in Brabant. On the other hand, such a positive influence could be counter-acted by the negative effect of low world prices for industrial products on artisans' incomes in the Brabant towns as far as their products were sold on the markets.

71

numerous, once again in contrast with the rest of Europe. Agricultural prices in Brabant were not proof against the fall or stagnation of European prices and reflected them even if incompletely and with important gaps. Excessive splitting up of acreage and the pressure of slackening food prices, in time, had serious consequences for rural incomes, which could not be compensated by the continuous flow of money between town and country. On the other hand, in more advanced agricultural areas like Brabant, the authority of the landlords was no longer strong enough to recuperate losses in income at the expense of dependent farmers, thus leaving some incentive for initiative in the small peasantry. In these circumstances the institutional factor also became crucial in the agricultural sector: the threat to the farmers' income generated a powerful creative impulse towards technical innovation by intensifying farming and introducing rural industry. The renewal was slow because the rural sector was more rigid than the urban and because taxation and war had considerable influence in the last third of the fifteenth century. But it was clearly present during the whole century.

Sixteenth-century development in urban and rural Brabant followed the same pattern of the previous century, yet it was much more intense. The marked increase of population accentuated still more the shortage of land and the relative abundance of labour. The threat to real wage incomes was again very strong, but in contrast to trends in less developed parts of Europe, this threat was overcome by very substantial nominal wage increases. This successful action by wage-earners showed group consciousness, but was also helped by the powerful guild structure and favoured by the growing export demand. It means that the modern character of the economic structure and of the institutional environment was most responsible for the successful artisan. The time-lag of world prices for industrial products behind grain price increases certainly affected prices in Brabant and therefore became a new threat to wage evolution there. But in an ambitious economy such as that of Brabant this new difficulty only acted as a stimulus for creative innovation, for a further astonishing development of physical and economic productivity in the newly developed artisanal sectors. The continuing flowering of specialized urban industry throughout the critical years of the Revolt is a striking proof of this.

The situation in agriculture was the same. The rising trend in the economic rent on land favoured a large section of the rural population because the extensive parcelling of ground in developed areas like Brabant implied a widespread fragmentation of private property resulting in a distribution of the increasing returns on land over a very large number of independent farmers. Important flows in money between town and country also continued. On the other hand, the threat to the farmer's income, because of the danger of diminishing returns when private exploitation became too small, was compensated by the introduction of new techniques of intensive husbandry, by the quick growth of rural industry, and by important wage increases, similar to those in the towns and in spite of the relative abundance of labour in the countryside. This creativity helped the rural sector, similar to the urban sector in Brabant, to withstand the storms of the Price Revolution and the Revolt.

From 1600 onwards the situation was entirely different. Brabant had deteriorated into one of the less developed areas, while England began to assume a more advanced position. Population gradually became the strategic variable in Brabant : the drastic reductions in population caused by the first years of war and emigration resulted in relatively too much land and too few workers. The result was a rise in the real *per capita* wage income from 1587 onwards. The vigorous demographic revival during and after the Twelve Years Truce resulted in a spectacular fall of the real *per capita* wage income during the second quarter of the century. Demographic stagnation and even decline from the 1660's onwards reversed the trend until the new exceptional conditions of war at the end of the century disturbed the process once again.

The Eighty Years War was clearly an important factor in the structural decline of the economy in Brabant: it gradually stifled the possibility of further creativity, particularly in the countryside but also in the towns. Yet it would be a mistake to identify the war as the sole explanatory variable in the economic decay of Brabant. In the first place the Revolt was itself the result of the economic, social, intellectual, and religious emancipation of the inhabitants of the Low Countries during the preceding decades; moreover, a second factor was the growing mercantile policy of the European nation States, who considered import substitution a necessary condition for national economic progress and therefore stimulated the production of luxury or semi-luxury goods within their own borders. Finally within the artisanal structure of existing specialized industries, the potential for further technological innovation and diversification was bound to become increasingly limited. Hence the much higher wages in Brabant in comparison with the rest of Europe gradually failed to be justified by continuing industrial progress and turned into a cost disadvantage for the region.

In England, on the other hand, falling real wage rates in the sixteenth century had long helped the export of traditional textiles. At the beginning of the seventeenth century, however, the wage cost factor as a result of relative abundance of labour could no longer be exploited, the subsistence level being reached. Gradually the institutional factor emerged and became the most important. First, the threat of industrial decline provided the stimulus necessary for a structural renewal of export industry. Helped by emigrants from the

73

southern Netherlands and the commercio-maritime expansion of the seventeenth century, England developed an industrial growth-dynamic, which allowed her to combine a high level of population, in other words a relative labour surplus, with a growth in the purchasing power of wage earner's incomes (graph III). Meanwhile it may not be forgotten that seventeenth-century commercio-maritime expansion was nourished largely by the surplus values that originated in industry. The very low sixteenth-century wage level opened wide prospects of extra profits for those entrepreneurs who succeeded in developing and launching new products. Even when nominal and real wages rose, this favourable situation continued because the new products still contained a vast potential for increasing returns. This was the beginning of England's move into a modern economy.

CONCLUSION

Our proposed working hypothesis is an abstract framework derived from the historical facts. Yet the synthesis might be somewhat too general for adequate empirical testing. Carving out several subhypotheses and testing them in turn seems to be the most promising avenue. This however is clearly beyond the scope of the present study. Our main purpose was to demonstrate that descriptive statistics derived from price and wage series are useful building stones for a tentative theory.

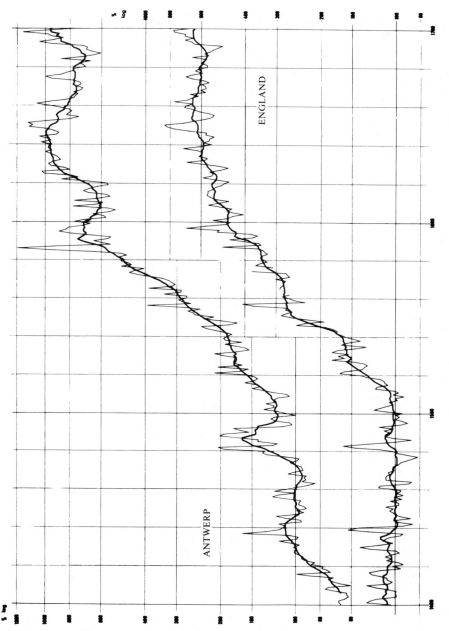

GRAPH I. *Weighted nominal price index of a packet of essential consumer goods in West Brabant and Southern England, 1400-1700: annual indexes and moving interquartile medians per 13 years (semi-logarithmic scale)*

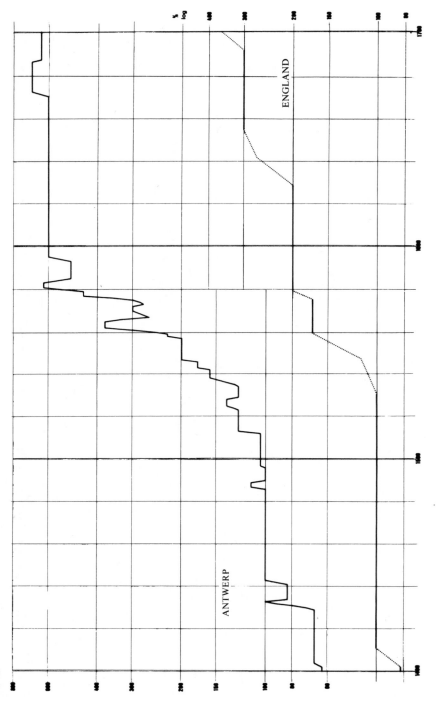

GRAPH II. *Nominal daily wage index of a master-mason in Antwerp and Southern England 1400-1700 (semi-logarithmic scale)*

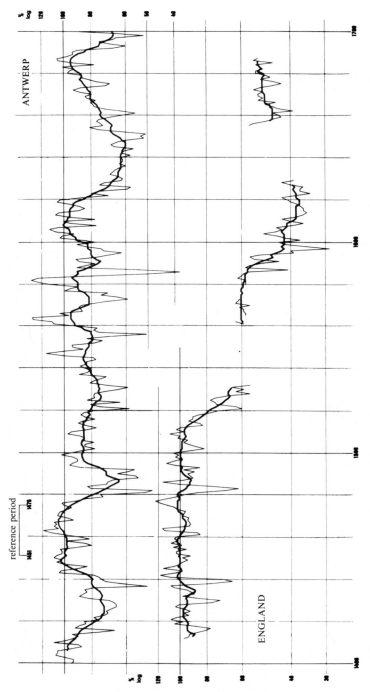

GRAPH III. *Index of the purchasing power of the annual wage of a master-mason expressed in a packet of essential consumer goods in West-Brabant and Southern England 1400-1700: annual indexes and moving interquartile medians per 13 years (semi-logarithmic scale)*

77

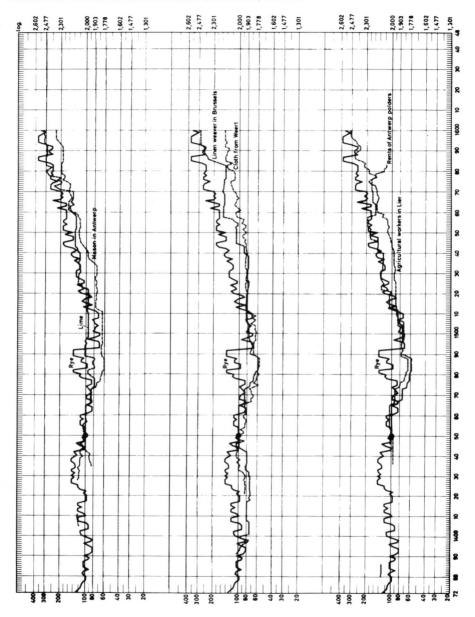

GRAPH IV. *Trends in rye, lime, textile prices and agricultural rents in West-Brabant, masons' daily wages in Antwerp, linen weavers' piece wages in Brussels, and rural piece wages from around Lier, 1372-1600 (silver equivalents, transposed logarithmically) (calculation of the trend by J. Meuvret's option method on moving 13 yearly averages)*

An Inquiry into the Behaviour of Wages in the Dutch Republic and the Southern Netherlands, 1580-1800 *

JAN DE VRIES

I

The quantitative evidence on labour compensation, because of its scarcity, has long been a particularly weak component of the economic historian's statistical arsenal. Unfortunately, our curiosity about what other people earn is usually coupled by an unwillingness to discuss openly and honestly our own earnings. This was no different in earlier times. The weakness of the data on labour compensation has not, however, prevented several scholars from erecting elaborate theoretical edifices on this shaky foundation. A recent attempt to argue from the record of wages paid in pre-industrial Europe is found in *The Modern World-System*, by Immanuel Wallerstein.[1]

The 'European world economy' whose creation Wallerstein describes and analyzes is characterized by a three-fold division of the 'world' into core, semi-peripheral, and peripheral countries. Each of these categories has its special role to play and each has its distinct forms of labour control. An obvious question presents itself to the readers of Wallerstein's book: how do countries find their appropriate niche in this world economy, and on what basis do countries move from one to another of the zones?

The author is not particularly generous in offering clarifying answers to these questions. There exists one notable exception to this unclear situation. Wallerstein devotes considerable attention to the course of real wages in the various European countries. He does this not only to identify a source of capital accumulation (*à la* E.J. Hamilton) but also to identify a mechanism that can help explain which States became core, semi-peripheral, and peripheral. He says, 'In the light of the [price revolution and profit inflation] we shall be able to explain the particular division of labour that the European world economy

* Paper delivered at the Colloque Franco-néerlandais, Paris, Maison des Sciences de l'Homme, 2-3 June, 1976.
1. Immanuel Wallerstein, *The Modern World-System. Capitalist Agriculture and the Origins of the European World-Economy in the Sixteenth Century* (New York, 1974). Another recent study that makes use of wage statistics is Dougless C. North and Robert Paul Thomas, *The Rise of the Western World* (Cambridge and New York, 1974).

arrived at by the end of this epoch' (69). Because we have here the only real differentiating mechanism in the book, it deserves careful examination.

He begins by noting the disastrous plunge of English building craftsmen's real wages as charted by Phelps Brown and Hopkins. This, he claims, was a European-wide phenomenon except in the old centres of the European economy, Italy and Flanders. In the latter, workers were relatively strong and could protect their interests. Inevitably, these economies fell into semi-peripheral status as their industries became uncompetitive. Ultimately, Wallerstein claims to have identified the pattern of real wages in the early seventeenth century: Italy and Flanders were on top, followed by England and Holland, followed in descending order by France, Spain, and Poland. On this basis Wallerstein established (84) what might be called the 'Goldilocks and the Three Bears' theory of wages: in Italy and Flanders wages were too high to allow for profits; in France, Spain, and Poland they were too low to create a home market; in England and Holland they were just right. Here the local investing class could profit from 'medium wages in their area' plus 'low wages in the periphery.'

What is the evidence for this bold theory? On Italian wages Carlo Cipolla is cited. But Cipolla mentions only that Italian businessmen complained of high wages in the seventeenth century. On Flemish wages, Verlinden is cited. But Verlinden argues that the reason Flemish real wages did not fall was that they were already at an irreducibly low subsistence level. On Holland no one is cited. One could go on. The fact is that all of Wallerstein's evidence is non-comparative. That is, it assesses the amount of decline of real wages in a given country relative only to earlier wages *in the same country*. No evidence is provided that might permit cross-country comparisons. Even if there were such evidence, Wallerstein's argument would still be of little value because he uses real wage comparisons to assess the competitive effects of wages on export production. For this purpose nominal — not real — wages are the relevant variable. Finally, Wallerstein ignores productivity and, hence, unit labour costs, which ultimately determine labour's contribution to an economy's export competitiveness.

And we are still not finished. Apparently Wallerstein believes that during the sixteenth century real wages fell in most of Europe (although at different rates), that the common people's meat consumption fell, that workers paid for economic growth with a lowered standard of living (44). But in almost the same breath he asserts that the sixteenth century witnessed 'an expansion [rise?] of agricultural productivity [which] opened the way to the expansion [rise?] of real income' (85). He says essentially the same thing again several times (for instance, 101, 116, 118).

A full untangling of this confusion exceeds my capacities, but by focusing on the course of wages in Flanders and the Dutch Republic it may prove possible to test the reasonableness of Wallerstein's theory. Here, after all, we have the case of a core State that descends to the semi-periphery (Flanders) and a State that rises to core status. In the course of my research I have, quite by accident, encountered a considerable number of wage rate quotations. By combining them with existing published wage data I hope to 1) provide a provisional sketch of the development of Flemish and Dutch wage rates from the mid-sixteenth to the late-eighteenth century; 2) test Wallerstein's theory; and 3) go on to identify some important characteristics of wage behaviour in the Dutch economy of the seventeenth and eighteenth centuries.

II

Thanks to the painstaking research of E. Scholliers the wage rates of sixteenth-century Antwerp are well known.[2] They were characterized by increases that, in the long run, prevented the purchasing power of most workers from falling. In this struggle to keep pace with inflation the unskilled and semi-skilled workers did somewhat better than the guild masters. Antwerp wages distinguish themselves from nearly all other available evidence of sixteenth-century wages (including other Flemish evidence) by not inflicting a massive erosion of purchasing power on the wage earners. This fact quite rightfully has attracted Professor Wallerstein's attention. But the sixteenth-century inflation did not end with the sixteenth century. It continued, at gradually decreasing rates until the mid-seventeenth century. What happened to Antwerp wages after 1600? Scholliers' evidence for the post-1600 period is not voluminous, but it does not have to be. The wage levels attained in the last five years of the sixteenth century were never permanently changed in the two centuries that followed.[3] Consequently, real wages fell in the first half of the seventeenth century, recovered in the second half, and fell again in the late eighteenth century.

From the 1590s until the end of the *ancien régime* master carpenters and bricklayers earned 24 *stuivers* per day, bricklayers' assistants earned 14 *stuivers*, and common day labourers earned 12 *stuivers*. Scholliers has recently published an article in which he notes that the wage for construction labour, 14 *stuivers* per day in Antwerp, was only 12 *stuivers* in other towns of the southern Netherlands and often no more than 10 *stuivers* in the small towns and in the

---

2. E. Scholliers, *De levensstandaard in de XVe en XVIe eeuw te Antwerpen* (Antwerp, 1960) 143-48.
3. *Ibidem.*

countryside. This is confirmed by eighteenth-century evidence for the Kempen region of Brabant (near Antwerp), where day wages for agricultural workers ranged from 8.5 to 10.3 *stuivers*.[4]

Now, how do these wage rates compare to those prevailing in the Dutch Republic, whose position as a core State was being consolidated in the first decades of the seventeenth century? We can begin to answer this question by examining the wage rates for assistant bricklayers. Scholliers based much of his analysis on their wages, holding them to be representative of other wage developments and particularly sensitive to price changes. We are fortunate that N.W. Posthumus, in his massive study of the Leiden textile industry, has presented tables of daily wage rates as paid by the Leiden municipal government for several occupational categories, including assistant bricklayers.

In the decade beginning with 1580 — the first year for which Posthumus offers wage data — these workers earned just over 9 *stuivers* per day. In the 1590s their rates rose to 14 *stuivers*. So far the Leiden wages follow the Antwerp wages almost exactly, as Figure I shows. But Figure I goes on to show that after 1600, when Antwerp wages are frozen, Leiden wages continue to rise. Only after 1640 do the Leiden rates display the petrification that is so characteristic of seventeenth- and eighteenth-century wages. But by then they have risen to over 21 *stuivers* per day, or over 50 per cent above the Antwerp level.[5]

This one example does little to support Wallerstein's belief that Flemish wages were too high to sustain competitive export industries while Dutch wages, because of their moderation, gave employers unique opportunities to accumulate capital and capture foreign markets. The wages in Antwerp and Leiden were roughly equal in the late-sixteenth century, and in the seventeenth century the Leiden wages rose far above the Antwerp level. But one occupation and two cities do not provide a sufficiently solid foundation on which to base far-reaching generalizations.[6] We should, at least, have data for a few other

4. E. Scholliers, 'De materiele verschijningsvorm van de armoede voor de industriële revolutie', *Tijdschrift voor geschiedenis*, LXXXVIII (Groningen, 1975) 451-67; P.M.M. Klep, *Groeidynamiek en stagnatie in een agrarisch grensgebied* (Tilburg, 1973) 158-60. A summary of official wage rates in six towns and four provinces of the southern Netherlands is available in E. Scholliers, e.a., eds., *Prijzen- en lonenpolitiek in de Nederlanden in 1561 en 1588-89. Onuitgegeven adviezen, ontwerpen, en ordonnanties*. Koninklijke Commissie voor geschiedenis (Brussel, 1962).
5. N.W. Posthumus, *De geschiedenis van de Leidsche lakenindustrie* (Leiden, 1939) II, 217, 1014-7.
6. A few scraps of evidence that bear on this issue can be mentioned here. The official daily wage for assistant bricklayers in Amsterdam was set in 1664 at 24 *stuivers*, about 2.5 *stuivers* above the Leiden rate and 10 *stuivers* above the Antwerp rate. (A.J. Deurloo, 'Bijltjes en Klouwers', *Economisch- en sociaal-historisch Jaarboek*, XXXIV (The Hague, 1971) 28-9.) The sixteenth-century wages of assistant bricklayers in Amsterdam are not known. Thus, we cannot be certain that they followed the same upward course as the Leiden wage rates. It is known that the wages paid for construction labour by five municipalities in the eastern provinces of the Netherlands followed

occupations and other locations. Here my research in the economic history of canal transportation can be of service, for, as noted above, it has yielded as a by-product wage quotations from many locations.

They are most numerous for carpenters — who built and repaired sluices and bridges, — and common labourers — who dug and maintained the canals and embankments. Tables I and II summarize the available evidence.

In the case of master carpenters the gap between Antwerp and the Republic is less than the 50 per cent observed for bricklayers. Only in Amsterdam did the carpenters at the shipwharves — who were organized in an effective guild — enjoy something like a 50 per cent advantage over their Antwerp counterparts. Common labourers, on the other hand, received wages at least 50 per cent above those prevailing in Antwerp (which were, in turn, higher than in the rest of Brabant). This advantage was only enjoyed by labourers in Holland. As one leaves Holland in any direction the wage levels quickly decline. Thus, in Friesland, Kampen, and Arnhem common labour received a wage comparable to that in Antwerp. Even these wages were apparently higher than those prevailing further to the east. In Twente, a day labourer, earned only 8 *stuivers* in the eighteenth century, and the wage levels prevailing in Friesland, for instance, were sufficient to attract every summer thousands of Westphalian seasonal migrants to dig peat and harvest hay.[7]

The wage gap that existed between Flanders and Holland can also be observed among salaried employees. The evidence presented in Table III does not permit direct comparisons to be made of the compensation in the two regions for the same work, but it does suffice to indicate the existence of a large gap: the stablemen in Holland not only earned more than crew members on the Flemish passenger barges, they earned more than the manager of one of those barges.

closely (but with a lag of a few years) the upward course of Antwerp wages between 1550 and 1599. What happened thereafter, when Leiden wages continued to rise while Antwerp wages remained fixed, is not known. See P.H.M.G. Offermans, *Arbeid en levensstandaard in Nijmegen omstreeks de reductie (1550-1599)* (Zutphen, 1972) 147-50, 201-3. The five towns for which the wages of assistant bricklayers are published are: Utrecht, Zutphen, Arnhem, Nijmegen and Venlo.

7. B.H. Slicher van Bath, *Een samenleving onder spanning* (Assen, 1957) 604. The eighteenth-century wages of common labourers in the 'Achterhoek' (eastern part) of Gelderland did not exceed 7 *stuivers*: A.H.G. Schaars, *Bosbouw in de achttiende eeuw* (Zutphen, 1974) 72. Johannes Tack, in his study of German migrant labour to the Netherlands, cites eighteenth-century sources to the effect that work in the hay harvest in Friesland paid 18 *stuivers* per day. Even after subtracting travel and maintenance costs while away from home (which amounted to two-thirds of the gross pay) this amount was capable of attracting tens of thousands of seasonal migrants from northwestern Germany: Johannes Tack, *Die Hollandsgänger in Hannover und Oldenburg* (Leipzig, 1902) 158-60.

Because of the characteristic petrification of so many wage rates in the late-seventeenth and eighteenth centuries, it may not be entirely inappropriate to conclude this reconnaissance of wage rates by summarizing the results of an economic survey conducted in 1819 in all the provinces of the Kingdom of the Netherlands, which then included modern Belgium (see Map I). Here, once again, Holland stands out as a region of high wages while Flanders and the region around Antwerp are conspicuous for their (incredibly) low wages. By then the Belgian economy had already begun its industrialization while the Dutch economy remained mired in stagnation. Nevertheless, the divergence that finds its origins in the tumultuous period 1580-1620 was still plainly apparent.

BRITISH WAGES

It may be of interest to add England, another State that achieves core status in the course of the seventeenth century, to this comparative discussion. The few available wage quotations for pre-nineteenth-century England cannot sustain far-reaching generalizations, but they can help put the level of Dutch wages in perspective. The overly famous wage series of Phelps Brown and Hopkins for southern English building craftsmen shows wage rates — converted into guilders and stuivers at the exchange rate of eleven guilders to one pound sterling — which were below even the Flemish rates in the first decades of the seventeenth century, but which gradually rose to equal the Flemish rates by the early eighteenth century and to exceed them in the course of that century.[8] The late-eighteenth-century wage quotations of E.W. Gilboy show day labour rates of 15 *stuivers* in the southwest, 17 *stuivers* in Lancashire, and 22.5 *stuivers* in London. Craftsmen's wages ranged from 17 to 22.5 in areas outside London; within the metropolis they earned 34 *stuivers*. The upper end of the late-eighteenth-century English range equalled Dutch rates, which had by then prevailed for at least 150 years.[9] Once again, it is the marked regional differences that are most striking in any investigation of pre-industrial wage rates. As late as 1867-70 differences of 50 per cent continued to exist between the regional *averages* of agricultural wages in the highest and lowest paid regions of England.[10] It seems likely, however, that English wages were

8.   E.H. Phelps Brown and Sheila V. Hopkins, 'Seven Centuries of Building Wages', *Economica*, XXIII (London, 1955) Table I.
9.   E.W. Gilboy, *Wages in Eighteenth-Century England* (Cambridge, Mass., 1934) 219-20.
10.   E.H. Hunt, *Regional Wage Variations in Britain, 1850-1914* (Oxford, 1973) 64. Hunt divides Great Britain into 13 regions and calculates average wage rates for each region.

as far below Holland's wages as were Flemish and Dutch wages outside Holland in the mid-seventeenth century. Then (in 1667) a publicist for the Leiden textile industry could complain that the 'day wages in combing, carding, spinning, and weaving are about half as much in England as must be paid here'.[11] By the mid-eighteenth century, when England's economic dominance had become well-established, it is unlikely that urban wages in southern England and Holland differed a great deal. The observations of eighteenth-century English travelers tend to confirm this generalization: they generally found nominal wage rates to be about equal to the English rates with which they were familiar.[12] It is interesting to note that the British navy and the Admiralty of Amsterdam hired common sailors in the eighteenth century at exactly the same monthly salary — 11 guilders. This equality dated from a much earlier time, however: in Holland this wage had prevailed ever since 1636 while in England it dated from 1653.[13]

Rural wages, in contrast to urban wages, may have been much lower in England than in Holland. Arthur Young presented figures for 1772 that showed day wages in agriculture to be no higher than 14 *stuivers* once one had traveled 20 miles from London.[14]

III

What does this evidence tell us about the role of wage rates in the development of the Dutch and Flemish economies, and the struggle for core status in general?

1. Wallerstein's belief that Dutch wages were lower than Flemish wages in the first half of the seventeenth century cannot be confirmed. The opposite was surely true. Correspondingly, the belief that high wages helped drive Flanders into a semi-peripheral status by undermining her export capacity is without foundation.

2. To the extent that low-wage labour offered profit opportunities available in a region of high wages such as Holland, capitalists did not have to go far afield to make profits. The surrounding territories both within and beyond the borders of the Republic offered labour at 30 to over 50 per cent less than the prevailing wage rates in Holland. One might question the usefulness of

11. Gemeentearchief Amsterdam, L.C. 8, N. 8. 'Vertoogh van d'onmooghlijkheidt van 't maken der Engelsche manufacturen hier te landen'.
12. J. Marshall, *Travels through Holland, etc. in the Years 1768, 1769, and 1770* (London, 1772) I, 160.
13. J.R. Bruijn, *De Admiraliteit van Amsterdam in rustige jaren* (Amsterdam, 1970) 160-1.
14. Cited in Donald R. Adams, Jr., 'Some Evidence on British and American Wage Rates, 1790-1830', *Journal of Economic History*, XXX (New York, 1970) 505.

tripartite division of the world economy when a State as small as the Dutch Republic can itself be divided into such zones. (France was apparently not the only State that was, as Wallerstein puts it, 'neither fish nor fowl,' *i.e.*, divided between two of his zones.)

3. The rise of the Dutch Republic to 'core status' went hand in hand with the bidding up of wage rates to what were probably the highest in northern Europe. Whether this helped or hindered the achievement and maintenance of core status depended in large part on the productivity of Holland's expensive labour — a matter not considered in Wallerstein's study.

It is worth noting here that a standard argument used to account for the rise of the American economy in the early-nineteenth century regards the high wages of North America as an advantage rather than a disadvantage.[15] Because labour — particularly unskilled labour — was expensive relative to Britain, the technological development of American industry acquired a strong bias toward the introduction of capital intensive techniques. The potential of technological development to reduce unit labour costs was not as great before the mid-eighteenth century as thereafter. Still, the observations of seventeenth-century visitors to the Dutch Republic that every manner of available labour-saving device was employed in Dutch industry is consistent with this Anglo-American argument. Dutch industry made intensive use of non-human energy sources in the forms of windmills and peat. The former — applied to the production processes of dozens of industries — is well known; the latter deserves much more attention than it has received. A long list of Dutch export industries were highly fuel intensive and existed in the Dutch Republic in large part because of the existence of a large peat industry capable of supplying Holland's towns at a far lower cost than other European towns could be supplied with alternative fuels.[16] In short, the Dutch labour force was endowed with *per capita* energy supplies that had no equal until the coming of the steam engine. This endowment obviously affected the productivity of labour. There is, therefore, no necessary inconsistency between high wages and profitable industry, even before the rise of modern industry.

15. See H.J. Habakkuk, *American and British Technology in the Nineteenth Century* (Cambridge, 1962).
16. The high level of *per capita* energy consumption in the Dutch Republic is demonstrated in the forthcoming article of J.W. de Zeeuw, 'Peat and the Dutch Golden Age: the Historical Meaning of Energy-Availability', *A.A.G. Bijdragen*, XXI (Wageningen, 1978). His necessarily rough estimate of average annual peat production in the seventeenth century amounts to 4 million kcal. *per capita*. This can be compared, says De Zeeuw, to the 1973 *per capita* availability (from *all* non-animate energy sources) of 50 million kcal. in the Netherlands and 2 million kcal. in India.

IV

What factors played the largest role in determining the level and pattern of wages in an early-modern economy? Until we can answer this question it will remain difficult to draw far-reaching conclusions about the meaning of a given wage level.

The most common explanation for wage levels is the cost of living. If the costs of necessities are high, the wage that must be paid to maintain the labour force in good health must also be high. In principle there is likely to exist some relationship between the cost of living and the level of wages, but that relationship is less direct than is often thought. The belief that workers were paid a subsistence wage which the employer's self-interest required to be raised when living costs rose is too simplistic to be of much use. At any rate, it cannot be regarded as intellectually satisfactory when it is a high-wage rather than a low-wage economy that is being analyzed.

When the subsistence wage theory is recast in the form of an 'historical subsistence wage' — unique to each locality and based on its past experience (and its position in the world economy) — it gains the tactical advantage of subjectivity. But it does not necessarily help explain anything.

The high cost of living characteristic of the Dutch economy has almost always been regarded as the product of the Republic's onerous tax burden.[17] By levying heavy excise taxes on nearly all consumption goods, so the argument goes, the cost of living — particularly in the towns — rose above that of other countries. Therefore labour in the Dutch towns had to earn more than labour elsewhere — as much more as the extra tax burden.

The theoretical and empirical unreasonableness of this argument has recently been exposed by Professor Joel Mokyr.[18] Theoretically this argument is unsound because an *ad valorum* tax of, say, x per cent on consumer goods will be borne entirely by consumers in the form of higher prices *only* in the extreme case of very elastic supply and inelastic demand. Moreover, the increase in consumer prices — almost surely to be less than x per cent (say y per cent where $y < x$) — will result in increased wages of y per cent *only* in the extreme case of highly elastic supply and highly inelastic demand for labour. Thus, except in extreme cases, an x per cent tax on consumer goods results in a y per cent increase in prices, which causes a z per cent increase in nominal wages, where

17.   See, among others, Charles Wilson, 'Taxation and the Decline of Empires, an Unfashionable Theme', in Charles Wilson, *Economic History and the Historians* (London, 1969) 114-27; Elias Luzac, *Hollands Rijkdom* (Leiden, 1783) IV, p. 82.
18.   Joel Mokyr, *Industrialization in the Low Countries* (New Haven, 1976) 190-3.

$x > y > z$. Theoretically, the impact of a given excise tax burden on wage rates is almost always smaller than the tax burden itself. Empirically, it has been demonstrated, again by Mokyr, that the share of excise taxes in the total Dutch wage bill was, under the most generous assumptions, no more than ten per cent. Thus, even in the extreme case where $x = z$ (and no excise taxes were levied in other countries) the tax argument cannot account for more than a small proportion of the substantial wage differentials that existed between Holland and the surrounding countries.

In addition, it should be noted that the upper-limit burden of taxes as estimated by Mokyr refers to the eighteenth century, when the tax burden had reached its peak. In the first half of the seventeenth century, when wages attained their peak levels, the tax burden was still considerably smaller. This chronological discrepancy must cast further doubt on the significance of taxes as a major cause of high wages in the Dutch Republic.

In searching for other factors that can help explain the high Dutch wage level, attention should be paid to the peculiar geographical and occupational differentiation of wage rates displayed by Tables I, II, and III and Map I. First, the gap between urban and rural wages is small or non-existent. This was apparently not the case in Flanders. Second, the 'skill premium' was smaller in Holland than in Antwerp. Master carpenters in Holland earned around 40 per cent more than common labourers while in Antwerp their wage was twice that of common labourers. Third, the smaller range of Dutch wages does not mean that skill was not important in determining a given worker's wage rate. The documents show a large number of separate wage rates being paid to workers who apparently worked together at essentially the same tasks. That is, within the petrified long-run wage rates, a considerable scope existed for discrimination among individual workers.

Further research will be needed before generalizations can be made with confidence, but I would like to suggest that the above mentioned characteristics reflect two important determinants of Dutch wages. First, productivity was important in setting wage rates. Dutch wages could rise in the early-seventeenth century because capital investment and the development of workers' skills made labour more productive than it was elsewhere. Second, basic wages were high because agriculture in the region was productive. The 'opportunity cost' of labour in a society with a large rural sector can be considered to be the marginal productivity of labour in agriculture. Where this was low — for example, in the overpopulated Flanders of the eighteenth century — the industrial wage could also be extremely low. But everything we know about agriculture in the maritime provinces of the Dutch Republic points to the existence of high productivity. Agriculture was capital intensive, farm size was large, and the role of rural industry as a source of extra earnings was very small. For this reason rural wages were high and, for obvious reasons, urban wages could not be lower.

V

Once wage rates had reached their maximums, around 1640, they stayed there. Through good times and bad, through rising and falling prices, the wage structure of the Dutch Republic showed no long-term changes until at least the end of the eighteenth century. One could speak of fossilization. This absence of change strikes me, for some reason, as a more interesting phenomenon than the increase of wages in the sixteenth and early-seventeenth centuries. After the 1670s, and with great force in the early-eighteenth century, the Dutch Republic experienced a profound economic decline. Industrial production was the most hard-hit sector and those branches of the economy which did not decline were characterized by a relatively low demand for labour. Consequently, the aggregate demand for labour in the Dutch urban economy declined very markedly in the 70 years after about 1675. In the same period the overall price level tended to decline. Through all of this Dutch wage rates stayed at the peak levels attained in the early-seventeenth century. (Indeed, there is some evidence that wage rates actually rose temporarily just when the industrial collapse had reached its nadir.) In short, wage rate played no constructive role in restoring equilibrium to the rapidly changing labour market.

How, then, did the economy adjust to the collapse of the industrial sector of the economy and the resulting reduction in the demand for labour? Two types of evidence beckon us to look to the supply curve of labour for the adjustment mechanism. First, the population of the maritime provinces declined, probably by about 10 per cent in the 70 years after 1680. Most of this decline occurred in the industrial towns (Leiden, Delft, Haarlem) and the important North Holland peninsula.[19] This population decline cannot be attributed to emigration. Instead, adjustments in the birth and death rates seem to account for the largest part of this population decline.

Consider for a moment the case of the North Holland towns of Hoorn and Enkhuizen. Their seafaring and fishing economies all but collapsed in the century after 1650. But the progressive impoverishment of these towns finds

19. For analyses of demographic trends in the Dutch Republic see J.A. Faber, e. a., 'Population Changes and Economic Development in the Netherlands: a Historical Survey', *A.A.G. Bijdragen*, XII (1965) 47-113; A.M. van der Woude, *Het Noorderkwartier* (Wageningen, 1972) I; Jan de Vries, *The Dutch Rural Economy in the Golden Age, 1500-1700* (New Haven, 1974) ch. iii.

no reflection in their prevailing wage rates. These not only held constant, but were the equal of those elsewhere in Holland. The population adjusted to the contraction of the demand for labour by wasting away. Everywhere in this region household size became unusually small.[20] In the century after 1650 Hoorn's population fell by half while Enkhuizen's fell by two-thirds. By saying that the population 'adjusted by wasting away' I am making an assertion that is not inconsistent with the evidence but, it must be added, not proven either. Further analysis is surely called for. A non-agricultural economy facing grave difficulties where wages remain among the highest in Europe while it sinks away into insignificance — including numerical insignificance — is an evocative spectacle of potentially great importance to our understanding of labour market behavior.

The second category of evidence refers to the problem of unemployment in the domestic labour force. Contemporary observers, municipal ordinances regarding poor-relief, and Church charity records all speak of a growing problem of unemployment in the eighteenth century. Yet at the same time the phenomenon of seasonal migration of Germans to work in Dutch industries (Haarlem bleaching and Harlingen ribbon factories, for example), agriculture (Frisian hay harvest) and peat digging assumed its greatest quantitative importance. Besides this *Hollandgängerei* the stream of permanent migrants from Germany also grew in this period. Finally, to complicate matters still further, the shortage of manpower in the Dutch navy became progressively more acute, so that by the 1740s handsome bonuses had to be offered to attract labour, and even then the number of recruits remained woefully inadequate.[21] To summarize, we have here a labour market phenomenon (not unfamiliar to modern industrialized societies) which combined high unemployment, acute labour shortage in some sectors, and the influx to the labour force of foreigners who were accustomed to a low standard of living.

If the Dutch labour force offered much more labour than the economy was prepared to employ, this would have resulted in unemployment and the generation of a downward pressure on wage rates. There was unemployment, but wages did not fall. This fact, combined with the phenomenon of the *Hollandgängerei* and the labour shortage in specific sectors, suggests the hypothesis that the Dutch labour force had, in effect, reduced the volume of its offered labour. In other words, the observed unemployment was in large part a

---

20. For evidence on the unimportance of emigration and on the size of households, see A.M. van der Woude, *Het Noorderkwartier*, 132-33, 232, and ch. iv.
21. Tack, *Hollandsgänger*; J.A. Faber, *Drie eeuwen Friesland* (Wageningen, 1972) I, 229, 231-34; Bruijn, *Admiraliteit van Amsterdam*, 161.

consciously chosen leisure, and the wage levels did not fall because the labour force was, despite appearances, *on* and not below, its labour supply curve.[22]

There are two arguments that could uphold the hypothesis of a leftward shift of the labour supply curve. The first is one often made by contemporaries, although I am unaware of it being made with regard to the Dutch Republic. A backward bending labour supply curve was thought to characterize the reaction of workers to increased real wages. It was argued that workers strove to achieve a target income. If increased purchasing power made this target attainable with less work, the amount of labour offered would be reduced. Since the purchasing power of a 20 *stuiver* daily wage was considerably greater in 1740 than it had been in 1670, this argument would predict that most workers in the later period, would refuse work that they would have accepted in 1670. As an anonymous Englishman bluntly put it in the eighteenth century:[23]

> Scarcity, to a degree, promotes industry ... the manufacturer [i.e., the worker] who can subsist on three days work will be idle and drunken the remainder of the week ... The poor in the manufacturing counties will never work any more time than is necessary just to live and support their weekly debauches.

One could not, of course, use this argument in the second half of the eighteenth century when the real wage fell considerably. But besides this limitation, the existence of this behaviour pattern remains to be demonstrated. In my opinion the expansion of the range of consumer goods available to the common man that was noticeable in the decades after 1650 gradually undermined what there was of a backward bending labour supply curve.[24]

The second possible argument focuses on the impact on the labour market of charity and poor-relief. The reasoning is, once again, familiar to the inhabitants of industrial societies: when unemployment relief approaches the minimum wage it has the effect of preventing wages from falling during periods of high unemployment and of shifting the supply curve of labour to the left, requiring higher wages to be paid than would otherwise be the case.

The charitable institutions of the Dutch Republic are justifiably famous for their number, their wealth, and their efficiency. None the less, it would come as a surprise to most people to learn that they could have had the sort of effect on the labour market that has generally been thought to be achievable only by the twentieth-century welfare State. This argument, too, still has to be proved

---

22. This suggestion is also made by Mokyr, *Industrialization*, 195.
23. Quoted in Paul Mantoux, *The Industrial Revolution in the Eighteenth Century* (London, 1928; reprinted, New York, 1961) 62.
24. For an elaboration and defense of this argument see my book *The Economy of Europe in an Age of Crisis, 1600-1750* (London and New York, 1976) 179-82.

(although Mokyr was persuaded that it was of considerable importance),[25] but one feature of the Dutch Republic's economy lends it credence — the massive accumulation of capital. The Republic remained rich long after if had ceased being prosperous. That is, when the economy lost its dynamism and the demand for labour declined, there continued to exist a large capital stock and the passive income that flowed from it. Thanks to the bourgeois fashion of founding and endowing charitable institutions, a large portion of the Dutch capital stock came to be administered by these institutions. One of the ironic legacies of the Golden Age was, thus, a stock of capital whose dedication to charitable purposes stood as an obstacle to the reform of the economy needed to reduce the problem of unemployment and poverty.

VI

The evidence and observations presented in this paper must be regarded as provisional and tentative. Much remains to be done before we can pretend to know the price of labour only half as well as we now know the price of wheat in the pre-industrial European economy. What little we do know urges upon us the need to take the labour markets of those portions of Europe with free labour forces seriously. The geographical pattern of 'average' wages may well have played a role in the functioning of a world economy, but the skill and occupational differentials and rural-urban differentials were probably at least as important, and not necessarily correlated to the geographical pattern of 'average' wages. Once an integrated and comparative analysis of wage patterns comes to supplant the rather naive studies of the past (studies which have concerned themselves mainly with the determination of real wages), we will be in a position to learn a great deal about the character of pre-industrial labour markets and perhaps even about the trends in the distribution of income.

25. Mokyr, *Industrialization*, 197.

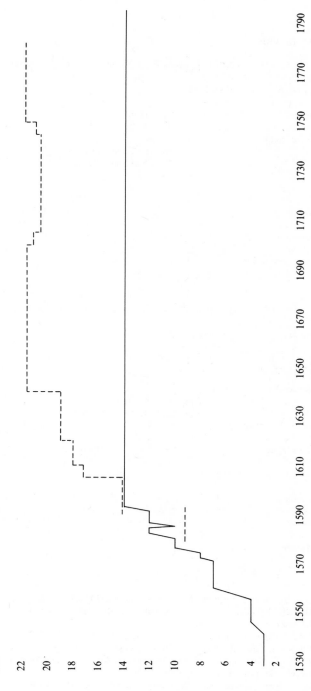

GRAPH I. Assistant Bricklayers Wages in Antwerp and Leiden, 1530-1800

Antwerp ———
Leiden – – – – –

Stuivers
per day

26. Posthumus, *De geschiedenis van de Leidsche lakenindustrie*, II, 1014-17; Scholliers, *De levensstandaard*, 143-48, appendix XXI.

TABLE I. *Daily Wage Rates of Master Carpenters (in stuivers)* [27]

Antwerp	1596-1735			
	24			
Leiden	1637	1680	1704	1732
	31	30,28	28	31,26
Amsterdam	1664-1869			
	36 (building ships) ⎫ at private wharves			
	34 (building barges) ⎭			
	30	at the wharves of the Admiralty and the VOC		
Ter Aar				1813
				27
Weesp			1759	
			30,28	
Buiksloot			1776	
			28	
Alkmaar-Hoorn	1660			
	28			

TABLE II. *Daily Summer Wage Rates of Common Outdoor Labour (in stuivers)* [28]

Antwerp	1596-18th century						
	12						
HOLLAND							
Dordrecht	1641						
	15 (30 per cent of observations)						
	20 (70 per cent of observations)						
Nieuw Beijerland		1674-77			1763-95		
		15			20		
The Hague				1694-1720	1732-37		
				20,18	23,22		
Delft	1638						
	22						
Leiden	1637	1659	1677	1684	1730	1759	1780
	24	26,24	25	24	24,18	20	22,20
Weesp				1691-1711	1729		
				16	16		
Muiden						1750-51	
						16	

27. *Antwerp*: Scholliers, *De levensstandaard*, 143-48; *Leiden*: Gemeentearchief (GA) Leiden, Oud Archief, Trekvaarten en Jaagpaden, 60, Bijlagen tot de rekeningen; *Amsterdam*: Bruijn, *De Admiraliteit van Amsterdam*, 159; Deurloo, 'Bijltjes en klouwers', 28-29; *Ter Aar*: G.A. Amsterdam, Part. archief, 16, Commissie over wegen en vaarten, 13; *Weesp*: G.A. Weesp, Oud Archief, Bijlagen tot de rekeningen; *Buiksloot*: Rijksarchief (RA) Haarlem, Archieven Zes Noord-hollandse steden, 22, Kwitanties; *Alkmaar-Hoorn*: GA Alkmaar, Oud Archief, 1882 'Hoornse vaart'; *Haarlem*: RA Haarlem, De Boedelpapieren, 1739.
28. *Antwerp*: Scholliers, *De levensstandaard*, 143-48; *Dordrecht*: Algemeen Rijksarchief (ARA) The Hague, Grafelijkheid Rekenkamer, 5240.
Nieuw Beijerland: C. Baars, 'Boekhoudingen van landbouwbedrijven in de Hoekse-waard uit de

| Haarlemmerliede | | 1674-75 20 | | | | | | |

Haarlemmerliede   1674-75 / 20

Buiksloot   1775-1812 / 18

Purmerend   1751-55 / 18

Edam   1667-69 / 22   1677-78 / 24

Hoorn-Alkmaar   1660 / 18   1663-67 / 20,18   1676 / 18,16   1688 / 20   1784 / 22   1797 / 18

Enkhuizen   1784 / 18   1796 / 22   1797 / 18

OTHER PROVINCES

Montfoort (Utrecht)   1793 / 14

Sneek (Friesland)   1760-1774 / 14

Drachten (Friesland)   1773-81 / 14   1793 / 10   1801-1810 / 14

Groningen (Groningen)   1635 / 15   1690 / 16,14   1730 / 16   1750 / 18,14   1810 / 16

Arnhem (Gelderland)   1629-52 / 12

Kampen (Overijssel)   1663 / 14,12

Baronie van Breda (Noord Brabant)   1780-1800 / 14-10

zeventiende en achttiende eeuw', *A.A.G. Bijdragen*, XIX (Wageningen, 1975) 21, 50, 81; *The Hague*: GA The Hague, Oud Archief, 5198, Rekeningen, Delftse straatweg; *Delft*: GA Delft, Oud Archief, 1899; *Leiden*: G.A. Leiden, Oud Archief, Trekvaarten en Jaagpaden, 60, Bijlagen tot de rekeningen; *Weesp*: G.A. Weesp, Oud Archief, Bijlagen tot de rekeningen; *Muiden*: G.A. Naarden, Oud Archief, 672; *Haarlemmerliede*: Hoogheemraadschap Rijland, Oud Archief, 2825; *Buiksloot*: R.A. Haarlem, Archieven Zes Noord hollandse steden, 26, Kwitanties; *Purmerend*: GA Purmerend, Oud Archief, 247, Rekeningen Vijf-steden trekvaart. These workers received a 2 stuiver-per-day supplement to their 18 stuiver wage. The supplement was called 'drinkbier' (intended to replace the actual provision of beer?) and is sometimes encountered under this or similar names, in other records, particularly in Leiden; *Edam*: RA Haarlem, Archieven Zes Noord-hollandse steden, 57-62, Edam kasboeken; *Hoorn-Alkmaar*: GA Hoorn, Oud Archief, 610 (1910) and 611 (2589); GA Alkmaar, Oud Archief, 1882, 'Hoornse vaart'; *Enkhuizen*: RA Haarlem, Archieven Zes Noord-hollandse steden, 93, Correspondentie betreffende Hoorn-Enkhuizen straatweg; *Montfoort*: RA Utrecht, Staten van Utrecht, 928, Bijlage tot de rekening van den kameraar van het zandpad van De Meern naar Montfoort en Oudewater; *Sneek*: GA Sneek, Oud Archief, 592; *Drachten*: GA Smallingerland, Oud Archief, 33, Rekeningboek voor de gecomitteerde tot de slaating van 't Dragt; 34, Rekeningboek van de gecomitteerde tot de Kletstervaart; *Groningen*: GA Groningen, Oud Archief, 332^b r, Bijlagen tot de Stadsrekeningen; *Arnhem*: GA Arnhem, Oud Archief, 3263; *Kampen*: GA Kampen, Archief der commissarissen Kampen-Zwolle trekvaart, 3; *Baronie van Breda*: P.M.M. Klep, *Groeidynamiek en stagnatie in een agrarisch grensgebied* (Tilburg, 1973) 159.

TABLE III. *Annual Salaries of Salaried Employees (in guilders)*[29]

Ghent-Brugge	1760-1779		1780-19th century		
Barge manager (*Baas*)	360		360		
Brugge-Ghent					
Barge manager	240		240		
Brugge-Ostende					
Cook (*Cock*)	120		150		
Servant (*Knecht*)	120		150		
Young servant (*Hulpe*)	72		90		
Haarlem-Leiden	1723-30	1759	1780-1818		
Stablemen (*Stalknecht*)	264	312	264,240		
Leiden				1677-1790	
Toll collector (*Commissaris op de Neksluis*)				279	
Enkhuizen	1711-1726	1726-1748	1748-1772	1787-1798	
Street-paver (*Straatmaker*)	550	550*	550	500	

* In the period 1726-1748 the street-pavers' monthly pay varied considerably, but never fell below the annual rate of 550 guilders. It is not impossible that the monthly payments in this period included reimbursement for materials.

29. *Ghent-Brugge*: RA Ghent, 1989-2010; *Haarlem-Leiden*: GA Haarlem, Oud Archief, 1097 (Kast 24, 45, 46); *Leiden*: GA Leiden, Oud Archief, Trekvaarten en Jaagpaden, 60, Bijlagen tot de rekeningen; *Enkhuizen*: GA Hoorn, Oud Archief, 626 (1926-1928).

MAP I.   *Average Adult Wages in the Kingdom of the Netherlands, 1819*[30]

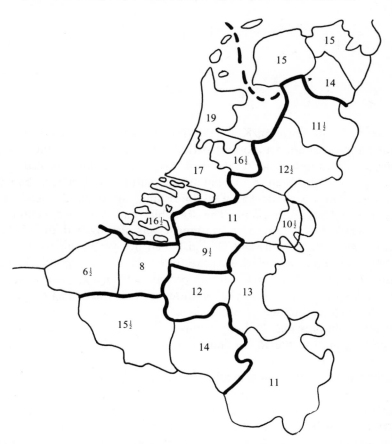

Province	Daily wage in *stuivers*	Province	Daily wage in *stuivers*
North Holland	19	Hainault	15½
South Holland	17	Namur	14
Utrecht	16½	Liège	13
Zeeland	16½	South Brabant	12
Friesland	15	Luxembourg	11
Groningen	15	Limbourg	10½
Drenthe	14½	Antwerpen	9½
Gelderland	12½	East Flanders	8
Overijssel	11½	West Flanders	6½
North Brabant	11		
Northern average	15	Southern average	9½

30.   I.J. Brugmans, ed., *Statistieken van de Nederlandse nijverheid uit de eerste helft der 19ᵉ eeuw.* Rijks geschiedkundige publicatiën, XCVIII (The Hague, 1956) 247-417. Compiled by Joel Mokyr, *Industrialization*, 177.

Poverty in Amsterdam at the Close of the Eighteenth Century*

PETER JANSEN

According to the historian Kluit, the third quarter of the eighteenth century was 'the happiest and most glorious period ever experienced by the Republic'.[1] There is still much to be said in favour of this view. It is quite probable that on the average the Dutchman in the eighteenth century lived better, than did his forefathers.[2] The economic life was flourishing, although the lead over the outside world had disappeared. The Republic had remained neutral in the Seven Years War. The *Doelisten* movement was already a thing of the past; *Patriotten* (anti-Orangemen) and Orangists had not yet begun to oppose each other and everything was relatively peaceful on the national political front.

A superb view of Amsterdam in this period is afforded by the collection of about one hundred townscapes that is known as the *Atlas Fouquet*.[3] When one studies the pictures one sees a well-balanced, prosperous city which makes an almost idyllic impression. Nobody seems to be in a hurry, although there is much activity and on the *Rokin* and the *Spui* fowls are still to be seen in the streets.

In 1795 the old Republic was in all respects virtually bankrupt. The stadhouder regime disappeared and the policy of neutrality that had rendered yeoman services for the greater part of the century was no longer useful. For some time industry had not been faring well, but trade was declining too and would not witness a return to the good old times. Even without the serious disturbances which the wars after 1795 brought in their wake the mediating role of the Republic in Europe was played out.[4] The social effects of the decline were not

* This article is a slightly revised version of P.C. Jansen, 'Armoede in Amsterdam aan het eind van de achttiende eeuw', *Tijdschrift voor geschiedenis*, LXXXVIII (Groningen, 1975) 613-25.

1. J. en A. Romein, *De lage landen bij de zee. Geïllustreerde geschiedenis van het Nederlandse volk* (4th ed., Zeist, 1961) III, 21. Kluit (1735-1807) was professor of history at Leiden University.
2. Boxer holds a contrary view. C.R. Boxer, *The Dutch Seaborne Empire 1600-1800* (London, 1965) 294.
3. I.H. van Eeghen, 'De Atlas Fouquet', *Maandblad Amstelodamum*, XLVII (Amsterdam, 1960) 49-59. Of course, topographical prints that are meant for the market exhibit a distinctive kind of reality. The weather is always fine so that many people are out on the streets and on the five winter-landscapes the ice is so thick that it could bear a number of skaters. On the other prints the trees are in leaf and almost always a beautiful coach is crossing the bridge in the distance.
4. On the neutrality of the Republic see the interesting book of A.C. Carter, *Neutrality or*

long in coming. Thousands became unemployed, tens of thousands were forced onto poor-relief, hundreds of children were abandoned on the streets annually.

It is not necessary to analyze cause and effect once again. Joh. de Vries has done this in respect of the economic decline[5] and Van den Eerenbeemt has investigated the social consequences.[6] What is not known is the extent to which Amsterdam suffered from the economic deterioration and when the social effects of it became noticeable.

It has only been in the past few decades that historians have discovered that economic and demographic developments are closely related to one another.[7] This starting-point does not however help us much since there is almost nothing known about the size of the population of Amsterdam. The only firm piece of evidence is the first census of 1795 (about 220,000 inhabitants).[8] About the development of the population we know a little more, although the data are far from adequate. Ideally the number of births, deaths, immigrants and emigrants should have been recorded to enable us to reconstruct the size of the population. In actual fact there is only information about the number of deaths, the number of marriages and migration.

Because all prospective brides and bridegrooms had to state their place of birth on notification of their intention to get married it is also possible to calculate which percentage of them were born outside Amsterdam. In Table I the number of notices of intended marriages and the percentage concerning the place of origin have been posited together.[9]

Commitment: the Evolution of Dutch Foreign Policy 1667-1795 (London, 1975). The reader is warned, though, about her excessive interest in the ship-worm (*teredo navalis*) as cause of the economic deterioration of the Republic (65, 72 and 114). On the mediating role of the Republic: J.G. van Dillen, *Van rijkdom en regenten. Handboek tot de economische en sociale geschiedenis van Nederland tijdens de Republiek* (The Hague, 1970) 657.

5.   Joh. de Vries, *De economische achteruitgang der Republiek in de achttiende eeuw* (2nd ed., Leiden, 1968).

6.   H.F.J.M. van den Eerenbeemt, 'De oorzaken van het pauperisme in Nederland in de 18e eeuw', *Maandschrift Economie*, XXVII (1963) 156-66.

7.   A.M. van der Woude, 'De historische demografie in de ontwikkeling van de geschiedweten-schap', *Tijdschrift voor geschiedenis*, LXXXII (Groningen, 1969) 195-92.

8.   E. Boekman, 'De bevolking van Amsterdam in 1795', *ibidem*, XLV (1930) 278-92.

9.   The baptismal and burial registers have been preserved but the number of entries has never been counted. Contemporary statements about the number of baptisms do not appear to be reliable. S. Hart, 'Bijlagen van het rapport Bronnen voor de historische demografie in de 17e en 18e eeuw' (Amsterdam, 1965. Mimeographed. Available in the library of the Gemeente Archief in Amsterdam).

TABLE I. *Number of notices of intended marriage in Amsterdam in the period 1750-1800, divided in five-yearly periods and the percentage of individuals concerned (prospective brides and bridegrooms) not born in Amsterdam*

	number of notices	percentage not born in Amsterdam
1751-55	11,220	50.2
1756-60	11,787	50.0
1761-65	13,064	49.1
1766-70	12,457	51.1
1771-75	11,690	52.4
1776-80	12,770	53.2
1781-85	13,718	53.8
1786-90	12,144	53.6
1791-95	11,385	51.7
1796-1800	10,268	47.4

In the second period the number of marriages (or rather, notifications of intended marriage) increased gradually, in the third period much more rapidly. Then follows a decade with fewer marriages; thereafter an upward trend is noticeable again. The percentage of those who did not come from Amsterdam runs at first counter to, but since 1771-75 parallel with, the number of those intending to get married.

Because of the high death rate the population of a pre-industrial town could only grow or maintain its level if there was a constant influx of immigrants.[10] Accordingly in the seventeenth and eighteenth century usually more than fifty per cent of the prospective brides and bridegrooms were not born in Amsterdam.[11]

In the period with the most marriages (1781-1785) the percentage of immigrants among those who had given notice of their intended marriage is also the highest.[12]

There are also data available about the number of congregants of the Dutch Reformed Church who arrived in, and left, the town annually. Because the Reformed church-goers made up about half of the population these figures

---

10. Cf. J.-P. Bardet, 'La démographie des villes de la modernité (XVIe-XVIIIe siècles); mythes et réalités', *Annales de démographie historique* (Paris, 1974) 117.
11. Hart, 'Bronnen'.
12. As has been indicated above, it is only after 1771-5 that there is a direct relation to be seen. In the first period after 1750 the prosperity which results in a greater number of marriages seems first of all to influence those who are already living in the city, whereby the number of marriages of immigrants drops relatively.

could very well be regarded as representative. It appears that in the period 1781-85 the net immigration surplus was likewise the greatest.[13]

A third indication of the *trek* to Amsterdam is the number of immigrants who had purchased burghership. In this regard too the greatest numbers are recorded in the same period.[14] Hart has therefore drawn the conclusion that the population of Amsterdam increased till the period 1781-85 and had decreased thereafter.[15] We must now investigate whether the economic tide had shown the same movement.

The sources for the history of the economic life of Amsterdam are of the same character as those relating to the population. The changes are in some cases easily to be seen but comparing the situation obtaining in 1750 with that in 1800 is very difficult. The first census of the number of businesses in Amsterdam dates only from the beginning of the nineteenth century.

As regards the Republic as a whole there is the classic doctoral dissertation of Joh. de Vries.[16] It appears that the trade-turnover during the second half of the century had remained more or less constant. In relation to the outside world there is certainly a relative deterioration. In industry and in fishery there is a definite, irretrievable decline. The financial sector and agriculture are flourishing. Within the Republic the position of Amsterdam has improved absolutely and relatively. De Vries has designated this phenomenon as 'internal contraction'. Yet even for Amsterdam, the statistics show a clear decline towards the end of the century.

For Amsterdam there are in the first place the annual statements of the convoy and licensing fees (import and export duties) of the office of Amsterdam within the admiralty of the same name,[17] and there are data on the business transactions within the town, the combined imposts.[18] If the annual proceeds

13. S. Hart, *Geschrift en getal. Een keuze uit de demografisch-economische en sociaal-economische studiën op grond van Amsterdamse en Zaanse archivalia, 1600-1800* (Dordrecht, 1976) 125-6, 175.
14. Gemeente Archief Amsterdam, (GAA), Archief Aalmoezeniersweeshuis, no. 88, fo. 49.
15. S. Hart, 'Een sociale structuur van de Amsterdamse bevolking in de 18e eeuw', *Jaarboek Amstelodamum*, LXV (Amsterdam, 1973) 77. An extensive discussion took place in the past on the question as to whether Amsterdam did not have more inhabitants about 1750. See J.G. van Dillen, 'Omvang en samenstelling van de bevolking van Amsterdam in de 17e en 18e eeuw', *Mensen en achtergronden* (Groningen, 1964) 484-97 and Hart, *ibidem*.
16. See note 5.
17. De Vries, *Economische achteruitgang*, 19 ff. The figures on 189-90. For the five-yearly averages use was made of the figures in J. Hovy, *Het voorstel van 1751 tot instelling van een beperkt vrijhavenstelsel in de Republiek. Propositie tot een gelimiteerd porto-franco* (Groningen, 1966) 9.
18. W.F.H. Oldewelt, 'De Hollandse imposten en ons beeld van de conjunctuur tijdens de Republiek', *Jaarboek Amstelodamum*, XLVII (1955) 48-80; List of the total annual yields of the combined imposts (*waag, rondemaat, grovewaren*) in the *ontvangerschap* (receivership) of Amsterdam on 72-3.

of the two classes of duties are compared with each other at five-yearly intervals
and the period 1751-5 is put at 100, then the following picture emerges (Graph I).

GRAPH I. *Convoy and licensing fees (duties) and combined imposts, 1750-1800. Five-yearly
averages; index number (1751-5 = 100)*

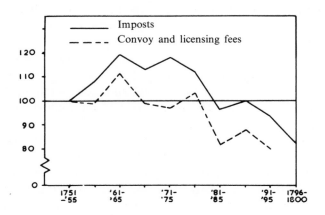

GRAPH II. *Bankruptcies, 1750-1800. Five-yearly averages; index number (1751-5 = 100)*

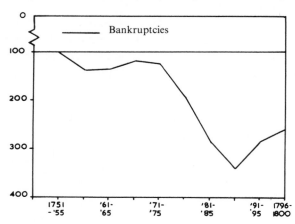

Over the first five years the imposts move on a somewhat higher level than
the convoy and licensing fees. In both cases the period 1761-5 provides the
highest yield. After the period 1776-80 a gradual deterioration sets in.

A third category of data is the annual number of bankruptcies.[19] If these are presented in the same manner — index numbers (1751-5 = 100) of the averages of the five-yearly periods but on a different scale and plotted inversely so as to facilitate comparison — then it also turns out that the position remains more or less the same till the period 1776-80, while it deteriorates thereafter (Graph II). In the last two periods there are then again fewer bankruptcies, though the other series do not show any improvements. The number of entrepreneurs was probably already so thinned out that in consequence an absolute decline in the number of bankruptcies was bound to occur.

Very little is known about the economic structure of Amsterdam in the eighteenth century. An attempt was made for the first time in 1800 to draw up an inventory of all businesses.[20] The first fully-fledged official inquiry dates from 1808.[21] In both inquiries comparisons are made with the eighteenth century. In the inquiry of 1800 the column in question is even headed 'impediments or reasons for decline', while in 1808 the more neutral term 'previous state' has been substituted. Unfortunately there is in the most cases only reference to the good old days in the most general of terms. With regard to the two most important branches of industry, ship-building and sugar-refining, there are more data available.

In 1800 ship-building does not appear in the inquiry; in 1808 it is stated that there is hardly work for 500 men, while in 1784 the yards had provided a *ruym bestaan* (comfortable living) to more than 3,000 persons. It was furthermore pointed out that the ruin of ship-building 'must inevitably result in the closing down of so many other works'. Mentioned are rope-makers, sail-makers, block-makers, pump-makers, smiths and compass-makers. The years of the Fourth Anglo-Dutch War must indeed have been a prosperous period for ship-building.[22]

The deterioration of the sugar-refining industry can be seen even more clearly (Table II).

19. *Idem*, 'Twee eeuwen Amsterdamse faillissementen en het verloop van de conjunctuur (1636 tot 1838)', *Tijdschrift voor geschiedenis*, LXXV (1962) 421-35.
20. Algemeen Rijksarchief, The Hague, Collectie Goldberg no 50. 'Generale tabelle van het getal der onderscheiden fabrieken en trafieken in de verschillende plaatsen van 't Departement den Amstel'.
21. GAA, Nieuw Stedelijk Bestuur, no. 238a, 'Generaale staat der fabrieken en trafieken binnen Amsteldam en der zelver jurisdictie in het Departement Amstelland. Anno 1808'.
22. A.J. Deurloo, 'Bijltjes en klouwers. Een bijdrage tot de geschiedenis der Amsterdamse scheepsbouw, in het bijzonder in de tweede helft der achttiende eeuw', *Economisch- en sociaal-historisch jaarboek*, XXXIV (The Hague, 1971) 47.

TABLE II. *Number of sugar refineries in Amsterdam*

year	number
about 1783	112[23]
1787	108[24]
1796	80[25]
1808	71[26]

With regard to the 71 sugar-refineries in 1808 it is moreover reported that they 'must at present remain almost idle'. The refining of sugar had a great influence on employment — directly and indirectly. In the inquiry of 1800 it is stated that six to fifteen men worked in each refinery, but that employment in many other crafts was involved. Mentioned are potteries, moulder's workshops, copper-smiths, iron-smiths, carpenters, bricklayers, plumbers and so forth. Reference is furthermore made to the supply of coal, paper mills, rope-yards, coopers, packing-case makers, bargees and the inland and overseas shipping. One of the reasons for the reduced sales, apart from the foreign competition about which everyone was complaining, was the high price of sugar.[27]

The inquiry of 1808 is one enormous lament. About the smoke-houses it is remarked that most workmen have already 'been reduced to the *Huiszittenhuis*', that is, dependency upon poor-relief, or begging; of the silk-factory it is reported that hardly a twentieth of the former workers are still employed there; the syrup-manufacturers have nothing to do, for sugar-refineries are almost idle and in the column 'present condition' but for a few exceptions, 'flagging', 'in decline' or 'idle' have been filled in.

If we finally compare the development of population with the economic situation it appears that after the period 1781-5 a definite deterioration is noticeable on all fronts. At first sight it seems remarkable that the peak of the population growth was reached during the dark years of the Anglo-Dutch War. Most of the persons from outside the town who gave notice of their intention to marry, most of the Reformed congregants and new burghers come in the years 1783 and 1784 when the peace with England is, to be sure, not yet been made but when, thanks to the truce, there is a revival of business. It is

23. 'Generaale staat 1808'.
24. J.J. Reese, *De suikerhandel van Amsterdam van het begin der 17de eeuw tot 1813* (Haarlem, 1908) 72.
25. *Ibidem*, 229.
26. 'Generaale staat 1808'.
27. In another article I have expressed the supposition that the high prices at the close of the eighteenth century were partly responsible for the decline in the Republic's trade. P.C. Jansen, 'Het ritme van de dood. Sociale conjunctuur in Amsterdam 1750-1800', *Ons Amsterdam*, XXV (Amsterdam, 1973) 90-1.

probable that the *trek* to Amsterdam in the last two years of the war could be explained by a desire to make up leeway, as it were.

Part of the immigrants who came to Amsterdam in the second half of the eighteenth century left their home towns because they were unable to find employment there anymore. The opportunities for employment in Amsterdam probably remained the same or decreased only slightly till the Fourth Anglo-Dutch War. The migration to Amsterdam was a result of the process of internal contraction, as has been shown by De Vries.[28] When after the Fourth Anglo-Dutch War the economic situation worsened also in Amsterdam the town drew fewer immigrants, with the result that the population decreased.

Now that it has been established that the economic situation worsened progressively after 1784 we should examine what social effects this had on the population. For this purpose the poor-relief figures are the first to be considered. It is true that the number of people on poor-relief does not tell us much about the real extent of the poverty, as De Bosch Kemper has remarked more than a hundred years ago already.[29] If, however, instead of isolated figures series of annual figures are available then the increase in poverty can in any event be determined with relative accuracy.

At first sight it is striking that there are so few figures extant on the question of poor-relief.[30] That the contemporaries did not have at their disposal a statistical summary of the economic situation goes more or less without saying. For that purpose an administrative machinery was needed which was only built up painstakingly after the revolution.[31] An adequate central registration of all persons on poor-relief should in any case not have produced insuperable difficulties, while one would moreover expect that the town administration would have been interested in some such information. Anyone who did not belong to a religious community could apply for assistance to one of the two *Huiszittenhuizen* (poor-relief centers), if he had lived in the town for at least seven years and had furthermore satisfied the required conditions.[32]

28. De Vries, *Economische achteruitgang*, 40 ff.

29. J. de Bosch Kemper, *Geschiedkundig onderzoek naar de armoede in ons vaderland, hare oorzaken en de middelen, die tot hare vermindering zouden kunnen worden aangewend* (Haarlem, 1851) 10.

30. The many figures in De Bosch Kemper, *ibidem*, table XI F, do not yield much either. In other cities too a similar dearth of information has been encountered up to now. Cf. C.W. van Voorst van Beest, *De katholieke armenzorg te Rotterdam in de 17e en de 18e eeuw* (The Hague, 1955).

31. W.M. Zappey, *De economische en politieke werkzaamheid van Johannes Goldberg* (Alphen a.d. Rijn, 1967).

32. W.F.H. Oldewelt, *Inventaris van de archieven tot 1808 van de colleges van regenten over het Oudezijdshuiszittenhuis en over het Nieuwezijdshuiszittenhuis en van 1808-1870 van het college van regenten over de Huiszittende Stadsarmen* (Amsterdam, 1929) introduction.

The *Huiszittenhuizen* were directly subsidized by the town, but the trustees were, except for the submitting of annual accounts, completely independent. This created no problems as long as the subsidies that were asked for did not become too large. When these amounts began to rise exorbitantly after 1780 the burgomasters instructed the treasury to examine the accounts more carefully. The trustees were moreover given instructions to draw up the accounts in such a manner so that it could easily be established which items had gone up since the previous year. Nevertheless, the trustees of the *Nieuwezijdshuiszittenhuis* continued with the old practice of rendering an account only of the incomes and expenditures, without mentioning how many families had profited from the poor-relief. When the treasurers enquired in 1793 why the number of people receiving poor-relief was not stated they replied: 'That has never been the practice or ever demanded'.[33]

On the parish poor-relief in the eighteenth century there is nothing to be found.[34] The poor-relief records of the *Huiszittenhuizen* have likewise been lost. For that reason the figures, insofar as they are still available, had to be compiled from the minutes. When the financial position of the town deteriorated rapidly during the last years of the ancien régime and the subsidies came to be paid out later and later, the trustees became communicative: in 1794 they wrote a letter to the burgomasters in which they even threatened 'to discontinue supplying aliment to the poor, unless ... an adequate supply of funds ... was forthcoming'. At the same time they showed on the basis of figures that at the *Nieuwe Zijde* (the western part of the town centre) the number of people in receipt of poor-relief had increased almost annually between 1783 and 1793.[35] Since 1786 the trustees of the *Oudezijdshuiszitten-huis* specified in their annual accounts the number of families receiving poor-relief.[36]

Although there are no figures available on the parish poor-relief, it is none the less possible to gain an overall view of the total number of people in receipt of poor-relief in the town. For, the *Huiszittenhuizen* did not only have to care for their own poor, but they furthermore supplied all parish poor-relief recipients with peat.[37] The total number of families receiving poor-relief from

33. GAA, Archief Burgemeesteren, no 595, Inv. Scheltema L.H. 14 13b, d.d. 26 april 1793.
34. For the Catholic system of poor-relief: H.C. de Wolf, *Geschiedenis van het R.C. Oude-armenkantoor te Amsterdam* (Hilversum, 1966) 129 ff.
35. GAA, Archief Huiszittenhuizen, Inv. Oldewelt, no. 259, 184; notulen 31 juli 1794.
36. *Ibidem*, no. 37.
37. *Ibidem*, no. 259, 314. In 1794 the ratio among the poor-relief recipients was as follows:

Reformed	16.59%
Roman Catholic	14.95%
Lutheran	9.68%
Portuguese jews	3.63%

the two *Huiszittenhuizen* therefore provides an approximation of all families on poor-relief in the city. For the years between 1782 and 1808 it has been possible to compile a set of figures that is almost complete.[38] One figure from the preceding period concerning the year 1764, as recorded by Wagenaar, enables us to make a comparison with the 'good (old) times'.[39]

GRAPH III. *Poor relief families at Oude- en Nieuwezijdshuiszittenhuis and amounts of grain used in Baking at Nieuwezijdshuiszittenhuis, 1764-1808; index number(s) (1764 = 100)*

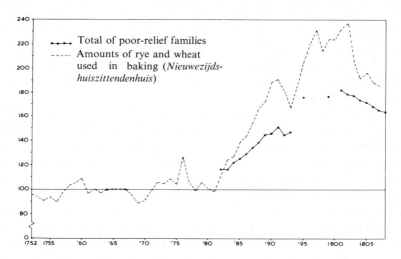

Besides there is still a complete set of the quantities of wheat and rye that were used in baking annually at the *Nieuwezijdshuiszittenhuis*.[40] Both sets have been presented diagrammatically in Graph III, with the year 1764 put at 100. From this it is clear that the number of poor-relief recipients had already in the

German jews	17.73%
Mennonites	0.43%
Remonstrant	0.09%
Huiszittenhuizen	36.88%
(municipal poor-relief recipients)	

In all there were then 33,833 recipients of poor-relief, cf. *infra* n. 42.

38. See the appendix.

39. J. Wagenaar, *Amsterdam in zijne opkomst, aanwas, geschiedenissen etc.* (Amsterdam, 1760-8) II, 273. There were then 7,100 'parties'.

40. The idea to use these figures is derived from E.E. de Jong-Keesing, *De economische crisis van 1763 te Amsterdam* (Amsterdam, 1939) 183-5. GAA, Archief Huiszittenhuizen, Inv. Oldewelt, no. 276.

seventies risen above the isolated figure for 1764. The rapidly progressing process of pauperization only begins to set in after the Fourth Anglo-Dutch War, at the same time as the economic deterioration. After 1800 the number of people receiving poor-relief decreases, undoubtedly as a result of the exodus from the town to the countryside. It has been estimated that between 1798 and 1811 the population of Amsterdam decreased by about 14,000 persons.[41] What now is the relation between the number of parties or families receiving poor-relief from the *Huiszittenhuizen* and the number of individual recipients? Fortunately there exists a statement about the total number of people in receipt of poor-relief in March 1795. There were then 18,961 adults and 14,872 children receiving relief, in all 33,833 persons. They constituted about 11,000 families.[42] A party or household therefore consisted on the average of three persons. This seems to square with other reports from which we know the number of households as well as the number of persons. It should be obvious that there were many single persons.

The number of those receiving poor-relief provides only an approximation of the real extent of the poverty. The same source from which the number of poor-relief recipients is obtained, also gives us the number of persons who wished to be considered for a share of the money raised through a special collection: 32,769 persons, almost just as many as the number of people on poor-relief. Four years later 81,080 individuals applied for this special assistance, while the number of poor-relief recipients, according to our estimation, amounted to about 37,500.[43] The best index, though, remains the number of people receiving poor-relief: the amounts that were issued as extra allowances were very small, in fact 25 cents per person! It is thus not without good reason that Brugmans has warned against the uncritical acceptance of the astronomical numbers of persons on poor-relief that have sometimes been reported: 'Indeed, one ought to bear in mind that the number recorded also includes those in receipt of partial poor-relief'.[44]

41. I.J. Brugmans, *Paardenkracht en mensenmacht. Sociaal-economische geschiedenis van Nederland 1795-1940* (The Hague, 1961) 59.
42. GAA, Archief Huiszittenhuizen, Inv. Oldewelt no. 7, 171. The report dates from March 1795, but it records the situation as it obtained the previous winter. Unfortunately the number of people who received winter poor-relief at the *Nieuwe Zijde* in 1794 is not known, but from a comparison with the figures for 1793 and the number of poor-relief recipients at the *Oude Zijde* we can deduce that there must have been about 11,000 'parties'. About 15% of the population was therefore in receipt of poor relief. C.M. Cipolla, *Before the Industrial Revolution. European Society and Economy, 1000-1700* (London, 1976) 18, gives 14% as the corresponding figure for Venice in 1780.
43. GAA, Archief Huiszittenhuizen, Inv. Oldewelt, no. 7, 451.
44. Brugmans, *Paardenkracht en mensenmacht*, 63.

One of the most hideous effects of the condition of poverty was the fate of the children who had been abandoned, deserted or thrown into one of the canals after birth. Graph IX shows that the number of foundlings between 1770 and 1800 had increased from 30 to almost 500 per year.[45] After the Fourth Anglo-Dutch War it reaches a very high level. This constitutes the best proof that society had been thrown completely out of balance. In the period between 1726, when figures first become available, and 1770 the number of foundlings always remained less than 30 per annum. The abandonment of children had become a more or less institutionalized possibility of ridding oneself of unwanted children. It is certainly true that this practice was prohibited, but every resident of the town knew the colossal building where these children were taken in — the present Palace of Justice on the Prinsengracht.

GRAPH IV. *Foundlings etc. and grain prices, 1770-1800. Semi-logarithmic scale*

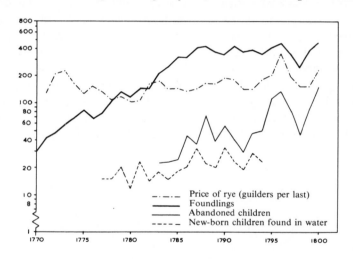

Far more severe were the measures taken against mothers who had murdered their children. In 1743, 1765 and 1770 the bye-law concerned was once again promulgated with examples containing gruesome details.[46] When the poverty became widespread the town administration chose the lesser of two evils. In the personal notes of J.B. Bicker, who had been alderman since 1772, the

45. The numbers of foundlings are to be found in N.S. Calisch, *Liefdadigheid te Amsterdam etc.* (Amsterdam, 1851) 88. The correct number for 1792 should read 366, see GAA, Archief Aal-moezeniersweeshuis, no. 391.
46. L. van Nierop, 'De keuren tegen 'het ombrengen van jonge-gebore kinderen' in de 17de en 18de eeuw', *Maandblad Amstelodamum*, XL VI (1959) 154-5.

following observation has been found: 'The abandonment of children is current-
ly being connived at, in order to keep people from doing away with their
new-born children, as has recently become much in vogue'.[47] Nevertheless the
number of children who were found in the water in the second half of the
period 1777-1794 was greater than in the first half, as is clear from Graph IV.[48]

In the figure the number of deserted children is also presented.[49] In the
eighteenth and the nineteenth century a distinction was made between foundlings and deserted children; in the former case it was a question of mostly
new-born children of whom the parents were not known, in the latter the
identity of the parent(s) was known.[50] The curves in the graph run more or
less parallel. From this it is obvious that poverty was the main reason for
the fact that these children were left to their fate. In Amsterdam, as is the case
elsewhere,[51] one can moreover ascertain the connexion with the cost of living,
here presented by the price of rye.[52]

Finally, the number of patients that were weekly treated in the *Binnen- en
Buitengasthuis* (hospitals) is an indicator of the situation in the city.[53] It
increased from 500 to 800 between 1785 and 1796, despite the fact that the
population probably declined in this period. Such a rising trend cannot be
ascribed to accidental factors like epidemics. The increasing spread of poverty
must be the principal cause. In Graph V it can be seen that as the price of rye
rises the number of patients in the hospitals increases.[54] The decline in the
number of poor-relief recipients, noticeable at the beginning and at the close
of the 1790s, is moreover to be observed in the number of patients as well.

47. I.H. v[an] E[eghen], 'Vondelingen', *Maandblad Amstelodamum*, XLIII (1956) 130. From this
article it is clear that the bye-law was indeed enforced previously and that the small number of
foundlings in the eighteenth century must be attributed, at least in part, to police supervision.
48. GAA, Doop-, trouw- en begraafboeken, Inv. Veder, no. 1271, Register van haaldoden. To
what extent these figures are representative of all murdered children is questionable.
49. GAA, Archief Aalmoezeniersweeshuis, no. 391.
50. P.C. Jansen, 'Geschiedenis van het Aalmoezeniersweeshuis in Amsterdam' (Unpublished
essay, Economisch-Historisch Seminarium, University of Amsterdam).
51. C. Delasselle, 'Les enfants abandonnés à Paris au XVIIIᵉ siècle', *Annales*, XXX (Paris, 1975)
207-9; J.P. Gutton, *La sociéte et les pauvres en Europe (XVIᵉ-XVIIIᵉ siècles)* (Paris, 1974) 88.
52. Derived from N.W. Posthumus, *Nederlandsche Prijsgeschiedenis*, I (Leiden, 1943) Table 7.
The price of rye has been shifted one year in the graph.
53. GAA, Archief Gasthuizen, Inv. Veder, no. 77 (new number 1272).
54. Price of rye : see note 52. The correlation coefficient is 0.79.

GRAPH V. *Hospital patients (weekly average) and grain prices, 1770-1796. Semi-logarithmic scale*

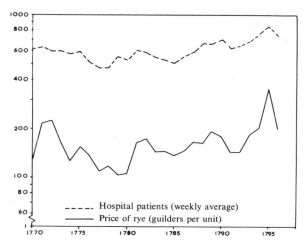

The economic retrogression and the concomitant increasing unemployment are not the only causes of the great poverty at the close of the eighteenth century. Far more serious was the constant rise in the cost of living. This rise in prices was a European phenomenon. The cause must be sought in the rapid growth of the European population in the second half of the eighteenth century which was not accompanied by a commensurate increase in the production of food.[55]

The effects would not have been so serious had the wages followed the same movement or rather had risen faster than the prices. Unfortunately almost nothing is known about the wages, while the data concerning the prices are available on an annual and sometimes weekly basis. Still, there are enough indications that the wages in the Republic in the second half of the eighteenth century did not rise. From various sources it can be concluded that the wages in the countryside remained the same.[56] Likewise the pay for the sailors on the

---

55. W. Abel, *Massenarmut und Hungerkrisen im vorindustriellen Europa. Versuch einer Synopsis* (Hamburg, 1974) 191 ff.; B.H. Slicher van Bath, *De agrarische geschiedenis van West-Europa. (500-1850)* (Utrecht, 1960) 243.
56. Slicher van Bath, *ibidem*, 247-8: the money wages did not undergo any change between 1697 and the middle of the 19th century. Recently this has been re-affirmed once again for the South Holland countryside: 'The wages remained at the same level in the 17th and the 18th century, despite the big differences in the purchasing power of the money!. The wages in question cover the periods 1674-1677, 1763-1773 and 1801-1802; C. Baars, 'Boekhoudingen van landbouw-bedrijven in de Hoeksewaard uit de zeventiende en achttiende eeuw', *A.A.G. Bijdragen*, XIX (Wageningen, 1975) 3-135. The quotation is from p. 132.

fishing-fleet did not undergo any change.[57] As far as the towns outside of Amsterdam are concerned, we have data only from Leiden at our disposal. The wages of some workmen employed by the town administration carpenter's and bricklayer's assistant, hodman, slater's mate and road-maker — did not change at all between 1750 and 1800.[58]

For Amsterdam the data are just as scanty. Deurloo has established that the wages of shipyard carpenters did not rise between 1664 and 1869.[59] That is a very important fact because the shipyard carpenters constituted a large group of highly skilled artisans who were in the employ of the biggest industry in Amsterdam. Moreover these workers were very active and were organized into a guild. These *Bijltjes* (Small Axes), as the shipyard carpenters were called, resorted on several occasions to armed action.[60] If there had been one group which would have been able to get their wages adjusted to the increased prices then it would have been the shipyard carpenters. Finally we know that the wages of the Amsterdam road-makers had not been raised between 1779 and 1808.[61] If wages are not increased while the prices are rising the real wages drop.[62] The greater part of the wages was spent on food.[63] Bread was by far the cheapest; potatoes were not yet consumed on a large scale.[64] For that reason

57. H.A.H. Kranenburg, *De zeevisscherij van Holland in den tijd der Republiek* (Amsterdam, 1946) 203.
58. N.W. Posthumus, *De geschiedenis van de Leidsche Lakenindustrie*, II, *De Nieuwe Tijd* (*zestiende tot achttiende eeuw*), part III, 1088-9. Only the wages of unskilled labourers who were in the employ of the Leiden *gestichten* (institutions) showed any movement. How these wages have been calculated is not known. It is worthy of note that two other categories of wages that were paid out by these institutions, namely the *maalloon* (milling) and *bakloon* (baking), exhibited the same immobility as the wages of the city workers.
59. A.J. Deurloo, 'Bijltjes', 28, note 2.
60. *Ibidem*, 54 ff.
61. GAA, Archief Thesaurieren Ordinaris, Inv. no. 71. Van der Woude who has conducted a cursory investigation into the wages of other city officials in Amsterdam gained the 'impression' that these did not change. A.M. van der Woude, *Het Noorderkwartier. Een regionaal historisch onderzoek in de demografische en economische geschiedenis van westelijk Nederland van de late middeleeuwen tot het begin van de negentiende eeuw*. A.A.G. Bijdragen XVI (Wageningen, 1972) 734, note 56.
62. 'By and large all workers are no longer in a position, as in former days, to earn a decent living through diligent labour because of the low wages and the high prices of foodstuffs', Algemeen Rijksarchief, Collectie Goldberg, no. 50, 'Tabellen der statistieke opgaven betrekkelijk de industrie. Ongedateerd, na 1800'. The (original) quotation comes from Leiden.
63. Abel, *Massenarmut*, 395-6; A bricklayer in Berlin about 1800: 72.7%. W. Minchinton, 'Patterns of demand', in: C.M. Cipolla, ed., *The Fontana economic history of Europe*, III (London, 1973) 116; agricultural labourers in England (1787-1793): 72.2%. Similar figures are not available for the Netherlands.
64. According to De Vooys, the potato was the staple food in the third quarter of the eighteenth century; A.C. de Vooys, 'De verspreiding van de aardappelteelt in ons land in de 18ᵉ eeuw', *Geographisch Tijdschrift*, VII (Groningen, 1954) 5. In 1781 it was however still necessary to publicize its use in Amsterdam: 'Advice to the common man, containing the means (by which)

the currency depreciation can best be illustrated by the price of bread. If we put the period 1750-54 at 100 then the price of bread in the period 1795-99 is 174. That means that the real wages, expressed in terms of bread, had dropped from 100 to 57 points or by almost half.[65]

At the close of the eighteenth century there are so many independant reports to the effect that poverty was on the increase that their reliability need not be questioned. Only by using sets of comparable annual figures is it possible to present the development in time more or less accurately. A single figure does not tell us anything. It is only through comparison with other data that, in Schöffer's words, the dead figure can be transformed into a living number.[66]

to live cheaply and healthily in these times of high prices and unemployment — times of manifold adversity. By a friend of his country'. Available in the Gemeente Archief of Amsterdam.
65. Calculated on the basis of the figures in Posthumus, *Leidsche Lakenindustrie*, III, 1083. According to M.C. ter Weer, 'De Broodzetting' (unpublished essay, Economisch-Historisch Seminarium, University of Amsterdam) the town government of Leiden took over the Amsterdam bread-price because the grain price was fixed at the Amsterdam Exchange.
66. I. Schöffer, 'Het dode cijfer en het levende getal. Een en ander over kwantificeren in het historisch onderzoek', *Tijdschrift voor geschiedenis*, LXXVIII (1965) 157-72.

APPENDIX

Number of households in receipt of poor relief: *Oude- en Nieuwezijdszittenhuis* (winter 'parties') 1782-1808. (Index 1764 = 100[67])

	Parties	Index
1782	8,234	116[68]
3	8,208	116
4	8,683	122
5	8,861	125
6	9,186	129[69]
7	9,582	135
8	9,864	139
9	10,286	145
1790	10,400	146
1	10,691	151
2	10,274	145
3	10,434	147
4	..,....	
5	12,467	176[70]
6	..,...	
7	..,...	
8	..,...	
9	12,549	177[71]
1800	..,...	
1	12,951	182[72]
2	12,678	179
3	12,652	178
4	12,358	174
5	12,222	172
6	12,011	169
7	11,784	165[73]
8	11,611	164[74]

67. J. Wagenaar, *Amsterdam*, II, 273; 7,100 'parties'.
68. *Oude zijde*; GAA, Archief Huiszittenhuizen, Inventaris Oldewelt, no. 6, p. 307 over 1782-86. *Nieuwe zijde*: GAA, Archief Burgemeesteren no. 594, Regenten aan Burg., 23-2-1787 (1782-6).
69. *Oude zijde*: GAA, Archief Huiszittenhuizen, Inv. no. 37 (over 1786-1807). *Nieuwe zijde*: *Ibidem*, inv. no. 259, 184 (over 1783-93).
70. *Nieuwe zijde*: *Algemeene Konst- en Letterbode* (1804) 359, note. The number quoted for the *Oude Zijde* is the same as in the archives.
71. *Nieuwe zijde*: GAA, Archief Huiszittenhuizen, inv. no. 260, 157.
72. *Nieuwe zijde*: *Ibidem*, 509 (over 1802-06).
73. *Nieuwe zijde*: *Ibidem*, inv. 322, no. 107B.
74. GAA, Huiszittende-Stadsarmen, inv. no. 305, 145.

Gijsbert Karel van Hogendorp 1762-1834

Gijsbert Karel van Hogendorp, born on October 27th, 1762 in Rotterdam of an aristocratic but impoverished regent family, received a military education in Berlin, returning to his native land in 1781. In 1783-4 he accompanied the first Dutch mission to the United States. On his return he studied law at Leiden, graduating in 1786. In 1787 he took a leading part in the conservative revolution brought about with the help of Prussia. He was rewarded with the office of *pensionaris* for his birthplace but was forced to resign in 1795 when the republic was occupied by the troops of the French Revolution. He spent the entire period of the French occupation in retirement, devoting himself to the study of political and constitutional questions. It was at this time that he wrote his *Schets eener grondwet* (Sketch of a Constitution) which was to form the basis of the constitution of the Kingdom of the Netherlands set up in 1814. But the State to whose rebirth he had contributed so much gave him no significant part to play, since the first king, Willem I (1813-1840), could bear no man beside him who was as ambitious and headstrong as himself and moreover more learned and more acute. From 1816 onwards Van Hogendorp lived more or less in retirement once more, though he was a member of the Second Chamber until 1825. He died in The Hague on October 5th, 1834.

Gijsbert Karel van Hogendorp in America, 1783-1784 *

J.W. SCHULTE NORDHOLT

Assis dans un coin de ma chambrette, dans l'enveloppe d'un grand manteau, puisque la pluie perçoit de differents cotés, et sourd au bruit des vents et de la mer, sans me ressentir des mouvements incommodes du vaisseau... je me suis occupé pendant des heures de suite de l'ouvrage intéressant de cet écrivain élégant et judicieux.[1]

This is the impressive pose assumed by the hero of our story, whose formal written French makes it seem all the more a conscious attitude, though at the same time it is more than a pose, for he is plying his pen while the tempest roars and rages about him, for days and, finally, weeks on end, in mid-Atlantic, literally *saevis tranquillus in undis*.

This is Hogendorp to the life, adopting a pose, but a pose not without reality, courageous, but conscious of his courage. His heroic attitude may be seen as common form in an age of classicism but it is above all his own character that makes our hero so brave and so rhetorically aware of his bravery, so that as the mainmast topples with a deafening crash he even recites Horace's famous lines: 'Iustum et tenacem virum...'.[2]

He is twenty years old at this moment of our first meeting, it is the year 1783 and the young man has exposed himself to such deadly perils because of his overwhelming urge to see the new world, the dream beyond the horizon. America is a dream for him, as for so many young men of his era,[3] but at the same time he is realistic enough to have prepared himself thoroughly; the 'écrivain élégant et judicieux', whose book he has in his hand in mid-ocean is the then well-known Scots historian William Robertson, and the book itself his most recent work, *The History of America*, published in 1777. It is not primarily idealism which has inspired the young man to this major voyage. Ambition is a deeper motivation. Romein, in his fine essay on Van Hogendorp, has cited ambition as his predominant characteristic and even spoken of a debt

* This article is the slightly shortened version of J.W. Schulte Nordholt, 'Gijsbert Karel Van Hogendorp in Amerika 1783-1784', *Tijdschrift voor geschiedenis*, LXXXVIII (Groningen, 1975) 39-62.
1. Algemeen Rijksarchief, The Hague, Van Hogendorp Archief (abbreviated: ARA, v. H) 50 (1783).
2. *Ibidem*.
3. J. and A. Romein, *Erflaters van onze beschaving* (3d ed., Amsterdam, 1941) III, 217-8.

to be repaid, the negative bequest of his grandfather and father.[4] This may well be true; it does much to account for the tensions inherent in the man's life. It must be added that ambition led to isolation. In his boyhood Gijsbert Karel already felt different and at the same time unsure:

> That I go about alone is because I prefer to live apart from my fellows rather than squander others' goods with them, frequent whorehouses or gamble. Hence I know no middle way since I care nothing for their faro-banks, pretty girls and understanding wasted on trifles.[5]

He was easily irritated, even by strangers:

> In a post-coach with a man and his wife in their forties, full of stupid chatter and so tedious. At length (having no book in my pocket) I began to rehearse to myself various plays, chiefly those of Voltaire.[6]

This play-acting goes deeper than might appear; indeed Gijsbert Karel always feels himself an actor on stage, set apart from the public but always a focus of attention: no gesture is unconsidered. In a 'Pleidooi' (Plea) written in Boston 'the first December evening by a warm fire' he imagines how people will talk of him and judge him when they hear that his ship was lost. Most people will dismiss him.

> But I seem to see somewhere in a corner, unnoticed, a man sitting, a man whose sound understanding goes out from his poor garret to comprehend the whole land and who in his poverty is more than rich in his high aim to do his country some essential service. He reflects on my voyage and while he hears the true report and believes the loss to include my own, I hear him sigh quietly and say to himself: 'Tis pity'. A young man with no greater wish than to serve his country, refusing nothing that might fit him for the task — and so to die'.

Then follows a description of all Van Hogendorp's good intentions in America leading up to the dramatic finale:

> But ah! my hopes are deceived and of all his fine intentions not even his good name survives; he is condemned because he is judged too soon.[7]

How typical this piece is of our hero, this obituary with indeed nothing but praise for the departed. In it his projects and intentions are set out in detail; his whole character may be read in it, the characteristic double vision from which the overwhelmingly self-conscious so often suffer is clearly expressed. For who is this man of understanding in his garret if not Van Hogendorp himself, as he hopes he is, passing judgment on himself: 'tis pity I should so die, a grievous loss.

4. *Ibidem*, 210-3.
5. ARA, v. H, 50 (1782).
6. *Ibidem*.
7. *Brieven en Gedenkschriften van Gijsbert Karel van Hogendorp*, ed. by F. and H. van Hogendorp (7 vols, The Hague, 1866-1903) I, *1763-1786*, 260-1 (1 Dec. 1783).

A man of this type is always out to make an impression, he feels himself the cynosure of all eyes, he must and will be noticed. When before his great voyage, he discusses his plans with an American merchant living in Utrecht, a certain Peterson, he writes, full of satisfaction: 'I saw that in our brief conversation I had made an impression on him'.[8] And on the same journey, turning up to see his uncle Duco van Haren at Scherpenzeel, he notes complacently : 'Accepted by Haren and received as a man with whom business may be discussed'.[9] The youth is becoming a man; with naif pride he announces from Boston to his mother that he is learning to do without help from others: 'I can even, he assures her, 'me lier mes cheveux de la queue'.[10]

But however great his need for recognition, he is on the other hand in-dependent enough — more and more so as his voyage proceeds — to realize himself. His sensitivity may make him insecure from time to time but is not so romantic as to unbalance him, except, as we shall see, on one single occasion. He believes in a plan for his life, clearly outlined, his ambition is controlled. When he sits alone at his desk reflecting on his life it is with unusual judgment. He sets out his plan almost prophetically:

> It is to make myself capable under an ambassador; to study law; to obtain good fees; to acquire a thorough understanding of all the tasks of government; to unite the mechanical and the commercial; to despise fools who try to sound me; to convince everyone in time of what I feel; to be of use; to benefit society; to put an end to abuses; to oppose idiots and good-for-nothings; to help good to triumph and in so doing to inscribe my name indelibly in the memory of my country as long as it exists.

The young man who can write like this, knowing how vulnerable he is, has confidence that he can hold out, that his vocation sets him apart. And he concludes his reverie with the words:

> To which I have nothing to add but God save me from ever disclosing these thoughts to anyone incapable of appreciating them, even from myself after the same judgment.[11]

The first step in the grand project, then, is: 'to make myself capable under an ambassador'. 'Under' is not to be taken too seriously; to be an underling hardly corresponds to this young man's ambition. But the ambassador is necessary to reach the distant land of the young man's dreams — America. In that very year of 1782 when Van Hogendorp, returned the previous year from his long cadet period in Germany, was seeking a purer goal for his ambition than a career in the army ('I admit it, in Prussia my longing was to

---

8. ARA, v.H 50; cf. L.G.J. Verberne, *Gijsbert Karel's leerjaren* (Amsterdam, 1931) 108, note 5.
9. *Ibidem.*
10. *Brieven Van Hogendorp*, I, 281 (16 Dec. 1783).
11. *Ibidem*, 225-7 (1782).

become a great general'),[12] the Republic of the Netherlands, after long hesitation and consideration and above all impelled by overstrained economic speculation arrived at the decision to recognize the young republic coming into existence in the new world. This was just the opportunity Van Hogendorp had been looking for. When in 1783 Pieter Johan van Berckel was named as first Dutch ambassador to the United States, the young man requested to be allowed to travel with him. There were some difficulties to be overcome — Van Berckel was not so enthusiastic about the idea; he had already arranged a post in the embassy for his son and another relative (Gijsbert Karel's father was his cousin) was in no way welcome. In the end the young man was allowed, at a suitable remove, in the ambassador's suite, aboard one of the ships of the squadron accompanying his excellency. This was the Erfprins, a small, ill-built ship; Van Hogendorp was the sole passenger. It was a disastrous voyage. We have already seen how our hero bore himself in the storm and solemnly deliberated how he would be mourned after his death. In the end he was one of the few to survive the adventure and after five months to set foot in the new world. Three days before, after months of difficult voyaging, the captain had taken the opportunity of hailing an American schooner just off the New England coast and had charged Van Hogendorp to go aboard and to lose no time in getting help from Boston. The help came too late; on the day he landed the ship went down and of the 350 men no more than 40 could be saved.

It is not easy to tell what effect this striking event had on our hero's inner life. The pose he struck amid the storm was so genuine that he kept it up to the end. There is a curious document to be found among his salvaged papers; a couple of small leaves of paper with a prayer inscribed in that precarious situation. Even then, in that existential situation, in the face of God, death before his eyes, not a word of his betrays the slightest feeling of dread, guilt or whatever. In this moment of need he does not resort to his mother tongue. With a good deal of circumlocution and in the most wooden French he informs his Creator of his acquiescence in his fate. He was on his way 'pour être le témoin de la plus grande leçon qu'un peuple puisse donner aux autres, celle de former son Gouvernement après avoir combattu pour sa liberté'. But:

> S'il n'est pas dans l'ordre des choses que je poursuive ma carrière, je me resigne sans murmurer. Je n'ai pas étouffé le germe de bien que tu formas en moi; peut-être veux tu le faire éclore dans une autre sphère ou Ta Sagesse me placera; sans doute est-ce pour mon bonheur mais c'est un bonheur que j'ignore et ne puis comprendre.

12. *Ibidem.*

Only at the end is there a tone of honest emotion after this confession of his ambition, extending to another planet. I acquiesce, he writes, since I am nothing in the Universal Scheme, since acquiescence is all the good I can now do, since I have no fear of death, but I would rather live: 'ne condamne point le voeu secrèt que je forme de jouir encore de cette vie'.[13] In a letter of some two or three weeks later to his brother Willem he allows himself more scope, or, let us say, is more successful, in putting on paper what he has gone through. He tells how he landed, first completely disoriented and above all concerned about the fate of his shipmates. He hears that help has been sent, he himself is hospitably received at table by an American family and then, suddenly, emotion breaks through, the long tension finds relief:

> In the evening, while I was pursuing my journey through a dark pinewood and from a hilltop could see land and sea around me in the moonlight I was overwhelmed by a feeling of bliss and raising my eyes to heaven I cried out with deep emotion: 'Thanks. Thanks'.[14]

The hardships had been great, but expectations were now all the higher. The voyage had been long, but had afforded the young man the opportunity to prepare himself really thoroughly. The lists of the titles of the books he had with him are impressive, with the classics and the philosophers and for relaxation the poets, particularly the English ones since in addition to the official French, the German mastered in Berlin and his somewhat neglected mother tongue the young man must make himself familiar with the language of the land now becoming the greatest power in the world, a land, too, which in those early days of romanticism had a fascinating literature to show; Van Hogendorp responded eagerly to the Shakespeare renaissance; he had the complete works with him, enjoyed reading them and often quoted from them.

What is not to be gathered from the book list but is clear from the correspondence is that Van Hogendorp had devoted a good deal of study to the country of his destination. Franklin and Robertson appear in his catalogue, but his letters also mention Buffon and Raynal. The taste of the time gives Franklin pre-eminence, he had 'des talents supérieurs et des grandes vertus' and everyone knows 'son grand métier littéraire' and Van Hogendorp hopes to meet him,[15] though this was never to happen. His admiration for Robertson, the most solid Americanist of the age, is typical. It is his balance that attracts Gijsbert Karel and inspires him to paeans of praise.[16] About Raynal, the author of the immensely popular *Histoire des Deux Indes* our Dutch reader,

13. ARA, v.H 50 (Aug. 1783).
14. *Brieven Van Hogendorp*, I, 263 (6 Dec. 1783).
15. ARA, v.H 12 (2 Aug. 1783).
16. Cf. H.S. Commager and E. Giordanetti, *Was America a Mistake? An Eighteenth-Century Controversy* (New York, 1967).

like so many of his contemporaries, is in two minds — sometimes he quotes him,[17] but he must also have realized how abstract much of that sort of writing was, if he did not hear as much from Jefferson and other American friends. I believe it was of Raynal and suchlike philosophers that he was thinking when he wrote to his father that it was necessary to expose the 'faux jugements de voyageurs où d'écrivains ignorants et superficiels'.[18]

What is in any case typical of our scholar is his urge to increase his knowledge, to correct, to inform both Europeans with a false impression of America and Americans, whom he intended to compliment on their simplicity but not to spare criticism. He would appreciate the 'brave fellows' and question them and so be able to 'discover their shortcomings'.[19]

One can visualize him, the young man ready to go for the Americans with Socratic dialectic, to discover himself — thus providing the new world with one of the first examples of European pedantry.

Everything that Van Hogendorp hoped to see and hear he wanted to check, everything interested him. This is why he gives us such a collection of data, a source of information about the new world. He himself is always involved, part of the bargain, as it were. America was where he exercised himself, a step in his career at home. Like so many travellers, he was unable to see it as anything but a reflection of Europe and for that reason interesting. The great question was whether that new beginning over there could really serve as an example to the old world. And whether he himself had a role to play.

Could there have been a more appropriate moment to act as observer than that very year of 1783, when the new nation received recognition, came into existence? 'The new State of thirteen provinces', he wrote on the way,

> will within a few years be flourishing and will offer a pleasing example to the eye of the wise; but never will America be more remarkable to me. To see a State arising is a happiness that falls to few, and what a lesson for him who cares to profit from it.[20]

And his high-pitched expectations were much more personally expressed in a letter just before his departure to his fatherly friend and the mentor of his German years, Biester:

> I am collecting material from books, knowledge of men and experience. When I am one of the first to come back from the country, that will be the moment to make myself known, to show that I am capable of observation and investigation, to make my object

17. Cf. Anatole Feugère, *Un précurseur de la révolution, l'abbé Raynal (1713-1796)* (Angoulème, 1922).
18. *Brieven Van Hogendorp*, I, 318 (10 March 1784).
19. ARA, v.H 50 (Aug. 1783).
20. *Brieven Van Hogendorp*, I, 419.

known and to prepare in advance to the change I hope shortly thereafter to carry out. May this journey extend to the greatest possible benefit.[21]

Here we have it, naif and full of purpose Gijsbert Karel journeyed to America, conceived as a means to his own end, his great dream. Coming from the old world of position, style and etiquette, he saw it with the critical eye of a stranger. His description of social life there is all the more interesting. In letters to his mother and sisters he talks about the casualness in social behaviour, in dress:

On s'habille simplement ... On ne conçoit pas en Amérique à quoi sert de porter une épée hors de service et l'on se moque de ceux qui achètent un chapeau pour le tenir sous le bras,[22]

in table manners: 'D'ailleurs on ne se gêne pas à table comme chez nous',[23] in short in everything that is done. Life is 'sans beaucoup de cérémonie'.[24] All this agrees with the general observation of the time. But Van Hogendorp surprises us by going further. The Americans, he maintains, are not merely casual but careless. They live from day to day: 'On n'accumule pas: on n'épargne point, mais on vit à son aise'.[25] They do everything the easiest way, putting off important matters five or six times. As a portrait of the Yankee — he is the subject, most of these observations are set down in Boston — this is, to say the least, remarkable and did much to surprise the nineteenth-century Dutch historian Fruin, who remarks how important it is for the historian to attend to eye-witnesses who say something we do not expect.[26] Of course we must remember that Van Hogendorp had arrived in a country that was drawing its breath in relief after a long war and was therefore enjoying life.[27]

But there is also a deeper explanation for this particular observation. Behind it lies the whole discussion of the difference between the old and the new world. The debate, engaged in above all in France, as to the advantages and disadvantages of the discovery of America, was one with which he was familiar. The opposition implied in the argument has since then become classic. Europe and America are the two poles of Western civilization, distinguished by such contradictions as old and young, complex and simple, theoretical and practical,

---

21. ARA, v.H 112; cf. Verberne, *Gijsbert Karel*, 110, note 2.
22. ARA, v.H 50.
23. *Brieven Van Hogendorp*, I, 281 (16 Dec. 1783).
24. ARA, v.H 50.
25. *Brieven Van Hogendorp*, I, 279 (14 Dec. 1783).
26. R. Fruin, 'De jongelingsjaren van Gijsbert Karel van Hogendorp', in: *Verspreide Geschriften*, V (The Hague, 1902) 263-74.
27. P.J. van Winter, *Het aandeel van den Amsterdamschen handel aan de opbouw van het Amerikaanse Gemenebest* (2 vols, The Hague, 1927-33) I, 98. (An English translation of this work has been published by Arno, New York: *American Finance and Dutch investments*, 1 vol.).

experienced and primitive. Buffon and his followers maintained that the new world was indeed so new that it was bound to be backward in all ways, that not only were the aborigines the most primitive people on earth, savage and feeble, but that immigrants too would be weakened by the as yet unbalanced damp climate. But admiration for the American revolution completely changed this image; defenders arose on all sides, characterizing what had seemed feeble and simple as pure and genuine. Sometimes the complete volte-face can be observed in a single writer, the great example being Raynal.

What Gijsbert Karel observes fits into this picture. His attitude is ambivalent, influenced both by his observation and by his reading. This is clear enough if one reads the context of his remarks as to the carelessness and indolence of the Americans. The echo of the French examples in these is unmistakable. He too maintains that the immigrants, once across the Ocean, lose their energy. 'Ils se font à la fin à cette vie aisée et tranquille, que nous autres appelons indolente',[28] but this makes them no less happy. But we, 'nous autres' naturally cannot feel at home in this simple world. He writes to reassure his disquieted mother that of course he will not stay in America. Whether you choose to call it 'perfection' or 'corruption', the developed European cannot satisfy the needs of his soul in a land of indolence, where the passions themselves pale, where 'l'amour même n'a pas un ombre de sa violence dans d'autres climats'.[29] And elsewhere he concludes: 'Voilà comme le sol rend l'une nation active, laborieuse, entreprenante, et l'autre douce, indolente et paisible'.[30] And, indeed, by this gentle, lazy, peaceful nation the young philosophe means the Americans!

In other words, quite classically stereotyped: the Americans are children. While in Europe all matters are complicated, 'elles sont ici dans leur enfance'.[31] The people too:

> some of them seem perfect children; it is agreeable to see a company laugh, be cheerful, eat and drink with relish, then talk, walk, ride, play, etc. But I have noticed in various foreigners, myself above all, that this joy is less strongly felt, if at all, not because we are more serious but because our understanding is riper and draws from other sources of cheer.[32]

Van Hogendorp's whole vision of the American people is thus determined by his European background and half-theoretical. With an amiable arrogance he expresses his detachment: 'C'est un grand bonheur pour les Américains de se croire le peuple le plus heureux de la terre'.[33]

28. *Brieven Van Hogendorp*, I, 398 (summer 1784).
29. *Ibidem*, 279 (14 Dec. 1783).
30. *Ibidem*, 302 (21 Jan. 1784).
31. *Ibidem*, 298-9 (21 Jan. 1784).
32. *Ibidem*, 287 (26 Dec. 1783).
33. ARA, v.H 50-b.

The great question inevitably arising from the assessment of social life, one posed by many observers, was to what extent more equality was to be found in the new world than in the old. It is a problem which not only occupied the people of that time but has kept historians busy ever since. Particularly in recent years, now that insecurity and dissatisfaction with what has been achieved is so great in America a good deal of attention has been devoted to the shortcomings of the new society. The posthumous work of the historian Hofstadter, which gives a social cross-section of the American situation in 1750,[34] shows how in every colony, from New England to the deep South, an élite developed which set the tone, merchants in Massachusetts, big landowners in New York, Quakers in Pennsylvania, planters in Virginia and South Carolina.

But in spite of this there was a feeling of equality unknown in Europe, what Hofstadter calls 'a middle-class quality of life', indeed, he says, a consequence of the lack of such tone-setting factors as court, nobility and established Church. Even if the equality was only relative, America was still a society centred on the average.[35] Social differences were no bar to equal opportunity. In other words, American society was from the outset ambivalent, 'a society strangely in conflict with itself' as another modern historian has put it. The whole of life seemed a race to overtake the next man but at the same time there was a general fundamental distaste for every manifestation of status or superiority.[36] Or, as John Adams said: 'All that we can say in America is that legal distinctions, titles, powers and privileges are not hereditary'.[37]

Gijsbert Karel, with his own starting-point and his own outlook, tackled the great problem of equality. In Boston on Boxing Day 1783 he tried to draw some conclusions under the heading 'Eenige opmerkingen omtrent de Zamenleving' (Some Observations on Society). He begins firmly with the principle:

Nature and law create inequality. However equal before the law, men are unequal by nature in strength, beauty, spirit, eloquence, upbringing and behaviour. In most countries there is also a hereditary distinction and everywhere that of wealth. Even here in the most liberal of States, freedom is greater or less according to the rights conferred on a man by his property.

But no sooner is this written than objectivity offers the other side.

Nonetheless equality before the law in this State may be regarded as complete, being carried further than anywhere else and possibly even determined by the nature of things.

---

34. R. Hofstadter, *America at 1750. A Social Portrait* (New York, 1971).
35. *Ibidem*, 131-2.
36. Gordon S. Wood, *The Creation of the American Republic 1776-1787* (Chapel Hill, 1969).
37. *Ibidem*, 573-4.

There is, so he notes further, a definite distinction in America between two classes: 'Gentlemen' and 'persons in lower life' is here a general division. 'To dress and behave like a gentleman' is a very common description. The distinction is rooted in property:

> Independence of others is based on possessions and so the richer and more independent, the more 'genteel'. Coach and horses, fine clothes, receptions attract all eyes here as everywhere else. The poor step back willingly enough.[38]

But the difference between America and Europe is at least as striking as this apparent similarity. The barriers in America are less rigid, the positions are indeed not hereditary, not fixed. They are known in everyday life, but not recognized. Van Hogendorp expresses it as follows:

> The difference between these two classes of people is however not always in evidence. So for instance in business. Everyone who has something to say even to the Governor goes and sits and drinks punch or porter with him.[39]

And elsewhere:

> Il n'y a point de rangs ici. La fortune d'un homme lui assigne communément la place dans la société. Car peu d'emplois donnent du lustre, et la noblesse est assez inconnue en Amérique qu'une fortune constante pendant trois générations. Le grand-père d'un homme riche se trouve la plupart des temps avoir été pauvre et celui du pauvre un richard.[40]

The critical Dutchman resorted for preference to the society of the distinguished. But he still has many comments to make on them. It is striking how strongly he opposes all the luxury and light-heartedness he comes across. 'All kinds of comfort and excess flatter the weaknesses of the rich. They enjoy them and are corrupted'. The degeneracy he claimed to observe he attributed to the influence of the French, at the time the most numerous foreigners in America. He himself wants no part of it but lands in it nevertheless inexperienced, awkward, all too heavy-handed. He is doing it as part of his plan of life, because it is what his mother wants. He writes to her

> Je me persuade de plus en plus que vous formez un jugement juste, en prétendant que pour être bien avec les hommes, il faut être bien avec les femmes.[41]

But after all he is only twenty, unsure, afraid of himself.

As to whether it was only his personal awkwardness that made him so unsure and thus so strict in his judgment on a relatively friendly and innocent social life is not easy to say. It might be ascribed to his Dutch calvinism,

---

38. *Brieven Van Hogendorp*, I, 284-5 (26 Dec. 1783).
39. *Ibidem*, 285-6 (26 Dec. 1783).
40. ARA, v.H 50 (1784).
41. *Brieven Van Hogendorp*, I, 296 (21 Jan. 1784).

but he was not brought up in that school. I would suggest that here too his reading had its influence. Perhaps in his strict censure something can be heard of the discussion of the philosophes as to the value of luxury. It is possible that his view is influenced by Montesquieu and the physiocrates.[42] But he will not pursue it too rigidly. The excess of wealth is after all only made possible by the blessing of property.

All this investigation of social life has one end in view; what is its influence on the constitution of the State? Where does all this equality lead in government? Does property still play a part? And if not, what is the power that holds a free community together? Pondering such questions Gijsbert Karel investigates the working of democracy, visiting every executive meeting that he can. In Boston he attends a 'town-meeting', the typical New England representative body, but is disappointed by it.

> It struck me that this was a slow way to do things. That there was much misunderstanding and the Moderator must have great influence, that but few speak, that the most distinguished, equal though the places are, sit nearest the Moderator... and that there were few there, a hundred at most, still fewer of the best people.[43]

He was no more edified by the meeting of the legislative assembly of Massachusetts, where democracy already meant that 'Few speak. Few appear to understand all that is going on'. It is true that it remains a peaceable spectacle, but this leaves the critical young man only half-satisfied.

> On the whole I am as impressed by the calmness of the proceedings as I am unimpressed by the acuity of the members.[44]

In Philadelphia it is even worse, the Pennsylvania Assembly is

> worse than Boston, really bad, all talk and nothing concluded, confusion, Senate slow, sitting with hats on, smoking, walking about the chamber.[45]

Van Hogendorp is irritated by the lack of style and maintains that there is not even a real democracy, two or three people have the real power. In the Legislature of Massachusetts government offices are secretly shared out

> by ten or twenty of the leaders who put their heads together and then distribute notes to their supporters. The people seem not to realize that they have a right to these offices. Their attention is fixed on money.[46]

---

42. Feugère, *Précurseur*, 133.
43. ARA, v.H 54-d.
44. *Ibidem*, 50-b (6 Febr. 1784).
45. *Ibidem*, 54-e.
46. *Ibidem*, 50-b (1 Febr. 1784).

What is lacking in this democracy is a real authority, that is Van Hogendorp's conclusion. The lawgivers are slavish or corrupt or both and this is true even of the highest body, the Congress, whose members are on the whole not 'des hommes d'un mérite ou de talents distingués'. Most of them seldom come, everything goes slowly. Rich young men, stupid farmers and retired officers put up for election but true patriots are few and far between.[47]

The one way out of the chaos may be provided by the merchants, the new élite. Van Hogendorp may grumble about riches but deep down he believes that property alone can hold the State together. He hears from merchants that they do indeed want a stronger authority, that they are aiming at a 'Gentleman party', so one of them tells him.[48] In Philadelphia he has an interesting meeting with John Dickinson, one of the most important, but most conservative theoreticians of the revolution, now president of the Executive Council of Pennsylvania, who tells him that two parties are being formed. The people, who have evil in their minds, want no improvement in the Constitution, maintains Dickinson. 'The man became somewhat passionate', writes his Dutch visitor.[49] Party politics leads to emotion.

Indeed it is possible in Van Hogendorp's notes to be aware, so to speak, of the birth of the Federalist party. He sees how men with money unite, how one's fortune indeed determines one's political preference and how men who become rich change from democrat to aristocrat.[50] To J.C. van der Hoop, the advocate-fiscal of the Amsterdam Admiralty, who has asked him to report on the 'Prospects for Commerce' he declares what happens.

> Everywhere merchants assemble to devise means to obtain a say on commercial topics in Congress. The merchants are the most important residents; they are not taken in by pure government by the people and would like to see the Great Administrators more powerful, aware as they are of their influence, which always goes hand in hand with Riches. But the people glory in the power they have gained and will retain it as long as possible.[51]

His remarks rank the Dutch observer with such Federalist leaders as Alexander Hamilton (whom he met) and John Adams. Equality 'cannot survive as long as one human generation' he writes; inequality, according to Adams at the same time, is 'common to every people and can never be altered by any, because they (the differences) are founded in the constitution of nature'.[52]

---

47. *Brieven Van Hogendorp*, I, 345 (Apr. 1784).
48. ARA, v.H 54-d and e (Febr. 1784).
49. *Ibidem*, (20 Febr. 1784).
50. *Brieven Van Hogendorp*, I, 337 (26 March 1784).
51. ARA, v.H 36-10 l.
52. Cf. John R. Howe Jr., *The Changing Political Thought of John Adams* (Princeton, 1966) and Wood, *Creation*, ch. xiv, 567-92.

That government is thus founded on property is 'a principle of civilization'.[53] So America remains reasonably like Europe, the only difference being that there are after all more people in America who may aspire to government since although there is no absolute equality there are many more men of property than in the old world. This is something that Van Hogendorp admires; he appreciates it that hereditary differences are no longer decisive:

> Tout l'héritage de sagesse et de folie qui laisse a ces enfants ce premier Européen [*i.e.* the first colonist] se réduit par conséquent à l'idée de propriété, idée heureuse qui est la mère de toute civilisation.[54]

But the prophet of austerity, whose warnings as to luxury were so clear, cannot on the other hand so easily drop his distrust of the rich. If the aristocracy of the distinguished, which is 'une suite assurée du système mercantile', take authority into their hands, this may pose a threat to society. If the people must delegate their authority to the few, what guarantee is there against the possibility that 'ces représentants rentrent dans la classe des riches et deviennent de nouveaux oppresseurs'?[55] In the manner of Montesquieu Van Hogendorp pleads for a balance, achieved through the institution of a strong excutive power, a *tribunus plebis* like the stadhouder or the king of England.[56] Which leaves him, like John Adams and so many other contemporaries, with the much-admired example of the British constitution, the *imperium mixtum*.

But the authority problem had another particular aspect which interested him as a Dutchman. He was familiar with it from experience. The America of 1783, very loosely united by the 'Articles of Confederation' seemed to be about to repeat all the mistakes made by the old Dutch Republic. The central authority was not merely unable to control the people, it was not even in a position to hold the States together. This was owing to various factors, such as the conflicts of interests between the States and to the sheer extent of the country. Montesquieu's warning to America that democracy could exist only in a homogeneous society was taken up by many, Van Hogendorp included. Back in Holland, in audience with the stadhouder, he assented to the latter's eager supposition that America was too big to remain united and confirmed this once again in an extended report; the States would break this weak union to form two or three federative republics of the size of the European kingdoms.[57]

53. ARA, v.H 71-a, 'Tegen Price's Burgelijke Vrijheid' (spring 1785); cf. Verberne, *Gijsbert Karel*, 185-8.
54. *Brieven Van Hogendorp*, I, 397 (summer 1784).
55. *Ibidem*, 411.
56. *Ibidem*.
57. *Brieven Van Hogendorp*, I, 384, 387, 391 (13 July 1784). The idea that it was only the struggle against England that held the American colonies together is one that Van Hogendorp may have heard from such spokesmen as Robert Morris or Governor Morris, cf. M. Jensen,

This is not just based on observation, Van Hogendorp had already heard it before he left, from his vaguely informed uncle Duco van Haren, who had told him that the 'oil and wine growing' South could not remain one with the commercial North. 'Separation then. Country too big. He will yet see America divided into various free States and kingdoms'.[58]

The difference between North and South was something Van Hogendorp was able to see clearly. His itinerary, completely revised after the shipwreck, took him from Boston in New England to Annapolis in Maryland and from the latter town he made excursions further in the south, into Virginia. This gave him the opportunity to make comparisons, which he did sharply and powerfully. His sympathies lay with the Northerners. He may have complained about the frivolity of the Yankees, but it was in the South that he saw real indolence and indifference. Already from Philadelphia he had written to his father characterizing the New Englanders as 'les Hollandais de l'Amérique', and from Annapolis he remarked to his mother how much he had been struck there by the difference between rich and poor, freeman and slave. What a different world from that of the North, from New England 'où la fortune égale ne prodigue ses faveurs et ne refuse la subsistance à personne'.[59] To the prince of Orange he gave a fuller account of the difference, praising the development of the North, where the universities were certainly inferior to those of Europe but 'les écoles du peuple sont supérieures aux nôtres'.[60] In his 'Considérations sur la Révolution en Amérique', written in Breda in the summer of 1784, he returned to the topic of the high level of general development:

> dans les maisons des paysans, par toute la Nouvelle Angleterre, vous trouverez une bible, qu'on lit souvent, une collection des lois de l'État, dont on fait usage fréquent dans l'achat et la vente des terres, enfin vous y trouverez quelquefois les écrits de Locke, dont on a sucé les principes.[61]

How different from the South! There most of the land is in the hands of a few men and there is not even equality of opportunity.[62] Slavery is the great

---

The New Nation, A History of the United States during the Confederation 1781-1789 (New York, 1950) 66; cf. Wood, *Creation*, 499 and Andrew Burnaby, *Travels through the Middle Settlements in North America in the years 1759 and 1760*, 113 as to the problem of democracy in a large territory.
58. ARA, v.H 50.
59. *Brieven Van Hogendorp*, I, 332 (26 March 1784).
60. *Ibidem*, 387-80 (13 July 1784).
61. *Ibidem*, 397-8 (summer 1784).
62. *Ibidem*, 332-3 (26 March 1784).

curse of the whole region. It is a mediaeval society and it is striking that commerce is despised.[63]

Both for white men and black the system is disastrous. As for the first, it makes them indolent and even proud of it: 'On y dit fièrement: 'Un homme libre, un blanc ne travaille guère, à moins que, faute d'esclave, ce ne soit pour lui-même'.[64] If they are poor they are downtrodden and suspicious. Some few are educated but 'les hommes en général sont ignorants'. Jefferson, to whom Van Hogendorp showed this note on 'L'esclavage', largely agreed, but by this last remark he made a note in the margin: that might hold good for the slaves, but the poor whites, he says, have 'the first elements of learning equally with the poorer citizens of Massachusetts'.[65]

As for the negroes, what struck Van Hogendorp was their listless dependence, their lack of enjoyment of their work. However fine some Southerners might find the system (he meets a planter who explains to him the blessings of slavery but naturally cannot tolerate the Dutchman's liberal logic: 'Il se fâcha, s'impatienta et lorsque sa confusion fut complète je le quittai avec un regard du plus profond mépris'),[66] he has no faith in it. The negro you meet on your way, 'vous craint comme un de ses tyrans'.[67] It would be better to free them, but is that possible now that they have become so dependent? Some of them convert their fear into hatred and think that the whites who take all the fruits of their labours 'méritent d'être volés par eux, vol légitimé par la loi de talion'. But they have no prospects, they die in their misery.

When Van Hogendorp writes about the character of the blacks he accepts the stereotyped idea that they are children, but he does not accept that this is inherent, it is due to their position. Precisely because they are children, he reasons, they can safely be raised 'au rang d'hommes. libres'. Once they are elevated to the level of their fellow-citizens, 'ils prendront leurs sentiments, ils auront les mêmes intérêts, ils trouveront leur avantage dans la félicité publique'. This goes further than Jefferson, who accepts that the background of slavery is responsible for many shortcomings but deems nevertheless that negroes in general are inferior to whites in 'reason' and 'imagination', having at the most certain gifts of musicality. Our Dutch observer goes much further, in his unpublished notes on slavery arriving at a prophetic vision of the future, so

63. *Ibidem*, 390-1; cf. ARA, v.H 54-g.
64. *Brieven Van Hogendorp*, 313 (March 1784); cf. ARA, v.H 54-g.
65. In Van Hogendorp's papers two essays on slavery are to be found, the first ARA, v.H 36-10d, published in *Brieven Van Hogendorp*, I, 313-5 and in J. Boyd, ed. *The Papers of Thomas Jefferson*, VII (Princeton, 1953) 216-8; the second, entitled 'Nègres esclavage', in ARA, v.H 54-a.
66. *Brieven Van Hogendorp*, I, 313 (March 1784).
67. *Ibidem*, 333 (26 March 1784).

surprising and impressive that I cannot resist quoting from it here at some length. They must some time be freed, he says, but the great question is what will happen then:

> J'ai demandé: mais quoi, ci ces nègres acquièrrent des biensfonds, s'ils augmentent en nombre comme en richesses, si convaincus des avantages de l'éducation ils font instruire leurs enfants, si des générations futures s'avisent de demander l'entrée dans vos jurys, une voix dans vos élections, si une parti pour se fortifier par leur accession appuie leur demande, qui paroit juste, et si par ce moien ils obtiennent une place dans vos assemblées, quelle loi pour prévenir un mélange arrêtera le torrent, qu'est ce qui pourra séparer les genres.

These words give a clear picture of the future; this is precisely what was to happen, much later, in 1865. From the freeing of the slaves onwards the fear of integration did indeed determine the policy of many whites, while on the other hand the rise of the negro was in no small way attributable to political interest on the other side. But unfortunately our prophet does not follow up this line of thought, he seems in what follows to allow himself to be convinced that there is nothing to be feared. White spokesmen assure him that the negro is weaker and can never rise in society, 'qu'ils sont fidèles, humains, généreux, qu'ils ont le génie de la musique, mais que leur jugement est au dessous de la nôtre'. Once freed they would go under, just like the Indians surviving among the whites. Undoubtedly one of the whites who explained this to him was Jefferson.[68]

Van Hogendorp comments as fully on the red minority as on the black, naturally enough in that era of enthusiasm for the noble savage. But his remarks are based on comparatively little direct observation; only once did he meet a couple of perfectly tame indians in Connecticut, whom he asked: 'What is your nationality? Indian? What tribe? Indian. What is your religion? Jesus Christ is our Saviour. Do you pay them taxes? No'.[69] What might well be called a brief survey.

The rest of what he writes on the subject is part of the contemporary discussion and is borrowed from others. The admission 'Les sauvages sont plus intéressants que les nègres' is part of it, but on the whole Van Hogendorp does not accept the myth of the noble savage. He is too sensible and hears in America that the ideas of Buffon and De Pauw are mere fantasy. The indians are 'fidèles, bienfaisants, généreux', but incapable of looking after themselves and thus 'avec tout leur génie, leur éloquence, et leurs vertus' inferior to the whites.[70] Yes, he comes to the conclusion that it is now their simplicity, their

68. ARA, v.H 54-n; cf. T. Jefferson, *Notes on the State of Virginia* (Harper Torchbooks, 1964) 132-8 and D.B. Davis, *Was Thomas Jefferson an Authentic Enemy of Slavery?* (Oxford, 1970).
69. ARA, v.H 54-d (4 Febr. 1784).
70. *Brieven Van Hogendorp*, I, 339; on Van Hogendorp's reading of De Pauw cf. Verberne, *Gijsbert Karel*, 164-5.

purity, that puts them at a disadvantage. In an essay, 'Wilden' (savages) written on his return home, he collects his ideas, praising and criticizing simultaneously. This can be seen in their eloquence, which is so famous. They lack the capacity for abstraction,

> that is why their language is so picturesque. This shows that what we call thinking is very little practised by the indians, since they must constantly support their understanding with objects of sense.

Then they live in society and cultivate the land, 'a practice that stifles industry'. They are thus doomed to decline.

> as to whether they in their primitive state are happier than we, that is a matter for Him alone who without experiencing their feelings or ours yet knows them, for He has created them; but in no way for us who cannot judge the extent of the pleasure felt in the wild other than according to external manifestations which are deceptive.[71]

The decline of the indian is inevitable; in the West there is a future in store, 'un empire formidable, une Union à laquelle de nouveaux peuples, qui n'existent pas encore, accèderont dans la suite des temps'.[72] The whole history of mankind from trapping to civilization can be observed simultaneously.[73] A new kind of man is coming into being, with a 'caractère original', that is indeed not 'sublime', not a model for us, but out there in the wilderness has its place and can create a world empire. It is almost a 'frontier' theory that our Dutchman is here adumbrating.[74]

There was nothing from which the young man expected so much as from contact with the sages who governed the New World. He envisaged it as a kind of Plato's Republic. His first-class letters of recommendation would allow him to view it from close by.

> Over there the best letters of introduction, for instance from Franklin to Washington, Livingston, Morris, will give me access to the first in that land, where every one has taken his part in this great event, the first in wisdom and perhaps in virtue.[75]

Expectations as high as this were doomed to disappointment. It is true he writes from Boston of the 'steadfast Character' and 'unshakeable adherence

---

71. ARA, v.H 50.
72. *Brieven Van Hogendorp*, I, 333 (26 March 1784).
73. ARA, v.H 36-10f.
74. *Brieven Van Hogendorp*, 384-95 (summer 1784). One aspect of the frontier theory, the idea of the safety valve that keeps wages high through the shortage of manpower can be found in a letter to his brother Willem, 6. Dec. 1783, *ibidem*, 263 ff: 'The reason there are no factories here is the amount of a day's pay; day-workers are scarce and soon leave an employer to buy a few acres to the west and live independent'.
75. ARA, v.H 112.

to wise principles', of the leaders, but there is already a fly in the ointment, for this wisdom is simplicity, they have it 'because they are raised little above these (*i.e.*, the common people) in understanding'.[76]

When the young critic settles down to write character sketches of the wise leaders he has met, little of his high hope remains. He strips them with pedantic superiority, accurately and mercilessly. John Hancock, his cordial host, is 'un homme d'un caractère faible et d'une vanité extrême', Samuel Adams 'un caractère inquiet et turbulent', General Benjamin Lincoln, who had received him on his farm, a brave man who 'ne possède ni de grands talents, ni de goûts élevés'.[77] Governor Morris, the New York politician, comes off even worse; he has a good deal of talent but is vain and characterless.[78] It is vanity that Gijsbert Karel most censures, discovering it in many of those he meets. As the Persian couplet says:

What you say of another you say of yourself;
A jug will pour out nothing it does not hold.

But he is capable of appreciation. A few escape being guillotined by his pen. There is the generally praised secretary of the Congress, Charles Thomson who admittedly 'conçoit lentement' and is very meticulous, but whose character is 'doux, mais ferme et toujours égal'.[79] And there is the controversial Robert Morris, the great financier of the revolution, of whom his Dutch guest gives an attractive portrait, praising his industry and his character.[80]

Finally Van Hogendorp comes face to face with the highest in the land, Washington, Jefferson, Hamilton. He tells us little of the latter but much of the other two. With what longing did he set out on the journey to see the great Washington and once in America he asks again and again after the hero. He is warned that the general is rather reserved, but he judges that a fine trait in his character.[81]

The event forms so curious a contrast with the expectation as to give the effect of a sort of tragi-comedy. Armed with letters of recommendation from Franklin and Jefferson (Mr. de Hogendorff is the best-informed man of his age I have ever seen')[82] the young man approaches the shrine of Mount Vernon and as he sees it far off on its hill his heart thumps with excitement. But the

76. *Ibidem*, 54-d (22 Dec. 1783).
77. *Brieven Van Hogendorp*, I, 346 (Apr. 1784).
78. *Ibidem*, 349 (Apr. 1784).
79. *Ibidem*, 347-8; cf. Jensen, *New Nation*, 361-3.
80. ARA, v.H 36-10l; cf. *Brieven Van Hogendorp*, 348-9 and also J.C. Miller, *Triumph of Freedom 1775-1783* (Boston, 1948) 446-51 and Jensen, *New Nation*, 366-71.
81. ARA, v.H 54-d (31 Dec. 1783).
82. Boyd, *Papers Thomas Jefferson*, VII, 83-4 (6 Apr. 1784).

ensuing reception is cool, almost unfriendly. The general, evidently bored by the umpteenth curious visitor, shows not the slightest interest in him, does not respond to his opinionated questioning:

> Je tâchai d'expliquer au Général mes doutes sur la revenue des terres que le Congrès se propose de vendre. Il me comprit mal, ou ne me comprit pas. Il ne sut s'expliquer ni avec concision, ne avec élégance, ni avec facilité.

Gijsbert Karel is quite thrown into confusion, suddenly he is no longer the critical rational observer but a pure Romantic, a *Sturm-und-Drang* youngster.

> Cette scène à laquelle je m'attendais si peu, me plongea dans une profonde rêverie, et je fus prendre l'air pour me livrer à mes réflexions. Cent fois je répétai ce passage de Hamlet: 'Quel chef-d'œuvre que l'homme! Que sa raison est sublime, etc... et qu'est-ce à mes yeux que cette quintessence de poussière? — L'homme ne me plaît pas!' En effet j'étais brouillé avec le genre humain.[83]

When he calms down he concludes that his god has fallen, that Washington 'n'était pas un homme de génie, qu'il n'avait pas de grands talents'. Now he can be objective, he finds, and the riddle is solved: 'il n'y a plus de miracle, plus d'admiration'. He soon comes to a more general conclusion: it is not the hero who leads the multitude; on the contrary heroes are only the exponents of a greater movement.

> Je considère Washington comme l'instrument de l'indépendance, qui trouve sa source dans le génie des habitants, dans leur situation et dans celle des puissances de l'Europe.

He is a good man, brave, cool, but without much spirit or understanding and without ambition, which is also, typically enough, a shortcoming in Van Hogendorp's eyes.[84]

An interesting aspect of the criticism that the young man spouts in such measure is that he can call on a vital witness. In his papers can be found an essay entitled 'War', with a note added much later, when he was old. He had shown this piece he wrote on 11th May 1830

> to an authorized judge whose opinions are appended. That his name is erased is no doubt because I wanted to show the piece to one or more others. As far as I recall it was Colonel Hamilton, General Washington's adjutant, author of the outstanding journal *The Federalist* and finally secretary of State for Finance. I met no quicker wit nor opener character on my whole journey.

And indeed, in spite of the erasures in two places it is easy to read that it was Hamilton who had commented on Van Hogendorp's observations. On the latter's remarks on Washington's 'hidden unpopularity' Hamilton notes that

---

83. *Brieven Van Hogendorp*, I, 350. The passage is from *Hamlet* II, ii, 295-300.
84. *Brieven Van Hogendorp*, I, 351, 354-5 (Apr. 1784).

the commander-in-chief was popular because 'the gentlemen of his family' had agreed

> to conceal his faults and to extoll his merit. His insensibility makes him unpartial. His size commands respect to the vulgar. He chose the best Officers to be his aid de camps. He appeared seldom. When the last year of the war he did appear, and acted more himself from want of 50 able officers, he decreased a little in popularity.

When one knows that Hamilton himself was Washington's chief adjutant but in the penultimate year of the war came into conflict with his commander and resigned, the venom here expressed is particularly evident in all its subjectiveness. But Van Hogendorp accepted it enthusiastically as confirmation of his own iconoclasm.[85]

There is another interesting element in his sharp reaction to the general's Olympian calm. The fact is that he measures Washington against his own weakness, transposed into over-evaluation of himself. But what to some extent compensates for this is that he himself is sometimes aware of it. Less than a month before he went to Mount Vernon, in Philadelphia on 17th March 1784, he made a note characteristic of the intensity of his self-concern, forecasting with astonishing clarity what he was to experience a couple of weeks later:

> That I am at last acquiring confidence in my own powers is an unspeakable comfort to me. Only contact with many men can give me this. I found myself too weak, too ignorant. Now I see others are weaker, more ignorant and, oh, infinite privilege! I am young, I am not yet standing still and I am burning with desire to progress quickly.
> This desire has been a good deal purified by experience. It has often led me astray. For I was always over-eager to display my knowledge, to please those I esteemed to do what I did passionately. Then it would happen that were my expectations never so slightly deceived, because I felt myself misjudged or insufficiently noticed, the upshot would be dejection or even embitterment which set me back considerably.

A scenario for his historic meeting with 'un des plus grands hommes que la nature ait formé'.[86]

Not Washington but Jefferson was the American statesman on whom Van Hogendorp lavished all his admiration. This may seem strange at first sight, since we know in retrospect how far the political views of the two were to diverge but at the moment under consideration, with the young Dutchman still open and unformed, it was not so extraordinary. They had certain things in common. Jefferson shared Van Hogendorp's unquenchable thirst for knowledge, having if possible an even greater passion for anything worth knowing on any topic, for facts and figures. Shortly after Gijsbert Karel arrived in

---

85. ARA, v.H 36; cf. J.C. Miller, *Alexander Hamilton, Portrait in Paradox* (New York, 1959) for the really ambivalent attitude of Hamilton to Washington (35) and the conflict between the two (63-79).
86. ARA, v.H 50-a; *Brieven Van Hogendorp*, I, 350.

Annapolis they had become friends, meeting frequently and discussing all their common interests. The account of all this talk on paper fills page after page in the Van Hogendorp archives.[87] More, a mutual understanding grew. Jefferson's earnestness finds an echo in the soul of his young guest when he writes 'que son esprit, nourri de grandes idées, répugnait au babil des oisifs'. He thinks highly of the style and the principles of the Declaration of Independence. He is struck by the shyness, timidity almost, of his older friend. 'Il a la timidité du vrai mérite, qui gène dans le commencement, et qui éloigne de lui ceux qui recherchent sa connaissance'. This conforms perfectly with other descriptions of Jefferson. Of course Van Hogendorp would not have been Van Hogendorp if he had had no comment to make. There is always something that he knows better than his admired friend who 'parait ne pas avoir les idées les plus claires au sujet du commerce considéré relativement à la population'.[88]

But he is truly happy that Jefferson wants to be his friend, he writes him all-too-flattering letters about his 'love and esteem', elucidating somewhat reserved answers from the older man. No doubt it hurt him that the young man expressed what he preferred to keep veiled, writing to him about his grief (Jefferson was recently widowed) so openly: 'One evening I talked of love, and then I perceived you could still feel and express your feelings'.[89] He wrote back that the 'sentiments' that his correspondent expressed were 'too partial': 'Your observation on the situation of my mind is not without foundation; yet I had hoped it was unperceived'. But he does go so far as to invite a regular exchange of letters, he values the young Dutchman's thirst for knowledge: 'your capacity to acquire it, your dispositions to apply it to the good of mankind give your country much to hope from the continuance of your life'.[90]

Gijsbert Karel must have read these lines with glowing cheeks. This was the recognition he had sought. In his reply a fortnight later he was in an ecstasy of gratitude: 'The esteem of a man of Your character is a great reward of my endeavours to deserve it, but his affection makes me happy'. At the end of the letter he again opens his heart, shyly urging the use of Christian names, writing under his signature, G.K. van Hogendorp, 'K. means Karel, that is Charles, which signature if you will accept it I shall employ in the future'.[91]

Not very much was to come, however, of the 'correspondence for the remainder of our life'. And that in spite of the fact that Jefferson came that year to Europe, as ambassador in Paris. From there he wrote once or twice,

87. Boyd, *Papers Thomas Jefferson*, VII, 207-21.
88. *Brieven Van Hogendorp*, I, 346-7 (Apr. 1784).
89. Boyd, *Papers Thomas Jefferson*, VII,80-3 (6 Apr. 1784).
90. *Ibidem*, 208-9 (4 May 1784).
91. *Ibidem*, 283-4 (22 May 1784).

no longer quite au fait: 'if I recollect rightly you are a native of Holland, but an officer in the Austrian service'.[92] Van Hogendorp hastened to set this right and there are a few more occasional letters. Jefferson even sent his *Notes on Virginia* to his friend and more data are exchanged relating to politics and finance. In the last letter, dated 25 August 1786, Jefferson helps his Dutch correspondent to information for his thesis in Leiden dealing with the finances of the federal State.[93] And that is that. They seem to have completely forgotten each other. When the American arrived in Holland in the Spring of 1788, and visited Rotterdam, he made no effort to look up his Dutch acquaintance, probably did not even know that he was *pensionaris* (Town clerk) of that very city. And on the other side there is in Van Hogendorp's papers no further trace of Jefferson's presence. The friendship had completely faded away, for good.

Gijsbert Karel's return voyage in the summer of 1784 was as successful as his outward voyage had been disastrous. On June 4 he took ship in New York and on June 25 he was in Falmouth. He stayed for a short time in London where he heard Pitt, 24 years old, speaking in the House of Commons, and was full of naif admiration. In July he was home. There he had the prince of Orange's permission to take a month's rest, a real need after so many impressions, even though his ambitious mother was anxious lest he should have been contaminated by 'indolence Américaine'.[94] What he had to do, he believed, was to set his papers in order and attempt some sort of summing-up of his experiences. The dominant note was that of disappointment. Going through his notes he found a piece written before his departure, sparkling with hope of seeing the new State coming into being, in which he had even played with the thought of taking instruction from 'Washington and his school for heroes'. Now he wrote an accompanying afterword, clearly formulating his disillusionment.

> I can now affirm that I found America different from what I had expected and that the word liberty has acquired another meaning for me. In America itself I have had my views on America changed and that is perhaps more useful than finding everything as I had hoped. In America, men in the same circumstances are no more virtuous than here, but the circumstances are up to now better. American Liberty has had a bad influence on our own. This much I have learned and that is better than seeing a heaven on earth.[95]

92. *Ibidem*, 545-6 (20 Nov. 1784).
93. The further exchange of letters: *ibidem*, 609-10; VIII (195) 324-5, 501-5, 631-4; X (195) 190-1, 297-300.
94. ARA, v.H 81-f (12 July 1784).
95. *Brieven Van Hogendorp*, I, 418-20 (22 June 1786).

The European ambivalence towards America is fascinatingly embodied by Van Hogendorp, it would seem. In his experiences can be seen a pattern often to be found : initial expectations transformed into disappointment and censure. The Dutch historian Presser, in the introduction to his book *Amerika*, has made fun of the European tendency to condemn everything American, quoting the German philosopher Count Keyserling who in a famous book on the Americans wrote: 'Beinahe alle ihre Problemen sehen sie bis heute falsch', to which Presser adds 'Why not put it more shortly — I, Keyserling, see them all clearly'?[96] Among Van Hogendorp's papers lie a couple of notes that remind us of this, two little leaves, one covered with: 'Advantages of America. The American View', the other with: 'Disadvantages of America. My view'. They were written while he was still in the New World itself, in Philadelphia on 1-2 March 1784, and make up a good summary of his ideas. The Americans believe in their isolation, their simplicity, their liberty, but he sees the jealousy of the States, the North's lack of natural resources, the dependence on Europe in taste and thus in industry, again the indolence, the 'Natural Distaste for Work among the settlers' and finally the 'Tyranny in the Southern States of a few masters over many negroes'.[97]

But in the end he does not bog down in criticism. In an almost Hegelian way the thesis of hope and antithesis of disappointment are followed by the synthesis of appreciation. This too is a pattern that repeats itself. But as far as Van Hogendorp is concerned it is dependent on what actually happened in America. The acceptance there in 1787 of a new constitution with a strong central authority was a striking fulfilment of hopes he had scarcely dared to entertain. And when in France a revolution much more savage than the American broke out, he could not refrain from comparison. In the years 1792-3 he wrote various long but never published essays on these topics. In one of these essays, entitled 'Gelijkheid der menschen (door Pieter Paulus) weerlegd'[98] (Equality of Man (by Pieter Paulus) Refuted) he turns against egalitarian ideals, calling America to witness. Every form of government, he writes, is dependent on the social circumstances. In America there is more equality because property is more widely distributed. But even this is not complete equality. I am in a position to know, he asserts, I 'spent seven months among Americans in the heart of the country, from Boston to Alexandria'. He is enthusiastic about the new constitution, which has created a balance, so that the 'supreme power is in a certain sense distributed among the settlers in

96. J. Presser, *Amerika, Van kolonie tot wereldmacht* (Amsterdam, 1949) viii.
97. ARA, v.H 36-10.
98. *Ibidem*, 71.

general, the men of property in particular and the wisdom and virtue of one'. As regards the theory of equality,

> North America has known this theory and rejected it. It was as incapable of taking root there as anywhere else. It remained in the speculative brains of eccentric philosophers or in their long-forgotten pamphlets. But the people of North America, that wise and good nation, for morally they are superior to any people in Europe, that nation has built on other foundations than the chimerical theory of equality.

It almost seems as though Van Hogendorp is making a plea for the Federalist party, his ideas are so close to those of Hamilton and Adams. It is with great satisfaction that he reports how Gênet has failed and Paine's influence is over.[99] But he goes still further. What is acceptable in North America will not do in Europe, where the people are 'differently disposed'. In America the vastness of the territory (now invoked as a positive, cohesive factor) has led to a 'generality of goods and chattels' unknown in Europe. We with our great differences can never be as free as the Americans. How glaringly events in France contrast with the American experience. In America during the Revolution there was no need of force:

> In the war the community of purpose was so great that all the requests of Congress to the different States had as much force as orders elsewhere — and more — and that the States could obtain anything from the settlers without applying any pressure; in France the reverse is true — it is the guillotine that inspires the service of the Fatherland and the Gouvernement Révolutionaire takes the place of community of purpose. In America the community of purpose came to an end only after the war, so that there was a need for a stronger authority, now fortunately provided by the constitution, not abstract but a properly constituted Representation of persons and properties, with an outstanding Head.

Here we find a different Gijsbert Karel, more mature, full of assurance, as can be seen from his now firm and flowing handwriting. And heard in the powerful tone, clear and definite, of his argument. He concludes roundly: equality does not exist, cannot exist, 'unless every citizen, of his own volition did what was good, without prescription of law or pressure of Authority', but this is impossible 'as long as men are not angels, that is, as long as men are men'.

This whole argument makes Van Hogendorp an early representative in Europe of a new vision of America, in which the constitution is not the logical consequence of the revolution but on the contrary a reaction against it. And with this knowledge he is able to transform his own negative impressions into positive appreciation, the first Dutchman to defend America, the idol of the

---

99. Gênet was the French representative who came to America in April 1793 and there began to launch privateers against England and in general to campaign for a more democratic pro-French attitude. The American government requested his withdrawal but refused to relinquish him when shortly afterwards Jacobin leadership asked for his arrest.

progressives, from the conservative point of view. His admiration is so great precisely because the Americans are following the British example, are not unique, not a new example, but traditional. Among Van Hogendorp's writings of 1793 is an essay on 'Omwendingen' (Revolutions) with a special section on the revolution in North America,[100] in which he comes to the conclusion that

> after they had broken with Britain they instituted a system of government based on the same principles and diverging from it only in so far as was demanded by local conditions and as the youth of the people admitted of improvement.

The whole essay constitutes a remarkably objective survey of the origins of the American Revolution, with as much understanding of England's critical financial position after 1763 as of America's grievances. Once more he praises the constitution as the crowning work, for gratitude is due to 'the moral nature of the people'. That people is now extolled, they are

> more enlightened than in Europe, they speak a better language, almost without dialects, write and read well in general, understand the newspapers, are quick in arithmetic and apply their understanding to all kinds of subjects.

He draws on his old observations to judge American education and the general standard of development with 'in every farmhouse... a Bible, a code of law, perhaps the works of Locke'. All is forgiven and forgotten. What he once wrote about New England apparently now holds good for the country as a whole. There is no end to his praise. Wealth, peace and security reign and if there are shortcomings the good far outweighs the bad.

As regards the future, however, Van Hogendorp is not quite so sanguine. He has evidently heard of more democratic tendencies (on the part of his friend Jefferson's Republican party) and writes anxiously: 'There is then a worm already gnawing at this flourishing State and liberty and equality become the cry, to repay the wise liberty of that prosperous land'. So far, things are going well, but what happens when the country is full? What he then writes is once more truly prophetic, albeit merciless.

> Whereas the number of the people increases daily, land will eventually become scarce, it will become more and more difficult to make a living, there will be more exploitation of one man by another, the poor will have to work harder, mutual dependence will increase, money will be accumulated more in particular piles instead of being generally distributed as it is now. Then there will come into existence a class of men such as we have, forced to spend every hour of the day in heavy labour, to make their own children work with them, with no time to spare for them or for themselves to acquire or to retain knowledge, but from father to son, the scope of understanding, the impression of religion, the good traditions of life will more and more decay until they form that pitiable section of the people known as the dregs of society.

100.   ARA, v.H 71.

What the writer fears above all else is that this group may be bought by a party and made use of. 'The rule of right and reason will then give way to that of might and majority'. And men may then call themselves lucky if one party does not

> convince the commonalty that they are the true people, the true nation, that they must rule and thus through the commonalty overthrow all authority and all the natural rulers. Then all is up not only with the State but with society as a whole.

There is an element of bitterness, of fatalism, in Van Hogendorp's conclusions. He praises the new nation because it is not completely democratic, he expects great prosperity, which will be a blessing to Europe as well. He has no fear for the future. What contemporaries of his already feared, that America would become so great a power as to threaten or at any rate to overshadow Europe, holds no terrors for him. To the great discussion as to whether America was to be a blessing or a curse for the old world he contributes the wise words: 'ceux qui disent que ce nouvel empire va nous dévorer, devraient penser que pendant plusieurs siècles il nous doit nourrir'.[101] No, factually, practically viewed, there are chances and possibilities.

But Van Hogendorp is, almost in spite of himself, a philosophe as well, even if a concrete one. He writes so appealingly in a letter from Boston to his mother: 'Rien ne me donne plus de satisfaction que d'observer la marche des hommes à travers ce monde tour à tour horrible, aimable, ridicule et sublime'.[102] And with this attitude no paradise is to be found on earth and America itself, however reasonable in its beginnings, will have its part to play in mankind's history of disaster and folly.

What he learned from his sojourn in America was precisely

> that I have arrived at the proper conception of liberty in the civil State and am now for ever guarded against being led astray through idle tales to nonexistent chimeras ending in anarchy and arbitrary authority.[103]

It is in this undoubted negative sense that he is thankful for the opportunity offered him. But one positive element is certainly there, one he has in common with many travellers in the new world, one he expresses as follows: 'I dwell with some pleasure on this material, since I am so happy to express my feeling of respect and affection for that hospitable and generous nation which so cordially entertained me'.[104]

---

101. *Brieven Van Hogendorp*, I, 413.
102. *Ibidem*, 284 (17 Dec. 1783).
103. That is certainly not quite the same as R.R. Palmer concludes in *The Age of Democratic Revolution* (2 vols., Princeton, 1959) I, 335, as to Van Hogendorp's trip: 'he thought of Americans as rustics from whom nothing in politics could be learned'.
104. ARA, v.H 71.

Some Remarks on the Cultivation System in Java

C. FASSEUR

There is probably no other topic in Dutch colonial historiography which has been the subject of so much written discussion as has the cultivation system in Java. The importance of the literature on the topic, however, is not proportionate to its extent.

In the first place the literature is strongly influenced by the political struggle in the Netherlands which preceded the liquidation of the cultivation system. If the system was praised by the conservatives it was condemned by the liberals. The mainstay of the system was government pressure — the obligation laid on the Javanese people to grow particular export crops such as coffee, sugar-cane, indigo, tobacco and tea, these being turned into money at the auctions of the Nederlandsche Handel-Maatschappij (Netherlands Trading Company) for the benefit of the treasury. For every nineteenth-century liberal a compulsory system of this kind was necessarily a thorn in the flesh. When at long last the system collapsed under the liberal onslaught this disapproval was general in literature.[1] The cultivation system was moreover an essential instrument in the pursuit of a policy of economic exploitation which made of the years from 1830 to 1850, in the words of Gonggrijp 'the most shameful pages in our colonial history'.[2] No wonder the system finds no favour with the majority of writers. To mention only the best-known of them: Van Soest,[3] Pierson,[4] Clive Day,[5] Colenbrander,[6] Stapel,[7] Gonggrijp,[8] they have given a verdict against the cultivation system and often judged and condemned it in emotional terms.

1. Cf. W.Ph. Coolhaas, review of Clive Day, *The Dutch in Java*, ed. by J. Bastin (1966), *Tijdschrift voor geschiedenis*, LXXX (Groningen, 1967) 541.
2. G. Gonggrijp, *Schets ener economische geschiedenis van Indonesië* (4th edition; Haarlem, 1957) 82.
3. G.H. van Soest, *Geschiedenis van het kultuurstelsel* (3 vols, Rotterdam, 1869-71).
4. N.G. Pierson, *Het kultuurstelsel* (Amsterdam, 1868).
5. C. Day, *The Policy and Administration of the Dutch in Java* (Kuala Lumpur, 1966).
6. H.T. Colenbrander, *Koloniale Geschiedenis*, III (The Hague, 1926).
7. F.W. Stapel, *Geschiedenis van Nederlandsch Indie*, V (Amsterdam, 1940).
8. Gonggrijp, *Schets*.

In certain dissertations written before the Second World War under the guidance of Gerretson there can be found a belated conservative reaction against this liberal criticism, but the one-sidedness of this reaction makes it equally untrustworthy. Gerretson boldly characterized the cultivation system in 1938 as 'the greatest benefit ever conferred by the Dutch on their East Indian possessions'.[9] Coolhaas too appears for the defence of the system, for instance in the tenth volume, published in 1955, of the *Algemene Geschiedenis der Nederlanden*. Nevertheless he would seem to have been somewhat hesitant in his quest for arguments to justify the system, considering his remark that 'it is not yet possible to provide conclusive arguments demonstrating the importance of the system'.[10]

There is another reason for the out-of-date impression made by the literature on the cultivation system. Research into archives and other source material was for a long time no more than minimal. Until some years ago virtually all the relevant literature was based on material assembled from the colonial office archives by S. van Deventer, an East Indian civil servant on home leave, in his *Bijdragen tot de kennis van het landelijk stelsel op Java* (contributions to the understanding of the landrent system in Java).[11]

The *Bijdragen* appeared under the auspices of and by order of the liberal colonial minister, I. D. Fransen van de Putte. They provided ammunition used by the minister in his campaign against the conservative protectors of the cultivation system. Van Deventer regarded himself as the 'instrument' chosen by the minister to deal the cultivation system its 'death-blow'.[12] When Fransen van de Putte resigned in 1866, Van Deventer was also obliged to cease his activity. The tempo at which he had worked until then may be gauged from the fact that within a single month (May 1866) the third and last volume of the *Bijdragen* was compiled and printed.[13]

Although it is thus difficult to see Van Deventer's work as objective or unprejudiced, it nevertheless provided the basis for all serious publications on the cultivation system for a whole century. It was relatively late before the archives of the colonial office, which Van Deventer had used as his source, were transferred to the Algemeen Rijksarchief and thus became public. For the records from 1830-50 this was done in 1929 and with those for 1850-1900

9. C. Gerretson, *et alii*, *De sociaal-economische invloed van Nederlandsch-Indië op Nederland* (Wageningen, 1938) 18.
10. W.Ph. Coolhaas, 'Nederlands-Indië van 1830 tot 1887', *Algemene Geschiedenis der Nederlanden*, X (Utrecht, 1955) 240.
11. S. van Deventer, *Bijdragen tot de kennis van het landelijk stelsel op Java* (3 vols, Zaltbommel, 1865-6).
12. S. van Deventer to I.D. Fransen van de Putte, 8-22 December 1867. Private archives Fransen van de Putte, in the possession of Mr W.A. Storm de Grave at Huis ter Heide (Utrecht).
13. *Ibidem.*

not until about 1950. The dissertations of Roosenschoon[14] and Reinsma[15] on the cultivation system, which appeared in 1945 and 1955, were still entirely based on source material already published and had very much the character of a study of the literature.[16]

Only the American historian Robert van Niel, in several valuable studies published in various periodicals and difficult to come by in Dutch libraries has made any systematic use of the almost incalculable amount of material still waiting to be dealt with in the Algemeen Rijksarchief.[17] The importance of this material for a fresh investigation of the cultivation system is clearly demonstrated by the so-called cultivation reports, in which the office of cultivations in Batavia during its existence from 1832 to 1866 gave from year to year a detailed survey of the results of the cultivation system for the information of the East Indian administration and for the colonial minister.[18] Although Van Soest in his *Geschiedenis van het kultuurstelsel* (history of the cultivation system) had focussed attention on the importance of these reports it was as late as 1959 that they were rediscovered in the records of the colonial office.[19]

Another important source is the 'semi-official' correspondence exchanged between minister and governor general from 1840-61. All kinds of matters of current interest are dealt with in these monthly letters, which thus provide a valuable key to the conduct of the colonial administration during these years.

The development of western estate agriculture in Java can be traced in detail in the so-called *staten van cultuurinrichtingen*, the surveys of enterprise activities drawn up every year from 1844 onwards by the office of cultivations.

Finally, attention must be drawn to another important source of data on the cultivation system: the Parliamentary Reports, in particular the reports printed for the benefit of the members of the States General, not included in the official *Verslag der Handelingen* (report of proceedings), owing to their bulk or to their confidential nature. To the best of my knowledge there is only one surviving collection of these 'white papers', which with time have dropped

---

14.   J.M. Roosenschoon, 'De westerse cultures op Java vóór 1870' (doctoral thesis, Utrecht, 1945, unpublished; cyclostyled copies in the university libraries at Leiden and Utrecht and in the Koninklijk Instituut voor de Tropen, Amsterdam).

15.   R. Reinsma, *Het verval van het cultuurstelsel* (The Hague, 1955).

16.   Roosenschoon's unpublished study of the cultivation system was not known to Reinsma.

17.   See in particular: R. van Niel, 'Measurement of Change under the Cultivation System in Java, 1837-1851', *Indonesia*, XIV (Ithaca, Oct. 1972) 89-109.

18.   The cultivation reports after 1851 were not found in the records present in the Netherlands. In so far as they were separately compiled, however, their content is dealt with in the yearly colonial report to the States General laid down by the Constitution of 1848.

19.   Cf. Reinsma, 'De kultuurprocenten in de praktijk en in de ogen der tijdgenoten', *Tijdschrift voor geschiedenis*, LXXII (1959) 57-83. Statistical material from the cultivation reports is further dealt with in P. Creutzberg, *Changing Economy in Indonesia*, I, *Indonesia's Export Crops, 1816-1940* (The Hague, 1975).

into oblivion, and that collection is to be found in the library of the Second Chamber of the States General.[20]

CROP PAYMENT AND LAND-RENT

Van Soest in his *Geschiedenis van het Kultuurstelsel* more than a century ago maintained that there would be no difficulty in dealing with the subject: 'The history ... of the cultivation system covers a modern period which leaves no dark or doubtful points to be cleared up'.[21]

The extent to which he here missed the mark can be seen from the obstinate misconceptions that there have been over a quite essential part of the cultivation system, the payment received by the Javanese themselves for the work they did.

Van den Bosch in his well-known 'Zakelijke Extracten', which appeared in the *Indisch Staatsblad* in 1834,[22] sums up the basic principles of the cultivation system as follows: A *desa* (village) which sets apart 1/5 of its rice fields for the cultivation of government crops — this refers in particular to sugar and indigo[23] — shall be excused from payment of the land-rent. Moreover this *desa* shall receive the difference between the greater worth at taxation of the crop and the land-rent. Finally in the event of crop failure the Javanese are to be indemnified by the government in so far as they themselves are not responsible for the loss.

In this concept the people's recompense for their services to the cultivation system thus lay primarily in their immunity from land-rent. This land-rent was, as is well-known, a duty on the rice crop paid by the *desa* as a whole. How payment was distributed among the villagers was a question for them and the *desa* headman, a question in which the Dutch authorities did not intervene. As a standard it was taken, as laid down by Raffles, who had introduced this land-rent, that the average rent should amount to 2/5 of the market value of the rice crop. The authorities had however no reliable data as to the extent of, or the productivity of the taxable ground. Tentative efforts to begin the gigantic task of registering and classifying the Java rice fields soon had to be abandoned owing to the lack of staff and of appropriate means.

20. For further description of the source material mentioned above, cf. C. Fasseur, *Kultuurstelsel en koloniale baten. De Nederlandse exploitatie van Java 1840-1860 (The Cultivation System and Colonial Profits. The Dutch Economic Exploitation of Java 1840-1860)* (Leiden, 1975).
21. Van Soest, *Geschiedenis kultuurstelsel*, II, ix.
22. 'Staatsblad van Nederlandsch Indie', 1834, no. 22, in: *Staatsblad van Nederlandsch Indië*, I, 1816-1845 (Zaltbommel: J. Norman en zoon, 1847).
23. Coffee was grown on land not used for other cultivations.

The advantage derived by the Javanese from the cultivation system was thus that on paper — and no paper was more forbearing than that of the *Indisch Staatsblad* — they need cede no more than 1/5 of their *sawas* (rice fields) with a more or less constant work contribution (assessed at 66 days work per year) to be immune from land-rent.

The *Zakelijke Extracten* with their splendid promises were gratefully taken up by liberal critics of the cultivation system as a measure of Van den Bosch's unreliability. 'Almost absurd is their insincerity' is Gonggrijp's judgment.[24] Was this condemnation always justified? It is true that there was a world of difference between the cultivation system in practice and the picture given by Van den Bosch. The Dutch government did not feel bound to adhere to the principle that a *desa* need plant no more than 1/5 of its *sawas* with crops for the European market, though there is some excuse for them in that concentration of a particular crop was unavoidable in cases such as sugar and indigo, where the harvested crop was destined for factory processing. Industrial efficiency required that these factories should operate on a reasonably large scale. Thus the number of sugar factories processing cane planted under government orders was never after 1836 more than a hundred or so. Nor were there ever very many Dutch officials available to oversee the planting (a task which it was felt should not be left to the factory-owner). As late as 1860 the supervision of the government crops throughout the whole of Java was in the hands of some 90 controllers, who had many other duties to carry out in addition to this.[25] This fact too was a reason to prefer crop planting concentrated in a small area which was easier to control than patches of crops spread over a large area.

The promise that in the case of crop failure the government would bear the loss was never kept either. It was in fact impossible to keep since the government derived its revenue largely from the sale of produce grown under the cultivation system. Crop failure, unless very much localized, was thus inevitably in itself a considerable loss for the government, let alone any notion that the government might over and above that indemnify the peasants. Moreover, the idea of crop insurance, with the risk borne by the government, was quite at variance with the spirit of the time.

And finally, as regards exemption from land-rent, the idea of paying the peasants out of a closed purse proved impossible to carry out in practice, leading to very inequitable results even for the Javanese themselves.[26] It would

---

24. Gonggrijp, *Schets*, 93.
25. Figures taken from the *Almanak van Nederlandsch-Indië* (Batavia, 1860). There were a further 100 or so 'European' supervisors employed (non-officials) but principally for the minor crops.
26. For a summary of the objections to exemption from land-rent: *Bijlagen tot het Verslag der*

happen that a *desa* with a high land-rent assessment would be exempted although it took less part in the cultivation than a *desa* that owned comparatively little land and thus came low in the tax scale. The cultivation system was in any case not so much a fixed burden on the land as a due exacted in labour. In 1850, for instance, as appears from the cultivation reports, some 20 per cent of the population in the residencies of Java where the system had been introduced were employed in sugar or indigo cultivation, while no more than 4 per cent of productive ground was set aside for these crops.[27] Even within the *desa* injustices might arise, when *desa* members who owned no fields and thus made no contribution to land-rent were pressed into labour in the sugar-cane fields. Exemption from land-rent, moreover, proved insufficient stimulus to adequate care for the crops. That incentive was there only when the Javanese peasants were offered payment proportionate to the quantity and quality of the crop.

Quite early therefore — in any case from 1836 — there was a general rule (except in the Central Javanese residencies of Madiun and Kediri and a few other smaller administrative areas) that the local population employed in the cultivation system should receive a separate crop payment for produce delivered (any work in sugar factories and the like was paid separately) while land-rent was to be paid as before the introduction of the cultivation system.[28] From the cultivation reports it is evident that the crop payments were considerably greater than the amount collected in land-rent. See Appendix I, which gives a survey of the gross assessment in land-rent in the period 1836-60 and the crop payments made for the three most important products, coffee, sugar-cane and indigo.

There can be no doubt that a considerable proportion of the crop payment never reached the individuals to whom it was due but disappeared into the pockets of coffee-warehouse employees, headmen of the *desas*, dishonest officials and the like. In 1850 the director of cultivation, S.D. Schiff, during a tour of duty through Java, set up an inquiry into the way in which crop payments were made.[29] He was obliged to conclude that payment depended completely on 'the whim of the officials' and might consequently be differently

Handelingen van de Tweede Kamer der Staten-Generaal 1862-1863 (The Hague, 1863) 348[34]. Cf. D.H. Burger, *De ontsluiting van Java's binnenland voor het wereldverkeer* (Wageningen, 1939) 137-8; *idem, Sociologisch-economische geschiedenis van Indonesia*, I (Wageningen, 1975).

27. Fasseur, *Kultuurstelsel*, 16. For the year 1840 the figures were 25 and 6% respectively.

28. See the government decree of 14th July 1837, no. 4, cited by Van Deventer, *Bijdragen*, III, 73. In Madiun and Kediri the exemption from land-rent was continued and in addition the population received a small reimbursement for the products they provided. This atypical state of affairs lasted until 1859.

29. Report of 26th August 1851, no. 2809/12, appendix to government decree of 15th October 1851, no. 4. A copy of this report, to be found in the Arsip Nasional in Jakarta, was made available to me by Mr. J. Erkelens.

carried out even in different *afdelingen* (divisions) of the same residency. Thus payment in Besuki, in contravention of the regulations, was carried out by *desas*, *i.e.* to all peasants at the same time, except for one division where the controller had introduced individual payment. In Pasuruan payment to individuals was carried out according to distribution lists on which each peasant engaged in cultivation was mentioned by name. Where the transport of the great quantities of cash needed for crop payments was a difficulty, however, the peasants had to come to the capital of their division to receive the money due to them. In Surabaya the land-rent owed by the *desas* was settled with the crop payment, although this had been forbidden in 1837. In the residency of Rembang, finally, payment of the money earned in sugar cultivation was carried out irregularly, either to individuals (in the division of Bojonegoro) or by *desa* (division of Tuban).

In 1851, therefore, the government brought out new ordinances which laid down that crop payments for sugar, indigo and tobacco were to be made from then on in all parts of Java before the *assistent-resident* (deputy resident) or the controller, in the presence of the *regent* (a Javanese high-up civil servant) and the district head, to each planter in person, without any deductions or other charges connected with land-rent and wherever possible on the basis of lists giving the name of every man engaged in cultivation.[30]

Notwithstanding the often irregular payment system in which the reality did not always correspond with the picture evoked by the cultivation reports, it may be taken for granted that the government crop payments represented an important source of income for the Javanese people and that in relation to the land-rent the government crops brought them a certain profit. Thus Van den Bosch's promise in the 'Zakelijke Extracten' is as far as this goes a good deal less absurd than Gonggrijp assumes.

It is remarkable that in the literature on the cultivation system so little attention has been devoted to the crop payment and its important influence on the further development of the Javanese money economy. Commentators have not been able to take their eyes off the *Zakelijke Extracten* in which, as we have said, there is no mention of a specific crop payment. This has given rise to the obstinate misconception that the cultivation system was simply a new burden laid on the Javanese people in addition to the land-rent, without any recompense worth mentioning being given for the work of cultivation. This misconception may be illustrated by Colenbrander's outcry: 'Most outra-

---

30. Government decree of 15th October 1851, no. 4, 'Staatsblad van Nederlandsch Indië', 1851 no. 53, in: *Staatsblad van Nederlandsch Indië*, II, *1846-1860* (Zaltbommel, 1852). There was no need to make particular regulations for those growing coffee, since they were paid on delivery of the coffee at the warehouses, every grower delivering his own. The scope for cheating when weighing the coffee gave employees the opportunity to enrich themselves at the people's expense.

geous of all: land-rent is still exacted from the villagers subject to compulsory cultivation service'![31] Gonggrijp too mentions the 'double load' of cultivation service and land-rent laid on the people contrary to the promises made to them.[32] The same misunderstanding may be found in Wertheim in the 1959 edition of *Indonesian Society in Transition*, where he remarks: 'The work had to be performed without pay'![33] Only work in the sugar factories and the transport of sugar-cane is supposed to have been paid.

A question these writers failed to answer, however, was how in spite of the double burden of cultivation service and land-rent the consumption of such commodities as linen and salt rose so considerably after 1830.[34] Nor do they explain how the land-rent throughout this period could be fixed higher almost every year (see Appendix I).

Gonggrijp is pleased to assume that only the land set apart for the government crops was exempted from land-rent.[35] He evidently relies on an incorrect quotation of Colenbrander's from the *Zakelijke Extracten*.[36] Colenbrander in his turn borrows his wisdom from the *Encyclopaedia van Nederlandsch-Indië*. The second edition (1917)[37] of this standard work includes an article on the cultivation system by a certain L.E. Dom van Rombeek, mentioned in the list of contributors as inspector of government coffee cultivation in the Dutch East Indies. It is striking that the summary of the *Zakelijke Extracten* given by this 'authority' is copied by Colenbrander word for word, including the false statement that 'the ground set apart is exempted from land-rent'. The same false statement is to be found in Hall's *History of South-East Asia* (1955).[38] It is typical of the often uncritical way in which writers on the cultivation

---

31. Colenbrander, *Koloniale Geschiedenis*, III, 39. Burger, *Ontsluiting*, 138, also points out the inaccuracy of this quotation.
32. Gonggrijp, *Schets*, 92; idem, *Enige oude en nieuwe meningen over het cultuurstelsel* (Rotterdam 1940) 20, n. 13.
33. W.F. Wertheim, *Indonesian Society in Transition. A Study of Social Change* (second edition, The Hague, 1959) 61, 243. Wertheim, *ibidem*, 93 ascribes the origin of money economy in the interior of Java to the payments supposedly made by the sugar factories to their labourers. However, at a big factory like Pandji in Besuki the so-called labour-payments in the years 1853-1862 came to no more than 28% of the amount paid out in crop-payments. Cf. Fasseur 'Van suikercontractant tot Kamerlid. Bouwstenen voor een biografie van Fransen van de Putte (de jaren 1849-1862)', *Tijdschrift voor geschiedenis*, LXXXVIII (1975) 339.
34. An exception must be made for the work of Burger, which I rate among the best on the cultivation system to have appeared before the Second World War.
35. Gonggrijp, *Schets*, 92.
36. Colenbrander, *Koloniale Geschiedenis*, III, 37.
37. *Encyclopaedie van Nederlandsch Indië I*, (2nd edition, The Hague, 1917) 548. My attention was drawn to the agreement between this article and the writings of later authors by Mr. Frank Nieuwenhuys.
38. D.G.E. Hall, *A History of South-East Asia* (London, 1955) 469.

system have transmitted certain misconceptions to one another without consulting the original document.

In Furnivall we have a favourable exception. He gives a correct account of the *Zakelijke Extracten*. The passage in his *Netherlands India* devoted to the payment received by the Javanese planters for the work they did is, however, one of the least clear in his book. His final conclusion is that 'apparently it became the rule, if not the practice, to pay the cultivators for their labour, instead of remitting land-rent, which was collected as usual'.[39]

Roosenschoon, in his unpublished dissertation on Western cultures in Java before 1870 is no more informative as to the relation between crop payment and land-rent. Since he has drawn primarily on the colonial reports presented to the Dutch parliament which began to appear only after 1849 he has little in the way of new data on the development of the cultivation system before that year. He contents himself with a reference to the well-known works of Van Deventer, Van Soest and Pierson.[40] Nor does Reinsma give a clear account of the function of the crop payment. In his analysis of the decay of the cultivation system he cloes acknowledge the large sums of money circulated among the Javanese population as wages paid for the work in the sugar factories and crop payment but he fails to place these payments in the proper perspective.[41] Elsewhere he contradicts himself when he states that as recompense for cultivation services the population enjoyed exemption from land-rent and thus the crop payment was just an additional profit.[42] Finally Reinsma subscribes to the assumption maintained in the old literature but in fact untenable, that the cultivation system was an obstacle to raising of the land-rent.[43]

In actual fact, as shown by the figures in Appendix I the income from land-rent rose considerably after the introduction of the cultivation system. Moreover the fields planted with sugar-cane and indigo were on the average much more heavily taxed than the others, since for the government crops the most fertile rice-fields were singled out and the amount due on land depended on the productivity of the soil. Thus the amount due on sugar-cane fields in the years 1857-60 averaged 12 guilders per *bouw* (0.7 hectares) as against a good 6 guilders on fields planted with rice.[44]

39. J.S. Furnivall, *Netherlands India. A Study of Plural Economy* (Cambridge, Mass., 1944) 133. Clifford Geertz, *Agricultural Involution. The Process of Ecological Change in Indonesia* (Berkeley, 1963) 54-5, on the other hand, maintains that the cultivations were 'imposed as substitutes for money taxes'.
40. Roosenschoon, 'Westerse cultures', 128.
41. Reinsma, *Verval*, 114-5.
42. *Ibidem*, 45.
43. *Ibidem*, 82. Cf. Pierson, *Kultuurstelsel*, 171.
44. Fasseur, *Kultuurstelsel*, 25.

The sharp rise in land-rent is easily explicable in terms of income from the crop payments which brought money into the *desas*. Again and again after 1830 we find instructions to the *residenten* to raise the land-rent in view of the way in which the expansion of government cultivation is said to have increased the standard of living of the population. The cultivation system thus provided at the same time the means of and the alibi for raising the land-rent. In the report already cited from the director of cultivations in 1851 this is admitted in so many words :

> The land-rent was readily increased at will in the belief that year by year more could well be paid, since large sums had been received for coffee, sugar and indigo.[45]

The extent of the influence of the crop payment on the yearly rate of the land-rent can be seen from the graph in Appendix II; crop payments given to, and land-rent owed by, the *desas* concerned with sugar and indigo cultivation in the years 1836-51 are there set against the other. The increase in land-rent after 1836 may further be ascribed to the rising market price of rice under the inflationary pressure of the crop payments. This market price was one of the basic factors taken into account in assessing the land tax.[46]

The screwing-up of the land-rent and further monetary taxation bore heavily on the Javanese people and brought much of the money disbursed in crop payments streaming back into the coffers of the government. Governor General J.J. Rochussen in 1847 estimated the percentage at as high as 60 to 70 per cent.[47] This heavy burden of taxation, increased by some years of crop failure, will account for the famine and destitution in large tracts of Java in the years 1845-50. Moreover, when the yield of the government crops proved disappointing and the crop payment thus fell short of expectations, this affected the levying of the land-rent only after some time. This phenomenon may be seen most clearly in the graph of crop payment and land-rent in the growing of indigo (see Appendix II). In 1845 the crop payment fell behind with the land-rent exacted on *desas* where indigo was cultivated. This recurred in 1847-8 and in 1850-1.

Van Niel expresses the view that the land-rent determined the amount of the crop payment :

---

45. Report of 26th August, 1851, cf. above, n. 29.
46. For details of rice prices in the years 1831-46 see Fasseur, *Kultuurstelsel*, 48-9.
47. Rochussen to J.C. Baud, 25th April 1847, no. 60, Algemeen Rijksarchief, The Hague, archives of the colonial office, 2nd section, 4566. The income from the taxes leased out, including the oppressive *bazarpacht* rose from under 6 million guilders in 1830 to almost 15 million in 1845. The only typical European tax (on riding-horses) brought in, in contrast, less than 80,000 guilders.

The assessed land-rent remained the measure against which export crops were to be delivered; if a village grew export crops valued at more than the land-rent which it owed, it would receive payment from the government for that amount in excess of the land-rent; but conversely, if the value of the crop grown on the portion of the village lands did not equal the amount of the land-rent, the village was expected to make up the shortage in cash or kind. The land-rent remained the *quid pro quo* for all goods and services which the village delivered.[48]

From what has gone before it will be clear that I cannot subscribe to this opinion. The crop payment was not determined by the land-rent but the land-rent by the crop payment. If for sugar cultivation the land-rent provided a possible standard in the first years for the payment to be allotted to the cultivators, this link was in any case broken in 1836. In that year the first model sugar contract was drawn up. According to this standard agreement the crop payment was in future to be calculated on the basis of the quantity of sugar actually obtained from the cane.[49]

Van den Bosch himself had in fact recommended as early as 1833 another criterion than the land-rent as standard for the crop payment for sugar. The cultivators were to receive such a sum as would give them more profit from their ground than if they had used it to grow rice.[50] This proposal formulated by Van den Bosch, which however took no account of the fact that sugar-growing occupied the ground for a longer period, is found in a new regulation laid down in 1860 for the government sugar cultivation ('Algemene Grond-slagen'). The minimum crop payment per *bouw* of sugar-cane was then fixed at 75 guilders, 'as at least equalling the average income from a one-*bouw* paddy field'.[51]

For the rest I ascribe only a limited value to all judgments of the principles alleged to be fundamental to the introduction of the cultivation system. Van den Bosch himself took the same attitude: in 1833 he put it to the director of cultivations that when there was a preference for acting according to general theories and principles the whole cultivation system would soon collapse. 'What is good for the smith doesn't always suit the carver and this is nowhere so true as in the profession of agriculture'.[52] Within the cultivation system there were only local and no generally operative rules. 'An interlocking set of local accommodations' is what Van Niel has called the cultivation system.[53] This is

48. R. van Niel, 'The Function of Land-rent under the Cultivation System in Java', *Journal of Asian Studies*, XXIII, (Ann Arbor, Michigan, 1964) 366.
49. Cf. Fasseur, *Kultuurstelsel*, 63 ff. In the 'forties some contracts actually fixed a minimum crop payment.
50. J. van den Bosch to B.J. Elias, 23rd November 1833, no. 407, Algemeen Rijksarchief, The Hague, archives of the colonial office, 2nd section, 3203.
51. *Nederlandsche Staatscourant*, 1860, no. 138 (The Hague, 1860).
52. See note 50.
53. Van Niel, 'Measurement of Change', 93.

what makes investigation into the practical working of the cultivation system and its importance for the Javanese people so difficult.

THE DECLINE OF THE CULTIVATION SYSTEM

The literature also contains a good deal of misunderstanding as to the origins of the 'decay' of the cultivation system. See for instance the following quotation from Wertheim's *Indonesian Society in Transition*:

> After 1848 ... the Dutch bourgeoisie represented in Parliament gained a significant voice in colonial affairs. The bourgeoisie, which had been able to build up considerable capital from the profits derived from the culture system, now looked for investment in the colony. The culture system, which reserved almost all economic activities to the state, was considered an impediment to private enterprise. Moreover, in that period the source of profits from the culture system gradually dried up as a consequence of the increasingly oppressive character of the system, which had caused famines in several regions. The conscience of the Dutch people, awakened by the famous novel *Max Havelaar* by Multatuli (Douwes Dekker), reinforced the campaign of the liberals against the abuses of the culture system.[54]

From almost every point of view this statement of the situation is incorrect. In the first place it is difficult to maintain that the cultivation system excluded private enterprise. Several government cultivations could only exist because of co-operation from private enterprise. Sugar provides the best-known and most important example. The government made sure of co-operation from private enterprise by concluding sugar contracts with its representatives. In a sugar contract of this kind — they also existed for tea and tobacco[55] — the government bound itself to see that the Javanese peasants within the range of the prospective sugar undertaking planted a certain area (usually 300-400 hectares) of sugar-cane for a given number of years. The entrepreneur — almost always a Dutchman or a Chinese — contracted to build a factory in which the sugar-cane would be processed into sugar. Part of the sugar had to be delivered to the government warehouses at a price fixed in the contract while the remainder — usually one third — was for the factory owner to dispose of as he wished. He could sell the 'free sugar' at the market price which was of course higher than the contract price, unless there had been a collapse in the sugar market. By such contracts the government cheaply acquired great quantities of sugar without having to be directly involved in production.

Generally speaking, the building and equipping of the factory was financed by means of an interest-free government advance to be repaid in sugar. In about 1845 there were some 10 million guilders outstanding, advanced by the

54. Wertheim, *Indonesian Society*, 61-2.
55. Reinsma, *Verval*, 137, assumes in addition the existence of indigo contracts in the period after 1840. The last indigo contract, however, was dissolved in 1837.

government on sugar-, tea- and tobacco-contracts.[56] After 1847 Governor General Rochussen put an end to the provision of government loans for the building of sugar factories, but most of these were by then already in business and the borrowed capital need only be paid back in stages.[57] Moreover, the government continued to offer annual credit for the running expenses of the undertaking.[58] In so far as there was need after 1847 for new investment in machinery and other permanent goods, money could be supplied by capital-owners on Java itself, usually by pledges on 'free sugar'. The suppliers of capital were the Factorij of the Nederlandsche Handel-Maatschappij in Batavia, import and export firms, Chinese grown rich on opium smuggling and so on. In the Netherlands there was certainly little interest until the 'sixties in investment in Indonesia which was considered too much of a risk.[59] I.D. Fransen van de Putte, for example, later minister for the colonies (1863-6), who had become rich as a sugar manufacturer in Eastern Java, invested a great deal of the million guilders and more he had earned in less than ten years in land in Holland. So did many another sugar magnate living on his capital in Holland. With the remaining money Fransen van de Putte bought 'Russians', 'Spaniards', 'metallics' and whatever the rest of the shares on the Amsterdam stock exchange might be called.[60]

Nor is it true that the profits from the cultivation system began to dry up after 1850, let alone that these declining profits were a consequence of the increasing pressure of the system on the Javanese people. The profits of the cultivation system were determined by the market price of coffee and sugar, since these two products accounted for no less than 96 per cent of the total profits of the system between 1850 and 1860. From 1848 onwards, in a period of boom and gold inflation the prices of the main colonial products went up considerably.[61] The East Indian surplus which flowed into the Dutch treasury in these years became enormous.

In the 'fifties the East Indian profits amounted to almost one-third of the total of the Dutch public revenue (31 per cent) as against less than one-fifth (19 per cent) in the period before 1850. The East Indian surplus had become the cork that kept the Netherlands afloat, a cork bobbing on a sea of rising and falling coffee- and sugar-prices. In a period when the cultivation system

56. Fasseur, *Kultuurstelsel*, 223, n. 41.
57. These repaid advances are most confusingly accounted for in the estimates of income and expenses of the Dutch East Indies under the heading of land-rent and cultivations, so that they are after all wrongly classed as part of the income from land-rent.
58. Reinsma, *Verval*, 159, takes no account of these advances for current expenses, which existed until 1861 and even after that date were occasionally extended.
59. Cf. Roosenschoon, 'Westerse cultures', 338.
60. Cf. Fasseur, 'Suikercontractant', 333-54.
61. Cf. J. Ridder, *Een conjunctuur-analyse van Nederland 1848-1860* (Amsterdam, 1935) *passim*.

was exposed to ever-increasing criticism, opposed as it was to every liberal principle of government, it was proving a more considerable source of income for the treasury than ever before. This explains why the liquidation of the cultivation system, even though most conservatives no longer gave it unconditional support, was the cause of so much political conflict.

Serious doubt may also be cast on the notion that resistance to the cultivation system was in fact much stimulated by the appearance of *Max Havelaar* in 1860.[62] The political influence of this book was more long-term than short-term. In any case Multatuli was attacking not so much the cultivation system — coffee and sugar-cane would not flourish in Lebak — as the colonial system as such, an arrangement in which government and the traditional Javanese administrative *elite* conspired to enrich themselves at the expense of the Javanese people. But this severe condemnation of the prevailing colonial policy could count on a favourable reception neither from the conservatives nor from the liberals. The liberals — Wertheim's moneyed bourgeoisie — were not willing to see the East Indian profits disappear since they were all too well aware that this would inevitably mean the introduction of an income-tax in the Netherlands. And 90 per cent of those East Indian millions came from the profits of the cultivation system. The remaining 10 per cent came from dealings in tin.[63]

The statement that the cultivation system declined because it offered no scope to private enterprise and investment directed from the Netherlands thus seems untenable. It is a myth, promulgated by liberal opponents of the system after its abolishment. Western large-scale agricultural enterprise in Java, in so far as it was based on 'free labour', that is, on voluntary arrangements with the population, was of very little significance before 1870.[64] There was no class of self-assured private entrepreneurs to make the cultivation system superfluous.

---

62. 'Multatuli' was the pseudonym of the East Indian civil servant E. Douwes Dekker. In 1856 he resigned as assistant-resident of Lebak in West Java because he was not allowed to proceed against a high-ranking Indonesian official guilty of extortion from the local population. His superiors considered his intervention too hasty and inappropriate to the system of indirect rule. In 1860 Douwes Dekker published a novel attacking the abuses in Dutch rule in Java. A recent English translation is: Multatuli; *Max Havelaar or The Coffee Auctions of the Dutch Trading Company* (with an introduction by D.H. Lawrence, Leiden, 1967).
63. The East Indian contributions to the Dutch treasury eventually ceased in 1878, though they continued for some considerable time to be registered 'pro memorie'. A tax on income from capital was introduced in the Netherlands in 1893.
64. Reinsma's views on free cultivation before 1870 can not be considered very convincing, based as they are on inaccurate estimates from the Centraal kantoor voor de statistiek. Moreover he concentrates too much on the figures for the area under 'free' cultivation, whereas it was not the area but the production figures that were decisive and the average production in the government sugar-growing area was much higher. See Reinsma, *Verval*, 134, 142; Fasseur, *Kultuurstelsel*, 142, 225 n. 82, 242 n. 108.

The private entrepreneurs in Java in the years in question were with few exceptions all sugar contractors and consequently operating within the cultivation system, which suited them admirably. A sugar contract — as we saw in the case of Fransen van de Putte — was the quickest way to riches in Java.

It was the changing climate of opinion in government circles that finally drove the entrepreneurs to seek a living outside the cultivation system. After 1853 no new sugar contracts were given out, so that the expansion of sugar cultivation came to a standstill. Why was the expansion of the lucrative sugar industry halted? The government in the Netherlands wanted first to wait for the findings of a large-scale local inquiry in Java into the question whether the sugar cultivation could not be organized in some other way, so that the population would be prepared in the course of time to co-operate voluntarily. This investigation took four years, after which it was not until 1860 that a new regulation was introduced — one no more satisfactory than its predecessor. The ban on concluding sugar contracts with new undertakings, however, remained in force.

These measures were inspired by political considerations. One of these was that the granting of sugar contracts had in the past given rise to a good deal of dissatisfaction since these contracts, usually so profitable for the manufacturer, were given for preference to the 'friends' of the East Indian administration or the minister of the colonies. Among those with sugar contracts were to be found relatives of highly-placed members of the government and former colonial civil servants, such as former *residenten* and a former director of cultivations. In the Netherlands this caused considerable scandal. The profits enjoyed by the sugar-contractors after 1850 became a 'national offence'. In the second half of the 'fifties a definite opposition can be seen forming between the liberal party in the Netherlands and the leading group of European entrepreneurs in Java — the sugar-contractors and their money-lenders.

The opinion of Clifford Geertz, who invokes Reinsma in this connection, that the 'fall' of the cultivation system and its gradual replacement by private enterprise

> were largely self-generated, because its success in establishing a serviceable export economy infrastructure made private entrepreneurship, originally so hampered by lack of capital, progressively more feasible,

is to say the least questionable.[65] The system went into decline because it came into conflict with the political views which came to dominate in the Netherlands after 1850.

---

65. Geertz, *Agricultural Involution*, 65.

A NEW APPROACH TO THE CULTIVATION SYSTEM

'He who generalizes', said Bertrand Russell, 'generally lies'. This dictum is particularly applicable to the cultivation system. One might maintain that there was never a *system* of cultivation. It was with justification that the government regulations of the Dutch East Indies never spoke of 'the cultivation system' but used a plural form:[66] 'the cultivations introduced by high authority'. Apart from the fact that they were imposed on the people by the administration, these government cultivations had little connection and little in common. The cultivation of each crop had its own organization and developed in its own way. When Reinsma in 1955 devoted a work of almost 200 pages to '*the* decay of *the* cultivation system' he was discussing a phenomenon that never existed and indeed never could.

If an effective analysis of the cultivation system is required we must abandon the area of generalizations and apply ourselves to the writing of regional and local studies. This is probably also the only way to detach ourselves from the Europacentrism which characterizes the existing literature, not that I would rule it out merely on this head. The new approach — that is, an Indonesiacentric approach, in which the development of Javanese social relations is seen as central — can succeed only when the topic of investigation is narrowly defined both in space and time, as Smail and Van Niel have already indicated.[67]

The material for such local studies is to be found in the first place in Indonesia itself. In Jakarta the records of the office of the director of cultivations have been preserved. The records are in very poor condition and not accessible to researchers. Further details as to completeness, access, etc., are, at least as far as my information goes, not at the moment available.[68] There are however measures taken to conserve the records. If these are once made available to the public, they will undoubtedly be seen to constitute a rich source of data for historians, sociologists and others.

The material present in the Netherlands which may be used for these local and regional studies is limited. The data in the cultivation reports are given on the basis of residencies and not of such smaller administrative units as regencies or districts. Material that might throw light on the situation in a

66. *Regeringsreglement*, 1854, art. 56, 'Staatsblad van Nederlandsch Indië', 1855, no. 2 in: *Staatsblad van Nederlandsch Indië*, II, *1846-1860* (Zaltbommel, 1856). In earlier *Regeringsreglementen* there was usually not so much as a mention of government crops.
67. J.R.W. Smail, 'On the Possibility of an Autonomous History of Modern South East Asia', *Journal of South East Asian History*, II (Singapore, 1961) 93; Van Niel, 'Nineteenth-Century Java: an Analysis of Historical Sources and Method', *Asian Studies*, IV (Quezon City, Philippines, 1966) 202.
68. Cf. M.G.H.A. de Graaff, *Verslag van een bezoek aan het Staatsarchief van Indonesië* (1974).

specific area of Java is on the whole lacking.[69] There is however an important exception with regard to the operation of the cultivation system. I have already mentioned the investigation instigated in 1853 into the government sugar cultivation. This time-consuming investigation had at any rate the consequence that 'two cartloads of paper' as a somewhat dismayed minister for the colonies put it in 1859 were despatched to the Netherlands. Every sugar factory in Java — and there were almost a hundred — received a full description. These descriptions gave details of how the work for every factory was organized, which *desas* were liable, the nature of the social structure of the Javanese population within the range of the sugar factory, how government services and cultivation services were divided, what influence the cultivation system exercised on local law and property rights, and so on. Examination of this material will enable future researchers to form a more accurate picture of the socioeconomic significance of the sugar cultivation for the Indonesian population.[70]

APPENDICES

The details as to land-rent are taken from the colonial report for 1866-8; see *Bijlagen Handelingen Tweede Kamer 1868-1869*, no. 38 (Bijlage no. 12). The data on crop payments are taken from the cultivation reports and after 1851 from the colonial reports. All amounts are given in so-called recepis-guilders, the monetary unit in circulation between 1846 and 1860.

The gross assessment for land-rent in general differed only slightly from the sums ultimately collected; cf. *Bijlagen Handelingen Tweede Kamer 1851-1852*, 176, where it appears that in the years 1839-48 a total of less than 120,000 guilders had to be written off.

The data on land-rent refer to the residencies of Banten, Karawang, Cirebon, Tegal, Pekalongan, Semarang, Jepara, Rembang, Surabaya, Pasuruan, Probolinggo, Besuki, Banjumas, Bageleen and Kedu, with the addition, for the years 1859 and 1860, of Madiun and Kediri. The 'fictive' land-rent in the two latter residencies (the tax was never actually levied, since it was cancelled out by the crop payment) also included the rate for 1849-1858.

69. Cf. Sartono Kartodirdjo, *The Peasants' Revolt of Banten in 1888. Its Conditions, Course and Sequel. A Case Study of Social Movements in Indonesia* (The Hague, 1966) 15.

70. See for these monographs, hitherto scarcely used as sources, Colonial Office (Schaarsbergen) 1176-1186 and C. Fasseur, 'Organisatie en sociaal-economische betekenis van de gouvernements-suikerkultuur in enkele residenties op Java omstreeks 1850', *Bijdragen tot de Taal-, Land- en Volkenkunde* (The Hague, 1977).

Appendix I

Land-rent and Crop Payments 1836-1860 (Dutch guilders)

Year	Land-rent (assessment)	Crop Payments			
		1. Coffee	2. Sugar	3. Indigo	Total columns 1-3
1829	5.016.272				
36	5.966.456	4.342.347	1.132.151	799.859	6.274.357
37	6.033.966	4.764.302	1.261.894	1.331.357	7.357.553
38	6.165.395	4.368.532	1.391.497	1.242.680	7.002.709
39	6.431.810	6.924.717	1.722.652	2.215.281	10.862.050
40	7.030.795	5.746.872	1.990.355	2.604.790	10.342.017
1841	7.470.839	7.170.810	2.038.825	2.116.280	11.325.915
42	7.899.264	7.400.275	2.335.925	1.738.225	11.474.425
43	8.291.350	8.337.025	2.416.895	1.878.675	12.632.595
44	7.941.619	6.610.250	2.645.320	1.765.405	11.020.975
45	8.799.142	4.580.640	2.774.310	1.710.900	9.065.850
46	9.416.246	6.198.250	2.816.135	1.971.733	10.986.118
47	8.854.389	5.332.263	2.926.492	1.449.224	9.707.979
48	9.500.823	6.079.357	2.911.380	1.330.829	10.321.566
49	9.200.544	3.363.275	2.906.939	1.113.490	7.383.704
50	8.331.834	6.929.579	3.343.703	731.524	11.004.806
1851	8.599.495	7.175.044	3.380.135	825.624	11.380.803
52	8.971.656	?	?	971.731	?
53	9.154.346	4.718.671	3.586.602	975.369	9.280.642
54	8.617.967	7.085.488	3.760.191	951.042	11.796.721
55	8.800.083	7.560.935	3.601.824	641.919	11.804.678
56	9.582.165	4.865.570	3.940.891	1.052.872	9.859.333
57	9.408.135	6.305.403	4.144.291	876.696	11.326.390
58	9.950.475	6.712.868	4.264.352	1.110.555	12.087.775
59	9.588.458	6.556.850	4.214.400	1.026.093	11.797.343
60	9.942.835	9.278.231	4.317.237	933.838	14.529.306

Appendix II

A. *Relation between crop payment and land-rent in sugar cultivation*

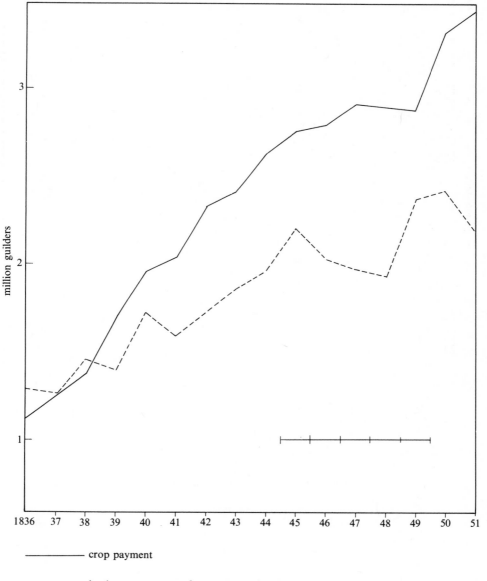

———————— crop payment

– – – – – – – land-rent assessment for sugar-growing desas

Source: Cultivation reports 1836-1851

B. *Relation between crop payment and land-rent in indigo cultivation*

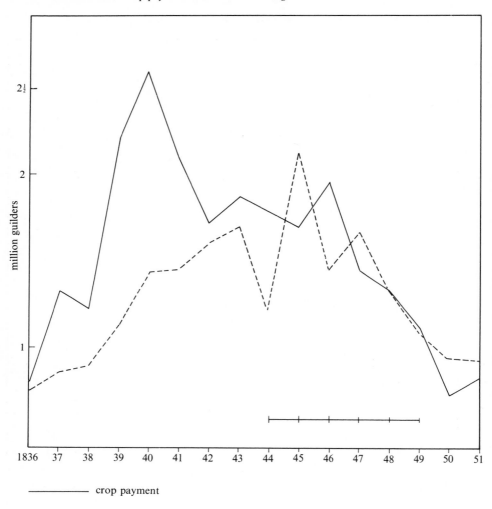

———————— crop payment

– – – – – – – – land-rent assessment for indigo-growing desas

Source: *Cultivation reports 1836-1851*

The Mutiny on Board De Zeven Provincien: Reactions and Repercussions in the Netherlands *

J.C.H. BLOM

On Saturday, 4th February, 1933, at approximately ten at night, mutiny broke out on board the Dutch warship De Zeven Provincien, as she rode at anchor in the roadstead of Oleh-leh near Kutaradja, at the north-west tip of Sumatra in the then Netherlands East Indies. A group of about ten native sailors seized the firearms and ammunition, surprised such officers as were on board (about half the officers were at a social gathering in the officers' club in Kutaradja), and took over the ship. Almost all the other native crew members aboard, about 180 men, unanimously joined in the mutiny, while the reactions of the European other ranks, about fifty of whom were on board, varied. Some immediately and enthusiastically joined the mutineers, others hesitated at first and subsequently tried to exercise a restraining influence, while some let themselves be forced to join or succeeded in holding themselves aloof.

After some hours of confusion the ship left Oleh-leh and set course for Surabaja, the central naval base in the Netherlands East Indies. The mutineers intended to hand the ship over to the authorities just before reaching Surabaja and to allow the commanding officer, who had been ashore at the outbreak of the mutiny, to come aboard. The naval chiefs, however, did not allow this to happen. They assembled an armed force of aeroplanes and warships in the Sunda Straits, between Java and Sumatra, which there lay in wait for the mutinous ship, by that time following the coast of Sumatra. On 10th February, at approximately nine in the morning, there was an engagement. A bomb, which officially had been intended as a warning, was dropped from an aeroplane and hit the mark. Twenty-three people died. The mutiny came to an immediate end.

In attempting to explain the mutiny, we must distinguish between general factors concerning conditions in the navy and factors related specifically to this particular incident. In this respect we wish to remark from the outset that the suggestion that a communist or Indonesian nationalist cell organized the

---

* The author summarizes part of his recent study *De muiterij op De Zeven Provincien. Reacties en gevolgen in Nederland* (Bussum, 1975; also thesis University of Leiden, Fac. of letters, 1975).

163

mutiny is highly improbable. This idea was already in circulation at the time of the mutiny and has been repeated in some recent publications.[1] There is, however, no reliable information whatsoever to indicate this and the entire course of events during the mutiny would seem to disprove such a contention.[2] Another, altogether different matter played a major role, the prelude to which began in mid-December 1932 when, in connection with the economic crisis, the government in the Netherlands East Indies decided to reduce the salaries of civil servants by seven per cent. In order to enforce this decision in the navy, consultations had to take place with the government in The Hague. Other problems arose and as a result the pay cut, which was originally to have taken effect on 1st January, 1933, was temporarily delayed. This decision more or less coincided with protest actions organized by navy personnel and although later on it turned out that there was no connection between the two,[3] at the time large groups of navy personnel assumed that there was. Moreover, there was a growing conviction that the cut in pay was to be put off for some considerable time.

Thus when the decision was taken to implement the pay cut, in a somewhat modified form, as of 1st February, 1933, this aroused great indignation, as well as renewed action on the part of the personnel, in which the employees' unions, who for that matter were forbidden at the time to hold meetings, lost control. In Surabaja, where practically the entire fleet was assembled when the decision was announced, there were cases of insubordination at the end of January and beginning of February, and several arrests followed.

The mutiny on board the ironclad De Zeven Provincien, even though Surabaja was a long way off, was clearly a reaction to the pay cut on the one hand, and to the connected arrests on the other. There had been some irregularities on board this ship before and the fact that the mutiny was successful can be attributed, among other things, to the presence of a few people with obvious leadership qualities and to the negligence of the superior officers, who ought to have known of the impending troubles but took no special precautions.[4]

In general to understand the mutiny it is important to pay attention to what might be called the 'climate' prevailing in the Dutch navy at the time. The economic, social and political situation in the thirties was certainly not favourable. Moreover, for the army and the navy it was unfavourable by virtue of the fact that until around 1936 'defence' was far from popular and was politically and financially neglected by the government and parliament. This

1. The clearest example of this is L. de Jong, *Het Koninkrijk der Nederlanden in de Tweede Wereldoorlog*, I, *Voorspel* (The Hague, 1969) 175-6.
2. Blom, *Muiterij*, 36-79.
3. *De ongeregeldheden bij de Koninklijke Marine in den aanvang van 1933* (The Hague, 1934) 23.
4. Blom, *Muiterij*, 78.

was detrimental to the atmosphere in the navy and although it is true that there was no obvious injustice, morale was low. Moreover, even though the great social distance which existed between officers on the one hand and petty officers and crew on the other was in fact taken for granted, it nevertheless led to a mutual lack of understanding and at times to tensions which in reality were unnecessary. Among the ratings unions with social democratic tendencies functioned in a way similar to that of a trade union in a factory or other enterprise, even though the former were not officially members of a trade union federation. They were the only ones in fact to serve the interests of the personnel, and acted as the mouthpiece of all malcontents. This was somewhat against regulations but, to the annoyance of many officers, the unions were usually able to do as they pleased without hindrance, thereby widening the already existing gap between officers and their subordinates.

The naval situation was alike in the Netherlands and in the Netherlands East Indies the sole difference being that in the colony it was complicated by the problem of the native personnel, whose position amounted to a kind of *apartheid*. Native navy personnel were always inferior in rank, had separate quarters, received special food, and were organized in their own separate unions, etc. Differences of language and culture reinforced their isolation. So it is quite understandable that conspiracies could take shape almost unnoticed by outsiders in precisely this circle. Given the general situation, as outlined above, in combination with any number of particular circumstances and events, these conspiracies ultimately ended in mutiny.

The mutiny on board De Zeven Provincien had its repercussions in the Netherlands. The Dutch government was of course primarily concerned with putting an end to the troubles in the East Indies — relations with the government in Batavia were very close — and also with preventing any similar developments in the Netherlands. To this end surveillance was intensified and special precautionary measures taken, in particular at the naval base at Den Helder. The Minister for Defence, L.N. Deckers, stated in the Second Chamber on 7th February, 1933, even while the mutiny was still going on, that

> drastic measures will be taken against the pernicious influences which have repined the minds of men to a violation by public servants of that same authority which they have voluntarily assumed the duty of serving.[5]

Such (drastic) measures were intended to strengthen government authority. Members of parliament and representatives of the liberal and denominational press, in the years preceding the mutiny, had repeatedly raised the problem

5. *Verslag der Handelingen van de Staten-Generaal 1932-1933*, II (The Hague) 1603.

of the maintenance of authority, while bourgeois and service circles had frequently called for that authority to be strengthened. Moreover, a number of measures to that very effect had already been drawn up or were in preparation. The mutiny intensified the need for such action and accelerated the process. In the thirties the government and the majority in parliament believed that government authority was being threatened by groups desirous of changing existing political and social relations, a danger which they feared came especially from groups on the left, such as the communists, revolutionary socialists, and to some extent also the social democrats. The above measures, which ultimately were rigorously applied also against right-wing groups, such as the fascists and nationalists, were originally aimed principally at the 'left'.

The measures in question can be divided roughly into two groups — those particularly affecting the fleet, and those of more general scope and in most cases only indirectly connected with the mutiny. The measures falling within the first category were designed on the one hand to purge the navy of undesirable elements and, on the other, to improve the existing conditions. The latter aim was only partially realized. A somewhat 'better' situation did not come into being until the second half of the thirties, when people in the Netherlands began to adopt a more positive attitude towards the armed forces. The 'purge' in the navy led to the dismissal of a large number of persons who, in connection with the mutiny and the preceding cases of insubordination had behaved incorrectly in the eyes of the government, eyes which had now suddenly become very sharp. The dismissals affected not only all the mutineers and many of those who had unlawfully neglected their duty, but almost all the committee members of the employees' unions as well. Besides trying to weaken the position of the navy unions,[6] the navy authorities were also especially bent on excluding social democratic influences. Communist and revolutionary socialist influences played hardly any role and hence were not subject to special control.

Even while the mutiny was still in progress, an injunction was issued forbidding servicemen to read newspapers favorable to social democratic ideas. Clearer still in its opposition to social democratic influences was a measure taken on 24th February, 1933, whereby the minister for defence prohibited servicemen from joining or supporting associations founded on social democratic principles. This provision was formally based on the servicemen's code, which contained an article prohibiting the support of associations which acted contrary to discipline in the armed forces.[7] According to the minister, this

---

6. J.L. Swarte, *Spreekpunt 1971. 25 jaar V.B.Z. en wat daaraan vooraf ging* (s. l., s.a) 92-9; Blom, *Muiterij*, 103-26.
7. Army order 1933 no. 59, in: *Militair-rechtelijk Tijdschrift*, XXVIII (The Hague, 1933) 528.

was the case with the socialists, who in those years still propagated anti-militarism.

The measures taken against the employees' unions were likewise directed in the first instance against unions with socialist leanings, on which in the course of February and March the minister had already imposed numerous conditions. The unions in question consisted of three associations combined into a federation, with its own weekly journal, a club house, and a great deal of activity. They were under the direction of professional administrators, mostly old navy men, no longer subject to naval authority. However, the unions were forced to dismiss these professionals and explicitly to subordinate their activities to military discipline, and from then on in fact losing thereby their originally fairly strong position.

A regulation issued on 18th April, 1933, and pertaining to associations concerned with the forces[8] placed the activities of the employees' associations under strict control, confining them to extremely rigid boundaries. This affected in the first place the unions of social democratic coloring, which in the eyes of the authorities were unreliable. They were disbanded, with the exception of one, which lingered on. In addition, however, the regulation also checked the freedom of movement of denominational associations, normally very emphatic in their loyalty to authority. In particular the Roman Catholic union conformed only after a long spell of passive resistance. From that time on the denominational unions, too, led a very precarious existence.

The so-called *Ambtenarenverbod* (Civil Servant's Prohibition), an amendment to the *Algemeen Rijks Ambtenaren Reglement*[9] (General Code for Government Civil Servants), is a good example of a measure taken to strengthen authority in a general sense. It also demonstrates fairly clearly the influence, albeit indirect, which the mutiny had on questions of policy. The prohibition came into force as early as 22nd May, 1933. Between that date and February 27 the text had gone with unusual speed through all the required advisory procedures and had passed all the proper official bodies. This measure entitled the government to dismiss those government servants who were members of particular organizations. Prior to this it had already been possible to dismiss government servants for behavior potentially dangerous to public order or State security. However, this provision had given rise to difficulties of interpretation. Hence it was now laid down that membership of associations regarded as undesirable for public servants (in practice always political parties and related organizations) could be viewed as potentially dangerous behaviour. The government was

8. Army order 1933 no. 138, *ibidem*, XXIX (1933) 93-8.
9. Royal Decree 22nd May 1933, no. 9, *Staatsblad van het Koninkrijk der Nederlanden* (The Hague, 1933) 294.

167

empowered to compile lists of those associations which could be regarded as dangerous to the State, the first list of this kind being published on 24th July, 1933.[10] Roughly speaking, it included all extreme left and extreme right parties. Moreover, by virtue of earlier measures it was prescribed that civil servants working in the defence department (both professional servicemen and departmental officials) were forbidden to join the Sociaal-Democratische Arbeiders Partij (SDAP - Social Democratic Labour Labour Party) and the NVV, the social democratic trade union. This particular prohibition remained in force until 1938.

The question is, of course, whether provisions of this type contributed much to increasing the reliability of government servants. For in this particular instance few such servants were actually dismissed, though many did resign their membership of the associations in question. These provisions did ensure, however, that open expressions of unrest and dissatisfaction among public servants no longer occurred.

The mutiny on board De Zeven Provincien and the measures which were taken as a result inevitably gave rise to heated political debates in the Netherlands, in particular in parliament and in the press. Reactions to events reflected current political and social relations.

The parties of the thirties can be roughly classified into four groups. In the first place, there were the large 'bourgeois' parties, which represented about two thirds of the electorate and which had together been calling the tune for some considerable time. They displayed all kinds of nuances and mutual contrasts, but were essentially positive in their attitude towards the existing social and political situation. These 'bourgeois' parties included the liberal Vrijheidsbond (Union for Freedom) and the Vrijzinnig-Democratische Bond (Liberal Democratic Union), the Rooms-katholieke Staatspartij (RKSP - Roman Catholic State Party) and the Protestant parties, viz. the Christelijk-Historische Unie (CHU - Christian Historical Union) and the Anti-Revolutionaire Partij (ARP - Anti-Revolutionary Party).

Secondly, there was the SDAP, which was going through a period of transition. At its inception the party had had a revolutionary tinge and was strongly opposed to society such as it was. But, and especially after the first World War, the social democrats had begun to see more and more positive elements in the existing situation, which had meanwhile also undergone all kinds of improvements. They had increasingly come to expect greater benefit from further reforms by gradual means rather than through revolution. They

10. Decision of the Council of Ministers 24th July, 1933, no. 327 Kab., *Bijvoegsel tot het Staatsblad* (1933) Gorinchem no. 175.

had assumed an ever greater shared responsibility in political and social developments, even though they were not as yet taking part in the government. During the thirties they held as a rule between twenty-two and twenty-four seats in the Second Chamber.

The two remaining groups consisted of extremists, who totally rejected the existing situation, either from a 'left' ideological viewpoint, usually called socialist, or else on the basis of a 'right' authoritarian, *mutatis mutandis*, fascist conviction. On the left a number of ideological trends were clearly organized into parties, together representing perhaps five per cent of the population. The situation on the right in the early thirties was less clear. There were a number of outspokenly fascist parties and all kinds of semi-organized groups and circles of people who were somewhat vaguely opposed to existing conditions. They often looked back on the past with a certain nostalgia rather than having in mind a radical image of the future. Politically, this latter group stood somewhere between 'bourgeois' and extreme right, and in the early thirties they were sometimes difficult to distinguish from the outspokenly fascist groups which were then beginning to appear.

Of the various reactions to the mutiny, those of the social democrats are the most interesting and the most characteristic. For the SDAP, the question of how to react to the mutiny was of fundamental importance, while for its political opponents it was above all how far the socialists could be regarded as politically reliable which was at issue. Some social democrats, in the early days after the mutiny evinced an emotionally charged enthusiasm for the mutiny's opposition to the prevailing system and tried without reserve to exploit the possibilities for propaganda which the situation offered. So Ch.G. Cramer, member of the Second Chamber, inadvertently let slip the remark that the incident 'gave him devilish much pleasure',[11] and the social democratic press showed more than clearly in pictures and writing that it regarded the mutiny as a just judgment on a discreditable policy. The fact that a bomb had been used to bring the mutiny to an end aroused great indignation. The terms 'murder' and 'murderers' were heard and artists drew pictures of hands dripping with blood. Many other social democrats, however, clearly rejected the mutiny. They emphatically took the side of authority and had no desire whatsoever to create the impression of being revolutionary. Professor Goudriaan, who left the party shortly after, expressed this viewpoint in the following words: 'Strong government authority is no reactionary slogan; it is a democratic requirement *par excellence*'.[12]

11. *Internationaal Instituut voor Sociale Geschiedenis*, Amsterdam, Archief Cramer no. 10, 93 and report in *Vooruit*, daily newspaper (The Hague, 6th February, 1933).
12. *De Groene Amsterdammer*, weekly (Amsterdam, 18th February, 1933).

A few weeks later, such extreme statements were no longer to be heard coming from the social democrat camp. By that time the social democrats had on the whole adopted a middle-of-the-road point of view, which was formulated very clearly by their leader, J.W. Albarda, in his speeches in the Second Chamber, in journal articles and in a pamphlet entitled 'Another light, another opinion on events aboard De Zeven Provincien',[13] which appeared at the beginning of March 1933. This pamphlet contained what can be considered as more or less an expression of the official party standpoint. The argument it presents has two main themes: an unequivocal rejection of the mutiny, in fact of any mutiny and in practice of all revolutionary action, and in addition a sharp criticism of the government. The author appealed to general common sense, but left no doubt that before and during the mutiny things had happened which were absolutely unacceptable to the social democrats; and he made it clear that in his opinion sweeping reforms were an urgent necessity. In particular, he criticized the way in which the mutiny had been brought to an end, the measures taken against unions of the navy personnel and the prohibition of membership of the SDAP and NVV. Albarda indicated emphatically that social democrats as such had had nothing to do with the mutiny and were aiming to defend the principles of the democratic system.

Meanwhile, however, the earlier radical statements had taken effect. Both the 'bourgeois' parties and extreme right circles violently attacked the SDAP, who in their eyes were untrustworthy, not only in this particular instance but in general when the maintenance of government authority was at stake. The very fact that they professed to actually want to maintain law and order — a deceptive and ambiguous position — left the social democrats open to objection in the eyes of their critics. The influential liberal daily, the *Algemeen Handelsblad*, gave the following sketch of the 'Janus'-like character of the SDAP:

> That twists and turns and stammers and brags so as nevertheless to have a front on both sides, and while one mouth pays homage to the pretended revolution (oh so carefully and just within the law so there is no risk), the other weakly regrets an attack on the lawful authority.[14]

This anti-socialist campaign, which formed part of the electoral contest for the parliamentary elections in April 1933, put the social democrats very much on the defensive, whereas in February they had still believed they could capitalize on events to the advantage of their own party.

Thus, in the first few months following the mutiny, the position of the social democrats on the national political level became even more isolated than it

---

13. J.W. Albarda, *Een ander licht, een ander oordeel over de gebeurtenissen op De Zeven Provincien* (Amsterdam, 1933).
14. *Algemeen Handelsblad* (Amsterdam, 9th February, 1933).

already was, although in the long run the effect was rather the opposite. The process of the integration of the social democrats into existing society, which had already begun before 1933, continued also thereafter, and precipitated a number of reports as well as changes in the SDAP program. An important step was the creation of a 'committee of review', after the SDAP had suffered a loss of two seats in the 1933 parliamentary elections. The committee's task was to reflect on the political line the SDAP should follow and to search for the reasons behind the electoral defeat. The mutiny was also something to be kept in mind in this connection, but it is difficult to determine exactly how much importance should be attached to it in comparison with other factors, such as the economic crisis and the rapid growth of fascism. In a certain sense the mutiny and the reactions that followed it stimulated a process of reflection which ultimately broke through the isolation of the social democrats, a breakthrough which was completed in 1939 when the SDAP, too, took part in the government coalition which was then formed.

In 'bourgeois' circles reactions to the mutiny were, certain nuances aside, quite clearly unanimous. What mattered here was in the first place, to suppress the mutiny as quickly as possible. Differences of opinion about the means to be used were of secondary importance. Colijn, ARP party leader, thought for example that the ship should be sent 'to the bottom of the ocean with a torpedo'[15] if necessary, but nevertheless agreed in principle with the opinion of H.P. Marchant, the leader of the progressive liberals (VDB), that 'What is needed are statesmanship, calmness, and political insight. Any display — display of force, display of courage — would be quite mistaken'.[16] And indeed all the 'bourgeois' parties supported the government in its actions against the mutiny and in the measures it took to strengthen authority. Any criticism remained marginal. The 'bourgeois' parties were equally united in their campaign against the social democrats. They all considered incidents such as the mutiny to be potentially lethal for the existing social system and they believed that only resolute and unreserved condemnation was appropriate. The denominational trade union movement also clearly took sides on this issue, and *De Volkskrant*, the paper of the roman catholic trade unions, spoke for example of 'the winding labyrinthian paths along which social democracy roams and wanders'.[17]

As such the 'bourgeois' parties were not concerned solely with the concrete case of the mutiny, but with Authority (often indeed written with a capital

15. Interview in the daily newspaper *Het Vaderland* (The Hague, 6th February, 1933).
16. *Verslag Handelingen Staten-Generaal 1932-1933*, II, 1647.
17. *De Volkskrant*, daily newspaper (Utrecht, 14th February, 1933).

'A') in general, which to them appeared to be a necessary condition for an ordered society. The mutiny presented a good opportunity to emphasize this once again. The absolute domination of authority was not desired, but rather a combination of authority and freedom as mutually complementary values. In such times as those one had above all to ensure that authority was not lost, nor overrun by freedom. On these points there was general agreement, even though opinions differed quite widely on details. Colijn believed that the demand to strengthen authority came from 'those who value not only order, but also freedom',[18] but that 'the worst that could happen would be for order and freedom, both, to be lost' and that therefore 'order will have to be maintained at the expense of freedom' in the unlikely event that a choice had to be made between the two.[19] From many sides, however, there also sounded a note of warning to the effect that government authority as such had of course to be maintained but that the means used to maintain it must be examined critically and the idea of a 'strong man' must be rejected. As the roman catholic daily *De Tijd* wrote, the important point was 'the exercise of authority purely on the basis of the legal principles of our democratic constitutional system'.[20] And according to the 'bourgeois' parties, the government had indeed kept to these principles in its actions of early 1933.

While the SDAP and the liberal and denominational parties, however big their mutual differences, tried to look at the problems in connection with the mutiny from various angles, both the right and the left extremist parties exposed respectively only one aspect.

According to the extreme right, the incident could be reduced to one cause, viz. the slackening of authority over many years had made the mutiny inevitable. Nor, in a political system where subversive left-wing forces were free to do as they pleased, could one expect anything different in the future. There was no question of the spokesmen of these groups advocating the preservation of a certain degree of freedom, and their campaign against the socialists was considerably more venomous than was that of the 'bourgeois' parties. Repeatedly they suggested that there was a connection between loss of authority and the 'decline of the nation' in general,[21] as it was put by A.A. Mussert, the leader of the Nationaal-Socialistische Beweging (NSB - National Socialist Movement), which at the time was still extremely small. In fact they had no real

18. H. Colijn, *Wankelen noch weifelen* (Amsterdam, 1933) 19-20 (speech of 9th March, 1933).
19. B. van Kaam, *Parade der mannenbroeders. Flitsen uit het protestantse leven in Nederland in de jaren 1918-1939* (Wageningen, 1964) 202.
20. *De Tijd*, daily newspaper (Amsterdam, 21st March, 1933).
21. *Rijksinstituut voor Oorlogsdocumentatie*, Amsterdam, Archief NSB, dossiers of the leader, 2g.

hope for improvement in what the fascist weekly *De Bezem* called the 'present corrupt parliamentary democratic State'.[22]

In extreme left circles, the reaction was the opposite. Here there was rejoicing at the mutiny and the hope that there would be a follow-up. They expressed their feelings of comradeship with the mutineers, compassion with the victims, and great indignation at the actions of the government and social conditions in general. The left tried to a large extent to exploit the events for their own propagandist purposes, and in this respect they were in fact practically unanimous in spite of all their other differences. In a pamphlet published on 5th February the 'revolutionary socialist' H. Sneevliet described what had happened as 'joyous events',[23] while 'respect, deep respect' was due the mutineers, as the communist L. de Visser stated in the Second Chamber.[24] Only a few anarchists and anti-militarists doubted the justness of so positive a judgment of the mutiny. Nevertheless, the entire left found the attitude of the government and pro-government parties repulsive and thought the same, perhaps even more strongly, of the social democrats, who had shown themselves once again to be traitors to the working class.

What, ultimately, were the consequences of the mutiny and the discussions it entrained for political relations in the Netherlands? The answer to this question must remain somewhat impressionistic for want of exact information. We have already referred to the position of the SDAP. A further indication is provided by elections to the Second Chamber, held in April 1933. The mutiny inevitably played an important role in the election struggle, and in the elections themselves fairly big shifts took place in view of the Dutch political situation at the time, though the results simultaneously confirmed the stability of the existing political system. Four of the five large 'bourgeois' parties each lost one or two seats (five altogether) out of a total of one hundred, but on the other hand the ARP won two seats under Colijn, who had shown himself to be a very strong advocate of the maintenance of government authority. The SDAP, as we have seen, had to accept a loss of two seats. The extremists gained ground — the communists went from two seats to four and for the first time the Trotskyist Revolutionary Socialists secured one seat. Their leader, Sneevliet, was in jail at the time of the elections because he had written a seditious pamphlet in connection with the mutiny. A new extreme right-wing party, the Verbond voor Nationaal Herstel (Alliance for National Recovery), which had placed a great deal of emphasis on the mutiny in the election campaign, also won one seat in parliament.

22. *De Bezem*, weekly paper, VI, no. 11 (The Hague, 18th February, 1933).
23. *Het proces Sneevliet* (Amsterdam, 1933) 3.
24. *Verslag Handelingen Staten-Generaal*, II, 1624.

The shifts which followed the elections are connected with the three big issues which were mainly under discussion in those years: the great economic depression and its aftermath, the rise of fascism and national socialism in Europe, and the problem of the maintenance of government authority. The last problem was not new but had become more important in the election campaign because of the recent mutiny. It is impossible to determine to what extent each of these factors — which are moreover interrelated — separately influenced the election results. We can assume, however, that the mutiny somewhat reinforced the tendency towards extremism, although it did not provoke any big shifts and was in the long run unimportant. However, for a short time it attracted a great deal of attention because of its spectacular character, and the discussions to which it gave rise present a good picture of political and social relations in the Netherlands in the early thirties.

Dutch Jews in a Segmented Society*

H. DAALDER

INTRODUCTION

Before 1795, the situation of Dutch jews differed greatly from one local community to another. The Union of Utrecht of 1579 had banned any form of inquisition. No stigmatizing jewish insignia were allowed. There was no numerus clausus on the number of jews admitted, or any restriction on their marrying. A decree of the States General of 1657 gave resident jews the status of Dutch subjects on a par with any other Dutchman in relations to foreign States or trading partners. But for the rest, everything depended on local magistrates. Some towns (like Utrecht and Deventer) excluded jews until 1795, although Utrecht made one exception for a rabbi teaching Hebrew at a university in the early eighteenth century. Amsterdam allowed free entry to poor and rich jews alike, but excluded them from citizenship. Other towns offered more freedom on that score. But only in 1795 was a framework established for national decisions.[1]

The new unitary State did not destroy old ideological diversities. Religious pluralism persisted and possibly became even more pronounced. Conflicts within the once-dominant Dutch Reformed Church about dogma and structure intensified. Protestant dissenters assumed a greater social importance. Catholics

* Text of an address given in Jerusalem, on 20th July 1975, on the occasion of the Commemoration of the Founding in 1275 of the City of Amsterdam and of the Opening in 1675 of the Portuguese Synagogue in Amsterdam, under the auspices of the Institute for Research of Dutch Jewry of the Hebrew University, Jerusalem. Since I gave this address, it has been my privilege to receive a large number of letters with extensive criticism, notably from Dr. L. Fuks, Max H. Gans, Dr J. Michman and his son D. Michman, Dr J.J. Woltjer and from Professors Th. van Tijn, Ph. de Vries and Val R. Lorwin. Their comments have covered the entire spectrum of views on the place of jews in Dutch society, from perspectives which have ranged from orthodoxy to agnostic assimilation, from political zionism to proletarian internationalism, and from any position in between. I have tried to do justice to their subtle insights, within the small amount of space which this article allows. All will undoubtedly acknowledge that I alone am responsible for any remaining errors of facts or interpretation.
1. For an analysis of developments in the Netherlands, see H. Daalder, 'The Netherlands: Opposition in a Segmented Society', in: R.A. Dahl, ed., *Political Oppositions in Western Democracies* (New Haven, 1966) 188-236.

slowly developed from a barely-tolerated minority with a clear sense of inferiority towards the calvinists, into a better-organized and somewhat more self-confident 'pillar' of Dutch society. Political conflicts of the nineteenth and the first part of the twentieth century centred to a considerable extent on the relation between the State and those various religious bodies. During a protracted struggle from around 1870 to 1930 a society developed which, for want of the better Dutch term of a *verzuilde samenleving*, has been termed a 'segmented society'.[2] A powerful majority coalition of calvinists and catholics broke the somewhat tenuous hold which liberals exercised on Dutch society in the latter part of the nineteenth century. Later, the socialists followed suit with the establishment of an integrated subculture of their own. They remained numerically weaker than almost any comparable European socialist movement, as the socialists did not succeed until very recently in winning over large sections of the calvinist and catholic working class. The co-existence of three powerfully organized 'segments' of orthodox protestants, catholics and socialists left the liberals and their like perforce relatively weak after 1900. Liberals had a recognized heritage and a secure place in policy making. They exercised an intellectual influence well beyond their numbers. But whenever heads were counted, liberals were seen to be numerically weak until at least the 1960's.

The main theme of this address will be to seek an answer to the question: How did Dutch jewry fare in the context of these larger social processes, of centralization, urbanization, democratization, and *verzuiling* or segmentation? This question is not an easy one to answer, for a variety of reasons. Obviously, much depended on the attitudes which various social groupings in Dutch society assumed towards the jews in their midst. This subject has been little studied and is intrinsically difficult to study because the pluralism of Dutch society made for many variations in attitudes — from one social group to another and within each group separately. There were also great differences in the attitudes which various sections of the Dutch jewish community adopted towards the new Netherlands State and nation. In all cases attitudes also changed considerably over a period. The analysis is inevitably influenced, moreover, by our present knowledge. We now know of the destruction of Dutch jewry in the Second World War. The initiative for this destruction may have come at gun-point from outside the Dutch borders. But we also know that this mass murder was made possible only through the partial, if generally reluctant, assistance — or at a minimum the passive toleration — on the part of many Dutch individuals and institutions: jewish

2. A number of general articles on 'segmented societies' have conveniently been brought together in K.D. McRae, ed., *Consociational Democracy: Political Accomodation in Segmented Societies*. The Carlton Library, LXXIX (Toronto, 1974).

and non-jewish alike.[3] Hence, the historiography of the post-1945 era emphasizes very different elements from pre-1940 writings. This is noticeable in at least three different directions:

First, one encounters a definite nostalgic tone, found in such different writings as Max Gans's *magnum opus*, the *Memorboek*,[4] and the reminiscenses of isolated survivers of the Jewish Quarter of Amsterdam, *e.g.* the many books of Meijer Sluyser.[5]

Second, there is in some writings a strong denunciatory element. These may be further divided into at least three categories:

1. There is the attack along 'class' lines which seeks to 'explain' pre-1940 jewry, as well as its destruction, in terms of the victimization of the poor and the proletariat by the egoism of an irresponsible jewish bourgeoisie.

2. There is the attack from a 'zionist' perspective which castigates the lack of realism of Dutch jews who forgot — or tried to forget — their jewish identity, let alone their special link to jews elsewhere. Or even worse: who denied to their eventual peril the inescapable momentum of antisemitism.

3. There is, finally, a type of denunciatory attack from a 'religious' perspective, which aims at the exposure of the presumed 'empty' and 'formalistic' qualities of much of jewish life in nineteenth- and twentieth-century Holland, and which implicitly accuses jewish authorities and followers alike of not living up to the tasks which the commandments of faith and history prescribed.

Third, there has been after 1945 a re-newed debate on the character of jewish-gentile relations in the Netherlands. In the perspective of pre-war times it was easy to visualize mutual relations in terms of the desirable 'emancipation' of jews, which for many could be identical with 'assimilation' — if one might use the latter term to characterize the development of jews who lived in Holland into Dutchmen of jewish origin, if no longer of clear jewish faith. There was in pre-war Holland an air of conscious satisfaction on the place of jews in Dutch society, almost to the point of self-congratulation. Such a view

3. Cf. A.J. Herzberg, 'Kroniek der Jodenvervolging', in: J.J. van Bolhuis, *e. a.*, ed., *Onderdrukking en Verzet* (4 vols, Amsterdam, 1949-54) III, 5-255; J. Presser, *Ondergang: de vervolging en verdelging van het Nederlandse Jodendom, 1940-1945* (2 vols., The Hague, 1965), shortened English edition: *Ashes in the Wind: the Destruction of Dutch Jewry* (London, 1968); L. de Jong, *Het Koninkrijk der Nederlanden in de Tweede Wereldoorlog* (vols. I-VII, The Hague, 1969-76, further volumes forthcoming).
4. M.H. Gans, *Memorboek: Platenatlas van het leven der Joden in Nederland van de middeleeuwen tot 1940* (Baarn, 1971). I am heavily indebted to this magnificent work, which has since been translated as *Memorbook: Pictorial History of Dutch Jewry from the Renaissance to 1940* (Baam, 1977).
5. Meijer Sluyser wrote a series of reminiscenses: *Als de dag van gisteren; Er groeit gras in de Weesperstraat; Hun lach klinkt van zover; Voordat ik het vergeet; De wereld is rond, maar mijn zolen zijn plat* (Amsterdam, s. a.); cf. for an anthology, drawn from these books; M. van Amerongen, *Meijer Sluyser, voordat hij het vergat* (Amsterdam, 1973).

is no longer tenable. We now know that whatever their desires, jews and non-jews were not alike when facing the new Haman, notwithstanding the unprecedented strikes of February 1941 when jews and non-jews joined in one massive protest against the beginnings of pogrom-like actions in Amsterdam.[6] In the end, even jews who had practically forgotten their jewishness — however defined — were to suffer a fate far different from any gentile, however anti-semitic, philo-semitic, or indifferent he might be.

Having thus lost, I trust, any pristine sense that we face an easy subject, let us try to reconstruct the developments of Dutch jewry between 1795 and 1940 — when an alien community living in the Netherlands transformed itself into a disparate group of jewish Dutchmen, with little affinity to either each other or to world jewry.

1796 AND AFTER

The legal emancipation of Dutch jews was marked by the famous decree of 2nd September 1796 passed by the first National Assembly, which granted jews full civic rights on a parity with any other Dutch subject. The decree is the highmark of a process which was full of controversy, among the powers of the day as well as among jews at the time. The initiative came after 1795 from a new revolutionary 'patriotic' club, *Felix Libertate*. Though jewish in origin, this club had consciously included christians as members. It consisted largely of members of the upper bourgeoisie who lived according to the philosophy of the Enlightenment, the lessons of a Moses Mendelsohn notably. The new club did not find an easy reception: it was soon excluded from the National Assembly of Patriot Societies, at the specific bidding of rival Amsterdam patriot clubs, among others. In a number of Dutch communities, jews had been admitted to vote for national and provincial elections and to service in the guards. But the municipal administration of Amsterdam had counted jewish votes on a separate list just in case they might be declared invalid. Amsterdam also banned jews from voting in its elections for the new town council. It barred jews from attendance at the Patriotic quarter meetings. And it did not admit jews to armed service in its guards.

Six members of *Felix Libertate* petitioned the newly elected National Assembly, to recognize jews as full Dutch citizens. The assembly appointed a special committee of inquiry and later held a seven-day long debate on its report. The pressures and debates, — in which a very large number of representatives took part have been extensively analyzed — albeit from a different perspective — by

6. B.A. Sijes, *De Februari-staking, 24-25 februari 1941* (The Hague, 1954).

S.E. Bloemgarten in an article published in *Studia Rosenthaliana*, and by M.E. Bolle in his 1960 doctoral dissertation.[7] A focal point of the debate was the question as to whether civil rights for jews were a natural concomitant of the Declaration of Human Rights which had been promulgated earlier — if so, civil rights were an inherent *individual* right to which every jew was as much entitled as any other individual Dutchman — or whether the issue was really that of the collective emancipation of the jewish 'nations' who for centuries had enjoyed a recognized life in the Dutch Republic. If arguments in favour of emancipation on an individualistic basis sat easily with the 'enlightened' members of *Felix Libertate*, they were resisted, often bitterly, by at least three groups: (a) by those who continued to regard the jews as an 'alien' enclave in Dutch society, (b) by the leaders of the jewish communities (*kehillot*), *e.g.* the *parnassim*, and by the more orthodox segments of the jewish 'nations' generally, who wished to retain their 'autonomy', and (c) by a number of Dutch Federalists, who unlike the Unitarian Patriots did not want the imposition of one central, national policy on once autonomous town corporations. The decree which allotted jews full civil rights was eventually voted unanimously, after a procedural move to stall the decision had been defeated, by 45 against 24 votes. It is worth noting that the majority of Amsterdam members in the National Assembly had resisted the early issue of the decree. It is equally worth noting that many catholics—who had also suffered from discrimination—voted in favour.

How to assess the importance of the 1796 decree?

It enfranchised Dutch jews, and gave them in principle access to public office. It formally abolished the bar against jews which virtually all existing guilds had traditionally maintained. The guilds themselves were abolished some time afterwards. Hence jews obtained in principle, though not always in practice, easier access to more varied employment. The decree did away with a number of other discriminatory measures, e.g. the practice of letting jewish couples wait at the townhall until first all marriages of gentiles had been performed. It did away with special fees levied on jews as jews (although Friesland continued to levy such a tax until 1807).[8] It made jews eligible for general poor-law relief, and freed them at least in theory from the authority

---

7. S.E. Bloemgarten, 'De Amsterdamse Joden gedurende de eerste jaren van de Bataafse Republiek, 1795-1798', *Studia Rosenthaliana*, I,i (Amsterdam, 1967) 66-96; I,ii (1967) 45-70; II,i (1968) 42-65; M.E. Bolle, *De opheffing van de autonomie der Kehilloth (Joodse gemeenten) in Nederland, 1796* (doctoral thesis Fac. of Letters, University of Amsterdam; Amsterdam, 1960); for a very critical review of this work cf. S.E. Bloemgarten, *Studia Rosenthaliana*, III,i (1969) 128-34. There is also an unpublished treatise by A. Halff, 'De emancipatie van de Nederlandse Joden' in Bibliotheca Rosenthaliana, Amsterdam.
8. R. Mahler, *A History of Modern Jewry, 1780-1815* (London, 1971) 99.

of their own *parnassim* : it did away with the co-ordinate powers which the *parnassim* had enjoyed together with the town authorities in matters of public order and which had extended deeply into worldly matters as well as in the religious sphere. It freed jews from a number of oppressive communal monopolies, such as that of the Askhenazi and Sephardi meat halls and public baths. It lessened somewhat the powers of the *parnassim* to lay oppressive taxes on 'forced' marriages, or on funerals.

Against such 'emancipatory' effects, a number of less positive developments could be noted.

The decree represented a fundamental attack on the existing structures of the two autonomous jewish 'nations'. It has been argued, with some force, that the corporate pluralism of the Dutch Republic made the existence of independent jewish communities relatively secure although it presupposed and confirmed their secondary status. Would tolerance automatically increase, now that jews had become equal citizens, although they still might remain aliens for generations?[9]

The 'New Order' (and not least the members of *Felix Libertate* who acted as an active and influential pressure group) deliberately attempted to extinguish elements of specific jewishness. For a time, the emancipated jews formed a separate community (*kehillah*), entitled *Adath Yeshurun*. Some of the modern jews began to speak with conviction of the blessings which the Supreme Being bestowed on mankind instead of evoking the God of Israel. They tried to be as alike to other Dutchmen as possible, and treasured signs of acceptance of jews into what was basically a christian world. The town authorities maintained their ban on small synagogue services (*minjanin*) and on the erection of eighth day feast tabernacles (*sukkoth*) on public streets, and they proscribed the benediction of new moon. Dignitaries of the various synagogues, like catholic clergy, should not wear their official clothing outside synagogue buildings. Mixed marriages between jews and gentiles were legalized, and even glorified.

More generally, the presumed 'privatization' of religion — henceforth regarded as an individual, and not a collective matter — was paradoxically to lead not to less, but to greater interference by the public authorities with organized religion. Thus, a number of new regulations were imposed — on all religious communities — by Napoleon's brother, Louis Napoleon, by Napoleon himself after 1810, and by King William I of Orange, who represented a clear 'Josephist' attitude in religious matters.

For the jewish communities this led in 1808 to the establishment of a Supreme Consistory. After the French annexation of 1810, the 'German' (Ashkenazi)

9. On continuing anti-jewish discrimination after 1796, see J. Michman, 'Gothische torens op een Corinthisch gebouw', *Tijdschrift voor Geschiedenis*, LXXXIX (Groningen, 1976) 493-517.

and 'Portuguese' (Sephardi) communities were brought together under one organization. According to new regulations, a chief rabbi should now either be Dutch-born, or have at least six years' of residence in the Netherlands before appointment. The government encouraged the translation of the Bible into Dutch, and insisted on religious and other instruction in the national language. In 1815 the king further appropriated a number of control powers, in such matters as the issue of Church regulations and the drawing-up of the budget. He also appropriated the right to cast a decisive vote on the appointment of rabbis if there was a tie in voting. All official correspondence and minutes, and all readings of official announcements in the synagogues should henceforth be in Dutch only. A chief rabbi, a *shammash* (verger) and a *chazzan* (cantor) should be familiar with the Dutch language, albeit in a decreasing order: the chief rabbi should speak, read and write Dutch, a *shammash* should be able to read and write, a *chazzan* need only be able to read the language. In 1827 an official royal decree promised awards for the best translation into Dutch of sermons and teaching material.

Such measures were symptomatic of the prevailing climate of a belated Enlightenment, rather than of actual religious practices. Until 1842, the Portuguese Synagogue held its proceedings mainly in Portuguese. Not until the 1850's did Yiddish fully disappear from jewish schools. As late as 1886 a number of older members of the synagogue in Leeuwarden left in anger when it was decided to drop the use of Yiddish. Yet these reforms imposed from above provided the framework for the eventual assimilation of the jewish communities into Dutch society — through their own religious institutions and practices, as much as through other public agencies.

THE MASS OF DUTCH JEWRY: SOME SOCIOLOGICAL DATA[10]

Before we turn to a more detailed consideration of these processes, however, greater attention should be paid to the great mass of Dutch jewry. One should not forget that the developments just described initially affected only the highest levels of the Dutch jewish communities. They barely touched the life of the great mass of the poor. One should stress this aspect in particular, because for almost a century after 1795 Dutch society in general remained a stagnant and very oligarchical society. Its 'pays légal' consisted of at most some 10 per cent

---

10. Cf. J.P. Kruijt, 'Het Jodendom in de Nederlandse samenleving', in: H.J. Pos, ed., *Anti-Semitisme en Jodendom* (Arnhem, 1939) 190-227; C. Reijnders, *Van 'Joodsche Natie' tot Joodse Nederlanders* (Amsterdam, 1969).

of the people. The great mass of the population had little hope for anything but the barest essentials of life.

The most glaring characteristic of Dutch jewry throughout the eighteenth and nineteenth century was their extreme poverty, even when compared with that of other Dutch poor around them.[11] If the French period might have helped to create an institutional framework for future emancipation, it also led to a further impoverishment of an already very poor community. Even the better-off (including the Portuguese jews) lost much of their capital by the abolition of the United East India Company, by Napoleon's introduction of the Continental System, by the cutting of the national debt, etc. Poorer leaders also had fewer means with which to practice their traditional philanthropy. Further impoverishment of the Amsterdam jews was probably the chief reason for a massive exodus of jews from Amsterdam which lost in the first decades of the nineteenth century as much as a quarter of the Ashkenazim, and 15 per cent of the Sephardim.[12] They probably went in search of alternative employment in the provinces where they were now legally free to settle. For a while, therefore, the *mediene* (the provinces) assumed an increasing importance over against *Mokum.* (Amsterdam) This process was reversed after the 1850's when jews increasingly migrated back to the western part of the country.

Alms statistics reveal that poverty among jews lasted a very long time. If in 1799 more than 80 per cent of Amsterdam Ashkenazi jews (but also 54 per cent of Sephardi jews) enjoyed support (mainly in kind: food and fuel), this figure was still as high as 62 per cent for the Sephardi, and 53 per cent for the Ashkenazi community in 1859. And even then, change was only very slow to come. It came mainly as a result of the multiplier effects of new developments in diamond manufacturing, cigar making, and to a lesser extent in the clothing industry. If these developments eventually made for greater social mobility — what prominent Dutch jew to-day, one is tempted to ask, is not the son or grandson of a former diamond worker? — and if all this resulted in increasing diversification of employment, there was no escape from the basic fact about Dutch jewry: the great majority remained poor. Within the jewish community social distances between the relatively rich (who generally were not very rich themselves) and the unmistakably poor remained vast.[13]

A look at demographic figures — the subject of a detailed study by the

11. S. Kleerekoper, 'Het Joodse proletariaat in het Amsterdam van de 19e eeuw', *Studia Rosenthaliana*, I,i (1967) 97-108, I,ii, 71-84.
12. Cf. Reijnders, '*Joodsche Natie*', *passim.*
13. Cf. Th. van Tijn, *Twintig jaren Amsterdam: de maatschappelijke ontwikkeling van de hoofdstad van de jaren '50 der vorige eeuw tot 1867* (Amsterdam, 1965) 125 ff.; Kleerekoper, 'Joodse proletariaat 19e eeuw', 98 ff.

late Amsterdam alderman E. Boekman[14] — reveals a number of further characteristics about Dutch jews before 1940. There was a slight temporary increase in the percentage share of jews in Dutch society through the immigration of Polish and Russian jews in the 1870's and 1880's. There was a very rapid urbanization of jews who left the provinces in disproportionate numbers, largely again for Amsterdam. There was a quick fall in the jewish birthrate so that the jewish community was greying strongly, and decreased after 1890 in relation to the fast-growing Dutch population as a whole. There was a strong loss in the earlier distinctiveness of the Sephardi and Ashkenazi communities who increasingly intermarried. There was an increase also in mixed marriages between jews and non-jews, notably in the provinces; there was also a growing reluctance on the part of persons of jewish descent to identify themselves with the jewish religion at census time.

Data on the domicile of Dutch jews further showed a large-scale *trek* away from the former jewish quarter in Amsterdam to neighbouring and other districts in the town: as a result the old Jodenhoek included only 18 per cent of Amsterdam jews in 1930.[15] This was the result partly of the demolition of the worst slum areas like Marken and Uilenburg. One of the districts cleared away was the Rode Leeuwengang, the alley from which the parents of Samuel Gompers had emigrated shortly before the birth in London of that later leader of the American Federation of Labor.[16] There was also a *trek* to suburbs of Amsterdam, away from the core of the town. If slum clearance did away with some of the worst and insanitary housing conditions in Dutch history, it also destroyed some of the intimacy and the face-to-face relationships which had characterized traditional jewish life in Amsterdam. The socialist leader of the Amsterdam diamond workers, Henri Polak, was to write unexpectedly lyrical reminiscences about life in the ghetto — ending with his famous nostalgic words: *En toch, en toch!* (And yet! And yet!).[17] And the demolition part of the old quarter was to inspire Jacob Israel de Haan to one of his most beautiful poems, which reads as follows:[18]

> Here, where for centuries we have dwelled,
> Humbly engaged in petty trade,
> Knowing bright moments and long hours of shade,
> The breaker's axe is hard at work.

14. E. Boekman, *Demografie van de Joden in Nederland* (Amsterdam, 1936).
15. Kruijt, 'Jodendom', 205 ff.
16. Cf. Gans, *Memorboek*, 668-9. Gompers was born in London in 1850.
17. H. Polak, cited in *Memorbook*, 639 ff.
18. De wijk, waar ons volk eeuwen heeft gewoond
    bij smal bestand van dagelijkschen handel,
    maar duldend steeds in wisselenden wandel,
    wordt door de felle sloopers neergeslagen.

Many who have rarely stepped outside,
Must wander now without a guide,
While children, pale-faced, sad and wan,
Revive like flowers in the sun.
Life carries on, an ancient ward's no more.
Does it spell freedom from old chains?
Or will dilution bring new pains?

THE DECLINING HOLD OF THE RELIGIOUS COMMUNITIES

By the middle of the nineteenth century, the religious organizations of Dutch jewry were in some disarray. From 1838 to 1874, and again from 1911 to 1916, the Ashkenazim had no chief rabbi, and the Sephardi community had none for a period as long as 1822 to 1900. In 1848, a change in the constitution brought a definite separation of Church and State. Soon afterwards the government invited the jewish communities to revise their statutes so as to bring them into line with the new constitutional situation. There followed a farcical period of twenty years' bickering and disagreement among the different *kehillot* which was brought to an end only by direct government pressure in 1870. The two main divisive issues were: 1. whether to retain or rescind the government-imposed unity between the Portuguese and the Ashkenazi communities — a matter which was finally solved by a return to the organizational independence which had existed earlier; and 2. the particular place of Amsterdam jews in the remaining religious organization. Amsterdam finally got its way: even though the organization of the Ashkenazi Nederlands Israëlietisch Kerkgenootschap (Netherlands Israelite Church Community) was to be built up from representatives of different *kehillot*, its Permanent Executive Committee was to consist of — and to be chosen by — Amsterdam Jews, and by them alone.[19]

In 1862 J.H. Dünner became rector of the Netherlands Jewish Seminary, and in 1874 he was also appointed chief rabbi of Amsterdam. Dünner's influence was massive and lasting. He built the seminary into a true training institute for Dutch rabbis — a group described in detail and with great love and

Menig moe man, die schaars zijn wijk verliet,
ontruimt zijn steeg, verbitterd van verdriet,
en kinderen, als een bleek bloeisel verkwijnd,
herbloeien in hun open lichte dagen,
het leven streeft: een oude wijk verdwijnt.
Is het geluk: bevrijding uit verenging?
Is het gevaar: bedreiging met vermenging?
(Jacob Israël de Haan, 1916, on the occasion of the exhibition 'The Vanishing Ghetto', quoted by Gans, *Memorboek*, 637. English translation by Arnold J. Pomerans).

19. A.S. Rijxman, *A.C. Wertheim, 1832-1897* (Amsterdam, 1961) 97-8; I. Lipschits, *Honderd jaar NIW: het Nieuw Israëlitisch Weekblad, 1865-1965* (Amsterdam, 1966) 90 ff.

piety by Gans in his *Memorboek*.[20] According to many observers, Dünner 'saved' the religions institutious of Dutch jewry. But in retrospect, his role has also come in for considerable criticism, in at least three directions. He has been accused of turning the seminary too much into a semi-university, by demanding a severe training in classics on a par with jewish training, leading one biased former pupil to the remark that it was turning out 'synthetic rabbis: 50 per cent Talmud, 50 per cent classics'.[21] It is alleged, secondly, that Dünner severed Dutch jewry from the great international centres of jewish learning, by not recognizing religious training obtained elsewhere and by being particularly severe on the use of Yiddish. And thirdly, his influence is thought to have made effective communion between most members of the intellectual rabbinate and the mass of poor jews more difficult, so that the religious organizations and institutions were unable to stem the large drift away of many of the ordinary one-time believers. Neighbourhood and *chevra-shuls* (synagogues of small associations) did something to stem this tide. Most jews, notably those in Amsterdam, retained some minimal emotional ties with religious institutions, but then of the kind of the man who said: 'I am a Dutchman of the jewish faith, who does not care about the jewish faith'. If circumcision, religious marriage and funerals might be kept up, the observance of sabbath or dietary laws declined rapidly.

There were other clear signs of loosening bonds. Counts of seats and of actual attendance of services revealed both in 1880 and in 1935, a massive disproportionality between nominal religious membership and actual practice. There were some 5,000 seats in Amsterdam synagogues in 1880, and some 3,000 in 1935, in either case sufficient for fewer than 10 per cent of Amsterdam jewry only. Even so, already in 1880 some 1,000 or more seats usually remained empty on sabbath.[22] There was also a sharp decline in jewish instruction.[23] In the beginning of the nineteenth century there had been a number of (admittedly poor) private jewish schools or teachers, and even some publicly financed jewish schools. These disappeared rapidly after 1857 when jewish children flocked massively to the government schools (even though in the phraseology of the Education Act these were to educate children to 'christian

---

20. Gans, *Memorboek*, 370-7.
21. J. Meijer, *Hoge hoeden/lage standaarden: de Nederlandse Joden tussen 1933 en 1940* (Baarn, 1969) 27; cf. Rijxman, *Wertheim*, 92 ff., 227 ff.
22. Meijer, *Hoge hoeden*, 42 ff.; cf. also Kruijt, 'Jodendom', 222-3.
23. Joseph Michman, who was himself the son of a teacher at a jewish school, holds that the dominant liberal jewish leaders in the Netherlands put charity before education in expressing their jewish identity; cf. his contribution on 'The Netherlands' in: *Encyclopaedia Judaica*, XII (Jerusalem, 1971) col. 983. On jewish schools, see also D. Michman, *Joods onderwijs in Nederland, 1616-1905. Geschiedenis samengesteld ter ere van de opening van nieuwe gebouwen van de Stichting Joodse Scholengemeenschap* (Amsterdam, 1973).

and social virtues'). At a time when catholics and calvinists began to rebel against these, demanding full financial support for separate denominational schools, jews on the whole embraced them with alacrity. Only a few isolated voices called for attempts to establish jewish denominational schools on a par with catholics and calvinists, including J.H. Dünner in his later life and also the Portuguese chief rabbi I. de Juda Palache. Although a few jewish schools were established, most vested interests in the jewish communities went against this trend. Only in 1939 did a minority report on the schools issue raise the banner for a massive expansion of separate jewish schools — much too late and too little to turn the tide of mass alienation.[24] Some attempt was made to fill the gap by the organization of special jewish schools, held on Sundays or after school time. But these were often of low quality, and they were inevitably very poorly attended.

Until as late as the early 1930's, the existing religious organizations did prove able to resist the establishment of separate reform communities. This was partly due to a curious *mariage de raison* between the orthodox on the one hand, and leading liberal elements on the other. It was the very liberal president of the Ashkenazi Kerkgenootschap, A.C. Wertheim (1832-1897) who at a critical moment in 1897 prevented the ousting of an orthodox majority from the governing boards of the Amsterdam community.[25] He set an example which was followed later by many leaders such as Abraham Asscher who occupied positions of authority in the religious governing bodies, notwithstanding the fact that they had themselves little actual identification with traditional religion in private life. Thus official jewry was both liberal and supportive of orthodoxy in official jewish life, and in most cases very definitely bourgeois — the work of some individual *rebbes* notwithstanding.[26]

JEWS IN DUTCH POLITICAL AND SOCIAL LIFE

What place did jews attain in Dutch political life? Immediately after 1796 there were some seemingly remarkable breakthroughs. Historians claim that the first two jews elected to any national assembly in western European

24. Meijer, *Hoge hoeden*, 80-1.
25. Cf. Rijxman, *Wertheim*, 226.
26. One might offer the hypothesis that the somewhat official character of the jewish religion under liberal influence in the Netherlands, and the absence of strong sectarian conflicts within the jewish community, may have been factors for alienating the jewish proletariat from all religion. For a parallel analysis explaining the early success of socialist propaganda in East Groningen by the dominance of liberal Church leaders in the Dutch Reformed Church which, unlike a more orthodox pietistic calvinism in other parts of the same province, had offered no solace to a starving proletariat, see: E.W. Hofstee, *Het Oldambt* (Groningen, 1937).

countries were H.L. Bromet and H. de H. Lemon who became members of the Second National Assembly in 1797. Twice a jew became a member of the Amsterdam town council in 1798, but not for long. There was the remarkable career of Jonas Daniel Meyer whose name is inextricably bound to a well-known square — now practically denuded and destroyed — near the remaining large Amsterdam synagogues. At sixteen a doctor of Leiden University, Meyer was admitted in 1796 as barrister to the Court of Holland. He became a leading counsellor to both Louis Napoleon and King William I. Perhaps the most interesting of his many appointments was that of secretary to the committee which drafted the constitution of 1815. This committee consisted of twelve protestants and twelve catholics. The king gave it a jewish secretary. In the nineteenth century the law[27] provided employment to numerous other prominent jewish lawyers, like A. de Pinto who became *landsadvocaat* (crown counsel). There were two famous dynasties of jurists: the Asser-family, beginning with Mozes Salomon Asser (who had been one of the founding members of *Felix Libertate*), and ending with Tobias Asser who won the Nobel Prize and became an apostate — and the Van Nierop-family. Typically, the only two professing jews who became cabinet ministers before 1940 were ministers of justice, and had it not been for their own refusal two others might have served in the same office. L.E. Visser was a well-known jewish president of the Supreme Court, from which he was dismissed during the German occupation. Similarly after 1945: another two jewish cabinet ministers, including the later burgomaster of Amsterdam, Ivo Samkalden, served in the ministry of justice.

On the basis of a Leiden University computer-file of all members of the Dutch parliament,[28] one can arrive at a clear picture of the successive election of jewish deputies, first as liberals ('uniting Thora and Thorbecke' as the phrase went in those days — Johan Rudolf Thorbecke being the leading constitutional liberal of the third quarter of the nineteenth century), then as radicals, then as socialists. Out of 100 members of the Dutch Second Chamber in 1940, eight were of jewish descent (four socialists, two radicals, one liberal, one communist). At the same time, our computer-file also exposes anew the sensitive problem of whom to define as jews. What about agnostics? What about apostates? If of some 1600 members of parliament in the file, we located 30 jews (three sons of a *rabbi*, one of a *shammash*, one of a *shochet* (a ritual slaughterer), we know of at least another twenty politicians of jewish descent

27. Cf. B.M. Telders, 'De Joodse geest en het recht', in: Pos, ed., *Anti-Semitisme*, 107-29.
28. A scanning of the Leiden computerized biographical file of over 1600 members of parliament since 1848 finds 11 liberals, 6 radicals, 10 socialists, 2 communists, and one dissident socialist. This number could probably be doubled if one were to include those who are known to have been of jewish descent, but who no longer reckoned themselves as belonging to the jewish religious community.

not registered as jewish, including Mr. Samkalden just mentioned and the present chairman of the socialist party in parliament, Mr. Ed van Thijn.

Should one conclude from this that there was something of a bar against professing jews in Dutch politics? Some symptoms might be adduced in evidence. How often did one not encounter the view that jews should not seek public office, lest they expose themselves to antisemitism? In 1933, that eminent example of the Dutch Yellow Press, *De Telegraaf*, condemned the simultaneous serving of four jewish aldermen in Amsterdam (although they represented different political parties). Jews were very definitely underrepresented in numerous public offices: there was not a single jewish mayor serving in Holland by 1940, and not a single jew was a prosecutor in that same year, to take only some examples.[29]

We can expand this statement further, to other parts of society. Even in the professions like the law, the medical profession, or journalism which have often attracted prominent jews, they never surpassed the 5 per cent figure. Marx's famous, and infamous, anti-semitic description of Amsterdam *Haute Finance* — which he described as better in finding their way about other people's cash than the smartest highwayman in the Abruzzi[30] — was far off the mark, even in his day. In the 1930's there were some small jewish banks. Two larger Dutch banks had one or two jewish directors. But jews were absent from the board of all other large banks. Not a single jew even worked in the Bank of the Netherlands. Jews found positive bars against them in such worlds as insurance, or shipping. Even in the universities, the number of jewish professors was far from numerous, with the law faculties as a possible exception.

Against such facts one might pose a long list of successful apostates in Dutch society : *e.g.* Marx's uncle, Lion Philips, who was to become the father of the Philips dynasty; the founder of the largest cigar-making factory Van Abbe in whose name the famous Van Abbe museum was established in Eindhoven; the president of the Jewish Seminary, S.P. Lipman who turned catholic in 1852; famous calvinists like the poet Isaac da Costa (1798-1860) and the physician Abraham Capadose (1795-1874); the Ephraim family of Tiel who as Tilanus were to end as leaders of a protestant party the Christian-Historical Union, and many others. Does this mean that baptism was vital as an entrance ticket in Dutch society? It is a hazardous statement. Paradoxically, many of the apostates remained known as being of jewish origin, and some did little to hide that fact. A former Sephardim like that famous apostate to calvinism,

29. H. Polak, *Het wetenschappelijk anti-semitisme: weerlegging en vertoog (s.l., s.a.)*; *idem*, in: *Volksblad voor Gelderland* (27 Dec. 1938) quoted in: Kruijt, 'Jodendom', 206 ff.
30. Marx's statement is only one of many in the same vein, cf. W.H. Chaloner and W.O. Henderson, 'Marx, Engels and Racism', *Encounter*, XLV (London, July 1975) 20.

Isaac da Costa, even prided himself on his jewish descent and essential jewishness,[31] thus strengthening the myth of the 'Hebrew coloration'[32] of Dutch society, and of Dutch calvinists as representing the 'Israel of the West'. Thus many calvinists regarded themselves as united to jews by a bond between two chosen people. Although such sentiments did not prevent anti-semitic utterances —not least those of the famous calvinist leader Abraham Kuyper—this factor may have contributed to making the calvinists the single most important communal group which was to harbour jews in hiding after 1941. A certificate of baptism was also not of great interest, because the census, as well as people generally, soon began to regard 'agnostics' of whatever earlier background, as perfectly respectable members of society.

DUTCH JEWS IN A SEGMENTED SOCIETY

What to conclude about the position of Dutch jews? One might single out a few main themes: first, the vague atmosphere of provincialism which characterized Dutch jewry in its relation towards world jewry; second, the marked contrast between the assimilatory tendencies of Dutch jews on the one hand and the simultaneous growth of powerful isolated subcultures of Dutch calvinists and catholics on the other hand; and finally, the somewhat deferential attitudes of many Dutch jews towards public authority.

1. The provincialism of Dutch jewry may be illustrated both by its relation towards other religious centres in the world, and by the somewhat special nature of the Dutch zionist movement.

As we have seen, both the Ashkenazi and Sephardi communities were successfully 'Netherlandized' in the course of the nineteenth century, even within their own day-to-day religious services and practices: by their successful integration into Dutch society, they partook of the provincial outlook which was characteristic of the Netherlands in world affairs generally. Both the Ashkenazim's loss of Yiddish and the clear atmosphere of self-satisfaction among Dutch jews thus alienated them from the great Talmudic centres in Eastern Europe, and also made them virtual strangers to the new centres of judaism across the Atlantic. Very often, jewish intellectual and religious leaders found their chief intellectual frame of reference more easily in secular Dutch or European culture than in living jewish culture in other lands.

A similar proposition may also be maintained with regard to the zionist movement. On the whole, the religious establishment, and also the jewish

---

31. Cf. M.J.P.M. Weijtens, *Nathan en Shylock in de Lage Landen: de Jood in het werk van de Nederlandse letterkundigen in de negentiende eeuw* (Groningen, 1971) 81 ff.
32. The phrase is Busken Huet's, quoted by Kruijt, 'Jodendom', 193.

189

press — such as the *Nieuw Israelietisch Weekblad*[33] — came down strongly against political zionism, as did a meeting of chief rabbis in a later much-criticized statement in 1904.[34] There were some early and notable exceptions among the rabbinate: again J.H. Dünner and particularly S.Ph. de Vries of Haarlem. Mizrachi, which sought to combine orthodoxy with zionism, had a Dutch branch from 1911. But when young Mizrachi activists introduced innovations like using the modern Hebrew pronunciation in prayers, they were officially condemned by older Mizrachi and other religious leaders for acting against jewish law.[35]

The Dutch zionist movement similarly failed to strike root among the large jewish proletariat in the Netherlands. When Herzl walked the Amsterdam jewish quarters, he had expressed the hope that its children would soon sing zionist hymns.[36] This was not to be. The jewish proletariat of Amsterdam followed socialism rather than zionism. In its initial emancipation, so it has been said, it even found in Henri Polak its own *rebbe* and in the General Diamond Workers' Union a secular substitute for a *chevra* synagogue. A Dutch Poale-Zion branch was established only in 1933, and it was never to acquire a massive following. One of its leaders, S. Kleerekoper, was to rationalize its failure to develop a mass following by insisting that this particular brand of zionism demanded more comprehension than any other ideology: *i.e.* a full understanding of the proletarian and of the national issue, both combined in a living synthesis. Presumably, only the elect could thus be counted upon...[37]

Zionism thus was mainly a movement of the secular younger intellectuals of bourgeois descent. The membership of the Nederlandse Zionistenbond (Netherlands Zionist Society) stood at a little over 4,000 in 1939, and the actual number of Dutch jews who had departed to Palestine must have been around 1500.[38] In as far as Dutch zionists were of significance to the International Zionist Movement this was mainly through the activities of particular individuals (who were often in opposition to the international Executive, for that matter). One can single out three outstanding figures by way of example: the banker Jacobus Kann who purchased the land on which Tel Aviv was to be built;[39]

---

33. Cf. Lipschits, *Honderd jaar NIW*, 228-53; Meijer, *Hoge hoeden*, 59-86.
34. Cf. L.A.M. Giebels, *De zionistische beweging in Nederland, 1899-1941* (Assen, 1975) 35ff.
35. Meijer, *Hoge hoeden*, 72.
36. Gans, *Memorboek*, 600, 607.
37. S. Kleerekoper, 'Het joodse proletariaat in het Amsterdam van de eerste helft der twintigste eeuw en zijn leiders', *Studia Rosenthaliana*, III,ii (1969) 216 and cf. Giebels, *Zionistische beweging*, 64-7, 184-92.
38. In Oct. 1939 the Nederlandse Zionistenbond put its membership at 4246: Giebels, *Zionistische beweging*, 171.

Fritz (later Perez) Bernstein who became a cabinet minister in Israel in 1948; and Nehemia de Lieme, who was prominent in the international as well as the Dutch zionist movement. De Lieme's special outlook has been described by one of his lieutenants in the following terms :

> No participation in religious organizational activities. No authority in the organization for those who supported the Zionist cause only with money. Immigration not for those who seek refuge in Palestine, but only for those who could contribute actively by their own labour to the economic development of the country — not quantity, but quality. Buying of land only in as far as financially responsible, and only if a profitable exploitation were guaranteed. Rejection of any political proposition which did not start from the idea of exclusive jewish control of the whole country.[40]

Chaim Weizmann dubbed Dutch zionism a *Geschäftszionismus* (commercial zionism) — a view provoked not least by De Lieme's financial strictures against the policies of the Jewish Agency in Israel.[41] One foreign jewish observer who was approached in 1942 about the plight of Dutch jews, cynically remarked: 'All I know about Dutch jewry, alas, is that the guilder was always good'.[42]

2. The development of Dutch jewry in the nineteenth and twentieth century stands in considerable contrast with developments in the same period of the orthodox calvinists and the catholics. The emancipation movements of the more militant calvinists and catholics expressed themselves in a strengthening of orthodoxy and a rapid development of a tight organizational network to buttress their particular systems of belief, their interests and social bonds. The typical mechanisms of the politics of *verzuiling* could have been used to some extent by jews as well, for instance by the establishment of a network of denominational jewish schools, and of State-subsidized welfare organizations. But Dutch jews used such potential instruments only sparingly. Some explanations may be advanced as to why they did not follow the example of other Dutch religious groupings:

(*a*) From the outset, the jewish community may have been too divided: originally, between Ashkenazim and Sephardim; within the elite, between the traditional parnassim and the emancipationists of 1795 and later years; and between the elite on the one hand, and the proletarian mass on the other. Moreover, such sense of identity as history had initially created was eroded to a great extent once social modernization resulted in increased physical and social mobility.

---

39. Gans, *Memorboek*, 611-2.
40. I. Kisch, review of L. de Jong, *Het Koninkrijk der Nederlanden*, 'Een bespreking, maar eigenlijk een bosje mémoires', *Studia Rosenthaliana*, III,ii, 264.
41. Gans, *Memorboek*, 613; Giebels, *Zionistische beweging, passim*.
42. Gans, *Memorboek*, 627.

(b) There was the comfort of existing jewish religious institutions which were always there, although they exerted few real claims. Jewish religion differed from calvinism and catholicism, moreover, in that it provided less of a dogmatic-ideological system, and more of a shared tradition of commands and customs. The latter lent themselves less easily to a process of defensive politicization than did calvinist or catholic dogma.

(c) There was a persistent fear on the part of many jews to press jewish claims, even in such a relatively favourable environment as Dutch society seemingly offered. The importance of this factor may be compared to similar anxieties, found among that other minority grouping in the Netherlands, which had suffered even more resolute discrimination in the past: that of the catholics. But in the case of the catholics large numbers, and strong regional bastions, eventually overcame clear qualms and fears, although even this process took in practice a century or more.

(d) There was always the possibility of the individual way out: baptism only rarely, agnosticism more frequently, indifferent jewishness more naturally.

(e) There was the rival attraction of political creeds: of liberalism and socialism above all (but also in the 1930's of the strong-man calvinist anti-revolutionary Hendrik Colijn). Though liberals and socialists often took jewish support too easily for granted, without a strong need for repayment in kind, they did make room for influential politicians of jewish descent: e.g. an I.A. Levy who was practically the founder of the Liberal Union in 1885, a Henri Polak who helped establish the Social Democratic Labour Party (SDAP) in 1894, and David Wijnkoop, one of the triumvirate which headed the beginning of the Dutch communist movement in 1909. One could argue, that jewish *verzuiling* was obviated, exactly because the jewish bourgeoisie integrated successfully into the liberal segment, the jewish proletariat (and also a number of jewish intellectuals of bourgeois descent) into the socialist subculture.

(f) Sheer size was another factor. Catholics and calvinists also had to fight the indifferent and the antagonistic in their midst, but the core of committed remained always credibly large. This was never true of the Dutch jewish community — so very much smaller in numbers in proportion to the rest of the Dutch population. The number of jewish leaders was almost too few to man the manifold jewish religious organizations, let alone to build these into an independent comprehensive subculture of its own.

(g) A final factor may have been the heavy concentration of jews in Amsterdam. There they could feel self-sufficient, in a way jews in other parts of the country could not. Jews outside Amsterdam were never strong enough in comparison to Amsterdam jews to go it alone. If Amsterdam lacked the incentive, jews in the provinces lacked the infrastructure for anything more than somewhat introspective jewish life.

3. As well as a certain provincialism, and an unwillingness to press minority status on a par with catholics and calvinists, a third characteristic trait of leading jews in the Netherlands was an overtly trustful — not to say deferential — attitude towards public authority. The force of this attitude may be illustrated, for instance, by the particularly strong adulation of the House of Orange in jewish circles. One need only compare the tone of Menasseh Ben Israels' elocution in the Portuguese synagogue to Frederick Henry and the English Queen Henrietta Maria in 1642[43] with the speech of Chief Rabbi A.S. Onderwijzer when he welcomed Queen Wilhelmina, her husband and daughter to the large Ashkenazi synagogue in 1924,[44] to find a consistent attitude.

A more portentous example can be found in the respectful attitude towards the Dutch authorities, demonstrated by the leaders of the Committee of Special Jewish Affairs, with Abraham Asscher and Professor David Cohen as its main leaders since 1933. There is a direct link between this organization and its attitude — at the moment when hell had already broken loose on the other side of the Dutch border — with the later attitudes of the Joodse Raad (the Jewish Council) under Asscher and Cohen after 1941.[45]

It is the bitter paradox of the combination of assimilatory and deferential attitudes that they could not prevent the forceful re-imposition of a jewish 'collectivity' once 'the jewish problem' began to make itself felt in the Netherlands. A number of events foreshadowed the coming holocaust. Was there not in the treatment of immigrants and refugees by Dutch and jewish authorities alike already visible something of a coalition of all the known against the nameless? Should one not regard the banning of all immigration of foreigners in May 1938, based on the alleged need to avoid economic competition and *Ueberfremdung*, as a first sign of discrimination against the really unprotected?[46] And should one be allowed to forget that the concentrationcamp of *Westerbork* was built by the Dutch government, originally as a camp for jewish refugees, far from the urban centres of the country, at the expense of Dutch jewry and jewish organizations? Most Dutch jews thought themselves secure in the

43. A contemporary text of the address in Portuguese was shown at the Exhibition on The Portuguese Jews of Amsterdam in Jerusalem, in the Jewish National and University Library, Jerusalem, 1975, catalogue no. 122.
44. Gans, *Memorboek*, 632.
45. Cf. De Jong, *Koninkrijk der Nederlanden*, I, 511 ff. D. Michman has prepared a doctoral dissertation for the Hebrew University of Jerusalem on jewish refugees from Germany and their fate in the Netherlands between 1933 and 1940.
46. Cf. B.A. Sijes, 'The Position of the Jews during the German Occupation of the Netherlands: Some Observations', *Acta Historiae Neerlandicae*, IX (The Hague, 1976) 173.

Netherlands, and they respected the authorities placed over them. Many would continue to do so, when the new German rulers began to use Dutch authorities — both jewish and non-jewish — as instruments first in the registration of the jews, later in their deportation.

Survey of Recent Historical Works on Belgium and the Netherlands Published in Dutch

ROSEMARY L. JONES and K.W. SWART, *editors**

INTRODUCTION

For the fifth year in succession Professor K.W. Swart and the members of the Dutch history seminar at the Institute of Historical Research, London University, have produced a bibliographical article covering the history of the Low Countries from the middle ages to the present day. They have been assisted by several Belgian and Dutch historians and a list of contributors is appended. The majority of books reviewed here appeared in 1974 and 1975. As before, no attempt has been made to cover French language publications on Belgian history and the reader interested in these is referred to *Acta Historiae Neerlandicae*, IX (1976) 187, where the details of relevant literature are given.

The National Archives in Brussels published a survey of material kept in the archive depositories of the Flemish provinces (Antwerp, Beveren-Waas, Bruges, Ghent, Hasselt, Kortrijk and Ronse), giving details of their history and of the contents and extent of the material preserved, as well as a survey of printed and hand-written inventories.[1] Similar volumes concerning Brabant and the Walloon area are in preparation. H. Coppejans-Desmedt investigated the extent to which the history of business firms can be studied on the basis of records kept in the national depositories, the municipal and university archives and museums.[2] In her report she points out that there appears to be enough material for historical research in the areas of heavy industry and the processing industry,

* The editors wish to record their special indebtedness to Dr. J.A. Kossmann for her assistance in preparing this article.
1. *Het Rijksarchief in de provinciën. Overzicht van de fondsen en verzamelingen*, I, *De Vlaamse provinciën* (Brussels : Algemeen Rijksarchief, 1975, 405 pp.).
2. H. Coppejans-Desmedt, 'De bedrijfsarchieven in België', in: *Economische geschiedenis van België. Behandeling van de bronnen en problematiek. De handelingen van het colloquium te Brussel, 17-19 nov. 1971 — Histoire économique de la Belgique*, ... (2 vols., Brussels: Algemeen Rijksarchief, 1972) I, 205-20. H. Coppejans has also published a guide to these collections: *Gids van de bedrijfsarchieven bewaard in de openbare depots van België — Guide des archives d'entreprises*, ... (Brussels: Algemeen Rijksarchief, 1975, 356 pp.). Collections of private papers, acquired by the Rijksarchief between 1950 and 1972, have been listed by D. Stobbeleir, 'Familiearchieven in het Belgisch Rijksarchief gekomen tussen 1950 en 30 juni 1972', *Archief- en bibliotheekwezen in België*, XLV (Brussels, 1974) 280-320.

but that with respect to other enterprises and to financial institutions the situation is less favourable although there is at present considerable pressure to preserve their records.

In 1974 Charles Verlinden completed the thirtieth year of a long teaching career, first at the University of Ghent and from 1957 at the Academia Belgica at Rome. A large number of friends, colleagues and former pupils have seized this opportunity to pay homage to this distinguished and versatile historian by presenting him with two volumes of learned contributions. *Miscellanea offerts à Charles Verlinden* contains 40 articles by scholars from all parts of the world, none of them written in Dutch.[3] They deal mainly with southern European and Latin-American history, thus reflecting major aspects of Verlinden's interests and activities. There is a most useful bibliography listing all the 535 publications which Verlinden published up to 1973. Craeybeckx, Van Houtte, Van Caenegem and others throw light on his many professional activities in short biographical notices.

In the other volume presented to Verlinden most of the articles are in Dutch and pertain to the history of the southern Netherlands.[4] Here we find a short, but interesting article by A. Verhulst on the growing participation, commencing in the thirteenth century, by wealthy citizens of the Tournai region in cattle-breeding as a profitable investment. Two contributions deal with the population of Ghent in the fourteenth century. The late professor Van Werveke, who in 1947 published an article on the subject, reconsiders the material in view of the criticism voiced in 1970 by D.M. Nicholas. Apart from one minor correction he keeps to his original evaluation of the source material and now proposes 60,000 as a probable total number of inhabitants. W. Prevenier is mainly interested in the structure of the population and the impact made upon it by the cloth industry. He estimates that some 60 per cent of the inhabitants (67 per cent of the craftsmen) were in some way engaged in cloth making. For the remarkable contribution by H. Van der Wee, comparing prices and wages in England with those in the southern Netherlands between 1400 and 1700, see above p. 58ff. An even longer period is covered in a substantial, well-documented article by C. Vandenbroeke, analyzing the ups and downs of wine consumption in Ghent from the fourteenth to the nineteenth century. He concludes that the consumption of wine *per capita* of the population (as high as 38 litres yearly in the 1360s) was already declining in the fifteenth century,

3. *Miscellanea offerts à — aangeboden aan Charles Verlinden à l'occasion de ses trente ans de professorat — ter gelegendheid van zijn dertig jaar professoraat* (Ghent: Universa, 1975, liv + 669 pp.). The articles published in this volume also appear in *Bulletin de l'Institut historique belge de Rome*, XLIV (Brussels-Rome, 1974).
4. *Album aangeboden aan — offert à Charles Verlinden ter gelegenheid van zijn dertig jaar professoraat — à l'occasion de ses trente ans de professorat* (Ghent: Universa, 1975, x + 478 pp.).

remained steady during the following centuries, but decreased sharply in the nineteenth century, when wine became more of an upper-class luxury article. The author relates this later development to the general decline of prosperity in the first half of the nineteenth century, but also takes into account the rising popularity of spirits and coffee since the eighteenth century. As to the origin of the wine, Vandenbroeke states that, whereas in the sixteenth century about 60 per cent came from France and some 36 from Germany, in the eighteenth, French wine dominates the market (88 per cent) with Spanish wines making steady progress. Whether the first signs of declining wine consumption, which the author found at the end of the fifteenth century, is in any way related to a dwindling of the domestic production of wine is a problem left unmentioned. In another contribution J. Craeybeckx brings out Alva's powerlessness against those who in 1572 opposed his 'tenth-penny' policy. K. Degryse deals with the attraction of Iberian trade to Antwerp merchants especially in the second half of the seventeenth century, whereas R. Baetens explains why the Ostend East India Company made such high profits in China compared with its meagre results in Bengal. M. Baelde, who is preparing a study of the High Court in Vienna, which supervised the administration of the southern Netherlands from 1717 to 1759, gives a preliminary account of the composition of this institution and its conflicts with the Austrian chancellor Kaunitz, which led to the abolition of the Court. H. Coppejans-Desmedt provides some new details on the benefits derived by the nineteenth-century cotton industry at Ghent from the economic policies of King William I. Although these and other articles are of unequal importance, the volume as a whole forms an impressive tribute to Verlinden.

To celebrate the retirement in 1974 of Antoine De Smet from his post as head of the maps department at the Albertine library, Brussels, friends and colleagues have compiled a selection from his many widespread articles, mainly on Belgian topography and cartography. The *Album Antoine De Smet* contains articles dating from the 'thirties as well as fairly recent studies, covering six centuries of history.[5] Deserving special mention is the interesting study on Flemish surveyors in the middle ages which first appeared in *De Leiegouw* (1966). Whereas no surveyor can be traced before 1190 — when a Bernoldus *landmetra* turns up — the profession is frequently mentioned in documents from the thirteenth century onwards.

The archivist of Ypres, O. Mus, has edited a volume of studies on the history of his town. Some have been published previously, others written for the occasion, and they cover the period from the thirteenth century to the present

5. *Album Antoine de Smet* (Brussels: Nationaal centrum voor de geschiedenis der wetenschappen, 1974, 526 pp.).

day, with an emphasis on social and economic history.[6] Here we find amongst others Mus's own contribution on Ypres wool merchants in England, A. Verhulst's study on the origins of the town and several contributions by J. Demey on the textile industry. There are also articles on the bishopric of Ypres, on sixteenth-century local printers and on the fortunes of the town in and after the First World War. J.A. Van Houtte wrote an introduction: a survey of the history of Ypres throughout the ages. The volume is excellently illustrated.

As a guide to the exhibition of Norbertine art treasures held at Park-Heverlee Abbey (1973) a catalogue was published which deserves our attention because it contains valuable introductory articles on the history of the Norbertines in the southern Netherlands.[7] N.J. Wyns surveys the spiritual history of the Norbertines in the Low Countries and deals with the origins and development of the order, as well as the administrative organization of the abbeys and monasteries. R. Van Uytven shows the influence of the Norbertine prelates in the States of Brabant (until *c.* 1750), where they came to the defence of Church autonomy against the increasing interference by the central government, whereas L. Van Buyten describes the efforts made by the government to control the politically and economically powerful abbeys, and follows the vicissitudes of the order under Emperor Joseph II, during the Brabant Revolution and the years of French domination. The role of the Norbertines in social and economic life is briefly dealt with by R. Van Uytven.

In 1375, the bishop of Utrecht, as a result of financial difficulties, granted the chapters, nobility and towns of his prince-bishopric, excluding his territories in the north-east of the Netherlands, a charter, called the *Landbrief*, which is regarded as the constitution of medieval Utrecht. This charter included provisions on warfare, taxation and the administration of justice which limited the bishop's freedom of action in these matters and can be seen as the basis for the development of the States of Utrecht. A commemorative volume, published by a combination of local history societies, contains articles on some critical periods in the history of these States.[8] C.A. Rutgers briefly explains what the *Landbrief* was about and how it concludes a series of fourteenth-century episcopal grants. An ungrateful task, since the subject was treated exhaustively by the late Enklaar years ago. Dr. Rutgers lends interest to his contribution by considering the relationship between bishop and States since 1375 and claims, moreover, for the chapters, nobility and towns a keener

6. J.A. Van Houtte and O. Mus, ed., *Prisma van de geschiedenis van Ieper. Een bundel historische opstellen* (Ypres: Town administration, 1974, 520 pp.).
7. *De glans van Prémontré. Oude kunst uit de Witherenabdijen der Lage Landen* (Heverlee, 1973, 384 pp.).
8. *Van Standen tot Staten. 600 jaar Staten van Utrecht 1375-1975.* Stichtse Historische Reeks I (Haarlem: Gottmer, 1975, 264 pp., ISBN 90 257 0272 4).

sense of patriotism than Enklaar allowed them. W.J. Alberts fits the *Landbrief* into a general pattern by surveying the development of the influence of the States in neighbouring countries — Guelders, Cleves, Münster and others, omitting, however, Holland and the bishopric of Liège. The bulk of the book is taken up by three articles falling in the period from the late-sixteenth to the early-eighteenth century. J. den Tex gives a straightforward sketch of the role of the States of Utrecht from the Pacification of Ghent to the fall of Olden-barnevelt, while D.J. Roorda provides an interesting discussion of the imposition by William III on the States of Utrecht of the *regeringsreglement* of 1674, after the liberation of the province from the French. Roorda outlines the historiography of this episode and indicates its complex political background and the ways in which the stadhouder was prepared to use the powers which the 'regulation' gave him. This is followed by an important article by M. van der Bijl which throws much light on the neglected topic of the opposition, first to the policies of William III, and particularly to the continued commitment to the war of Spanish Succession after his death, through concentrating on the role of the Utrecht noble, Welland. This account of the activities and motives of Welland and his associates in what might crudely be called the pro-French party suggests that here is a fruitful field for further investigation. The book ends with a personal account of the activities of the provincial States of Utrecht since 1958 by J. Schuttevâer.

Not unnaturally much of Dutch historical writing on the Republic has been centred upon Holland, whilst outside the Netherlands, both in common parlance and in historiography, the identification of the county of Holland with the whole of the Republic has been and still remains virtually complete. The result has been to obscure, even to overlook the contributions of the other provinces, and at times seriously to distort Dutch history. Regional history in the Netherlands, therefore, has a particular function in correcting a long tradition of imbalance. This is one reason for welcoming the second volume of the history of Gelderland, a work of collective scholarship, which takes the history of the duchy from 1492 to 1795.[9] The volume begins with five synoptic chapters, all showing evidence of archival work, some of it — as befits an area which for long periods of its history was of international concern — undertaken outside the Netherlands, in Brussels, Vienna, Düsseldorf, and Simancas. Two of these chapters deserve special mention: that by J.J. Poelhekke, whose coverage of the period 1609 to 1672 is luminous, evocative and elusive; and that by Dr. A.H. Wertheim-Gijse Weenink, which exactly reproduces — apart from an occasional re-arrangement of paragraph

9. P.J. Meij, W. Jappe Alberts, P.A.M. Geurts, e. a., ed., *Geschiedenis van Gelderland 1492-1795* (Zutphen: Walburg Pers, 1975, 564 pp., ISBN 90 6011 292 X).

structure and a few amendments to footnotes — her recent book on democratic movements in Gelderland from 1672 to 1795.[10] The synoptic chapters are followed by a chapter on the religious history of the whole period, and three chapters on cultural history. Because of the undeveloped state of research in the field of the cultural history of Gelderland the authors have had a difficult task: indeed, in the case of the arts, the struggle proved too much, and had to be abandoned at the eleventh hour in favour of the promise ultimately of a separate book. The other notable gap is the absence of any systematic treatment of social and economic history. Here, it seems, the struggle has yet to be joined. By a self-denying ordinance the editorial board deemed it better to do without, rather than to make do with the superficial treatment inevitable in the present state of ignorance. It is to be hoped that this large gap will be filled. It is certain that the present work has set a standard of scholarship it will not be easy to emulate.

As a participant in armed conflicts, the Republic developed a formidable fighting force. In fact, under Maurice, the States' army was the most modern in Europe. The navy adopted an individual style of combat, with varying success, in its conflicts with the English fleet. The organization and structure of the Dutch army and navy in the sixteenth and seventeenth centuries therefore play an important part in G. Teitler's sociological dissertation, which attempts to explain the evolution of the modern professional officer corps over the centuries by reference to changes in the society and politics of Europe since the middle ages.[11] In his interesting comparison of the Dutch, English and French forces, he is on safe military-historical ground, but the analysis of the long term process of professionalization demands a mastery of subjects which he knows only partially. In this way he becomes the victim of a circular argument. First of all he emphasizes that the co-existence of a 'noble' and 'bourgeois' ethos is a prerequisite for military professionalization, and then he takes from works on military history whatever suits his argument in order to prove his point.

The prestigious Hague Historical Society has celebrated its seventy-fifth anniversary with a volume of essays reflecting the interests of its membership.[12] L. Brummel's introduction tells the history of the Society itself, and the

10. A.H. Wertheim-Gijse Weenink, *Democratische bewegingen in Gelderland 1672-1795* (Amsterdam: Van Gennep, 1973; Thesis Faculty of Letters, Nijmegen, 1973). See *Acta*, VIII, 181.
11. G. Teitler, *De wording van het professionele officierscorps. Een sociologisch-historische analyse* (Rotterdam: Universitaire Pers, 1974, 309 pp., ISBN 90 237 6239 8; Thesis Faculty of Social Sciences, Rotterdam. With summary in English).
12. *Driekwart eeuw historisch leven in den Haag. Historische opstellen uitgegeven ter gelegenheid van het 75-jarig bestaan van het Historisch Gezelschap te 's-Gravenhage* (The Hague: Nijhoff, 1975, 216 pp., ISBN 90 247 1759 O).

following papers exemplify almost every branch of historical writing. Three papers deal with medieval topics: H. Enno van Gelder discusses the difficulty of currency transactions facing travelling merchants and dignitaries, while J. Fox compares the early development of Groningen with that of Bern in Switzerland, both in relation to neighbouring local authorities. In the third medieval paper H. Hardenberg studies the origins of the States of Holland in the fourteenth and fifteenth centuries, throwing light on the conflicting interests of and intermarriages between local noble families. Religious history is represented by a note by J.P. van Dooren on the fortunes of a protestant community in the predominantly catholic eastern Generality Lands in the mid-seventeenth century and later, showing that there still remain many unanswered questions about such communities. For military history we are presented with an exciting spy story of the period of the Spanish Succession War from A.J. Veenendaal, and F.C. Spits gives a lively paper on the attitudes of the enlisted man in the nineteenth-century Dutch army. The diplomatic historian C. Smit compares Dutch neutrality in the Seven Years' War with the position in the war of 1914-1918. In both contests, the writer concludes, profits from neutrality should not, and did not, compensate for limitations placed on government freedom of decision.

In recent years the number of students reading history at Dutch universities has increased rapidly. To provide these undergraduates with stimulating insights a group of Dutch historians have collected together some thirty essays covering the main aspects of their history from the early modern period to the twentieth century, written from differing historiographical standpoints.[13] The first section deals with general themes and includes Geyl on the development of Dutch national consciousness and Boogman on the decisive influence of Holland on the foreign policy of the Republic. From the numerous studies on the origins of the Revolt and the course of the Eighty Years' War the editors have selected well-known articles by Romein, Craeybeckx and Geyl together with recent revisions by J.W. Smit and Woltjer. Four authors discuss the seventeenth century, concentrating on the regent patriciate of Holland and the domestic and foreign policy of the United Provinces. Slicher van Bath and Van Dillen study the long-term trends in the demography and economy of the Netherlands. De Wit, Geyl and Kossmann assess the Patriots and the Batavian period. Bornewasser analyzes the changes in the concept and practice of ministerial responsibility before and after the constitution of 1848. The collection ends with a series of articles by Van Tijn and Schöffer on the growth of neutral and confessional political parties in the nineteenth and twentieth

---

13. G.A.M. Beekelaar, J.C.H. Blom, e. a., ed., *Vaderlands verleden in veelvoud. 31 opstellen over de Nederlandse geschiedenis na 1500* (The Hague: Nijhoff, 1975, 640 pp., ISBN 90 247 1757 4).

centuries. These enable us to appreciate the historical background of *verzuiling*, the division of Dutch society in politics, business, trade union and leisure activities along confessional lines. It is easy to cavil at the choice of articles, especially as they cover such a long span, but it is perhaps a matter for regret that almost all the articles have been published previously (several times in the case of Geyl's on 'Protestantization') and the great majority are comparatively recent. Nevertheless such a collection is especially useful to those interested in Dutch history outside the Netherlands, where Dutch historical periodicals are difficult to come by. Five articles appear in English, one in German and the balance in Dutch.

The scholarly study of the history of the jewish community in the Netherlands has been greatly promoted by the publication of a special periodical devoted to this subject, the *Studia Rosenthaliana*, which began to appear in 1967.[14] Besides many solid articles on the emancipation of the Dutch jews in the period of the French Revolution and Napoleon and on the condition of the jewish proletariat in the nineteenth century, it has published a number of important primary sources, such as the notarial records of the Portuguese jews in the first half of the seventeenth century, and some interesting historical accounts written by Dutch jews in the seventeenth and eighteenth centuries. A series of articles on the Dutch zionist movement which Ludy Giebels contributed to this periodical has now been published in book form.[15] This study contains a detailed account of the internal history of the Dutch Zionist Union from its foundation in 1899 until its dissolution by the Germans in 1941. It analyzes the tensions and conflicts with orthodox and socialist jews both within and outside the zionist organization and also discusses the role played by such prominent zionists as Jacobus Kann and Nehemia de Lieme and their frequent disagreements with the allegedly opportunist policies pursued by the leaders of the International Zionist movement in Berlin or London. While doing full justice to the idealism or zeal inspiring many Dutch zionists, the author points out that the appeal of the movement remained restricted to a relatively small social and intellectual elite who were generally conservative or paternalistic, frequently dogmatic and occasionally blindly nationalistic in their convictions, and who showed little or no concern for the plight of the mass of the less privileged jews. This lucidly written and richly documented monograph is in many respects a model of its kind, not only providing a penetrating analysis of the various political attitudes taken by Dutch jews, but also relating their attitudes to the political and social developments which took place in the Netherlands during the first half of the twentieth century.

14. Published by Van Gorcum, Assen.
15. L. Giebels, *De Zionistische beweging in Nederland 1899-1941* (Assen: Van Gorcum, 1975, 223 pp., ISBN 90 232 1274 6).

MIDDLE AGES

A number of studies of considerable interest have been recently published on various aspects of the political, cultural and social and economic history of the middle ages. Several publications of source material will certainly prove useful, although they do not open wide and new perspectives.

P.H.J. van der Laan has edited a handsome collection of documents on the early history of Amsterdam, 1275-1400,[16] starting with the freedom of toll granted by Florence V to the then insignificant settlement near the *dam* in the Amstel. The date of the latest document published was determined by practical, financial considerations. Although expertly edited the collection is slightly disappointing. The author has concentrated entirely on institutional, legal and topographical subjects, whereas the economic development remains in the dark. It is true that this development only got into full swing after 1400, but if the editor had not deliberately refrained from looking for relevant items in such records as those of the count's exchequer, he might have been able to throw some light on the town's early economic activities. It seems characteristic that while quoting the accounts of the *scultetus* of Amsterdam on matters of legislation and jurisdiction, Van der Laan omits passages referring to the sale of English cloth (1393). On the other hand much space is devoted to deeds concerning the transmission of immovable property in the town, although their importance from the point of view of legal history is limited and does not, in the reviewer's opinion, justify publication in this quantity. Was it really wise to include all of them, instead of reserving room for documents from a period historically more exciting?

The Frisian Institute of Groningen University has published about 200 documents from the town archives of Groningen, concerning the relations between the town of Groningen and various Frisian towns, abbots and noblemen in a period of political chaos (1416-97).[17] They show how Groningen, from 1422 onwards, tried to establish some order and security in the northern parts of the Netherlands by concluding peace treaties all over the region. The treaties granted Groningen the right to interfere where the local authorities failed to maintain law and order, and greatly increased the political weight of the town. Most important was the peace with the so-called *Vetkoper* party of Oostergo (1491), which opened prospects of a protectorate over most of the actual province of Friesland. Remarkably enough, such agreements, while mainly concentrating on the creation of peaceful conditions, usually included one paragraph on a matter of civil law — the right of landowners to lease out

16. P.H.J. van der Laan, *Oorkondenboek van Amsterdam tot 1400*. Publicaties van de Gemeentelijke Archiefdienst van Amsterdam, XI (Amsterdam: N. Israel, 1975, 652 pp., ISBN 90 60 72 117 9).

their land to whomsoever they pleased: presumably the peasants attempted to claim hereditary rights to the ground. Most documents are in the vernacular, some in Latin. They are carefully edited by O. Vries, who adds a small, but illuminating introduction on the complicated political situation of the period. The Frysk Ynstitut choose to publish *Pax Groningana* in the Frisian language. For the benefit of those who are not well-versed in modern Frisian, the introduction and a list of titles of the documents are also given in German, while a Dutch translation of geographical names is added. The *apparatus criticus* is, apparently, only meant for Frisian specialists. The 'Frisian' documents can be easily understood by those who read medieval Dutch or German.

Interesting source material of a more restricted character has been brought to light by F. De Nave, who has published the most ancient lists of newly accepted *poorters* (citizens) of the town of Antwerp (1390-1414).[18] Although it is always difficult to assess in how far such lists give a reliable picture of the actual immigration, the collection is very useful. Each entry up to 1409 mentions not only the name of the newcomer, but also that of the man who stood surety for him, and thus we get acquainted with thousands of late-fourteenth-century Antwerp citizens.

In his lively inaugural lecture delivered at Leiden University, *Holland's advance*,[19] H.P.H. Jansen comments on the paradoxical situation that in Dutch historiography the origin and early development of the county has for a variety of reasons attracted more attention than the late medieval period when Holland achieved an importance which clearly presaged its predominant position among the northern provinces at the time of the Republic. He stresses Holland's advance, recognizable from c. 1350 onwards, and welcomes recent signs of a growing interest in late-medieval Holland. The lecture is published in a slightly modified version in this volume, above, p. 1-19.

H.J. Kok, who in 1958 published a solid study on the patron saints of churches in the bishopric of Utrecht in the middle ages, has not lost interest in the subject, as can be seen from his recent article, an inventory of church *patrocinia* in the Zeeland part of the medieval bishopric of Utrecht.[20] From a

17. M.G. Oosterhout, P. Gerbenzon, B. Sjölin, Th.S.H. Bos, A.L. Hempenius, J. van der Kooi, A. Pietersma, O. Vries, ed., *Pax Groningana. 204 oarkonden út it Grinzer Gemeente-archyf oer de forhâlding Grins-Fryslân yn de fyftjinde ieu.* Estrikken, XLIX (Groningen: Fries Instituut der Rijksuniversiteit, 1975, 317 pp.).
18. F. de Nave, 'De oudste Antwerpse lijsten van nieuwe poorters (28 januari 1390-28 december 1414)', *Handelingen van de koninklijke commissie voor geschiedenis*, CXXXIX (Brussels, 1973) 67-309.
19. H.P.H. Jansen, *Hollands Voorsprong* (Leiden: Leidse Universitaire Pers, 1976, 21 pp., ISBN 90 6021 295 9).
20. H.J. Kok, 'Inventarisatie van de kerkpatrocinia in het Zeeuwse deel van het middeleeuwse bisdom Utrecht', *Archief. Mededelingen van het koninklijk Zeeuwsch genootschap der wetenschappen, 1972/3* (Middelburg, 1973) 151-233.

thorough inspection of the supplication registers at the Vatican the author has been able to unearth a number of hitherto unknown *patrocinia* and thus has brought the total of identified church patrons to 130 (from a total of 195 medieval parish churches). Results of this sort are helpful when it comes to dating the relevant churches and to tracing the spread of certain spiritual fashions.

K.A. Kalkwiek's study on castles in the history of Gelderland until 1543 is a pleasant and readable book, well-organized, provided with well-designed maps and graphs, and nicely illustrated.[21] The author's intention is to show the decisive importance of castles for the formation and consolidation of the *territorium* of the counts — from 1334 dukes — of Gelderland. To this effect he has listed all the castles and manor houses the count possessed as an *allodium*, as well as those held in fief from the count. He gives information about their foundation, their proprietors or occupants and about the military function of these fortified places, spread all over the land. The role of castles as centres of administration and jurisdiction is touched upon, although the author does not seem to feel much interest in this important aspect. Chapters on medieval conceptions of property and authority, as well as on castle-building in France and England — why not on the other Netherlands provinces and Germany? — provide readers who are strangers in this field with an easy introduction. In some ways however, the book remains unsatisfactory. The author is often imprecise in the use of special terms and there is a certain lack of logic in his conceptions. Is it by accident that the book is called 'The Duke and his castles' although it largely deals with the period before the count had been elevated to a higher rank? Dr. Kalkwiek is just as lighthearted in his use of the term *landsheer* (territorial prince) even for a period when the forming of a 'territory' had hardly begun. A sentence like (196) 'The idea of a county or duchy was still so vague that it was practically covered by the extent of power of the territorial prince' seems typical of his occasional lack of clarity. On the origin of the count's authority he is equally confused: on the one hand he devotes many pages to the *regale* of fortification as the basis of the right of castle-building, on the other hand he speaks (12) of authority (*overheidsrechten*) as linked to the castle and thus seems to opt for an otherwise undeveloped theory that the possession of real estate was the basis of the count's authority. And while he mentions *passim* the importance of castles for the policy of 'expansion' of the counts, he in fact only shows their importance for the strengthening of the count's position inside his lands. It is interesting, on the

21. K.A. Kalkwiek, *De Hertog en zijn burchten. Kastelen in de Gelderse geschiedenis tot 1543* (Zaltbommel: Europese bibliotheek, 1976, 248 pp., ISBN 90 28 85051 1; Also thesis Faculty of Letters, Utrecht University, 1976).

other hand, that Dr. Kalkwiek gives an insight into the rhythm of the count's policy in this respect and relates periods in which building or acquisition of castles is rare, to the apparent decline in the count's power at that time.

In 1974 Ename on the Scheldt (near Oudenaarde) celebrated its millennium. In a contribution to a commemorative publication L. Milis assesses the significance of the data concerning the origin of the *castrum*, probably of some importance in the struggle against the Norman invaders of the ninth century, the *portus*, and a Benedictine abbey, founded in 1063. Not these, but the establishment of a *marca* Ename by Emperor Otto II in 974 served as the point of departure for the celebration.[22] The village of St. Martens-Latem however can claim an even longer history. It commemorated the fact with a publication *Sint-Martens-Latem 824-1974*, to which A. Verhulst has contributed an article on the medieval period, and J. Van den Abeele one on the church that lent the village its name.[23]

Dr. J. Roelink, who retired in 1975 from the chair of medieval history in the Free (calvinist) University at Amsterdam, has written an interesting article on 'differences in social status in the ninth-century Frankish kingdom', more specifically on the attitude of Church and society towards slavery.[24] He stresses the point that the Church — like St. Paul — taught spiritual liberty for all men and their equality before God, without any intention, however, of bringing about a revolution in society. *Manumissio* was certainly stimulated by the Church but did not lead to a fundamental change in social hierarchy.

In a solid article E. Van Mingroot discusses the dating of the *Gesta episcoporum cameracensium*. He dates the *Gesta* I at around 1024 and rejects the arguments of earlier historians who have opted for 'after 1040'.[25] His conclusion is important since the chronicle serves as a *terminus ante quem* for the foundation or renovation of a whole series of ecclesiastical institutions, which can now be dated with more precision.

Among the twelfth- and thirteenth-century scholars who were most actively engaged in the translation of Greek philosophical, theological and scientific literature was Willem van Moerbeke (*c.* 1250), a Flemish Dominican sent to Byzantium, where he probably completed his translation of Aristotle's *Politica*,

22. L. Milis, 'Ename duizend jaar?' in: *Uit het rijke verleden van Ename, 974-1974* (Oudenaarde: Sanderus, 1974) 7-85.
23. *Sint Martens-Latem 824-1974* (Sint Martens-Latem: Heemkring Scheldeveld, 1974). J.P. Peeters has published a selection of his articles on Vilvoorde: *Bloei en verval van de middeleeuwse stadsvrijheid Vilvoorde* (Tielt, 1975, 227 pp.).
24. J. Roelink, 'Standsverschil en christendom in de negende eeuw in het Frankische rijk', *Tijdschrift voor geschiedenis*, LXXXVIII (Groningen, 1975) 6-26.
25. E. Van Mingroot, 'Kritisch onderzoek omtrent de datering van de Gesta episcoporum cameracensium', *Belgisch tijdschrift voor filologie en geschiedenis*, LIII (Brussels, 1975) 281-332.

Metereologia, and other works. G. Verbeke tries to evaluate his translations, which were severely criticized in Moerbeke's own time as well as by several humanist authors.[26] Verbeke explains that Moerbeke's main purpose was to further scholarship through his translations and that he therefore proceeded carefully and with a strong sense of responsibility, concluding that Moerbeke's work is more useful to modern Aristotelian studies than are the more elegant translations by the humanists.

In a substantial article D. Van den Auweele analyzes the lists of hostages from Bruges taken by the count of Flanders after the rebellions of 1301, 1305 and 1328.[27] He finds that about five per cent of the active male population was involved, mainly members of the bourgeoisie and of the textile guilds.

The *willekeuren* (laws) laid down by the judges of the Frisian Sealands, who used to assemble at the Upstal tree (probably near Aurich, Germany), were the outcome of meetings convened with the clear intention of keeping the prevailing anarchy within bounds and of strengthening the position of the Frisians with regard to the outside world. The *willekeuren* of 1323, meticulously studied by H.D. Meyering, were to serve as general rules of law to which the associated 'countries' should conform.[28] They deal with matters of both civil and criminal law. The judges felt compelled to fight the existing chaos and lawlessness by way of very severe punishments. Consequently, the *willekeuren* can well be compared with the peace agreements the Frisian lands concluded among themselves in the fifteenth century. Dr. Meyering supposes that the text originated from Friesland west of the Lauwers (that is, the present Dutch province of Friesland) and may have influenced the agreement of 1361 between Westerlauwers Friesland and the town of Groningen, considered to be the starting point from which the *Pax Groningana* developed.

An interesting contribution to Dutch agrarian history is R. Wartena's article on the reclamation and abandonment of land on the Veluwe (Gelderland) during the fourteenth century.[29] The author has made use of the fiscal documents of the county to determine the extent of land allotted to cultivators,

26. G. Verbeke, *Het wetenschappelijk profiel van Willem van Moerbeke*. Mededelingen der Koninklijke Nederlandse Akademie van Wetenschappen, Afdeling Letterkunde, Nieuwe Reeks XXXVIII, 4 (Amsterdam-Oxford: Noord-Hollandse Uitgevers Maatschappij, 1975, 30 pp., ISBN 72 048304 2).
27. D. Van den Auweele, 'De Brugse gijzelaarslijsten van 1301, 1305 en 1328. Een komparatieve analyse', *Handelingen van het genootschap voor geschiedenis Société d'Emulation te Brugge*, CX (Bruges, 1974) 155-167.
28. H.D. Meyering, *De willekeuren van de Opstalboom (1323), een filologisch-historische monografie* (Groningen: V.R.B. Offzetdrukkerij; Also thesis Faculty of Letters, Free University, Amsterdam, 1974).
29. R. Wartena, 'Ontginningen en 'Wüstungen' op de Veluwe in de veertiende eeuw', *Gelre. Bijdragen en Mededelingen*, LXVIII (Arnhem: Vereniging Gelre, 1975) 1-50.

and finds that from about 1310 till 1345 the marshy borderlands of the Veluwe were reclaimed, mostly by inhabitants of the district. He also studies the influence of 'bad times' from the second half of the century. He concludes that in this period various areas of the Veluwe ceased to be cultivated, especially in the high, sandy parts which suffered increasingly from sand drifts, while the lower ground, recently brought under the plough, seemed to thrive. Wartena supposes that a number of peasants migrated from the higher places to the nearby, more fertile soil which could support the cultivation of other crops besides rye.

In a lengthy article on 'the relationship between Leiden and Rijnland, 1365-1414', — a printing error seems responsible for the latter date — D.E.H. de Boer studies the relative density of population in the different parts of the country-side surrounding the town of Leiden in the late-middle ages.[30] He starts his research *c.* 1365, when the industrial development of Leiden was in an early stage, and ends in 1514, the year of the famous *Informacie* which after an *inquisitio* of 1369 provides us with the first opportunity for getting an overall impression of the demographic situation of the region. The author confirms earlier findings about a general decline of population within the period concerned and finds that this development was most obvious in the peat region east of Leiden, where agricultural conditions had worsened in the course of the fifteenth century. He also concludes that a definite shift in relative density of the population took place between 1369 and 1514, and establishes a correlation between the demographic decline in different parts of the countryside and contemporary immigration into Leiden. The not very surprising conclusion seems to be that the town drew most heavily on the most impoverished part of the surrounding countryside for filling its industrial vacancies.

R. Degryse has investigated the difficulties which the Flemish overseas trade encountered following the resumption of the Hundred Years' War in 1377.[31] In particular, ships heading for La Rochelle and Bordeaux often met with trouble and special measures were needed to ensure the safety of the Flemish vessels. The author has studied the documents concerning the consequent negotiations with the English and has found them to contain ample information on the nature of the Bordeaux trade. The Flemings mainly exported smoked or salted herrings and brought home wines, salt and sometimes subtropical fruit.

---

30. D.E.H. de Boer, 'De verhouding Leiden-Rijnland 1365-1414. Veranderingen in een relatie', *Economisch- en sociaal-historisch jaarboek*, XXXVIII (The Hague, 1975) 48-72.
31. R. Degryse, 'De Vlaamse Westvaart en de Engelse represailles omstreeks 1378', *Handelingen der Maatschappij voor geschiedenis en oudheidkunde te Gent*, XXVII (Ghent, 1973) 193-239.

The same author has also examined the role of the *buis*, a type of ship that appeared in 1405 in the Meuse delta, a developed form of the existing single-mast *buza*.[32] In the first half of the fifteenth century we find it not only employed as a coaster but also as a war vessel — for instance in 1418 in Jacqueline of Bavaria's fleet —, as a privateering vessel and as a fishing boat. From 1439 the *buis*, or buss, formed the backbone of the fleet that Philip the Good equipped for the protection of the Dutch and Zeeland fisheries. By the end of the fifteenth century, according to Degryse, the *buis* had found a place of its own as a fishing vessel, with facilities on board to clean and salt the herring at sea.

The eighth volume of *Hollandse Studiën*, a series published by the very active *Historische Vereniging Holland*, consists of four contributions on the history of the province, of which the first deals with the medieval period.[33] J.C. Besteman and H.A. Heidinga publish the results of an investigation into the vicissitudes of the monastery Galilea Minor near Monnikendam, founded in 1431, the remains of which were excavated by archaeologists in the nineteen sixties. Originally it adhered to the third order of St. Francis, but in 1465 it joined the reformed Cistercian congregation of Sibculo, which was sympathetic to the *Devotio Moderna*. Its brief period of prosperity had already come to an end by the beginning of the sixteenth century. The article reveals the composition of the monastery's real estate and the way in which this had been acquired. It also provides plenty of information on the architecture and furnishings of this modest convent, characteristic of a large number of monasteries that mushroomed in Holland in the years just before and after 1400.

In 1975 an entire issue of the *Tijdschrift voor geschiedenis* was devoted to the history of poverty and poor relief in the Netherlands. It contains an extensive and most valuable article by W.P. Blockmans (*lector* at the Erasmus University, Rotterdam) and W. Prevenier (Ghent) on poverty in the Netherlands from the fourteenth to the mid-sixteenth century, in which the problems presented by the relevant source material get full attention.[34] A shortened version is published in this volume, p. 20-57 and thus it is superfluous to summarize its contents in the present survey. The study is based on a wide selection of partly unpublished material, and the authors have taken care to approach the problems they deal with — the definition of indigence, the extent

---

32. *Idem*, 'De Zeeuwse-Hollandse buisnering en konvooiering omstreeks 1439-40', *Holland, regionaal-historisch tijdschrift*, VI (Haarlem: J.H. Gottmer, 1974) 57-86.
33. J.C. Besteman and H.A. Heidinga, 'Het klooster Galilea Minor bij Monnikendam. Een historisch en archeologisch onderzoek', in: J.C. Besteman, e.a., *Hollandse Studiën*, VIII (Dordrecht: Historische Vereniging Holland, 1976, 348 pp., ISBN 90 257 0514 6) 1-130.
34. W.P. Blockmans and W. Prevenier, 'Armoede in de Nederlanden van de 14e tot het midden van de 16e eeuw: bronnen en problemen', *Tijdschrift voor geschiedenis*, LXXXVIII (1975) 501-38.

of poverty in the late-middle ages and the early-modern period and the (in)-sufficiency of poor relief — from different sides, be it with some strict limitations. Their interest is exclusively focused on the 'small people', represented by the mythical bricklayer's assistant, star performer in so many studies of this kind. Other problems, like impoverishment in other classes of the population, are left untouched. In the original article the countryside has been treated somewhat more extensively than is the case in the translation.

R. Van Uytven's stimulating article on politics and the economy in the fifteenth century comes as a comfort to historians who like to see history as the result of a variety of interacting factors, including the events of political history held in such disdain by 'structuralists'.[35] The author's starting point is the apparent anomaly that, whereas in Europe the end of the fifteenth century is generally a period of economic recovery, it seems to be a time of decline in the Netherlands, albeit that some historians have recently expressed some scepticism about the supposed scope of the crisis. Demographic and other research, however, supports the contemporary complaints of the inhabitants of the Low Countries: the period is one of epidemics, of deserted villages, of steeply rising grain and meat prices, of impoverished peasants and fishermen. Van Uytven analyses these phenomena and relates them directly to the wars with France and the internal rebellions, which ruined the countryside, the herring fleet and the linen and wool industries. They interrupted the normal imports of grain, meat and wine, and the exports of herring, and benefitted few but the wine merchants from Cologne who found the shift from the temporarily unobtainable Burgundian wines to Rhine wines most profitable; in addition Antwerp, left untouched by the wars with Louis XI and not implicated in any rebellious movement, may have been able to strengthen its position as a commercial centre. In another article Van Uytven has explored the impact of Antwerp's growth on the towns of the Hageland at this time.[36] He concludes that far from acting as a spur to economic activity the rise of Antwerp suffocated the older established trades and industries of towns like Louvain, Diest, Tienen (Tirlemont) and Zoutleeuw.

In an article commemorating the establishment of the parliament of Mechlin (cf. *Acta*, VIII, 167) W. Blockmans re-examines the State-building policy pursued by the Burgundian rulers of the Netherlands.[37] The author stresses the

35. R. Van Uytven, 'Politiek en economie: de crisis der late XVe eeuw in de Nederlanden', *Belgisch tijdschrift voor filologie en geschiedenis*, LIII (1975) 1097-1149.
36. *Idem*, 'In de schaduwen van de Antwerpse groei: het Hageland in de zestiende eeuw', *Bijdragen tot de geschiedenis bijzonderlijk van het aloude hertogdom Brabant*, LVII (1974) 171-88. Summary in English.
37. W.P. Blockmans, 'De Bourgondische Nederlanden: de weg naar een moderne staatsvorm', *Handelingen van de koninklijke kring voor oudheidkunde van Mechelen*, LXXVII (Mechlin, 1973) 7-26.

need felt by the princes to reduce the power of the large towns, which had come to dominate, economically and politically, the smaller towns and the country-side. In the southern Netherlands the Burgundians consciously exploited the social unrest within the large towns with a view to weakening their burden-some mastery, the next step being the development of their own central power. The same author summarizes his unpublished doctoral thesis on representation in Flanders under the Burgundians.[38] He analyzes the process of the streng-thening of the central administration, which was accompanied by a gradual loss of influence by the representative assemblies. The critical moment seems to be 1430, when Philip the Good brought together several important, adjacent territories and started to centralize the administration within the individual provinces. Whereas until then the representative assembly of the Four Members of Flanders had taken decisions on such weighty matters as international diplomatic relations, economic regulations and, more rarely, on legal problems, a new system was now being developed, which reduced the power of the Four Members and favoured a representative assembly in which the large towns had considerably less influence.

W. Lourdeaux from Louvain University, who specializes in the *Devotio Moderna*, summarizes in a short study recent publications on the Brethren of the Common Life[39] and investigates a number of crucial problems concerning, among others, the relative importance of Gerard Grote and Florens Radewijns, and the cultural activities of the Brethren which, according to the author, can be regarded as anticipating those of the Jesuits.

In honour of the retiring archivist of Bruges, Albert Schouteet, an *Album* has been composed in which the local history of Bruges takes a prominent place.[40] Of particular interest is a short analysis by O. Mus of the financial administration of the agent and inn-keeper Amayede, covering the years from 1498 to 1507. Many bankers at that time had gone bankrupt and some of their tasks were taken over by the inn-keepers. In this context we may also refer to H.J. Leloux's short biographical article on Canon Gerard Bruyns, from De-venter, who acted as secretary in the Hanseatic office at Bruges from 1462 to *c*. 1500.[41] He took part in several diplomatic missions and personally showed a strong interest in canon law and Church history.

38. *Idem*, 'De volksvertegenwoordiging in Vlaanderen in de beginperiode van de nieuwe tijden (1384-1506)', *Wetenschappelijke tijdingen*, XXXIII (Ghent, 1974) 483-502.
39. W. Lourdeaux, *De Broeders des Gemenen Levens*. Historica Lovaniensia — Studien van leden van het departement geschiedenis van de Katholieke Universiteit te Leuven, II (Louvain, 1972). Also appeared in *Bijdragen. — Tijdschrift voor filosofie en theologie*, XXXIII (1972) 372-416.
40. *Album Albert Schouteet* (Bruges: Westvlaams Verbond van Kringen voor heemkunde, 1973, 262 pp.).
41. H.J. Leloux, 'Een Deventer kanunnik secretaris van de Oosterlingen te Brugge in Vlaanderen', *Verslagen en Mededelingen. Vereniging tot beoefening van Overijsselsch regt en geschiedenis*, LXXXVIII (Zwolle, 1973) 3-23.

In the series *Bijdragen tot de geschiedenis van het Zuiden van Nederland* M.A. Nauwelaerts has published his revised doctoral thesis (University of Louvain, 1946) on the grammar school and education in 's-Hertogenbosch until 1629, the year in which Frederick Henry conquered the town.[42] Nauwelaerts follows a familiar pattern in tracing the early history of the 'Latin school', collecting biographical details on the teachers and analyzing the type of education provided. The Latin school at 's-Hertogenbosch, unlike so many others in the northern Netherlands, was not taken over by the town government during the middle ages, but remained in the grip of the chapter of St. John's until 1629. In his solid study the author includes the boarding schools run by the Franciscan friars, who provided some additional teaching to boys visiting the Latin school, and he also draws attention to the different forms of primary education: the 'small' or 'duytsche' schools and, from 1525, a French school, founded at the special request of a group of citizens.

EARLY MODERN PERIOD

Cartography is a fashionable subject in the Netherlands at the moment. The bi-monthly periodical *Holland* devoted a special number to sixteenth-century maps and topographical sketches. C. Koeman provided a useful introduction, giving details on early surveyors and textbooks on surveying such as Gemma Frisius's edition of the *Cosmographicus liber Petri Apiani*.[43] The most interesting article is H. Schoorl's discussion of sixteenth-century surveying activities on the island of Texel in connection with demands for fiscal reductions by the inhabitants who had to reinforce their severely damaged dikes. As usual in *Holland* the illustrations are excellent. The career of Jaspar Adriaenz., a sworn surveyor and mapmaker in the service of the *Hoogheemraadschap* (Regional Drainage Authority) of Schieland and, afterwards, in the 1540s and 1550s, of the Great Council of Mechlin, is the subject of an article by S. Groenveld and A.H. Huussen jr.[44] They have collected interesting details on the practice of surveying in connection with law suits over property rights and territorial boundaries.

The religious upheavals of the sixteenth century have prompted several important studies. Pride of place must go to Decavele's weighty and impres-

---

42. M.A. Nauwelaerts, *Latijnse School en onderwijs te 's-Hertogenbosch tot 1629* (Tilburg: Stichting Zuidelijk Contact, 1974, 326 pp.).
43. C. Koeman, 'Algemene inleiding over de historische kartografie, meer in het bijzonder: Holland voor 1600', *Holland*, VII (Haarlem, 1975) 218-238. H. Schoorl, 'Texel in enige zestiende-eeuwse kaarten en opmetingen', *ibidem*, 239-290.
44. S. Groenveld and A.H. Huussen jr., 'De zestiende- eeuwse landmeter Jaspar Adriaensz. en zijn kartografisch werk', *Hollandse studiën*, VIII (Dordrecht, 1975) 131-177.

sively documented history of the Reformation in the county of Flanders to the eve of the Revolt.[45] Exploiting numerous previously unknown records, including the detailed accounts of that notorious inquisitor Pieter Titelmans, Decavele has constructed a wholly new chronology for the Flemish Reformation. Before the shortlived intrusion of Münsterite Anabaptism in the mid-1530s religious dissent in the county was characterized by the prominence given to the New Testament and the outright rejection of the real presence. During this period most 'evangelicals' did not openly break with the Roman Church and they continued to attend services in their parish churches, supplementing these with discussions about the Bible. By 1538 Münsterite Anabaptism had virtually disappeared and its adherents merged with the sacramentarians, with whom they had so much in common. Renewed persecution, however, polarized religious opinion, a process further hastened by the accommodation of fugitive dissenters in the Reformed congregation at Emden and the stranger-churches in England. Around 1550, the anabaptists, now under the influence of Menno Simons, made some headway, especially in and around Kortrijk (Courtrai), whereas the reformed won numerous converts in the industrialized countryside of the Westkwartier. The formative influences on reformed protestantism were several: Luther's writings had been important, especially in the early years, but A. Lasco and Bullinger as well as native theologians also made their mark. Geneva's impact was delayed until the early 1560s.

From the outset Charles V resolutely opposed the spread of heresy in his patrimonial provinces and this repressive policy cost the lives of 264 Flemish protestants by 1565, while rather more than ten times that number were indicted for offences against the heresy legislation. But this policy lacked the wholehearted consent of those responsible for the implementation of the edicts. In Bruges and Ghent the governing classes were amenable to the pleas of christian humanists for a piety purged of superstition. Nor as magistrates and merchants did they necessarily accept the axiom that heresy should be eradicated even if this meant depopulation and the overturning of cherished privileges. Traditional religious values were eroded by humanist schoolmasters, active even in the villages, and the chambers of rhetoric with their shafts directed at the clergy and their penchant for religious controversy. The printed word also exerted an incalculable influence: despite the draconian edicts threatening death for those who printed, translated, sold or possessed uncensored literature, the printers and colporteurs were still prepared to take the risks. In this climate the conservatives, led by the mendicants, found it hard to match the propaganda put out by their opponents.

45. J. Decavele, *De dageraad van de reformatie in Vlaanderen (1520-1565)*. Verhandelingen Koninklijke Academie België, LXXVI (2 vols, Brussels, 1975, I, lvi + 644 pp., II, 210 pp.).

213

Decavele next examines the correlation between social position and religious choice. At first anabaptism was restricted to the larger towns, though during the second phase, after 1550, it struck roots in the villages of the Leie valley. Sacramentarianism and reformed protestantism had a wider geographical appeal and no part of Flanders was immune except for the agrarian zone in the extreme north-west. No doubt material motives contributed to the advance of heresy, but so many entrepreneurs, intellectuals and magistrates sympathized with the 'new religion' as to rule out the possibility of protestantism being a vehicle of social protest. Usually reformed protestantism recruited higher up the social hierarchy, but the support given the anabaptists in Courtrai by prominent inhabitants proves that their appeal could, occasionally, extend to the upper reaches in a town. Finally, Decavele sets out the religious *Weltanschauung* of the dissidents. As might have been expected from a population exposed for so long to different religious influences, yet constantly harassed, firm confessional loyalties were slow to emerge. Luther is the formative influence, yet most heretics utterly rejected his doctrine of the real presence in favour of the memorialist or sacramentarian interpretation associated with Zwingli. Inevitably judicial sources form the backbone of this study, so that the anti-catholic aspects of dissent are emphasized. Students familiar with the recent historiography of the English Reformation will be interested by Decavele's tentative remarks about the connections between late medieval heresy and the rise of protestantism in Flanders.

The *Festschrift* for Professor C.C. de Bruin of Leiden contains, appropriately, several offerings on the medieval Dutch Bible and its Reformation successors. The Dutch Bible printed by Vorsterman in 1528 has been generally accepted as a close translation from the Vulgate, but Augustijn shows that the sources were more numerous and less orthodox than the printer pretended.[46] The career of the Amsterdam humanist and *Hebreeuwsche meester* Wouter Deleen (Delenus) spans the Dutch and English Reformations. Forced to leave Amsterdam in 1535 on account of his suspect religious affiliations, he subsequently came to London and entered royal service as *biblioscopus* around 1540. Trapman analyzes his *Novum Testamentum* of 1539 and reveals a heavy, sometimes literal, dependence on Erasmus, with a more specifically protestant flavour informing the annotations.[47] The appointment of this scholar, with his anabaptist sympathies, is not without its interest for students of the religious climate of the English court at this time.

---

46. C. Augustijn, 'De Vorstenmanbijbel van 1528', *Nederlands archief voor kerkgeschiedenis*, n.s., LVI (1975) 78-94.
47. J. Trapman, 'Delenus en de bijbel', *ibidem*, 95-113.

Probably nowhere was the impact of the anabaptists more enduring than in the Low Countries. In 1968 a committee was set up to undertake the publication of the extensive records left by the radical reformation down to the middle of the seventeenth century. As well as publishing the judicial sources concerning anabaptists, the committee envisages the edition of the principal writings, thus complementing the task begun by Cramer and Pijper in their *Bibliotheca Reformatoria Neerlandica* before the First World War. Now Dr. Mellink has produced the first volume in the series entitled *Documenta Anabaptistica Neerlandica* covering Friesland and Groningen to 1550.[48] Government edicts, municipal ordinances, court proceedings, official correspondence, chronicles and exchequer records form the staple sources. The texts are presented in strict chronological order and succinctly annotated. In both provinces anabaptism was early entrenched, but the response of the provincial authorities differed. In Friesland, where criminal justice was centralized, 82 heretics were executed, most of these at the time of the Münster episode,[49] as against one isolated capital sentence in Groningen. The editor emphasizes the close links between anabaptism in these provinces and neighbouring East Friesland and Westphalia. This series should provide a valuable Dutch counterpart to the older established *Quellen zur Geschichte der Täufer* for Germany and Switzerland.

Dr. Mellink has also distilled his researches on the radical reformation in the northern Netherlands in an important revisionary article.[50] He shows that Dutch anabaptist thought was lastingly modified by Melchior Hofmann's incarnational doctrine and eschatological emphasis. Joris emerges as the dominant force in anabaptist circles from the debacle of Münster to his flight in 1544 to Basel. The pacifist and revolutionary wings were also far less sharply differentiated than was once thought to be the case.

The Marranos continue to arouse interest. Dr. Vermaseren has explored in detail the career and family connections of Martin Lopez, who migrated to Antwerp.[51] Though his own religious propensities are obscure he was evidently an ardent admirer of Seneca. The children of his first marriage remained loyal

48. A.F. Mellink, ed., *Documenta Anabaptistica Neerlandica*, I, *Friesland en Groningen (1530-1550)*. Kerkhistorische Bijdragen VI (Leiden: Brill, 1975, xxviii + 200 pp., ISBN 90 04 04263 6).
49. For a constructive reassessment of the theology of the anabaptists in Munster see A.J. Jelsma, 'De koning en de vrouwen; Munster 1534-1535', *Gereformeerd theologisch tijdschrift*, LXXV (Kampen, 1975) 82-107.
50. A.F. Mellink, 'Das niederländisch-westfälische Täufertum im 16. Jahrhundert. Zusammenhänge und Verscheidenheiten' in: H-J. Goerts, ed., *Umstrittenes Täufertum 1525-1975. Neue Forschungen* (Gottingen: Vandenhoeck & Ruprecht, 1975, 314 pp., ISBN 3 525 55354 4).
51. B.A. Vermaseren, 'De Antwerpse koopman Martin Lopez en zijn familie in de zestiende en het begin van de zeventiende eeuw', *Bijdragen tot de geschiedenis bijzonderlijk van het aloude hertogdom van Brabant*, LVI (1973) 3-79. With summary in English.

to Philip II and the catholic cause, but this pattern was not followed by the offspring of his second marriage. One son, also called Martin Lopez, and a son-in-law were among the first signatories of the Compromise in 1565 and a daughter, Ursula, married another Marrano merchant, Marco Perez, who took a prominent part in the Reformed Church at Antwerp in 1566. The attraction of reformed protestantism for such men is unclear: perhaps they were swayed, like the great printer Plantin, by the prospect of the overthrow of catholicism. On the other hand by no means all persevered in the 'new religion' and the descendants of Marco Perez hitched their waggon to the rising star of the prince-bishop, Ernest of Bavaria.

Bohemia and the Low Countries are not usually yoked together, yet Nicolette Mout has studied their cultural and religious links in the sixteenth century.[52] In truth, the encounters from the Czech side were few and spasmodic, though here, as elsewhere in Europe, the course of the Dutch Revolt was followed with great interest by the partisans of the Spanish and the States. Far more important is the contribution made by Netherlanders to mannerist culture in Prague at the end of the century. Turmoil in the Low Countries compelled many intellectuals and artists to seek tranquillity and patronage outside their native land. The tolerance and affluence of the courts of Maximilian II and Rudolf II were undeniably attractive. Mout carefully analyzes the political and religious creed of those *émigrés*. Even in Prague they could not forget the Netherlands, and several retained their close links with the circle around Plantin and kept in touch with likeminded humanists in the Silesian town of Breslau. They were careful not to parade strong religious convictions, for these stood in the way of the restoration of peace in the Netherlands and could prove an obstacle to their own advancement. Though affiliation to the Family of Love is difficult to prove. Mout does show that they shared the attributes and outlook of these spiritualists. Especially interesting is her endeavour to reconcile their spiritualist mysticism, with its eschatological undertones, and their admiration for neo-Stoicism: since the end of the world was at hand, these humanists considered that the only dignified conduct was one of patient forbearance. But some of these refugees had pronounced religious opinions, which after 1609 they were not afraid to make public. Using the records of the reformed congregation for strangers at Prague, which have been preserved in the archives of the Walloon church at Dordrecht since 1635, Mout has been able to identify many of the leading members. Germans made up the bulk of the congregation but Netherlanders were also quite conspicuous. Several of

52. N. Mout, *Bohemen en de Nederlanden in de zestiende eeuw*. Leids historische reeks, XIX (Leiden : Universitaire pers, 1975, xiii + 206 pp., ISBN 90 6021 226 6). For ch. iv see *Acta*, IX, 1-29.

those active in the putsch of 1618 belonged to this reformed congregation, including Jacob Hoefnagel.

The first of a projected four-volume series, collecting the scattered essays of Fontaine Verwey on the history of the book, has now appeared.[53] It deals with the sixteenth century and includes contributions on Erasmus, the sects and the Revolt. Only one essay is entirely new, but it is a great convenience to have these illuminating articles brought together. His painstaking detective work gives this collection a special charm. He shows how the script type was employed in France and also in the Netherlands for textbooks with a heterodox flavour. Fontaine Verwey is well-known for his studies on the Family of Love and his hitherto unpublished essay on the sect and its publications is of great interest. In the debate surrounding the privileges, which preceded the Revolt, the *Joyeuse Entrée* of Brabant was a key document, for this seemed to imply that resistance was justified against a sovereign who violated his oath. Fontaine Verwey investigates the circumstances of the three editions of this charter, which were printed at Cologne between 1564 and 1566 by Godfried Hertshorn.

This brings us to the Revolt. Viglius, for all his importance in the central government, still stands in need of an adequate biography. For that reason the assorted collection of sources edited by Professor Waterbolk concerning this eminent Frisian is welcome.[54] These show that Viglius remained a loyal son of Friesland, despite being only able to visit the province infrequently. He used his extensive patronage to advance members of his own family in Friesland and elsewhere. Several of Viglius' accounts are also published in full. Other contributions deal with the home Viglius established for the elderly in Swichum in 1571. Though fragmentary these sources remind us of the importance of family connections and the ties with the province for even a seasoned administrator of the central government like Viglius. William of Orange, once a close colleague of the Frisian in the councils of the realm, developed into the leading opponent of the centralized State advocated by Viglius. The absence of a satisfactory life of William is a serious obstacle to our understanding of the Revolt. Many historians have tried, Rachfahl, Blok, Van Schelven and Miss Wedgwood being the most notable. But William's famous reserve and the ambivalence of his policies stand in the way. Van Roosbroeck has long been interested in the prince and his biography published in 1962 has considerable merits.[55] For that reason his lavishly produced *Willem de Zwijger* might have

---

53. H. de la Fontaine Verwey, *Uit de wereld van het boek*, I, *Humanisten, dwepers en rebellen in de zestiende eeuw* (Amsterdam: Nico Israel, 1975, 162 pp., ISBN 90 6072 110 1).
54. E.H. Waterbolk assisted by T.S.H. Bos, ed., *Vigliana. Bronnen, brieven en rekeningen betreffende Viglius van Aytta* (Groningen: Frysk Ynstitut en Historisch Instituut, 1975, ix + 132 pp.).
55. R. van Roosbroeck, *Willem van Oranje. Droom en gestalte* (Hasselt: Uitgeverij Heideland, 1962, 232 pp.).

been expected to break new ground.[56] Instead the reader finds a fairly pedestrian text, which scarcely advances our understanding of this statesman. But the abundant illustrations, many of them unfamiliar, do something to redress the balance.

In his inaugural lecture Woltjer seeks to explain why Flanders and Brabant, which had made the running in 1566, remained relatively quiescent in 1572, whereas the Beggars took control of so many towns in Holland and Zeeland.[57] He suggests that political and religious polarization had gone further in the south than in Holland and that, as a consequence, the catholics there were on the alert. Moreover the outrage aroused by the iconoclastic riots in the south removed some of the indignation against Alva for his high-handed policies. This is certainly a helpful perspective, though Woltjer seems to leave out of account the discrepancy between the morale and military strength of the central government in 1566 and 1572. In 1566 Margaret of Parma felt herself isolated and militarily impotent whereas in 1572 Alva commanded a large army and had a clear policy. In these circumstances the reluctance of the southern towns to declare for Orange in 1572 is understandable. But in Holland, virtually denuded of government forces, that threat seemed less substantial. Woltjer concludes his aptly entitled lecture 'small causes, profound consequences' by noting how often the destiny of the Revolt turned on quite minor occurrences. When everything is still in the melting-pot events, insignificant in themselves, can bring about fundamental changes.

Formsma reminds us how very differently things might have turned out in the north when he studies a little known episode in the history of the town of Groningen.[58] The attachment of this town to catholicism and Philip II has often been noted. But in 1592 the town offered sovereignty to the duke of Brunswick, whom it saw as an alternative protector to either Spain or the United Provinces. Interestingly, this move received some support in the United Provinces, yet another indication that Groningen was still not considered an indispensable part of the Dutch nation. It is one more reminder of how malleable the Netherlands still were at the close of the sixteenth century.

On the other hand historians have often emphasized the accidental character of the incorporation of a large part of the former duchy of Gelre in the Netherlands. But Rutgers believes this aspect has been overplayed and he

56. R. van Roosbroeck, *Willem de Zwijger, Graaf van Nassau, Prins van Oranje; een kroniek en een epiloog* (The Hague: W. Gaade — Antwerp: Mercatorfonds, 1974, 491 pp.).
57. J.J. Woltjer, *Kleine oorzaken, grote gevolgen* (Leiden: Universitaire pers. 1975, 18 pp., ISBN 90 6021 269 X).
58. W.J. Formsma, 'De aanbieding van de landsheerlijkheid over Groningen aan de hertog van Brunswijk in de jaren 1592-1594', *Bijdragen en mededelingen betreffende de geschiedenis der Nederlanden*, XC (1975) 1-14.

argues strongly, though not entirely convincingly, that the incorporation should be seen as the culmination of a longstanding development.[59] In support he points to the ecclesiastical ties with Utrecht and the mixed feelings in the duchy about too close an association with the Rhineland territories.

H.A. van Oerle has written a very thorough study on the urban development of Leiden until the end of the Golden Age.[60] The author deals first with the early history of the settlement on the Rhine, its topographical and institutional expansion and pays special attention to its role as the count's residence in the early years of Florence V. He then describes the growth of the town, which from 1294 onwards widened its intermural area in quickly succeeding phases. Van Oerle studies the medieval development, until 1580, of the old heart of the town and of each of the later additions separately, carefully collecting material from archives and comparing it with archaeological evidence, following a familiar pattern. But then he introduces a new element by using some — in fact, already well-known — fiscal and census documents from the late-sixteenth century for a remarkably visualized reconstruction of the population structure of each quarter. Numerous maps show the occupations and the estimated wealth of the inhabitants, the value of their houses and the density of habitation in the different areas. The town in 1580 had not yet attained its widest extent and was suffering badly from overpopulation inside its walls. By the end of the century most of the secularized ecclesiastical ground within the town was parcelled out to eagerly buying citizens, whereas the town council itself had cheap houses built on some of it to find room for textile labourers. Nonetheless it was necessary to widen the urban area once more in the first half of the seventeenth century. Inside the old town the number of houses had risen from 28.7 per ha. in 1581 to 66.9 in 1632. It was, as Dr. Van Oerle shows, only after 1659 that expansion came to an end. The book contains a wealth of details on public buildings, watercourses and fortifications, and on numerous minor subjects like street lighting, introduced in 1597, the distribution of industrial buildings such as breweries over the town, etc. The work consists of two magnificently produced volumes, one containing maps, the other the lavishly illustrated text.

One of the documents used by Van Oerle concerns the census of 1581, organized by the town government of Leiden for unknown purposes, questioning the entire population on the size and composition of households, name and occupation of the heads of families, lodgers and their occupations, origin and,

59. C. Rutgers, 'Gelre: een deel van "Nederland"?', *Tijdschrift voor geschiedenis*, LXXXVIII (1975) 27-38.
60. H.A. van Oerle, *Leiden binnen en buiten de stadsvesten. De geschiedenis van de stedebouwkundige ontwikkeling binnen het Leidse rechtsgebied tot aan het einde van de Gouden Eeuw* (2 vols., Leiden: Brill, 460 pp., ISBN 90 04 04283 0 & 90 04 04285 7).

in the case of recent immigrants, the number of years elapsing since their arrival. This document, to which Posthumus first drew attention in 1910, has been looked upon with a demographer's eye by the Belgian historian F. Daelemans during a stay at the Department of Agricultural History at Wageningen.[61] It provides full information on family structure and shows that the average household was limited to 3.86 persons; 55.6 per cent of the families consisted of two to four persons, not counting any servants, distant relatives and paying lodgers. Very large families were rare; in any case it was unusual for more than three children to live with their parents. As many as 37.7 per cent of the Leiden families were childless. No information on the age structure of the population is available. We do not know, for instance, how many of the children listed were over, say, twelve or eighteen years old. We get, on the other hand, details on the distribution of occupations, but the fact that information on this subject happens to be very incomplete detracts from the value of a number of Daelemans's industriously compiled graphs and tables. For instance, the 35 per cent heads of families whose occupation is not listed, suggest that the textile workers in a town with a predominant textile industry may have achieved a higher total than the 6.7 per cent Daelemans can lay hands on. Many of the 'unknowns' were, it is true, women, but it still seems improbable that none of them was occupied as spinsters and the like. Of the 'children' the occupation is mentioned in 40 cases only, mainly in fatherless families. The factor 'occupation unknown' also invites the reader to question the relatively low percentage of wage earners (11.5) which in Daeleman's view proves that the town's industry had not yet developed a capitalistic structure. On the other hand the author has been able to collect useful information on immigrants, especially on the relatively large size of recently arrived families. By combining details from the census with that of slightly later fiscal documents he reaches some interesting conclusions, among others, that the one-family house was predominant in all social groups (90.5 per cent of all houses).

The important role of the Holland nobility in the early years of the Revolt has been demonstrated by, among others, the late Enno van Gelder, but a full-scale analysis of their attitudes and conduct during the first decades of the Republic is still lacking. From a wide range of source materials the local historian A.G. van der Steur has documented the career of Johan van Duvenvoirde, heer van Warmond, an active collaborator of William of Orange and Prince Maurice.[62] After participating in the defence of Leiden, he served as

61. F. Daelemans, 'Leiden 1581. Een socio-demografisch onderzoek', *A.A.G. Bijdragen*, XIX (Wageningen, 1975) 137-215. With summary in English.
62. A.G. van der Steur, 'Johan van Duvenvoirde en Woude (1547-1610), heer van Warmond, admiraal van Holland', *Hollandse studiën*, VIII (1975) 179-273.

Admiral of Holland (1574-1603), as a member of the Council of State (1604-7) and of the States General (1607-10). Van Duvenvoirde also held high office at local and provincial level. Van der Steur devotes much attention to unravelling the complicated genealogy and chronicling the administration of the family properties at a time of revolt and change in religion. The author suggests that Van Duvenvoirde's personal inclination to allow freedom of religion was moderated by the influence of his family's loyalty to catholicism. He gave no active support to the old religion nor did he willingly admit the interference of the reformed church in the organization of religious affairs in his *heerlijk-heden*.

In the first half of the sixteenth century the Chambers of Rhetoric, which flourished especially in the towns of Brabant and Flanders, fell under the suspicion of the catholic church and were sometimes blamed for the image-breaking outburst of 1566. The reformed church realized that these clubs had assisted the spread of new religious ideas and yet when they came to power the protestants tended to be even more censorious of the Rhetoricians' activities and urged the civil authorities to prohibit their allegedly unedifying plays. J.G.C.A. Briels charts the fortunes of the four separate Chambers founded by refugees from the south in Haarlem, Gouda, Amsterdam and Leiden, where the magistrates, if not the ministers, were more tolerant.[63] In other towns where the Rhetoricians were not altogether prohibited the refugees, lacking the leadership of a Karel van Mander or a Jacob Duym for example, probably joined existing Dutch Chambers. In spite of official disapproval the southern Rhetoricians included many convinced reformed and the clubs split in the early seventeenth century, reflecting the divisions within the Dutch Reformed Church as a whole. The Chambers represented an essentially popular culture, drawing the bulk of their support from skilled artisans, though in Haarlem painters, printers and schoolmasters were also involved. Briels argues that they played an important part in raising the standard of the Dutch language. The article concludes with appendices containing extracts from archival material.

In recent years a remarkable vogue has developed for studies on royal entries and magnificences in the sixteenth and seventeenth centuries, for the interpretation of the symbolism employed in these spectacles can assist our understanding of the political ideas and controversies of the age. Although after the Revolt the northern Netherlands lacked a monarchy proper theatrical presentations and processions were devised to celebrate the visit of members of the house of Orange and other important dignitaries. In his thesis D.P. Snoep describes how these festivities developed from simple displays with triumphal

---

63. J.G.C.A. Briels, 'Reyn Genuecht': Zuidnederlandse Kamers van Rhetorica in Noord-Nederland 1585-1630', *Bijdragen tot de geschiedenis*, LVII (1974) 3-89. With summary in English.

arches decorated with greenery and painted cloth to the construction of elaborate *tableaux vivants* over arches or on floats on the canals.[64] The author explores the classical and contemporary sources of the *tableaux* and reconstructs the scene from etching and contemporaneously published commemorative books. He reveals the independent line taken by Amsterdam in fêting Marie de Medici in 1638 and Henrietta Maria in 1642, while in 1659 the town celebrated a visit from members of the Orange family, though the policy of the States party was hostile to Orange and the monarchical idea alike. The most detailed and interesting section of the book is the examination of the propaganda effort of Romein de Hooghe to present William III as the eminent leader of the European coalition against Louis XIV, when the stadhouder-king made a triumphal entry into the Hague in 1691. The book is abundantly illustrated with contemporary etchings.

Apart from the events surrounding the National Synod held at Dordrecht, the years 1617-18 were not perhaps among the most momentous in the history of the young Republic. It is therefore unfortunate that the resolutions of the States-General of these years, edited by J.C. Smit, are unable to shed much fresh light on the political background to the religious controversies: a search for the documents relating to the synod yielded nothing.[65] As usual the resolutions are most instructive on the Republic's relations with France, England and the southern Netherlands. Indicative of the United Provinces's growing prestige in the anti-Habsburg constellation was her close association with Venice at this time, resulting in Dutch military aid in return for subsidies. Other matters to preoccupy the States General were trade with the Indies and the Mediterranean, the latter made hazardous by the Algerian privateers. The index is very comprehensive, and references to individually numbered resolutions make consultation extremely straightforward.

An important anniversary publication celebrates the foundation of the University of Leiden in 1575: the catalogue of an exhibition at the Rijksmuseum, Amsterdam.[66] Short introductory articles by J. van Dorsten, J.J. Woltjer and Th. J. Meijer stress three themes — Leiden's Dutch (or, rather, Holland), humanistic and innovatory character, while the body of the catalogue gives much useful information and commentary on the finances, organization

---

64. D.P. Snoep, *Praal en Propaganda. Triumfalie in de Noordelijke Nederlanden in de 16de en 17de eeuw* (Alphen aan den Rijn: Canaletto, 1975, 186 pp.; Utrecht University Thesis. With a summary in English).

65. J.G. Smit, ed., *Resolutiën der Staten-Generaal*, nieuwe reeks, *1610-1670*, III, *1617-1618*. Rijks Geschiedkundige Publicatiën Grote Serie, CLII (The Hague: Nijhoff. xix + 662 pp., ISBN 90 247 1792 2).

66. *Leidse universiteit 400. Stichting en eerste bloei 1575-ca. 1650* (Amsterdam: Rijksmuseum, 1975, 186 pp.).

and teaching of the university. One example among many: with regard to theology, the point is made that whereas William of Orange had hoped that this would be based on the study and interpretation of the Bible, already before the beginning of the seventeenth century the emphasis in the Faculty of Theology had decisively shifted to a concentration on doctrinal matters, and Biblical studies were developed not here but in the Faculty of Philosophy and Letters.

A further contribution to the history of the University of Leiden is provided by a study of the Walloon College.[67] This college was founded on the initiative of the Walloon Synod to train ministers for their churches, as a French-speaking equivalent to the Staten College which provided ministers for the Dutch Reformed Church. In contrast to this latter, however, it was not under the control of burgomasters and curators but of the Walloon Synod, and in general its connections with the university were always weaker. Indeed, the author makes the point that such was its independence that the Walloon College was more akin to a separate Illustrious School for theology than an institute of the university. The College never had more than a few students and its *raison d'être* was undermined from about the 1640s by a greatly increased supply of ministers and students from France, which gave the Walloon Church the ministers it needed without the expense of having to pay for their training. Consequently, the synod began to lose interest in the college and it ceased to exist before the end of the century. This interesting study covers the activities of the regents of the college, the number of its students, its connection with the trustees of the Hallet-bequest (which also supported students at the college), and the teaching given.

Florentius Schuyl, after over twenty years as professor, remarkably enough of philosophy, at the Illustrious School in Bois-le-Duc, was appointed to a chair in medicine at Leiden in 1664, became rector magnificus in 1666, and died there three years later at the age of fifty. The biography of Schuyl by G.A. Lindeboom is therefore another work of interest to students of academic, as well as intellectual history.[68] He was not a major figure either in philosophy or medicine, but Lindeboom sees him as personifying a major shift in Dutch intellectual life — the acceptance of Cartesianism. He began his career as an orthodox Aristotelian, shown clearly by the theses he defended for his master's degree in philosophy, but soon became an enthusiastic advocate of the thought

67. G.H.M. Posthumus Meyjes, *Geschiedenis van het Waalse College te Leiden 1606-1699. Tevens een bijdrage tot de vroegste geschiedenis van het fonds Hallet* (Leiden: Universitaire Pers, 1975, 218 pp., ISBN 90 6021 2290).
68. G.A. Lindeboom, *Florentius Schuyl (1619-1669) en zijn betekenis voor het Cartesianisme in de geneeskunde* (The Hague: Nijhoff, 1974, 161 pp., ISBN 90 247 1640 3).

of Descartes. His acceptance of the new philosophy is expressed in his rectoral oration *De Veritate Scientiarum* (which is reproduced in full), and in what was probably his major work — a translation into Latin of Descartes' treatise *De l'homme*.

Though she spent only a few years in the Dutch Republic, Antoinette Bourignon, born in Lille (which was then in the Spanish Netherlands), is a significant figure in Dutch religious life in the later seventeenth century. Yet, as M. van der Does points out, the only works published about her in the Republic during her lifetime were translations of foreign pamphlets, and she argues that the role of Holland in the spread of Bourignon's ideas was only as the 'carrefour spirituel et intellectuel de l'Europe'.[69] This is one of the surprises which emerges from the valuable first part of her book, which consists of a check list of all the publications of her writings, both in the original French and in translation, and a discussion of published reactions to and comments on her teachings both by contemporaries and later. In the rest of the book, Van der Does gives a sympathetic account of the life and ideas of this not-altogether-attractive personality, who discovered that the orphans assigned to her care in 1654 had all made a pact with the devil, and who concluded that her rivals with similar ideas to her own — such as Jean de Labadie, Johannes Rothe and Quirinus Kuhlman — were false prophets and servants of Satan. What perhaps does not appear too clearly from this work is why such men as Comenius were so impressed by her.

A study by a scholar of Czech origins of the relations between the imperial court and the Dutch Republic in the years immediately preceding the French invasion of 1672 deserves particular notice for the fresh perspectives it has to offer on international relations in Europe at this time.[70] The author brings out subtly the difficulties these two powers had in coming together, even under the spur provided by an aggressive France. The Dutch Republic had, during the Thirty Years' War, been part of a group of alliances (which, of course, included France) opposing the power of the Spanish and Austrian Habsburgs, and attitudes inherited from this period were only reinforced by the ruthless recatholicising policies pursued by the emperor in his hereditary possessions. The imperial court, for its part, at the very least did not feel inclined to make sacrifices for this still-protestant former enemy. Moreover, the emperor did not consider himself to be directly threatened by French expansion, and was

---

69. Marthe van der Does, *Antoinette Bourignon. Sa vie (1616-1680) — Son œuvre* (Groningen: Verenigde Reproduktie Bedrijven, 1974, 218 pp.; University of Groningen doctoral thesis).
70. Václav Čihák, *Les Provinces-Unies et la Cour Impériale 1667-1672. Quelques aspects de leurs relations diplomatiques* (Amsterdam: Holland Universiteits Pers, 1974, 300 pp., ISBN 90 302 1102 4; Catholic University of Nijmegen doctoral thesis).

extremely reluctant to become involved in western Europe because of his constant preoccupation with the continuing Ottoman threat to his lands. It took the French invasion to bring about the *renversement des alliances* so significant for the succeeding period of European history. Čihák is often too allusive and indirect in his approach, but his book amply rewards careful study.

Another volume of the *Generale Missiven* of the governors general and councillors of the Dutch East India Company has been published, covering the years 1686-97, the last years of Johannes Camphuys and the first of Willem van Outhoorn as governor general.[71] It is impossible, of course, to indicate the content of such a publication, with so much material relating to so wide an area and covering so broad a range of topics, but one or two leading themes might be mentioned. Firstly, Camphuys in particular showed himself to be painfully aware of the seriousness of the endemic problem of corruption and inefficiency, and of his own inability to deal with it, in part at least because of his increasing ill-health. Another recurring subject is the activities of English traders and pirates, and the impossibility of excluding them from such regions as the west coast of Sumatra. These letters also give interesting information on the difficulties of defending the company's possessions in Asia after the outbreak of war with France, on the taking of Pondicherry from the French, and on Asian developments in general, such as the *coup* in Siam in 1688.

R.B. Evenhuis continues his detailed study of the Reformed Church in Amsterdam at a quickened pace. In his recently published fourth volume he covers the eighteenth century up to 1795, with a concluding chapter which goes just beyond this terminal date in order to take in, if not fully to take up, the separation of Church and State.[72] The sub-title of the volume — the great crisis — affirms the author's contention that the whole volume, and not simply chapter IV, which deals specifically with the Reformed Church and the Enlightenment, serves to make clear the challenge to the Church posed by the Enlightenment and the success of the Church in resisting that challenge. It may be suggested, however, that what the author's evidence, and some of his *obiter dicta*, serve to make clear, is less the success of the Church in resisting the challenge, than the weakness of the challenge in the Netherlands, at any rate until the last decades of the eighteenth century. Indeed, it might be argued that in some senses the Reformed Church may have suffered more damage from the activities of some of its own establishment than from the writings of its critics. However, if Dr. Evenhuis has not sustained his major

71. W.Ph. Coolhaas, ed., *Generale Missiven van Gouverneurs-Generaal en Raden aan Heren XVII der Verenigde Oostindische Compagnie*, V; *1686-1697*. Rijks Geschiedkundige Publicatiën, Grote Serie, CL (The Hague: Nijhoff, 1975, xv + 927 pp., ISBN 90 247 1700 0).
72. R.B. Evenhuis, *Ook dat was Amsterdam*, IV, *De kerk der hervorming in de achttiende eeuw: de grote crisis* (Baarn: Ten Have, 1974, 367 pp., ISBN 90 259 0096 8).

thesis, he has provided a wealth of information, gleaned from ecclesiastical records as well as a mass of ephemeral and secondary literature, which is used to good effect in illustrating such matters as the social origins, religious duties, and interests of ministers of the Reformed Church in Amsterdam; the administration of poor relief, and education in the town; the impact or, better, the lack of impact, of pietism and methodism; attitudes and policies towards the various dissenting groups; and the Patriot movement. In short this is a substantial and successful piece of *haute vulgarisation*, which illuminates not only the lives of ministers, elders, and deacons of the Reformed Church in Amsterdam, but also the lives — the sins and the pleasures — of the wider community of believers. Students of social history will find much of interest to them in the volume.

Joan Corver and his grandson Gerrit dominated the government of Amsterdam, Joan for fourteen years at the beginning of the second stadholderless regime until his death in 1716 at the age of 88, and Gerrit from 1744 right up to August 1748. Joan had been brought to the front in 1666 with the willing co-operation of Johan de Witt, supposedly in order to strengthen De Witt's position when William of Orange should reach his majority. Gerrit was really powerful only for a short time from 1744 since he was among those who lost power when the new Stadhouder William IV was sent for in the summer of 1748 to restore peace and order. A. Porta's book is founded on enormously wide reading and a tremendous amount of archive work.[73] We are given not only the local history of Amsterdam itself in these years but also much valuable information on the history of the Republic. This makes the absence, typical of such thorough and detailed Dutch studies as this, of a subject index a particular misfortune.

In 1747 the States of Holland, fearing a possible attack from the French, ordered the registration of all men aged between 16 and 60, capable of bearing arms and living in the country districts. The lists, put up by the village secretaries, have been preserved for the districts south of the IJ, and form an excellent starting point for demographic research. D.C. Noordam has studied one of the districts — Maasland near the town of Maassluis — meticulously, employing the method of family reconstruction, which was possible because the baptismal, marriage and death registers in Maasland happen to be in an excellent condition.[74] Thus Noordam could trace biographical details on 87 per cent of the listed men and their families. He studies their religion, profes-

73. A. Porta, *Joan en Gerrit Corver. De politieke macht van Amsterdam 1702-1748* (Assen: Van Gorcum, 1975, 376 pp., ISBN 90 232 1292 4).
74. D.J. Noordam, 'De weerbare mannen van Maasland 1747. Een historisch-demografisch onderzoek', *Holland*, VII (1975) 1-61.

sion, level of prosperity — Maasland was a district of more or less well-to-do husbandmen, — the age of marriage, child mortality, the structure of the household and so on, and compares his results with similar studies made in France and England. He finds a striking similarity on most points with findings about French eighteenth-century villages. He also shows the strong immigration into Maasland — nearly 70 per cent of the listed men were born outside the village and so were 57 per cent of their wives; emigration on the other hand took place on a smaller scale. The article is of considerably more than local significance.

A.M. Elias's Leiden doctoral thesis on the *Nationaal Sijndicaat* makes a useful if slender volume.[75] Based almost wholly on the three-men *Sijndicaat*'s records this work gives as clear a picture as the limited material allows of the operation of one part of the administration of the *Staatsbewind*. Too often however the case studies here described end with the ominous comment, 'nothing more is recorded in the minutes', and not surprisingly this institutional innovation did not reappear under the *Raadpensionaris*. The inspiration behind its introduction was uncertain, its major purpose unclear, and its powers circumscribed by subordination to an unsympathetic High Court and *Staatsbewind*, which mistrusted an institution charged with preserving constitutional integrity against central and local government abuses. Their lack of co-operation, compounded by that of the departmental and town governments on which the *Sijndicaat* depended for information, contributed to its failure. Nor was it assisted by the dichotomy between its role as constitutional watchdog and its second function on which most of its considerable funds were spent, surveillance of subversive activities by individual citizens. The tensions thus created proved finally destructive when most of the members of the *Staatsbewind* acquiesced in the idea of constitutional change. Elias explores and properly rejects the suggestion that here is an early version of the Ombudsman, but in so doing he produces a limited thesis lacking a full discussion of the insecurity of the regime the *Sijndicaat* had to protect against internal and external subversion. He explains the failure of the *Sijndicaat* in broadly functional terms although clearly it ought also to be linked to the lack of consensus about the principles underlying the *Staatsbewind*. Unlike the *Conseil d'État* and the Supreme Court, the *Sijndicaat* never became the collective repository of constitutional wisdom, or the institutional conscience of an assured government; nor could it develop into a much needed administrative weapon in the armoury of a precariously unified State. The relationship of these failures to the *Staatsbewind*'s own uncertain position is left unexplored. Also unexplained,

75. A.M. Elias, *Het Nationaal Sijndicaat, 1802-5* (Bussum: Fibula-van Dishoeck, 1975, 194 pp., ISBN 90 228 3528 6. Summary in French).

227

although partly described, is the surprising extent to which the *Sijndicaat*'s members succeeded in charting a course for the new institution. Nevertheless Elias has performed a service in putting together this record of ·a little-known and interesting constitutional experiment.

An issue on which feelings ran high between the *Sijndicaat* and the *Staatsbewind* was the instruction for the new High Military Tribunal, the first permanent college to exercise military and naval jurisdiction. Against the wishes of the *Staatsbewind* the *Sijndicaat* tried to enforce the principle that all justice should be exercised free of administrative intervention, including the execution of sentences. A recent publication, a Utrecht doctoral dissertation, surveys Marine Justice under the *ancien* and revolutionary régimes.[76] C.H.F. Simons provides another vivid operational picture, this time of justice and its administration in a specialized field, by the use of archive-based case studies which, together with extensive appendices, including a complete list of naval sentences, 1750-95, makes a particularly useful work of reference. Not surprisingly the original formidable project for a systematic survey of the development of naval justice up to the present has been pruned. Simons justifies his choice of period on the grounds that it encompasses the Batavian Revolution which 'left its stamp on the administration of justice as on so much else' and 'gives a long enough perspective to the work to validate the conclusions reached'. This slightly naive formulation results in a rather undigested work retaining the characteristics of a mere survey with a somewhat sketchy second part. The years 1750-95 are treated in 95 pages of text; 1795-1814 in 35 pages and the work effectively ends in 1806. There is a list of archive material consulted, but not of printed and secondary works.

LATER MODERN BELGIAN HISTORY

In his 'Companion to the Study of Topographical Maps of the Netherlands', published in 1963, C. Koeman stressed the importance of the Staff maps drawn up for military purposes after 1815, which show a remarkable precision of design.[77] Between 1815 and 1830 such maps were naturally also prepared for the southern part of the United Kingdom. These have now been studied by

---

76. C.H.F. Simons, *Marinejustitie: Ontwikkelingen in de strafrechtspleging bij de Nederlandse zeemacht, in het bijzonder gedurende de tweede helft van de 18e eeuw en het begin van de 19e eeuw* (Assen: Van Gorcum, 1974, xxv + 285 pp. Summary in English).
77. C. Koeman, *Handleiding voor de studie van de topographische kaarten van Nederland 1750-1850* (Groningen, 1963).

L. Hens-Vercauteren, who also pays attention to the preceding maps of Ferraris (1771-7) and the later ones by Vandermaelen (1837-53).[78]

In our previous survey we called attention to the publication of the first volume of the 'Encyclopedia of the Flemish Movement'. Meanwhile the second and final volume has appeared.[79] The previous format has been maintained; information concerning individuals, organizations, trends, newspapers and other periodicals are arranged alphabetically. There are a considerable number of more extended articles, which give general surveys of, for instance, education, the Flemish Movement and language laws. A serious effort has again been made to maintain the greatest objectivity possible. No doubt there are still some regrettable gaps but it is clear that this encyclopedia has developed into a professional tool of high calibre.

Another recently published reference work of major importance is a complete inventory of all periodicals on educational subjects published in Belgium between 1817 and 1895.[80] This work, consisting of two substantial volumes, has been produced through the co-operation of a great many researchers from Louvain and Ghent under the direction of M. De Vroede, professor at the Catholic University of Louvain. This publication is among the best and most important of its kind. The periodicals are dealt with in chronological sequence and for each of them information is provided on depositories, subtitles, title script, motto, price, format, number of pages per issue, periodicity, circulation and distribution, and address of administrative offices, all according to the system developed by the press section of the Interuniversity Centre of Contemporary History; this also applies to the information given concerning first and last publication dates, founders, publishers, owners, printers, boards of directors, managers, editors-in-chief, other editors, contributors and manner of financing and subsidizing. In addition the authors indicate in which years the editors and contributors were connected with the listed periodicals; they have also deciphered all initials and supply a wealth of information which in nearly every instance has grown into a full-fledged biography. De Vroede has provided the two volumes with excellent introductions which clearly illuminate the significance of schoolteachers in the political and cultural life of Belgium.

78. L. Hens-Vercauteren, 'De topografische kaarten van de Zuidelijke Nederlanden (1815-1830)', *Tijdschrift van de Belgische vereniging voor aardrijkskundige studies*, XLII (Brussels, 1973) 333-455.
79. J. Deleu, G. Durnez, R. De Schryver, L. Simons, ed., *Encyclopedie van de Vlaamse Beweging* (M-Z) (Tielt-Utrecht: Lanno, 1975, 1205 col. ISBN 90 209 9457 4).
80. M. De Vroede, e.a., ed., *Bijdragen tot de geschiedenis van het pedagogisch leven in België in de 19e en 20e eeuw* (2 vols., Ghent-Louvain; 1973-74) I, *De periodieken 1817-1878*, 658 pp.; II, *De periodieken 1878-1895*, 764 pp.; cf. M. De Vroede, 'De onderwijzersgezelschappen in België, 1816-ca. 1846', *Pedagogische studiën. Maandblad voor onderwijs en opvoeding*, XLVI (Groningen, 1969) 650-86.

I. De Troyer has published a list of treaties concluded by Belgium with other countries between 1830 and 1940.[81] He reports the title, the parties concluding the treaty, the subject, the place where it was signed, the dates of ratification and of the deposition of the ratified document, and of course the place where the treaty is now kept. His work is provided with useful thematic indices.

The governments of the Directory, the Consulate and the Empire favoured commerce and industry. Lieven Bauwen, who managed to build up an empire — although short-lived — in the cotton industry in Ghent and elsewhere, belonged to the social class which profited from this. His previous biographers were mainly concerned with the results of his work and paid scant attention to the way in which these were achieved. A.M. Suetens has now studied his correspondence and has come to the conclusion that Bauwen did not honour the contracts with his English technicians, that he paid the workers as little as possible and that he exploited prisoners released to him as labourers in a most revolting manner.[82] He used his political power to crush resistance against these policies and did not even spare his own family and relations in this respect.

The Treaty of Versailles of 1814 brought an enlightened despot to power in the southern Netherlands. The changes resulting from the policies of William I included the reorganization of higher education. B. Borghraef shows how he applied the same formula in the south that he had already used successfully in the north at an earlier date.[83] The universities of Ghent, Louvain and Liège were placed under strict State supervision with a secretary as well as an inspector general acting as co-ordinators. The task of the universities was limited to teaching; they were not granted a role in the area of scholarly research. During the 'twenties modern subjects such as agriculture and mining were added to the established faculties. It proved to be very difficult to find professors even for the small number of chairs that had been endowed.

The battle which the papacy waged in the 1860s to maintain its temporal power found its repercussions in Flanders, where many enlisted in the papal corps of the Zouaves. It is not yet clear what drove them to do this and from what strata of society they originated, but some light is thrown on these

81. I. De Troyer, *Repertorium van de door België gesloten verdragen — Répertoire des traités conclus par la Belgique, 1830-1940* (Brussels: J. Goemaere, 1973, 575 pp.).
82. A.M. Suetens, 'Lieven Bauwens — mythe en werkelijkheid', *Handelingen der Maatschappij voor geschiedenis en oudheidkunde te Gent*, XXVIII (Ghent, 1974) 77-114.
83. B. Borghraef-Van der Schueren, *De universiteiten in de zuidelijke provincies onder Willem I.* Mededelingen van de Koninklijke Academie voor Wetenschappen, Letteren en Schone Kunsten van België, XXXV, ii (Brussels: Paleis der Academiën, 1973, 22 pp.).

questions by L. Monbaliu's recent edition of the letters written by a young student who was later to become a famous missionary.[84]

The struggle after 1848 between catholics and liberals for dominance of the State proceeded with repeated ups and downs. The clerics, who had had to relinquish their position around 1848, did not definitely regain their dominance until 1884. The liberals were in uninterrupted control from 1857 to 1870 and again from 1878 to 1884. In both parties a radical wing developed which could not always be kept under control without difficulty. E. Coppens describes the development of such a radical left catholic nucleus in Ghent.[85] This group derived its ideas from François Huet, a Frenchman who taught at Ghent University. Huet found his followers among the former liberal catholics who had lost their struggle against the ultramontanes after being condemned by the bishop and had then gradually drifted towards the Liberal Party. In 1846 they welcomed the Parisian revolution enthusiastically and considered the possibility of forming their own political party. The conservative leadership of the Catholic Party intervened, however. Huet returned to his native country and the organization he had inspired crumbled as its members left to join the conservatives.

R. Lesthaeghe has investigated a particularly interesting problem in his article on birth control, marriage rates and socio-economic changes in Belgium in the second half of the nineteenth century.[86] He found that while all of western Europe showed a decline in fertility in wedlock and also in the age at which marriage was entered into, this did not happen in Flanders — in contrast to the Walloon areas — until a much later date. It is impossible to attribute this phenomenon simply to a lagging industrialization and urbanization. Other factors such as language, religion and culture have to be taken into consideration as well. The author does this in a 'co-variant analysis with some five variables' in what he terms 'correlograms' and 'scattergrams'. This explanation might easily have been extended by, for instance, including secularization and election results in the calculations.

A number of historians have concentrated on the position of the less fortunate in the nineteenth century. K. Welffens has studied a little-researched group, namely the civil servants of lower rank at Antwerp.[87] She found that

---

84. L. Monbaliu, 'Amaat Vyncke's zouavenbrieven, 1867-1869', *Rollariensia*, V (Roesselaere, 1973) 6-113.
85. E. Coppens, 'La société Huet, Tussen revolutie en reactie', *Handelingen Maatschappij Geschiedenis Gent*, XXVI (1972) 131-50.
86. R. Lesthaeghe, 'Vruchtbaarheidscontrole, nuptialiteit en sociaal-economische veranderingen in België, 1846-1910', *Bevolking en gezin* (Brussels, 1972) 251-305; (1973) 375-81.
87. K. Welffens, 'Poging tot benadering van de sociale toestand van de Antwerpse stadsbedienden in de negentiende eeuw', *Bijdragen tot de geschiedenis*, LVI (Antwerp, 1973) 157-95.

their income was not very different from that of common labourers but that they did enjoy certain advantages: a better education, a permanent position, more suitable working conditions and usually a pension. Much more unfavourable were the living conditions of the workers. Particularly in cities with a high rate of demographic expansion, conditions were deplorable. This was the situation in Antwerp where the economic structure was altered in the first half of the century through the decline of the textile industry and the rise of the trading port, with the latter able to provide work for only a portion of the able-bodied men available. A sharp increase of rents took place because the construction of new housing lagged behind population increase. The workers and the many unemployed could no longer afford a decent home. In her investigation C. Lis used the archives of the commission of public assistance and found an increase in the number of slum dwellings.[88] In order to protect the better neighbourhoods against this decline, the well-to-do bourgeoisie embarked upon a well-considered policy of demolition and new construction which forced the proletarians to draw back entirely to certain sections of the city, which then developed into true ghettos.

W. Steensels has approached the same problem from a different angle.[89] He traces how the government reacted to the increasing housing problem among the workers during the course of the nineteenth century, when the initiatives taken by private construction companies and industrial entrepreneurs (such as De Gorge-Legrand) were solely calculated to make a quick profit and seldom had the improvement of the welfare of the workers at heart. He establishes that the authorities only stepped in when definite emergencies arose. After the crisis of 1848, the cholera epidemic of 1866 and the Walloon revolutionary days of 1886, housing regulations were hastily passed by Parliament but culminated in few concrete results. A law of 9 August 1889, on the other hand, made both a quantitative and qualitative improvement possible in the housing available because it not only created a number of bodies for the purpose of inspection but also provided the possibility of obtaining credit.

In 1886, after labour unrest and numerous strikes in the Walloon districts, a commission was appointed by royal decree to investigate the socio-economic plight of the workers and to make proposals for improving their lot. The reports of the inquiries held fill many volumes with information concerning

88. C. Lis, 'Krotten en ghetto's: exponenten van verpaupering en polarisering. Een concreet voorbeeld: Antwerpen, 1780-1850', *Tijdschrift voor geschiedenis*, LXXXVIII (Groningen, 1975) 626-36; cf. *idem*, 'Woontoestanden en gangensanering in Antwerpen in het midden der 19e eeuw', *Belgische tijdschrift voor nieuwste geschiedenis*, I (Ghent, 1969) 93-131.
89. W. Steensels, *Proletarisch wonen. De woonsituatie in België in de 19e eeuw* (Antwerp: C.E.A.-C.E.R.E. Centrum voor Architektuuraal onderzoek en voor onderzoek van het environment — I.C.C. Internationaal Cultureel Centrum, 1975, 45 pp.).

the living conditions of the workers. Consulting this source, however, is not so simple, since the facts obtained are without rhyme or reason. L. Denys has grouped the material around a number of principal themes: working hours, household budgets, the organizing of labour, and the structure of the groups of workers in the various enterprises.[90]

U. Vermeulen has researched how the bourgeois press reacted to the activities of the First International.[91] He came to the hardly surprising conclusion that the press showed little understanding of this emanicipative movement and tore every aspect of it rather cynically to shreds. No means were spared to discredit the opponents. Vermeulen gives a very long list of examples of the invective and insinuations hurled from both liberal and catholic side. In this respect there proved to have been no difference between papers and periodicals written in French and those written in Dutch. After the dismemberment of the First International a considerable period of time elapsed before a revival of the political awareness of the workers manifested itself in the founding of the Belgian Workers Party in 1884. This gave the impetus towards a large movement pressing for the improvement of society by political means. The socialist labour movement was followed by that of the catholics, except that their success was not equally great in all parts of the country. Particularly in the province of Limburg, a predominantly agrarian area where the influence of the Catholic church was overwhelming, every attempt at social change was met with very strong opposition. The christian democrats also had great difficulty in establishing a foothold in this area. Social security, however, was nevertheless greatly extended after 1889 *via* the so-called *mutualités*, but the first labour union was not established in Limburg until 1909. The socialists began their propaganda in the province in 1889. Around 1895 they won a few local council seats in the south. W. Massin, who wrote a book on this subject, included a number of memoirs of militant socialists of that period in an appendix.[92]

The rural areas continued to be dominated by the Catholic Party. This is also the conclusion of the fascinating study by J. Craeybeckx about the agrarian depression at the end of the nineteenth century and the political struggle for the farmers' support.[93] First of all the author describes the crisis in agriculture, beginning at the close of the 'seventies, which resulted in the withdrawal of capital from rural areas — although rentals were favourable for large property

90. L. Denys, 'Trends in de sociaal-economische toestand van de Belgische arbeiders rond 1886', *Belgisch tijdschrift voor nieuwste geschiedenis*, V (1974) 361-426.
91. U. Vermeulen, 'Het beeld van de Eerste Internationale in de Belgische burgerlijke pers (1865-1877)', *Belgisch tijdschrift voor nieuwste geschiedenis*, V (1974) 447-92.
92. W. Massin, *De opkomst van het socialisme in Limburg ... 1890-1914* (Diest, 1975, 132 pp.).
93. J. Craeybeckx, 'De agrarische depressie van het einde der XIXe eeuw en de politieke strijd om de boeren', *Belgisch tijdschrift voor nieuwste geschiedenis*, IV (1973) 191-230, V (1974) 181-225.

owners — and in many farmer's sons leaving the land to seek a better living in the cities. The small family farms, whose members worked hard and lived frugally, were able to survive the crisis but not without becoming dependent upon money lenders. This last evil was counteracted on the part of the catholics by the founding of the Boerenbond (Farmers Union) and the Raiffeisenbanken (Farmers Banks). Craeybeckx emphasizes that the farming population in Flanders was concurrently being immunised against the socialist propaganda which began to infiltrate during the 'nineties. The socialists had taken a great deal of trouble to analyze the situation in rural areas but had found no response and were finally forced to adapt their Marxist model to the mentality of the farmers and to accept the continuance of small-property ownership. They did not gain any advantage among the farmers from the lowering and abolition of the property franchise tax.

The social movement revolving around the brothers Daens, on the other hand, did meet with success in rural districts. Up to now historians have devoted attention mostly to Aalst as the centre of Daensism and to its best-known protagonists. Now, however, two small volumes have appeared about Daens's supporters Hector Planckaert and Florimont Fonteyne. Planckaert, who worked in the arrondissement of Aalst, was one of the first to join Daens and his cause. Verdoodt describes this militant figure, who became a member of the German-sponsored Council of Flanders during the First World War and who unsuccessfully introduced a Daensist slate for the elections of 1936 at a time when Daensism was no longer mentioned by anyone.[94] The publication by K. Rosaert about Father Fonteyne and his Daensist activities in the area surrounding Bruges reveals nothing apart from a number of details about the childhood years of the author's hero.[95] Similarly the scholarly significance of M. Van Roey's biography of J. Cardijn, the founder of the Catholic Youth Movement (Katholieke Arbeidersjeugd), merely consists in the revelation of some documents from Cardijn's personal archives.[96] G. Depamelaere has on the other hand managed to avoid any form of hagiography in his study of Hugo Verriest, a priest (d. 1922) who exerted a profound influence on the Flemish catholic student movement both as a teacher and as a public orator.[97] The author arrives at a fairly objective assessment of Verriest; he is not blind to his less pleasant aspects nor does he overrate the literary merits of his prose.

---

94. F.J. Verdoodt, *Het Daensisme in het arrondissement Aalst* (Dendermonde, 1975, 123 pp.).
95. K. Rotsaert, *Priester Fonteyne en the Fonteynisme te Brugge* (Bruges, 1975, 104 pp.).
96. M. Van Roey, *Cardyn* (Brussels: D.A.P. Reinaert Uitgaven, 1972, 227 pp.).
97. G. Depamelaere, *Hugo Verriest, man van zijn tijd* (Tielt: Lanno, 1972, 105 pp.).

The socialists too honour their great leaders, particularly Camille Huysmans, secretary of the Second International, member of Parliament, mayor of Antwerp, twice minister, about whom the Standaard Uitgeverij intends to publish some nine volumes, in part biographical, in part a collection of documents. W. Geldolf and D. Deweerdt were responsible for the first volume which relates to Huysmans's activities prior to 1919, the period during which he was working in Brussels as a city councillor and as a member of the Chamber of Representatives.[98] Letters, newspaper articles and excerpts from his memoirs constitute the framework of the account, in which fringe figures and events are also placed very effectively.

A different principle is used as the basis of the publication of the work of Hendrik de Man (1885-1953) by M. Claeys-Van Haegendoren (who published a good biography of De Man in 1972), L. Magits and others.[99] They give their readers the opportunity of becoming acquainted with articles which have become virtually impossible to find and with the books of one of the most original socialist thinkers of the first half of this century, systematically arranged and translated where necessary. The first volume, arranged and edited by M. Claeys, consists of fragments of his memoirs *Après Coup* (1941), *Cavalier Seul* (1948) and *Gegen den Strom* (1953); the second volume, edited by Magits, contains parts of *Zur Psychologie des Sozialismus* (1926) and *Opbouwend Socialisme* (1931). A specialist will regret the fact that not a single text has been published in its entirety and will not always agree with the choice of extracts. Four volumes are still to follow. H. Brugmans provided the first volume with a brilliant introduction.

D.E. Devreese has investigated which factors prompted people to take a militant part in the labour movement.[100] She chose a number of figures and followed the course of their lives and on this basis she feels able to claim that consecutive generations each show their own pattern of behaviour. The intellectuals of the period prior to 1860 were stirred by a mixture of republicanism, the ideas of Lamennais and deism; after this date the positivism of Proudhon made more appeal. All militants were most active between the ages of twenty and thirty. Their social background varied. Most intellectuals came from

98. C. Huysmans, D. De Weerdt en W. Geldolf, *Geschriften en documenten*, I, *C. Huysmans te Brussel* (Antwerp-Amsterdam: Standaard, 1974, 143 pp.).
99. M. Claeys-Van Haegendoren, e.a., *Hendrik De Man, persoon en ideeën* (Antwerp-Amsterdam: Standaard, 1974ff.), vol. I, M. Claeys-Van Haegendoren, ed., *Autobiografie*. Introduction by H. Brugmans, 551 pp.; vol. II, L. Magits ed., *Psychologie van het socialisme. Opbouwend socialisme*, 611 pp.
100. D.E. Devreese, 'Een onderzoek naar beinvloeding en reactie: het voorbeeld van militanten van de arbeidersbeweging, België 1830-1884', *Mededelingenblad. Orgaan van de Nederlandse Vereniging tot beoefening van de sociale geschiedenis*, XLV (Amsterdam, 1974) 57-103.

middle-class families whereas the workers came from ordinary working-class families or occasionally from an impoverished skilled-trade background. What stands out is that the generation of intellectuals which came after 1860 managed to obtain a good position in society; the future prospects of the militants from a worker's background were significantly less promising.

During the First World War resistance to the French-language army command arose behind the front lines at the instigation of *alumni* of the Catholic University of Louvain, the so-called Front Movement. Officers of lower rank, non-commissioned officers and medical personnel took part in it. R. Vanlandschoot has studied the role played by one of the leaders, Joris Lannoo, and emphasizes once again how much influence Cyriel Verschaeve had on this expression of Flemish nationalism.[101] After the war many young intellectuals fell into a state of mental depression, the causes of which are analyzed by M. Sertyn in his article 'Sense of Decadence among the Avant-garde in Flanders after 1918'.[102] The violence of war, the diplomatic cattle trade in racial groups and peoples after the war and the Russian revolution had, according to the author, robbed them of their traditional certainties. Many artists and writers sought refuge in avant-garde periodicals and gave exaggerated praise to a difficult to define revolutionary idealism which was often both anti-militaristic and Flemish nationalistic. Among the artistic circles of a number of cities the internationalism of 'les esprits libres' à la Barbusse and Romain Rolland — the so-called Clarté group — was influential. However, this mixture of pacifism, Flemish radicalism and social concern was never channelled to the point of forming a co-ordinated left front.

Cardinal Mercier, a powerful proponent of a French-speaking Belgium nationalism, was a highly formidable opponent of the German forces of occupation during the First World War, and German appeals to the highest ecclesiastical authorities to have him silenced were in vain. R. Boudens has investigated data contained in the archives of Foreign Affairs at Bonn concerning Mercier and his influence in German-occupied Belgium.[103] The documents he has examined also contain information not previously known concerning the conduct of the Flemish 'activists' who collaborated with the Germans.

101. R. Vanlandschoot, 'Joris Lannoo en de eerste Wereldoorlog', *De Roede van Tielt*, IV (Tielt, 1973) 3-50.
102. M. Sertyn, 'Avondlandstemming bij de jonge avant-garde in Vlaanderen na 1918: inspiratiebron voor purito-flaminganten en marginale wereldverbeteraars', *Belgisch tijdschrift voor nieuwste geschiedenis*, V (1974) 547-80.
103. R. Boudens, 'Kardinaal Mercier volgens het archief van de Wilhelmstrasse', *Collationes Brugenses et Gandavenses*, II (Bruges, 1970) 506-45. On Mercier's attitude towards the Flemish Movement, see *idem*, *Kardinaal Mercier en de Vlaamse beweging* (Louvain, 1975), a work we will review in our next survey.

The military historian Weemaes has written an extensive technical treatise about the last stages of the war.[104] He describes in rather technical terms the successive battles during the offensive of 1918. What is especially interesting for non-specialists is that the author shows that King Albert was averse to the splitting of his troops among English and French units. The structure of authority which was accepted in the end conflicted with that of the king, whose say was reduced to virtually nothing.

Exceptionally interesting is the article by V. Janssens about the impact of the inflation after the First World War — a subject to which the author devotes even more attention in his subsequent work about the Belgian franc, which was published at the end of September 1975 and will be reviewed by us in a later survey.[105] In his first tentative contribution the author explains how after the First World War no-one knew how to handle the then unknown phenomenon of a galloping inflation. The few specialists posited that restoring the prewar gold standard together with maintaining the parity of the franc against the dollar could quieten things down. Attempts were made to find a solution by consolidating the floating debt, conducting a strict budget policy and restoring the balance of payments. Around 1925 the tide began to turn. The first plan to stabilize the franc initially met with a great deal of understanding but failed just the same. The author sees the reason for this in the refusal of the American Morgan group to agree to a loan of 150 million dollars. He does not rule out, however, that the hope with which Minister Janssens anticipated this loan attested to a misplaced optimism. His successor Franqui finally put the country's finances on a sound footing.

L. Brouwers, S.J., has written a substantial commemorative work in celebration of the fiftieth anniversary of the Christian Employers Association, to which he is the spiritual advisor.[106] It is a chronological report of conferences and stands taken, of leaders and members, of how the association is organized and of its effect at a national, regional and local level. The reader is not spared a single detail; what, however, the precise significance of the organization is remains obscure. It apparently served especially as a retreat for reflection and encounter for executives who wanted to bring their daily work in line with their religious beliefs. Nothing is revealed in the book of tensions or frictions.

104. W. Weemaes, *Van de grens tot Brussel. Het bevrijdingsoffensief van het Belgisch leger, 29 september 1918* (Brussels: Dienst voor de geschiedenis van de Belgische strijdkrachten, 1972, 454 pp. + 34 maps).
105. V. Janssens, 'De inflatie — de Eerste Wereldoorlog en de stabilisatie van de Belgische frank', in: *Economische Geschiedenis België*, I, 73-90; cf. *idem, De Belgische frank — anderhalve eeuw geldgeschiedenis* (Antwerp-Amsterdam: Standaard, 1976, 456 pp., ISBN 90 02 13428 2).
106. L. Brouwers, *Vijftig jaar christelijke werkgeversbeweging in België. Een bijdrage tot de sociaal-economische geschiedenis* (2 vols., Brussels: Unipac, 1974, 517 + 648 648 pp.).

It does, however, contain interesting biographical data about industrialists and may be useful in the study of the interaction between christian employers and the christian labour movement.

In 1830-31 North Brabant was in a difficult position, as the majority of the population was very sympathetic to the Belgians and to some extent disliked the protestant northern Netherlands, and yet did not wish to secede from the north. E.R.M. Hoffmann's dissertation explains why the North Brabanders wished to avoid a choice between north and south, and to preserve William I's United Kingdom as the framework in which to fulfil their political aspirations.[107] Their opposition was therefore not so far reaching. There was no collaboration between liberals and liberal catholics on the Belgian pattern, for North Brabant was in political terms as little advanced as the rest of the north — indeed in that respect it had more in common with it.

To mark the 125th anniversary of the Dutch parliamentary stenographic service N. Cramer published a collection of interesting fragments from the proceedings of the States General.[108] It is a collection of parliamentary speeches which recall a number of important political events, but more attention is paid to curious incidents and dramatic situations in parliament since 1849.

The memoirs of the liberal deputy Van Eck, edited by C.A. Tamse, give a glimpse behind the scenes of nineteenth-century political life.[109] They offer shrewd commentaries on the parliamentary treatment of bills, and on the attitude of leading ministers and deputies. The strained relationship between William III and his ministers is also discussed. Finally some passages and appendices shed light on the formation of clubs within the amorphous group of liberal deputies in the second chamber, efforts to strengthen the Liberal Party organization, and the championing of local interests in the days of the constituency system.

C. Smit devotes a number of diplomatic-historical sketches to important aspects of the often tense relations of the Netherlands with Great Britain,

---

107. E.R.M. Hoffman, *Noord-Brabant en de Opstand van 1830*. Bijdragen tot de geschiedenis van het Zuiden van Nederland, XXXI (Tilburg: Stichting Zuidelijk Historisch Contact, 1974, 263 pp.; Thesis Faculty of Letters, Nijmegen. With summary in French).
108. N. Cramer, *Wandelingen door de Handelingen*. Parlementaria, I (The Hague: Staatsuitgeverij, s.a., 352 pp., ISBN 90 12006155).
109. C.A. Tamse, ed., *Memoires van een enfant terrible. Politieke herinneringen van de Zeeuwse liberale afgevaardigde mr. Daniël van Eck aan vijfendertig jaar Kamerlidmaatschap 1849-1884* (Middelburg: Koninklijk Zeeuwsch Genootschap der Wetenschappen, 1975, 130 pp).

Germany, the United States and the Kerensky government during the First World War.[110] He describes how Queen Wilhelmina, her ministers and diplomats tried to give substance to the Dutch policy of neutrality, and thereby created a variety of tensions. It is clear how many limitations the belligerents imposed on small border neutrals without feeling too restrained by international law. London and Berlin made large demands on the Hague because they knew that the Netherlands wished to remain outside the war at all costs. The German General Staff wanted the Wilhelmstrasse to go to the limit against the Netherlands in order to secure the acceptance of its demands. Smit stresses that in Germany's policy towards the Dutch, the moderate line of the civil authorities consistently triumphed over the extremism of the military. One could wish that the author had explained why the Germans gave way to the relatively weak Netherlands but ended by forcing the mighty United States into the war, although the allied blockade had hindered free passage from Rotterdam so much that one important motive for Germany to respect Dutch neutrality was no longer valid by 1916.

In a substantial study A.J. Rasker analyzes the development of ideas and theological currents in the Dutch Reformed Church since 1795.[111] It is a *tour de force*, as all kinds of European philosophical and theological trends influenced Dutch protestant theology. Theological differences also had far reaching consequences for Church, State and society. For example, the increasing social and political pluralism of the Dutch people readily took on a theological guise, as is indicated by the founding of a number of autonomous protestant churches, the establishment of confessional political parties, newspapers, trades unions, universities and cultural organizations, and also the total alienation of the Church. Modern Dutch society still bears the traces of this curious interplay of theological and socio-economic factors in the previous century, *verzuiling* or the vertical division of society being the most striking. An integral history of the Dutch Reformed Church would therefore have to illuminate so many facets that it would be beyond the power of a single author. Rasker's study confines itself to ideas and thinkers. He sketches clearly the concepts of the enlightened theologians, the Groningen school, the Réveil and the 'ethical', 'modernist' and 'neocalvinist' tendencies. Also of interest are his discussions of the Church's resistance to the Nazis, the revival after the Second World War, ecumenism and the new theology. This book is of great value as a work of reference as it deals also with the twentieth century. However, social and

---

110. C. Smit, *Tien studiën betreffende Nederland in de Eerste Wereldoorlog* (Groningen: Tjeenk Willink, 1975, 159 pp., ISBN 90 01 80288 5).
111. A.J. Rasker, *De Nederlandse Hervormde Kerk vanaf 1795. Haar geschiedenis en theologie in de negentiende en twintigste eeuw* (Kampen: J.H. Kok, 1974, 455 pp., ISBN 90 242 2662 7).

political developments are not satisfactorily integrated into the argument. For example, the social importance of the violent conflicts within the Reformed Church, or the great intellectual and cultural role of preachers in the nineteenth century, do not receive enough attention.

The depth of interest in theology in the Netherlands in the nineteenth century and the degree to which theologians could become famous national figures, are revealed also in the interesting short biography which C. van der Woude devoted to E.A. Borger.[112] In his day Borger was a famous Leiden theologian and historian whose moderate rationalism and pragmatic historical views clearly illustrated the strong influence exercised by the eighteenth-century Enlightenment in the Netherlands in the first decades of the nineteenth century. Theological opinions such as those of Borger created an ideological gulf between the leading groups in the Reformed Church, and the more orthodox members on the lower rungs of the social ladder. They caused violent tensions which culminated in 1834 in the first schism in the Church. The emergence and growth of separatist congregations in the classis of Dordrecht is sympathetically described by C. Smits.[113] In 1971 he published a first volume on the Schism (*Afscheiding*) in and around Gorinchem. His second volume reveals the strength of the tendency in and near Dordrecht for simple unlettered Church members to form independent 'Churches under the Cross'. Sometimes they emigrated en masse from the hostile Netherlands with its stagnant economy, to the United States. Smits's work of piety offers a descriptive catalogue of the various communities rather than an analysis or explanation. It is clear that the author hardly feels the need to explain the foundation of a denomination with which he is in sympathy. This is a pity, for in this way one learns nothing of the often curious personal continuity which certainly existed in the South Holland countryside between the eschatological sectarianism of before 1834, and the schismatic communities thereafter.

How the formation of these eschatological conventicles acted as a training school for the later separatists, appears in A.J. Onstenk's many-faceted, but mainly literary-historical biography of C.E. van Koetsveld.[114] Van Koetsveld was a well-known court chaplain with a surprisingly warm appreciation for the social concern of Marx and the socialists. Onstenk's dissertation now shows how great the social and cultural importance of certain prominent

112   C. van der Woude, *Elias Annes Borger (1784-1820). Een geleerde-leven in het begin der 19e eeuw*. Kamper cahiers, XXVI (Kampen: J.H. Kok, s.a., 61 pp., ISBN 90 242 0867 X).

113.   C. Smits, *De Afscheiding van 1834, II, Classis Dordrecht c.a.* (Dordrecht: J.P. van den Tol, 1974, 440 pp).

114.   A.J. Onstenk, '*Ik behoor bij mezelf'. Cornelis Elisa van Koetsveld, 1807-1893* (Assen: Van Gorcum, 1973, 211 pp., ISBN 90 232 1119 7; Thesis Faculty of Letters, Utrecht. With summary in German).

preachers was at that time. For Van Koetsveld was a popular and able publicist who revealed the problem of poverty to a wide readership. He also set up a school for the physically and mentally handicapped, and launched an agricultural project. The author rightly devotes much attention to the fierce struggle between the various tendencies within the Reformed Church. Van Koetsveld did not wish to join any party and his theological opinions stood between those of the 'ethical' and Groningen schools; he was too independent to adhere to any group, but with his principled middle course, he represented an important section of the Reformed Church about whom most ecclesiastical historians, according to the author, say nothing. It is an interesting hypothesis which deserves more detailed elaboration.

H.P.H. Nusteling has joined the ranks of the economic historians questioning the traditional view of the Dutch economy of the nineteenth century.[115] In his substantial doctoral thesis he describes the drastic shifts in the interdependence of Dutch and West German economic life, with special reference to Rhine shipping and rail traffic. In the period 1831-1914 not only did the economic and political power-relationship between the Netherlands and their West German hinterland change, but Dutch and German transport and commercial policies and the structure of freight traffic also underwent great alterations. In 1851, under diplomatic pressure from the *Zollverein*, and in reply to sharp competition from French, Belgian and German ports, The Hague followed the example of England and liberalized its trade policy. From that date, free trade was as undisputed a part of the Dutch foreign policy catechism as neutrality. In the period 1850-75, the Netherlands experienced a drastic re-orientation. The government gave up protectionism and attempted to revive Dutch commerce and shipping by means of free trade, for which the transit traffic to Germany seemed to offer a suitable instrument. It was not until about 1875 that commercial circles in Rotterdam ceased to regard transit trade as inferior, and accepted the new situation in which transport of bulk goods to and from Germany dominated the port and Rhine shipping. Dutch economic growth in the second half of the last century depended to a great extent on German expansion and Rhine shipping. The well-known question of how and when the Netherlands reached the stage of autonomous economic growth remains to be solved. Nusteling's dating of this is still vague, but he emphasizes and gives precision to J.A. de Jonge's view that the shipping sector was one of the

115. H.P.H. Nusteling, *De Rijnvaart in het tijdperk van stoom en steenkool, 1831-1914. Een studie van het goederenverkeer en de verkeerspolitiek in de Rijndelta en het achterland, mede in verband met de opkomst van de spoorwegen en de concurrentie van vreemde zeehavens* (Amsterdam: Holland universiteitspers, 1974, 540 pp., ISBN 90 302 1101 6; Thesis Faculty of Letters, Nijmegen. With summary in German).

primary factors in the process of sustained economic growth. The author rightly considers the term 'industrial revolution' unsuitable as a description of the gradual transformation from a commercial and maritime society into an industrial one, which took place in the Netherlands in the second half of the nineteenth century.

Problems related to the improvement of the competitive position of the ports of Rotterdam and Flushing by means of hydraulic works and rail construction, are also raised in the commemorative volume of the Zeeland Steamship Company.[116] However, in this case the main interest centres on the efforts of Dutch business circles before and after 1875 to derive profit from the country's geographical position by means of a regular steamer service to England. In seven articles various authors deal with, *inter alia*, postal and passenger traffic between the Netherlands and England in the two centuries before 1875, the founding and sometimes chequered history of the Zeeland Steamship Company, and the routes from Flushing to Queensborough and Harwich to the Hook of Holland. Finally, technical aspects of the ferry boats, and the origins of the passengers are discussed.

The late J.A. de Jonge's long article on Delft in the nineteenth century is an integrated social history which will serve as a model for some time to come.[117] As the development of Delft was in many ways typical of Dutch economic and social evolution, the work is one of general importance. De Jonge's study reviews not only economic life and social and political developments, but also demographic structure, education, charities, administration and finance in Delft. In *c.* 1820, Delft was the centre of an agrarian district; industry played only a modest role in the urban economy. Until 1870 the old established families stood at the top of the social ladder. With the arrival of modern dynamic entrepreneurs in Delft, the economic bias shifted gradually in favour of industry. The new entrepreneurs were, however, unlike their counterparts abroad, not men who rose from 'the dunghill to the chariot' but came rather from the town establishment or commercial circles. At the end of the nineteenth century Delft was an industrial city where social and political relationships were in sharp contrast to the situation in the first three-quarters of the century. The old aristocracy no longer played any role in industry, and ceded its political functions to the propertied middle class. Furthermore a class of industrial workers had emerged, clearly distinguished from the unskilled

116. P.W. Klein en J.R. Bruijn, ed., *Honderd jaar Engelandvaart. Stoomvaart Maatschappij Zeeland, Koninklijke Nederlandsche Postvaart nv.; 1875-1975* (Bussum: Unieboek, 1975, 335 pp., ISBN 90 228 1910 8. With summaries in English).
117. J.A. de Jonge, 'Delft in de negentiende eeuw. Van 'stille, nette' plaats tot centrum van industrie. Enkele facetten van de omslag in een locale sociaal-economische evolutie', *Economisch- en sociaal-historisch jaarboek*, XXXVII (1974) 145-247.

poor. A substantial middle group of officials (especially teachers) and administrators from trade and industry had also come into existence.

According to certain economic theories industrialization and the associated process of autonomous economic growth in the nineteenth century were the result above all of the readiness of bank capital to invest on a large scale. P.W. Klein's article shows how the actual situation in the Netherlands diverged from this general theory.[118] In the years 1895-1914, so decisive for the industrialization of the Netherlands, Dutch industry covered its capital requirements mainly by internal financing. The Dutch banking system and industrialization developed separately, according to Klein. For that reason pre-industrial capital accumulation within existing enterprises was more important for industrialization than was capital formation in Dutch banks.

The coalmines of South Limburg were always of modest importance in Europe, and only became vital to the Dutch economy in the First World War and the decades after 1945. For Limburg itself, the mines had been important even under the *ancien régime*, and in the periods of French and Belgian rule, while the north Netherlands State gave no stimulus to the mining industry. It was not until the end of the nineteenth century that the number of mining concessions increased, but it was especially after 1901, with exploitation by the State, that mining in Limburg took on real importance. C.E.P.M. Raedts has collected a number of articles which together form a good introduction to the history of mining in Limburg.[119] Among other topics he illuminates the technical, legal, commercial and social aspects of mining. He describes developments during the two world wars, post-war prosperity and the fatal coal crisis of 1958 from his own experience.

Social history is gradually emancipating itself from political and economic history. This trend had been manifest for a long time in the Netherlands in the works of Rüter, Baudet, Slicher van Bath and Van Tijn among others. The separation was obvious when social history began to make use of the methods and techniques of the social sciences. Several universities have accordingly set up special chairs in social history, and the young specialism now has its own organ in the *Tijdschrift voor sociale geschiedenis*.[120] A separate periodical was to be expected. After all, social history does have some imperial-

---

118. P.W. Klein, 'Het bankwezen en de modernisering van de Nederlandse volkshuishouding tijdens de tweede helft van de 19e eeuw', *Economisch- en sociaal-historisch jaarboek*, XXXVI (1973) 131-146.

119. C.E.P.M. Raedts, *De opkomst en ontwikkeling en de neergang van de steenkolenmijnbouw in Limburg*. Maaslandse monografieën, XVIII (Assen: Van Gorcum, 1974, 239 pp., ISBN 90 232 1221 5. With summaries in German and French).

120. *Tijdschrift voor sociale geschiedenis* (Amsterdam: Van Gennep, Nes 128, subscription fl. 20.- p.a.).

ist traits, in particular its tendency to regard itself as an integral history of society, with economic history its handmaiden and political history its offshoot. Modern conceptions were long current among the members of the Netherlands Society for the Study of Social History, and it was natural for the society to transform its newsletter (*Mededelingenblad*) into the *Tijdschrift*. The new periodical tries to combine the need for publications on social history with the already existing interest in biographical sketches from the history of the Dutch working class movement. Because of the existence of various other Dutch professional periodicals it will not be easy for the *Tijdschrift* to spread its wings. The articles published in 1975 are virtually all related to the Dutch and Belgian workers' movement in the last 200 years. Perhaps the publication of the definitive report of a group set up to study Dutch society c. 1850 will break the magic circle to some extent. The *Tijdschrift* has already published an interesting discussion on the occasion of a preliminary report on social stratification.[121] The first annual volume also contains two interesting contributions. In a long article partly based on quantitative data P. van Horssen and D. Rietveld describe the organization and social composition of the Social Democratic League (1879-94).[122] The authors explain how the League grew from a small group of intellectuals and artisans in Amsterdam into a broad movement of the discontented in the towns and later in the countryside. In another article J.J. Giele shows that there was a measure of continuity between the social and political conceptions of Dutch radical journalists and agitators in the 1840s and the Dutch section of the First International.[123] The so-called *Volksmannen* (men of the people) formed the missing link according to the author; true, such figures as J. de Vries, Van Gorcum, Van Brussel, De Vletter, Van de Voo and Multatuli did choose one of the two most important 'bourgeois' parties in the 1850s and 1860s, but because of their social awareness they still adopted their own unique position. In the author's opinion the great expectations which a man of the people such as Multatuli had of royal intervention to improve political and social life show how the development of social views within the rudimentary Dutch workers' movement had stagnated.

Multatuli's varied literary work was not only important for the history of social ideas. The great writer, in his vain struggle for rehabilitation, satirized

---

121. J. Giele en G.J. van Oenen, 'De sociale structuur van de Nederlandse samenleving rond 1850', *Mededelingenblad*, XLV (mei 1974) 2-32; H.A. Diederiks, 'Klassen en klassenbewustzijn. Een commentaar', *Ibidem*, LXVI (november 1974) 109-118; J. Giele en G.J. van Oenen, 'Wel discussie, geen vooruitgang', *Tijdschrift voor sociale geschiedenis*, I (1975) 147-150; J. Lucassen en Th. van Tijn, 'Nogmaals: sociale stratificatie', *Ibidem*, II (1976) 74-91.
122. P. van Horssen en D. Rietveld, 'De Sociaal Democratische Bond', een onderzoek naar het ontstaan van haar afdelingen en haar sociale structuur', *Ibidem*, I (1975) 6-71.
123. J.J. Giele, 'De oppositie der 'volksmannen' (1850-1869)', *Ibidem*, I (1975) 171-218.

the most diverse abuses in the Netherlands and Indonesia, and got involved in all kinds of strange and difficult situations. Studies of Multatuli are therefore forced to consider the colonial policy of the period, the clash of liberals and conservatives in the Netherlands, and cultural and intellectual life. P. Spigt's collection of previously published articles therefore offers much of interest.[124] As Multatuli is still a controversial figure in literary circles, some of the articles unfortunately have an excessively polemical or eulogistic tone.

There are still many *lacunae* in the history of Dutch colonialism in the nineteenth century. No quantitative historian has yet analyzed the importance of the exploitation of the colonies for the Dutch economy as a whole in this period. More traditional historiography is also inactive, and there have been no biographies of important nineteenth-century colonial statesmen. The archives of the ministry of colonies had not even been systematically investigated for the study of such a well-known subject as the cultivation system until C. Fasseur made fruitful use of them for his dissertation.[125] Under the cultivation system, the Dutch administration in Indonesia compelled the population to grow certain export crops for the benefit of the Dutch treasury. On the basis of his interesting account of the evolution of the cultivation system, Fasseur concludes that it undermined the conservative intentions of its protagonists by introducing new social and economic elements into traditional Javanese society. The cultivation system also dug its own grave in another way. From 1850, government plantations stagnated and economic considerations therefore favoured the gradual introduction of private plantations. Fasseur's figures on the dependence of the Dutch treasury on the sale of Javanese coffee and sugar are a revelation. In this way this thorough study of a specific phase of colonialism is also important for the history of the motherland. The author also illustrates the interdependence of the Netherlands and her overseas possessions in a biographical article on the career in the Indies of the liberal minister for the colonies, Fransen van de Putte.[126] After a lucrative career as a sugar planter Van de Putte entered Dutch politics and used his colonial experience to push liberal policy in a particular direction, with all the consequences for the Netherlands and Indonesia. Van de Putte's Indonesian career is therefore of some general importance.

---

124.   P. Spigt, *Keurig in de kontramine. Over Multatuli* (Amsterdam: Athenaeum-Polak & van Gennep, 1975, 231 pp., ISBN 90 253 6509 4).
125.   C. Fasseur, *Kultuurstelsel en koloniale baten. De Nederlandse exploitatie van Java, 1840-1860*. Leidse Historische Reeks, XX (Leiden: Universitaire pers, 1975, 289 pp., ISBN 90 6021 253 3; Thesis Faculty of Letters, Leiden. With summaries in English and Bahasa Indonesia).
126.   C. Fasseur, 'Van suikercontractant tot kamerlid. Bouwstenen voor een biografie van Fransen van de Putte (de jaren 1849-1862)', *Tijdschrift voor geschiedenis*, LXXXVIII (1975) 333-354.

An edition of the sources relating to the slave rising in Curaçao in 1795 will certainly be read with much interest in these days. The objection to A.F. Paula's edition of government documents on 1795 is that officials usually judge a revolt from their standpoint, which is generally unsympathetic to the rebels.[127] Those who know the tensions of Curaçao society at that time and also take into account the disturbances in the rest of the Caribbean and the revolution in the Netherlands, will have no difficulty in forming a balanced picture of the 1795 slave revolt.

European Architectural Heritage Year was marked by the appearance of J.A.C. Tillema's comprehensive study of the history of the preservation of ancient buildings in the Netherlands. The book analyzes the various concepts which inspired the experts who advised the government on the restoration of monuments.[128] The restoration work which is the result of a hundred years of government care of monuments is illustrated by photographs and drawings. At the same time, a group of Amsterdam art historians produced a re-issue of Victor de Stuers' famous article which shamed the Dutch government into taking more active measures for the conservation of the country's architectural heritage.[129] The care of monuments in the last hundred years, and its absence in the first half of the nineteenth century, reflect not only changing principles in art-history but also Dutch society itself. Dutchmen of the first half of the nineteenth century could not see old buildings as monuments, as the gap between them and the past was clearly still too small. Throughout the nineteenth century many protestants disparagingly referred to medieval architecture as 'Romish'. In particular, when a number of prominent catholics led the movement to conserve monuments after 1870, protestant Netherlanders detected ultramontane influence in the work of restoration. Catholic emancipation was certainly not unconnected with this protestant sensitivity. In this way, these two publications offer much more than purely art-historical information.

The mutiny which broke out on the 'Zeven Provincien' in February 1933, when this armoured vessel was off the east coast of Sumatra, deeply disturbed public opinion in the Netherlands. In his well-written and richly documented thesis J.C.H. Blom first re-examines the causes and nature of the mutiny, concluding that the incident was caused by low morale and the tactless manner

127. A.F. Paula, ed., *1795. De slavenopstand op Curaçao; een bronnenuitgave van de originele overheidsdocumenten* (Curaçao: Centraal Historisch Archief, 1974, 344 pp).
128. J.C.A. Tillema, *Schetsen uit de geschiedenis van de Monumentenzorg in Nederland. Ter herdenking van een eeuw regeringsbeleid, 1875-1975* (The Hague: Staatsuitgeverij, 1975, 656 pp., ISBN 90 12 00614 7).
129. Victor de Stuers, *Holland op zijn smalst*. Ingeleid en toegelicht door een werkgroep van het Kunsthistorisch Instituut der Universiteit van Amsterdam (Bussum: Unieboek, 1975, 180 pp., ISBN 90 228 3564 2).

in which the government announced its decision to reduce the wages of naval personnel rather than by communist or Indonesian nationalist plots.[130] He also points out that the mutineers behaved with a remarkable degree of restraint which hardly warranted the suppression of the mutiny by submitting the vessel to an aerial bombardment. But the major and most interesting part of his work is concerned with the political impact of the mutiny. Since the author summarizes his book in an article published above, p. 163ff., it is superfluous to sum up its contents here. According to Blom, the mutiny, in forcing the Socialist leadership to re-examine their attitude toward governmental authority, hastened rather than retarded the transformation of the SDAP into a widely respected party accepting the basic rules of parliamentary democracy.

Much more debatable are the conclusions of S.Y.A. Vellenga's doctoral thesis attempting to account for the relatively high percentage of votes (more than four times the national average) cast for national-socialist parties (the NSB and the much smaller NSNAP) in the southern half of the province of Limburg in the elections of 1935.[131] The author briefly discusses such obvious reasons as the province's proximity to Germany and its incomplete integration into the economic and cultural life of the Dutch nation, but attributes the fascist electoral success primarily to the complacency and the conservatism of the dominant Catholic Party. He argues that this party made little or no effort to retain the traditional allegiance of the small farmers adversely affected by the Great Depression, or of the lower and middle classes in Limburg's mining areas suffering from the evils of rapid industrialization, and that for this reason many among these discontented groups decided to vote for a new party promising a radical reorganization of the existing political system. This explanation does not take into account that in North Brabant, the other province in which the Roman Catholic Party traditionally dominated political life, this party did not lose strength in the 1935 elections and the percentage of the votes cast for the national-socialist parties was the lowest in the country. In general Vellenga's conclusions are based on very slim evidence, almost all of which is taken from printed sources only. Another unsatisfactory feature of his work is that no attempt has been made to investigate the local history of the NSB in order to determine the extent to which its effective organization, or the influence of prominent personalities among its leadership, contributed to the party's electoral success.

---

130. J.C.H. Blom, *De muiterij op de Zeven Provicien* (Bussum: Fibula-Van Dishoeck, 1975, 367 pp., ISBN 90 228 3527 8, Thesis Faculty of Letters, Leiden. With summary in English).

131. S.Y.A. Vellenga, *Katholiek Zuid Limburg en het fascisme. Een onderzoek naar het kiesgedrag van de Limburger in de jaren dertig* (Assen: Van Gorcum, 1975, 175 pp., ISBN 90 228 12673; Thesis Faculty of Letters, Utrecht. With summaries in German and French).

The once burning question of whether or to what extent individual Dutchmen behaved as 'true' or 'false' patriots in the period of German occupation is still the leading theme in some recent publications. F. Visser has produced a detailed narrative of the activities of the highly unscrupulous German agent A. van der Waals, whose uncanny talent to infiltrate the Dutch resistance movement resulted in the arrest of numerous Dutchmen by the German secret police.[132] On the basis of new investigations the author concludes that at least 44 names should be added to the list of the 38 members of the resistance movement for whose death Van der Waals was held partly responsible by the post-war tribunal which sentenced him to the death penalty (not to mention the two persons whom he killed personally in order to be able to assume their identity). The main purpose of Visser's study is not so much to contribute to historical understanding as 'to pay a debt of honour' to Van der Waals's victims and 'to present a warning example to future generations'. His lengthy work does contain some interesting chapters vividly illustrating the almost unbelievably shrewd and deceitful manner in which this psychopath operated. Unfortunately we are given neither a clear indication of all the sources on which his account is based nor a discussion of the problems concerning the reliability of those sources he does mention.

It is a far cry from Van der Waals's ruthless egotism to the lofty idealism which inspired J.H. Scheps in his attitude toward the German invaders. This christian socialist was one of the first Dutchmen to take a strong stand against the German nazification policies but who refused to accept the view that the end of fighting nazism justified almost all means. In the first and only published volume of his memoirs he refutes the widely held notion that his party, the SDAP, failed to play any role of importance in the resistance movement.[133] His fair, if long-winded appraisal of the war-time record of the SDAP is less valuable for its factual information (most of which was already known from more reliable archival sources) than for the additional light it throws on the sentiments and convictions of an elite of the Dutch socialist party. Particularly welcome is the lengthy appendix consisting of a reprint of Schep's war-time pamphlets, many of which he dared to publish during the occupation under his own name in spite of the fact that they were devastatingly critical of the policies pursued by the German authorities and their Dutch henchmen.

---

132. Frank Visser, *De zaak Antonius van der Waals* (The Hague: Ad. M.C. Stok, Zuid-Hollandsche Uitgeversmaatschappij, 1975, 519 pp., ISBN 90 235 8091 5).
133. J.H. Scheps, *Scheps inventariseert* (vol. I, Apeldoorn: Semper Agendo, 1973, 736 pp., ISBN 90 6086 600 2).

With the appearance of its sixth volume L. de Jong's comprehensive history of the Netherlands during the Second World War is now half finished and even more likely to be regarded as one of the major works produced by Dutch historians in the twentieth century.[134] Once again the author has succeeded in writing a lucid and richly documented narrative partly based on hitherto unused sources while at the same time perceptively analyzing the course of events. This time covering the period from July 1942 to May 1943, he further develops the two subjects which were already the dominant themes in his two preceding volumes: the increasing terror to which the German occupation authorities resorted after they had realized that they had failed in their policy of winning over a substantial section of the Dutch nation for national-socialism; and the growing resistance to German rule among the Dutch population, increasingly outraged by German brutality and now fully confident of an Allied victory. This volume concludes with an account of the great strikes of May 1943 in which the popular resentment of German rule most clearly revealed itself. Although the Germans were forced to shelve some of their ambitious plans to introduce national socialist institutions, they continued to step up their measures against the jewish population of the country. In great detail De Jong describes the policies of deceit and intimidation practised by the Germans in carrying out their plan to deport most of the Dutchmen registered as 'full jews' to extermination and concentration camps in eastern Europe. De Jong's masterful if highly depressing account of the tragic fate suffered by the Dutch jews will constitute the most unforgettable passages for many readers of his latest volume.

The German design to exterminate Dutch jewry is also the main theme of the small volume of articles by B.A. Sijes, an historian noted for his definitive studies on the German conscription of Dutch labourers and on other important aspects of the German occupation in the Netherlands.[135] In two well-researched articles he establishes the extent of the responsibility which two leading members of the SS, Erich Rajakowitsch and Adolf Eichmann, bore for the various measures taken against the Dutch jews. Of a more general interest is his illuminating essay examining the helpless position of the Dutch jews during the last war (which appeared in English translation in volume IX of *Acta*). The volume moreover contains three articles dealing with various aspects of the persecution of the jews in Austria and Germany. It concludes with an

134. L. de Jong, *Het Koninkrijk der Nederlanden in de Tweede Wereldoorlog*, VI, *juli '42-mei '43* (The Hague: Nijhoff, 1975, 911 pp. in two parts; ISBN 90 247 1742 6; also available in an edition without scholarly apparatus, The Hague: Staatsuitgeverij, 1975).
135. B.A. Sijes, *Studies over Jodenvervolging* (Assen: Van Gorcum, 1974, 184 pp., ISBN 90 232 1204 5).

analysis of the post-war prosecution of the Germans who had committed war crimes or crimes against humanity in the Netherlands, in which Sijes forcefully argues against any release of the three SS-officials who are still being detained in the Breda prison. An opposite view on the same question is taken by C.F. Rüter in his doctoral dissertation assessing some important aspects of the procedures instigated against persons who were accused of having committed war crimes or crimes against humanity during or immediately after the last war.[136] Without regarding the Dutch war crime trials as a serious miscarriage of justice, the author exposes the confusion characteristic of much of Dutch legal thought on the subject. He points out for example that Dutch legislation failed to make a clear distinction between war crimes and crimes against humanity and that high officials in the German administration who bore a heavy responsibility for the crimes committed were not indicted at all, or received only light sentences, whereas relatively heavy sentences were meted out to lower personnel who acted in accordance with the guidelines drawn up by their superiors. In his discussion of the crimes committed by Dutch army personnel in the armed conflict with Indonesia the author is highly sceptical of the Dutch government's statements that justice had been done against the offenders. He is even more critical of the Dutch government's refusal to allow any further investigation of the archives pertaining to this question until after the completion of the publication of all official documents on Dutch-Indonesian relations by the historian Van der Wal. He convincingly argues that this decision is not likely to have been taken, as was said in its justification, in the interest of historical research and will certainly impede the introduction of the reforms needed to prevent the recurrence of any war criminality on a large scale.

Contributors to this article:

Mrs. Alice C. Carter (University of London, London School of Economics) eighteenth-century Dutch history.

W.P. Blockmans (University of Rotterdam) medieval Belgian history.

A.C. Duke (University of Southampton) sixteenth-century Dutch and Belgian history.

Professor R. Van Eenoo (University of Ghent) nineteenth- and twentieth-century Belgian history.

136. C.F. Rüter, *Enkele aspecten van de strafrechtelijke reactie op oorlogsmisdrijven en misdrijven tegen de menselijkheid* (Amsterdam; University Press, 1973, 244 pp.,: Thesis Faculty of Law, University of Amsterdam, ISBN 90 6042 144 2. With summary in German).

Mrs. Renée Gerson (City of London Polytechnic) eighteenth-century Dutch history.

G.C. Gibbs (University of London, Birkbeck College) eighteenth-century Dutch history.

Miss Rosemary L. Jones, ed. (Southampton) sixteenth- and seventeenth-century Dutch history.

Mrs. dr. Johanna Kossmann (Groningen) medieval Dutch and Belgian history.

Dr. J.L. Price (University of Hull) seventeenth-century Dutch history.

Professor K.W. Swart, ed. (University of London, University College) twentieth-century Dutch history.

Dr. C.A. Tamse (University of Groningen) nineteenth- and twentieth-century Dutch history.

SELECT LIST OF RECENT WORKS ON THE HISTORY OF THE LOW COUNTRIES PUBLISHED IN ENGLISH

H. van den Brink, *The Charm of Legal History* (Amsterdam: Hakkert, 1974, 344 pp., ISBN 90 256 0620 2 and 90 256 0708 X).
Pp. 123-216 of this lightly written book contain a series of lectures on the influence of Roman, common and canon law on the development of modern Dutch civil law, which were originally delivered to an audience of Scottish students in 1973.

H. Van der Wee, 'Structural Changes and Specialization in the Industry of the Southern Netherlands 1100-1600', *Economic History Review*, 2nd series, XXVIII (1975) 203-221.
Explains the growth of the cloth industry in the towns, the decline in the fourteenth century and the subsequent concentration on luxury cloth for the home market and the development of production of cheaper cloth for export.

D. Nicholas, 'Economic Reorientation and Social Change in Fourteenth-century Flanders', *Past and Present*, LXX (1976) 3-29.
Argues that the cities were able to overcome problems confronting cloth production and export in the later middle ages by diversifying their interests. To compensate for the inadequacy of domestic grain supplies for their enormous populations, towns began importing grain from northern France etc. Thus while the basis of urban wealth broadened, the depression deepened in the countryside, which fell increasingly under the influence of cities.

E. Warlop, *The Flemish Nobility Before 1300*, Part I (vol. 1 and 2): *Text* and *Notes*; Part II (vol. 3 and 4): *Annexes* (Kortrijk: Desmet-Huysman, 1975-6, 1332 pp).
Terminological and genealogical study of the Flemish nobility. The author examines its position from the mid-ninth century to the end of the thirteenth century and determines how long it was able to maintain its dominent role in the administration and society of the county. Translation of *De Vlaamse adel vóór 1300* (Handzame: Familia et Patria, 1968).

J. Isewijn, 'The Coming of Humanism to the Low Countries', in: H.A. Oberman with T.A. Brady, ed., *Itinerarium Italicum: The Profile of the Italian Renaissance in the*

251

Mirror of its European Transformations (Leiden: Brill, 1975, 471 pp., ISBN 90 04 04259 8) 193-301.
Emphasizes the religious character of humanism in the Low Countries and shows the concentration on philology rather than poetry. Points out that classical influences in the north did not affect art and architecture until the end of the sixteenth century.

G. Parker, 'Why did the Dutch Revolt last eightly years?', *Transactions of the Royal Historical Society*, 5th Series, XXVI (1976) 53-72.
Argues that the duration of the war is only explicable when consideration is given to Dutch involvement in Brazil, the Caribbean and the Far Fast.

Idem, 'Francisco de Lixalde and the Spanish Netherlands (1567-1577): some new evidence', *Tijdschrift voor geschiedenis*, LXXXIX (1976) 1-11.
Refers to an article by A.W. Lovett in the same journal, LXXXIV (1971) 14-23. Parker demonstrates the corruption of this Spanish paymaster, was by no means an isolated case of peculation in the Spanish régime in the Netherlands.

J.S. Bromley and E.H. Kossmann ed., *Britain and the Netherlands*, V, *Some Political Mythologies* (The Hague: Nijhoff, 1975. 212 pp. ISBN 90 247 1763 9).
The papers delivered to the Fifth Anglo-Dutch Historical Conference, among which the following are of special interest to the student of Dutch history: J.J. Woltjer, 'Dutch Privileges, Real and Imaginary' (during the Revolt of the Netherlands); K.W. Swart, 'The Black Legend during the Eighty Years War'; I. Schöffer, 'The Batavian Myth during the Sixteenth and Seventeenth Centuries'; J.A. Bornewasser, 'Mythical Aspects of Dutch Anti-Catholicism in the Nineteenth Century'.

H. De Schepper and G. Parker, 'The formation of government policy in the Catholic Netherlands under "the Archdukes", 1596-1621', *English Historical Review*, XCI (1976) 242-254.
Underlines the restraints on the absolute power of the Archdukes, by Spain in the matter of foreign policy and defence, and by the Estates and local officials in domestic affairs.

M.D. Feld, 'Middle-Class Society and the Rise of Military Professionalism. The Dutch Army 1589-1609', *Armed Forces and Society*, I (1975, Inter-University Seminar on Armed Forces and Society) 419-442.
Brings out the importance of the middle classes in the United Provinces, where broadly speaking, military strategy was determined by the politicians and the army, though specialised, did not give the aristocracy much political influence.

R. Feenstra and C.J.D. Waal, *Seventeenth-Century Leyden Law Professors and their Influence on the Development of the Civil Law. A Study of Bronchorst, Vinnius and Voet*. Koninklijke Nederlandse Akademie van Wetenschappen, Afd. Letteren, Nieuwe Reeks, XC (Amsterdam-Oxford: North-Holland Publishing Company, 1975, 124 pp. ISBN 72048296 8).
Mainly bibliographical study, which gives an idea of what the three professors taught their students and how their works were spread outside the Netherlands.

Th.H. Lunsingh Scheurleer and G.H.M. Posthumus Meyjes, ed., *Leiden University in the Seventeenth Century. An Exchange of Learning* (Leiden: Universitaire Pers/Brill, 1975, 496 pp., ISBN 90 04 04267 9).
A handsomely produced volume, containing essays, mostly in English, on a wide

variety of topics. While not a systematic survey, there is much here that is both useful and interesting, and the whole is indispensable for the student of Dutch academic, or even intellectual history.

W.D. Hackmann, 'The Growth of Science in the Netherlands in the Seventeenth and Early Eighteenth Centuries', in: M. Crosland, ed., *The Emergence of Science in Western Europe* (London: Macmillan, 1975, ISBN O 333 18217 O) 89-111.
This article is chiefly useful as a survey for English readers of the material available in Dutch on this subject.

C.R. Boxer, *The Anglo-Dutch Wars of the Seventeenth Century 1652-1674* (London: Her Majesty's Stationary Office for the National Maritime Museum, 1974, 68 pp. ISBN 11 2901697).
Deals with each of the three wars in succession concentrating on the tactics and results of the main engagements between the Dutch and English fleets in the Channel and North Sea, arguing that the English were unable to make their strategic and other advantages count in the second and third wars, as they had done in the first, because of De Ruyter's skilled leadership and the greater financial strength of the Dutch Republic. An enlarged Dutch edition of this work was published under the title *De Ruyter en de Engelse oorlogen in de Gouden Eeuw met een beschouwing door R.E.J. Weber over de zeeschilders Willem van de Velde de Oude en de Jonge* (Bussum: De Boer Maritiem, 1976, ISBN 90 228 1955 8).

J.E. Wills jr., *Pepper, Guns and Parleys. The Dutch East India Company and China, 1662-1681* (Cambridge, Mass.: Harvard University Press, 1974, 232 pp.).
A solid account of the Dutch failure to maintain any trading privileges in the Chinese empire.

A.P. Kenney, *Stubborn for Liberty, the Dutch in New York* (Syracuse, N.Y.: Syracuse University Press, 1975, 301 pp., ISBN 0 8156 0113 1).
A popular, readable and not always convincing attempt to demonstrate the nature and the importance of the Dutch contribution to the history of this State in the colonial and revolutionary periods.

G.C. Gibbs, 'Some Intellectual and Political Influences of the Huguenot Emigrés in the United Provinces, c. 1680-1730', *Bijdragen en mededelingen betreffende de geschiedenis der Nederlanden*, XC (1975) 255-87.
An interesting essay, suggesting the importance of the Huguenots in a number of fields, notably as publishers of French books, and as historians, publishing considerable bodies of material for the study of contemporary history and providing the rest of Europe with its image of the Dutch Republic.

A. Clare Carter, *Neutrality or Commitment: The Evolution of Dutch Foreign Policy, 1667-1795* (London: Edward Arnold, 1975, 118 pp., ISBN 0 7131 5767 4).
Refutes the contention of previous writers that the Dutch policy of non-alignment was the outcome of political weakness and argues forcefully that this strategy admirably suited the political and economic aims of the Republic.

Idem, Getting, Spending and Investing in Early Modern Times. Essays on Dutch English and Huguenot Economic History. Aspects of Economic History: The Low Countries I (Assem: Van Gorcum, 1975, 190 pp., ISBN 90 232 1243 6).
A collection of papers reprinted from various periodicals published over the last

forty years or so, mainly on eighteenth-century financial and other economic aspects of Anglo-Dutch relations.

M.C. Ricklefs, *Jogjakarta under Sultan Mangkubumi, 1749-1792* (London: Oxford University Press, 1974, 463 pp., ISBN 019 713578 1).
Drawing on Dutch colonial and Javanese archive material the author traces the foundation and early development of the sultanate of Jogjakarta in a period when the influence of the Dutch East India Company was in decline.

S. Schama, 'The Exigencies of War and the Politics of Taxation in the Netherlands 1795-1810', in J.M. Winter, ed., *War and Economic Development* (Cambridge: University Press, 1975, ISBN 0 521 20535 2) 103-37.
An excellent review of Dutch fiscal policies in the eighteenth century, arguing that the introduction of an adequate system of public finance was a fortunate by-product of the period of French dominance.

J.E. Helmreich, *Belgium and Europe. A Study in Small Power Diplomacy*. Issues in Contemporary Politics, III (The Hague: Mouton, 1976, 451 pp., ISBN 90 279 7561 2).
Discusses developments in Belgian foreign policy from 1830 to the present but fails to mention the favourite idea of many Belgian statesmen in the nineteenth century, namely a customs union with the Netherlands, and is superificial as regards Belgian irredentism after 1839 and the complete reversal of Belgian diplomacy during the Second World War.

H. Kroeskamp, *Early Schoolmasters in a Developing Country. A History of Experiments in School Education in 19th Century Indonesia* (Assen: Van Gorcum, 1974, 497 pp., ISBN 90 232 1093).
A detailed analysis of the changing education policy and the organization of primary schools and teachers training which the government and missionary societies provided for the Indonesian population.

The Authors

Dr. W. P. BLOCKMANS is Reader in Social History, Erasmus University, Rotterdam

Dr. J. C. H. BLOM is Lecturer in Modern History, University of Amsterdam

Dr. H. DAALDER is Professor of Political Sciences, University of Leiden, European University Institute, Florence

Dr. C. FASSEUR is Professor *extra-ordinarius* in the History of West-European Expansion, University of Leiden

Dr. H. P. H. JANSEN is Professor of Medieval History, University of Leiden

Dr. P. C. JANSEN is Lecturer in Economic History, University of Amsterdam

Dr. W. PREVENIER is Professor in the Auxiliary Sciences of History, University of Ghent

Dr. JAN DE VRIES is associate Professor of History, University of California, Berkeley

Dr. H. VAN DER WEE is Professor of Economic History, Catholic University of Louvain

Translations by:

Mrs. P. Van Caenegem-Carson (Afsnee near Ghent)
Miss M. van Doorn (Leiden)
C. C. Hibben (London)
D. S. Jordan (Wingham, Canterbury)
A. H. MacKinnon (Groningen)
J. J. Ravell (Bilthoven)